African Successes, Volume IV

National Bureau
of Economic Research
Conference Report

African Successes, Volume IV
Sustainable Growth

Edited by **Sebastian Edwards, Simon Johnson, and David N. Weil**

The University of Chicago Press

Chicago and London

SEBASTIAN EDWARDS is the Henry Ford II Professor of International Economics in the Anderson Graduate School of Management at the University of California, Los Angeles. SIMON JOHNSON is the Ronald A. Kurtz (1954) Professor of Entrepreneurship and professor of global economics and management at the MIT Sloan School of Management. DAVID N. WEIL is the James and Merryl Tisch Professor of Economics at Brown University. All three editors are research associates of the NBER.

The University of Chicago Press, Chicago 60637
The University of Chicago Press, Ltd., London
© 2016 by the National Bureau of Economic Research
Printed in the United States of America
25 24 23 22 21 20 19 18 17 16   1 2 3 4 5

ISBN-13: 978-0-226-31555-3 (cloth)
ISBN-13: 978-0-226-31569-0 (e-book)
DOI: 10.7208/chicago/9780226315690.001.0001

Library of Congress Cataloging-in-Publication Data

Names: Edwards, Sebastian, 1953– editor. | Johnson, Simon, 1963–
    editor. | Weil, David N., editor.
Title: African successes : government and institutions / edited by
    Sebastian Edwards, Simon Johnson, and David N. Weil.
Other titles: National Bureau of Economic Research conference report.
Description: Chicago ; London : Chicago and London, 2016– | Series:
    National Bureau of Economic Research conference report
Identifiers: LCCN 2015050080| ISBN 9780226316222 (cloth : alk.
    paper) | ISBN 9780226316369 (e-book) | ISBN 9780226316055
    (cloth : alk. paper) | ISBN 9780226316192 (e-book) | ISBN
    9780226315720 (cloth : alk. paper) | ISBN 9780226315867
    (e-book) | ISBN 9780226315553 (cloth : alk. paper) | ISBN
    9780226315690 (e-book)
Subjects: LCSH: Economic development—Africa. | Africa—Economic
    conditions—21st century.
Classification: LCC HC800 .A56873 2016 | DDC 330.96–dc23 LC
    record available at http://lccn.loc.gov/2015050080

Relation of the Directors to the
Work and Publications of the
National Bureau of Economic Research

1. The object of the NBER is to ascertain and present to the economics profession, and to the public more generally, important economic facts and their interpretation in a scientific manner without policy recommendations. The Board of Directors is charged with the responsibility of ensuring that the work of the NBER is carried on in strict conformity with this object.

2. The President shall establish an internal review process to ensure that book manuscripts proposed for publication DO NOT contain policy recommendations. This shall apply both to the proceedings of conferences and to manuscripts by a single author or by one or more co-authors but shall not apply to authors of comments at NBER conferences who are not NBER affiliates.

3. No book manuscript reporting research shall be published by the NBER until the President has sent to each member of the Board a notice that a manuscript is recommended for publication and that in the President's opinion it is suitable for publication in accordance with the above principles of the NBER. Such notification will include a table of contents and an abstract or summary of the manuscript's content, a list of contributors if applicable, and a response form for use by Directors who desire a copy of the manuscript for review. Each manuscript shall contain a summary drawing attention to the nature and treatment of the problem studied and the main conclusions reached.

4. No volume shall be published until forty-five days have elapsed from the above notification of intention to publish it. During this period a copy shall be sent to any Director requesting it, and if any Director objects to publication on the grounds that the manuscript contains policy recommendations, the objection will be presented to the author(s) or editor(s). In case of dispute, all members of the Board shall be notified, and the President shall appoint an ad hoc committee of the Board to decide the matter; thirty days additional shall be granted for this purpose.

5. The President shall present annually to the Board a report describing the internal manuscript review process, any objections made by Directors before publication or by anyone after publication, any disputes about such matters, and how they were handled.

6. Publications of the NBER issued for informational purposes concerning the work of the Bureau, or issued to inform the public of the activities at the Bureau, including but not limited to the NBER Digest and Reporter, shall be consistent with the object stated in paragraph 1. They shall contain a specific disclaimer noting that they have not passed through the review procedures required in this resolution. The Executive Committee of the Board is charged with the review of all such publications from time to time.

7. NBER working papers and manuscripts distributed on the Bureau's web site are not deemed to be publications for the purpose of this resolution, but they shall be consistent with the object stated in paragraph 1. Working papers shall contain a specific disclaimer noting that they have not passed through the review procedures required in this resolution. The NBER's web site shall contain a similar disclaimer. The President shall establish an internal review process to ensure that the working papers and the web site do not contain policy recommendations, and shall report annually to the Board on this process and any concerns raised in connection with it.

8. Unless otherwise determined by the Board or exempted by the terms of paragraphs 6 and 7, a copy of this resolution shall be printed in each NBER publication as described in paragraph 2 above.

Contents

Series Introduction

Sebastian Edwards, Simon Johnson, and David N. Weil

In the 1950s and early 1960s, there was a great deal of optimism about the prospects for economic development in sub-Saharan Africa. By early in the twenty-first century, the prevailing consensus had become much more negative—and for good reason. Decades of civil war, repeated state failure, corruption, and disappointing private sector performance characterized much of Africa's postindependence experience. A wave of prominent papers in the economic literature tried to dig more deeply into the causes of these problems, with some scholars putting them in a broader comparative perspective and others focusing on the specifics of the African experience. There was no shortage of deep causes suggested as explanations for repeated African disappointments, including weak rule of law, a lack of democracy, colonial inheritance, the impact of the slave trade, the burden of tropical disease, some form of "resource curse," and ethno-linguistic divisions among the population.

The NBER Africa project, conceived in the middle of the first decade of the twenty-first century, took a different approach. Rather than trying to understand the causes of underperformance in Africa, we decided to focus on finding and understanding more positive aspects of what was happening

Sebastian Edwards is the Henry Ford II Professor of International Economics at the University of California, Los Angeles, and a research associate of the National Bureau of Economic Research. Simon Johnson is the Ronald A. Kurtz (1954) Professor of Entrepreneurship and Professor of Global Economics and Management at the MIT Sloan School of Management and a research associate of the National Bureau of Economic Research. David N. Weil is the James and Merryl Tisch Professor of Economics at Brown University and a research associate of the National Bureau of Economic Research.

For acknowledgments, sources of research support, and disclosure of the authors' material financial relationships, if any, please see http://www.nber.org/chapters/c13651.ack.

on that continent south of the Sahara, along several different dimensions studied by economists. Our timing proved good for three reasons.

First, scholars were turning their attention increasingly to the details of what was working well or at least better with regard to African development. This new wave of research involved working with or, in many cases creating, data sets suited to careful analysis—including sophisticated use of econometrics. We are fortunate to have involved and supported many leading empirical researchers as they broke new ground in multiple directions. Most likely some of this work would have happened in any case, but at the very least we can claim to have provided an appropriate catalyst for many projects.

Second, Africa is changing—and the prospects for nearly a billion people are looking up. A decade or more of relatively good performance does not a miracle make, but across a wide range of countries there has been better economic growth, considerable progress with improving public health and other social indicators, and a range of attempts to improve the performance of the state. Many of the chapters in this series of four volumes address some aspect of this profound and important transformation.

Third, the study of Africa is becoming much more integrated with the rest of economics. Just as happened earlier with research on Japan and China, a line of work that previously might have been seen as of purely regional interest can now appear in top journals. The broader trend, of course, has been the resurrection of development economics as a vibrant field. But also encouraging—and a central part of the NBER Africa project—has been the increase in interest among nonspecialists regarding what is actually happening on this dynamic and fascinating continent.

Volume I in this series focuses on the most basic building blocks of economic development, including the rule of law, civil conflict, and institutions more broadly. Volume II contains chapters on human capital development in Africa, including some important work on public health improvements, but also research into education on the continent. Volume III examines whether Africa can glean any advantage from being relatively late to economic development, including being able to bypass some large investments (for example, in fixed-line telephones or in traditional branch banking) or being able to learn from others (for example, in the development of an export sector). Volume IV looks at whether recent growth can be sustained, in terms of agricultural development and more broadly.

The research presented in these volumes covers a wide territory, in geographic and intellectual terms. However, our project was never intended to be comprehensive. Rather we attempted to act as a catalyst for rigorous and innovative thinking applied to recent African development. The work published here far exceeds our earliest expectations—a reflection, primarily, of how many serious scholars are now deeply engaged with these issues.

It has been a great honor for us, as program directors and now as editors of these volumes, to participate in and help to facilitate this surge in serious interest. In terms of making this possible, we must thank, first and foremost, the Bill & Melinda Gates Foundation for their willingness to encourage economists in this endeavor. We have worked with a range of officials at the Foundation over the past decade; their support has been unstinting and their perspective on development is always refreshing. We would specifically like to thank Sara Sievers for many of our early interactions and Oliver Babson for his subsequent engagement. We also greatly appreciate the ideas and energy of Geoffrey Lamb, Kim Hamilton, Negar Akhavi, Adam Gerstenmier, and Mumukshu Patel.

We must also recognize the founding insight and energy of Martin Feldstein, who emphasized, among many other relevant and helpful points, that there is an important link between raising the quality of economic research on an issue and improving the odds that policy discussions will become more informed. Since becoming president of the NBER in 2008, James Poterba has also provided us with great leadership and encouragement—including sage advice at every stage of the process.

Our four published volumes present results from thirty-nine research teams, with the findings organized along thematic lines. Of the 100 authors whose names appear on one or more of the chapters in our collection, nineteen are from Africa and thirty-two are affiliated with the NBER as either Faculty Research Fellows or research associates. They range from experienced specialists on African development to scholars who had never previously worked on the continent; in seniority they ran the gamut from newly appointed assistant professors to distinguished, established thought leaders.

Every project included a significant on-the-ground component. Some research teams combined money we provided with other funds, for example, to support the collection of very large field data sets. In other cases, funding from the NBER made it possible for researchers to interview policymakers, business people (both large and small), farmers, health workers, or others engaged in the process of economic development.

Results from the research project were presented at a series of conferences in the United States and in Africa. Given the large size of our project and our explicit goal of including scholars who had not previously been working on Africa, we began with a background conference in February 2008, at the NBER in Cambridge, MA, bringing together researchers and policymakers from the United States, Africa, and Europe. The conference featured presentations on current research and an overview of available data, aimed especially at scholars who were new to the area.

Our next meeting, also in Cambridge, MA, in February 2009 was a preconference at which preliminary findings from ten papers were presented. This was followed by a conference in December of the same year, again in

Cambridge, MA, that took a hybrid form: final versions of five projects were presented, as were preconference versions of another twelve projects.

This was followed in July of 2010 by a conference in Accra, Ghana, held in cooperation with the Institute of Statistical, Social, and Economic Research (ISSER). Our final research conference was held in Zanzibar, Tanzania, in August 2011, in cooperation with the Bank of Tanzania.

One goal of our project from inception, with full support from the Gates Foundation, was to help connect economic research with the African policy community. We arranged some interactions along these lines throughout our project, but we were fortunate to be able to make a special effort at the end, with a meeting devoted specifically to the Next Macroeconomic Challenges in Africa, held again in Zanzibar, in December 2012, also in cooperation with the Bank of Tanzania.

There are many people to thank for the successful completion of this project. Benno Ndulu, governor of the Bank of Tanzania, provided wise guidance throughout the process and particularly helped us to focus on narrowing the gap between research and policy, including our two fruitful meetings in Zanzibar. His team at the Bank of Tanzania was most helpful in many ways, and we have special thanks for Patricia Mlozi, Mechtilda Mugo, Msafiri Nampesya, and Pamella Lowassa-Solomon.

Our conference in Accra benefited greatly from the engagement and support provided by Ernest Aryeetey, Kwesi Botchwey, and Robert Osei. And we had great cooperation in many ways across the entire project with African Economic Research Consortium (AERC); thanks to Olu Ajakaiye, William Lyakurwa, and Lemma Senbet for making this possible.

We would like to thank everyone who attended our various conferences and who worked hard on all dimensions of these research projects. We are also most grateful for all the inputs received from members of the Advisory Committee, formed especially for this project: Robert Bates, Paul Collier, Martin Feldstein, Benno Ndulu, Franklyn Prendergast, Antoinette Sayeh, Nicholas Stern, and John Taylor.

The entire project ran smoothly due to the hard work, precision, and attention to detail of Elisa Pepe at the NBER. Elisa was with us from beginning to end, and words cannot sufficiently express our gratitude for all she has done.

Others at the NBER provided outstanding help on a wide variety of tasks. Our meetings in the United States and in Africa were organized with exemplary competence by Carl Beck of the NBER's conference department. For all their help in the production, management, and dissemination of research, we would also like to thank Alex Aminoff, Laura Bethard, Daniel Feenberg, Helena Fitz-Patrick, Wayne Gray, Steve Harriman, and Alterra Milone. And for their assistance with the data portal, we are grateful to Binh Thanh Le, Dimitry Legagneur, and C. Michelle Tejada.

Volume Introduction

Sebastian Edwards, Simon Johnson, and David N. Weil

All the volumes in this series deal with some dimension of the broad question: Can recent African success—in terms of economic growth and human development—be sustained? At the time our research project was conceived, in the middle of the first decade of the twenty-first century, there were many skeptics who thought that recent African growth was primarily a flash in the pan, largely driven by resource exports. As we write this, in mid-2014, African economic success—and the contrast with previous failure—is undeniable.

But an entirely reasonable question—and one that we discussed in detail at all our research meetings—is whether sub-Saharan Africa can continue to grow as in the past two decades. Did the end of the Cold War provide an extraordinary one-off peace dividend, for example, because the superpowers stopped meddling or supporting proxy wars? Or is there some deeper transformation of African economies that proved elusive immediately after independence, but which is now firmly and irreversibly under way?

Volume I addresses this issue through chapters that look at the aftermath of civil war, the way in which political power operates, and how the private sector develops mechanisms to cope. Volume II focuses on the progress manifest in public health—including against both malaria and HIV/AIDS. On

Sebastian Edwards is the Henry Ford II Professor of International Economics at the University of California, Los Angeles, and a research associate of the National Bureau of Economic Research. Simon Johnson is the Ronald A. Kurtz (1954) Professor of Entrepreneurship and Professor of Global Economics and Management at the MIT Sloan School of Management and a research associate of the National Bureau of Economic Research. David N. Weil is the James and Merryl Tisch Professor of Economics at Brown University and a research associate of the National Bureau of Economic Research.

For acknowledgments, sources of research support, and disclosure of the authors' material financial relationships, if any, please see http://www.nber.org/chapters/c13432.ack.

this front, parts of Africa are already experiencing a breakthrough. Women's rights may also be on the rise, although here the progress is more tenuous. And whether existing educational systems can handle rising population numbers remains to be seen.

Volume III reports on the details of African development in the financial, mobile phone, and export sectors. The picture is mixed, but it is also far from gloomy. Africa's prospects seem real and the achievements to date are impressive. This is a huge reversal from what prevailed prior to the 1990s.

The current volume reports on research that looks more deeply at aspects of whether African growth will continue. We do not look at all aspects of sustainability—this project was not designed to produce a comprehensive picture, but rather to encourage outstanding research on questions of important current interest. The scholars we supported took a hard look at agriculture, market development, and some particularly informative case studies. They set high standards for quality research and we hope that other scholars will find it easy to stand on their shoulders.

The link between the chapters is that they all examine whether growth can be sustained. The recurrent theme is potential limits or constraints on growth, although each set of authors took a different approach to that issue. These chapters should be read, therefore, more as an inspiration to further high-quality work rather than as presenting any kind of definitive snapshot or comprehensive survey.

The authors obviously also disagree on what is most important in the next stages of African economic development. We view this disagreement as a strong indicator of competition between ideas. Providing we do not lose track of the most definite basics (covered in volumes I and II), it is healthy and even a good thing to have distinct ideas competing for the attention of policymakers. Hopefully, African governments will be able to learn from each other's experiences, for example, through the filter of high-quality applied economic research.

Agriculture

In chapter 1, "The Decline and Rise of Agricultural Productivity in Sub-Saharan Africa since 1961," Steven Block argues that agricultural productivity growth in sub-Saharan Africa has been much better than commonly supposed. The period immediately after independence witnessed slow or negative growth in output per worker and output per hectare in most of Africa, but total factor productivity growth increased rapidly from the early 1980s. In part, this is explained by higher spending on relevant agricultural research and development, but better macroeconomic and sector-level policies have also played a role. In addition to his cross-country evidence, the author provides some more detailed insights into the particular experience of Ghana.

In chapter 2, Douglas Gollin and Richard Rogerson root their analysis in the details of the quasi-subsistence sector in Uganda, but they also attempt to draw much more general implications. Specifically, in "Agriculture, Roads, and Economic Development in Uganda," they explore the links between high transportation costs, low productivity, and the size of the agricultural sector. Their model has the striking result that the number of Ugandans stuck in low-productivity agriculture is very much influenced by transportation costs. The possibility of strong positive complementarities between improvements in agricultural productivity and transportation needs more attention, particularly as this broadens the range of relevant potential policy actions.

One of the most dramatic success stories in this volume is contained in chapter 3, "The Sahel's Silent Maize Revolution: Analyzing Maize Productivity in Mali at the Farm Level." In Mali, production increased more than tenfold and yields grew by about 2 percent a year since independence. Jeremy Foltz, Ursula Aldana, and Paul Laris find that in southern Mali's maize-growing regions, farmer adoption of increased fertilizer use has driven much of the productivity growth. The adoption of new seed varieties by itself does not have huge impact; any move in that direction needs to be complemented by increased use of fertilizers. Interestingly, cotton production contributes to food security through making it possible to obtain credit, which can in turn be used to buy fertilizer for use in maize cultivation. New drought-resistant varieties have the potential to spread maize production into lower-rainfall regions of Mali and give farmers there the potential to access the higher fertilizer responsiveness of maize compared to sorghum or millet. Countries such as Senegal, Gambia, Guinea, and Niger have so far been left out of this green revolution for maize, but this could change—presumably if the right policies and incentives are put in place.

There is also evidence of new, more efficient institutional arrangements evolving. For example, in contract farming, the buyer and the producer commit in advance. In most cases, the buyer provides credit, monitors, and may be directly involved in part of the production process. In chapter 4, "Contract Farming and Agricultural Productivity in Western Kenya," Lorenzo Casaburi, Michael Kremer, and Sendhil Mullainathan use data from the administrative records of a large Kenyan sugarcane contract-farming scheme to study participation and productivity among participants.

Their analysis suggests that, in the presence of labor market imperfections that make plantations inefficient, contract farming can enable producers to take advantage of economies of scale, while preserving the existing allocation of land property rights. In the presence of monitoring costs, a contractual form that preserves decentralized land holdings has important advantages over a plantation estate. On the other hand, the contract-farming arrangement prevents some of the failures that would likely arise in a fully decentralized market, such as underinvestment in inputs due to credit constraints or lack of commitment ability for a monopsonist buyer.

Chapter 5 integrates thinking about agricultural development with the broader political economy themes that feature more prominently in volume I of our series. Nathan Nunn and Nancy Qian present evidence on what determines food aid, and report that some of the stated objectives of these programs have been met while others have not. In "The Determinants of Food-Aid Provisions to Africa and the Developing World," the authors examine the supply-side and demand-side determinants of global bilateral food-aid shipments between 1971 and 2008. Overall, domestic food production in developing countries is negatively correlated with subsequent food-aid receipts, suggesting that food-aid receipt is partly driven by local food shortages. However, food aid from some of the largest donors is the least responsive to production shocks in recipient countries. United States food aid is partly driven by domestic production surpluses, while former colonial ties are an important determinant for European donor countries, especially in the case of African recipients. Further, aid that flows to former colonies is particularly unresponsive to recipient country production.

Food aid and its impact on developing countries is a well-established topic. The impact of cellphones on development is a new topic, and one that was covered in part in volume III. In the context of their study, "International and Intranational Market Segmentation and Integration in West Africa" (chapter 6), Jenny C. Aker, Michael W. Klein, and Stephen A. O'Connell find significant international border effects dividing and disconnecting agricultural markets in Niger and Nigeria, but this effect is lower when participants in cross-border markets have access to mobile phones. As the authors put it succinctly, "the Walrasian auctioneer can be heard across the Niger-Nigeria border. Her voice carries especially well within her ethnic community, or with the aid of a mobile phone."

Country Studies

This volume, and in some sense our project, concludes with some case studies that shed light on particular sustained growth experiences. In chapter 7, "Cape Verde and Mozambique as Development Successes in West and Southern Africa," Jorge Braga de Macedo and Luís Brites Pereira provide a narrative of Cape Verde and Mozambique's long-term development. They stress the importance of moving toward a market economy, opening up to regional and global trade, increasing economic and political freedom, pursuing macroeconomic stability and financial reputation, ensuring policy continuity (especially in the industrial and trade sectors), and focusing on human development (especially education and poverty reduction).

Jeffrey Frankel draws broadly similar conclusions in chapter 8, "Mauritius: African Success Story." The country has mostly followed policies supportive of economic growth: creating a well-managed export processing zone, conducting diplomacy regarding trade preferences, spending on education, avoiding currency overvaluation, and facilitating business.

As is often the case, policies conducive to economic growth can in turn be traced back to the underlying institutional environment. In this case, the author emphasizes: forswearing an army, protecting property rights (particularly nonexpropriation of sugar plantations), and creating a parliamentary structure with comprehensive participation (in the form of representation for rural districts and ethnic minorities, the "best loser system," ever-changing coalition governments, and cabinet powersharing). But from where did the good institutions come? This is hard to say with great certainty, but it appears to help that the ancestors of everyone who lives on the island arrived from somewhere else during relatively recent historical times.

Chapter 9 uses the case study method to flesh out a mechanism through which colonialism may have had persistent negative effects on economic development. In "Indirect Rule and State Weakness in Africa: Sierra Leone in Comparative Perspective," Daron Acemoglu, Isaías N. Chaves, Philip Osafo-Kwaako, and James A. Robinson argue that a fundamental problem for economic development is that most poor countries have weak states, which are incapable or unwilling to provide basic public goods such as law enforcement, order, education, and infrastructure. In Africa this is often attributed to the persistence of indirect rule from the colonial period. The authors discuss ways in which a state constructed on the basis of indirect rule is weak and the mechanisms through which this weakness has persisted since independence in Sierra Leone. Indirect rule excessively empowered traditional rulers at the expense of postcolonial elites.

Conclusion

The six chapters in this volume that look at agriculture are, taken as a whole, among the most optimistic pieces of our project. No measure of economic success is more fundamental than whether people have enough to eat, and there are plenty of pessimistic observers of the African scene who worry about the continent's ability to feed itself in the long run.

Recent successes seem to have several causes. New technology, either directly related to agricultural production (new crop varieties) or useful in making markets more efficient (mobile phones in Niger) are part of the story. The same institutional changes that bear fruit in other economic dimensions—macroeconomic stability, reduced transport costs, improved communication—also lead to more productive farms. Similarly, contract farming—not a technology, but a potentially useful innovation—provides an efficient solution to many of the institutional problems in African agriculture.

Two of the three case studies included in this volume can also be said to be relatively optimistic. The cases of Mozambique and Cape Verde (taken together in chapter 7) show the benefits of sensible economic policies and reasonably good governance, accompanied by regional surveillance and "peer pressure," in terms of gross domestic product (GDP) growth (following, it must be acknowledged, a horrific civil conflict in Mozambique that ended in the early 1990s). The case of Mauritius is a more unalloyed success.

Of course we would not be fully representing the complexity and heterogeneity of the African experience if all the countries we studied were successes, and the final chapter, on Sierra Leone, certainly tells a mostly unhappy story regarding the persistence of weak state institutions.

As a fitting demonstration that economists rarely agree, that further research is always needed, and that only time really will tell, volume IV concludes with the relatively pessimistic view of Acemoglu, Chaves, Osafo-Kwaako, and Robinson, which stands in complete contrast to the chapter by Casey, Glennerster, and Miguel that opens the first volume of this project.

I

Agriculture

1

The Decline and Rise of Agricultural Productivity in Sub-Saharan Africa since 1961

Steven Block

> Measuring technical change is of interest because, in a sense, it defines our wealth and puts limits on what we can accomplish. . . . Since our ability to accumulate additional conventional resources . . . may be limited, the growth of the economy and of per capita income and wealth depends on the rate at which technological knowledge is expanding.
> —Zvi Griliches (1987, 1010)

1.1 Introduction

Agricultural productivity is central to the lives of most Africans. Two-thirds of the population of sub-Saharan Africa is rural, and the Food and Agriculture Organization (FAO) counts nearly half of sub-Saharan Africa's rural population as "economically active" in agriculture. For some countries, such as Burundi, Rwanda, Uganda, and Burkina Faso, the rural population share approaches 85–90 percent, with 45–50 percent of the total population counted as economically active in agriculture. Even among the most urbanized countries of sub-Saharan Africa, such as South Africa, one-third of the population remains rural. In addition, up to 80 percent of Africa's poor live in rural areas, nearly all of whom work primarily in agriculture (World Bank 2000). For these producer groups, agricultural productivity is the key determinant of welfare, and agricultural productivity growth is the key hope for poverty reduction (at least in the short to medium term). Nonfarm rural employment, too, is often closely linked to agriculture—either directly (as in the marketing of agricultural inputs and outputs) or indirectly (as in the provision of other services in rural markets). The indirect benefits of agricultural productivity growth, in the form of lower food prices, are also

Steven Block is professor of international economics and director of the Program on International Development at the Fletcher School at Tufts University.

The author wishes to thank the National Bureau of Economic Research Africa Project for supporting this research. He is particularly grateful to Keith Fuglie and Will Masters for detailed comments and suggestions, along with the feedback of participants at the NBER Africa Successes Project conference in Accra, Ghana (July 2010). The author also thanks Marina Dimova for her able assistance in constructing the data set. For acknowledgments, sources of research support, and disclosure of the author's or authors' material financial relationships, if any, please see http://www.nber.org/chapters/c13435.ack.

critical to the welfare of Africa's rapidly expanding urban populations, the poorest of whom devote 60–70 percent of total expenditures to food (Sahn, Dorosh, and Younger 1997).

From a macroeconomic perspective, as well, agriculture continues to play a central role in sub-Saharan Africa, accounting for 15 percent of total value added (20 percent, excluding South Africa). Of course, every generalization about sub-Saharan Africa masks the region's vast heterogeneity. In Liberia, for example, agriculture accounts for 66 percent of total value added, while in other countries, such as oil-rich Angola, agriculture accounts for only 10 percent of the value added (World Bank 2010).

African organizations, themselves, highlight these issues. The Comprehensive Africa Agriculture Development Program of the New Partnership for Africa's Development has stated that, "High and sustained rates of agricultural growth, largely driven by productivity growth, will be necessary if African countries are to accelerate poverty reduction. This is because agricultural growth has powerful leverage effects on the rest of the economy. . . . The poor performance of the agricultural sector explains much of the slow progress towards reducing poverty and hunger in Africa" (CAADP 2006, 7). Current efforts to promote a "new Green Revolution" in Africa face myriad environmental, institutional, and physical challenges in their quest to promote agricultural productivity growth in the region.

This chapter provides new estimates of cross-country agricultural productivity growth in sub-Saharan Africa. The resulting picture is one of qualified success. Total factor productivity (TFP) growth in African agriculture has accelerated dramatically since the early 1980s. By early in the twenty-first century, average annual total factor productivity growth in African agriculture was over four times faster than it had been twenty-five years earlier. The success is qualified by the finding that much of this acceleration represents a recovery from the substantial decline in TFP growth rates during the 1960s and early 1970s. In addition, levels of output per hectare and per worker in African agriculture remain low by global standards. Among a range of potential explanations for agricultural productivity growth in agriculture, expenditures on agricultural research and development (R&D) play a dominant role, followed by policy distortions at both the macroeconomic and sectoral levels. Improvements in the *quality* of the labor force, as indicated by average years of schooling, have also played a central role in driving productivity growth in African agriculture.

Many of these findings, gleaned from cross-country analysis, are also evident in this chapter's more detailed examination of agricultural productivity in Ghana.

This chapter is organized as follows. Section 1.2 reviews related studies. Section 1.3 describes data used in the cross-country analysis, as well as the approach used to aggregate agricultural output across multiple commodities. Section 1.4 provides a preliminary perspective on agricultural productivity trends in the form of partial productivity ratios (output per worker and per hectare). Sections 1.5 and 1.6 describe, respectively, my methodology for estimating total factor productivity growth and my results. Section 1.7 explores various explanations for the productivity results presented in the previous section. Section 1.8 presents a brief case study of agricultural productivity in Ghana, while section 1.9 concludes.

1.2   Related Studies

Within the broader literature on cross-country agricultural productivity, relatively few papers have focused specifically on sub-Saharan Africa. Block (1994) was the first to report a recovery of aggregate agricultural TFP in sub-Saharan Africa during the 1980s, a result confirmed by a number of subsequent studies. Block attributed up to two-thirds of this recovery to investments in agricultural R&D and to macroeconomic policy reform. Frisvold and Ingram (1995) provide an early growth accounting exercise for land productivity, concluding that most of it (up to 1985) resulted from increased input use (labor, in particular). Thirtle, Hadley, and Townsend (1995) highlight the role of policy choices, finding that an index of real agricultural protection played a significant role in explaining TFP growth in African agriculture for the period 1971–1986. Lusigi and Thirtle (1997) highlight the role of agricultural R&D in explaining TFP growth in Africa. They also highlight the role of increasing population pressure in driving increased agricultural productivity in Africa. Chan-Kang et al. (1999) focus on the determinants of labor productivity in a cross-country African setting. They, too, find land per unit of labor to be an important determinant of labor productivity.

Fulginiti, Perrin, and Yu (2004) estimate agricultural TFP growth for forty-one sub-Saharan African countries from 1960 to 1999, finding an average TFP growth rate of 0.83 percent per year, and confirming the finding from Block (1994) of an acceleration of the agricultural TFP growth since the mid-1980s. Their analysis concentrates on the role of institutions in explaining this growth. They conclude that former British colonies experienced greater rates of TFP growth, while former Portuguese colonies experienced lower rates. They also found negative effects for political conflicts and wars, and positive effects resulting from political rights and civil liberties. Three more recent papers conclude this review.

Nin-Pratt and Yu (2008) reconfirm the acceleration of African agricultural TFP growth since the mid-1980s. They find, however, a negative average growth rate of agricultural TFP (–0.15 percent per year) from 1964 to 2003, casting the recovery period as making up for negative productivity growth during the 1960s and 1970s. Specifically, Nin-Pratt and Yu find that average TFP growth fell at the rate of –2 percent per year from the mid-1960s to the mid-1980s, then grew by 1.7 percent per year between 1985 and 2003.

They, too, highlight the role of policy change in explaining this reversal in performance. In particular, they find that an indicator of reforms associated with structural adjustment played a positive role. In addition, they find that agricultural productivity in East and southern Africa benefited from the end of internal conflicts, and that agriculture in West Africa benefited from the devaluation of the CFA franc. They also provide suggestive evidence of the positive effect of investments in agricultural R&D.

Alene (2010) also focuses on the contributions of R&D expenditures to productivity growth in African agriculture. In contrast to the average TFP growth rate reported by Nin-Pratt and Yu (2008), Alene finds an average TFP growth rate of 1.8 percent per year for the period 1970–2004 (a difference that he attributes to an improved estimation technique). Alene finds strong positive effects of lagged R&D expenditure on agricultural productivity growth, arguing that rapid growth in R&D expenditures during the 1970s helped to explain strong productivity growth after the mid-1980s, while slower growth of R&D expenditures in the 1980s and early 1990s led to slower productivity growth since 2000. Alene (2010) also notes a 33 percent annual rate of return on investments in agricultural R&D in Africa.

Most recently, Fuglie (2010) examines agricultural productivity growth in sub-Saharan Africa from 1961 to 2006. His findings are mixed. While he reports an increased rate of growth in agricultural *output* during the 1990s and early in the twenty-first century, Fuglie finds that most of this growth in output is explained by expanding cropland rather than improved productivity. Fuglie (2010) stands out in this literature for his critical assessment of the standard data sources, for which he proposes various corrections. In contrast to previous studies, Fuglie does not find a general recovery of agricultural productivity in recent decades. For the period 1961–2006, he reports an average TFP growth rate of 0.58 percent per year, with the lowest rate occurring during the 1970s (–0.18 percent per year), and the highest rate occurring during the 1990s (1.17 percent per year).

Thus, recent estimates of the rate of agricultural TFP growth in Africa differ widely, though there is a general consensus surrounding a decline in productivity during the first two decades following independence and a recovery during the past two decades. These studies applied different methodologies to essentially the same data set, which may explain some of the conflicting findings cited above. As described below, the methodology applied in the present study differs from all of the studies cited above.

1.3   Data and Output Aggregation

This study combines data from a variety of sources. The core data on agricultural outputs and inputs are drawn from the FAO online database. While often regarded as being of limited quality, these data are ubiquitous in studies of international agricultural productivity, as they are the only comprehensive and detailed source of cross-country data over a long period of time. The central challenge in constructing a data set suitable for estimating a cross-country agricultural production function lies in aggregating the output of multiple agricultural commodities in a way that is comparable across both time and space. The fact that national-level data on key agricultural inputs—land, labor, fertilizer, tractors, and livestock—are provided as national totals, and not disaggregated by the crops to which they are applied, requires that agricultural output also be aggregated to the national level.

The most comprehensive discussion of agricultural output aggregation for international comparison is Craig, Pardey, and Roseboom (1991). Drawing on index number theory, they note that the ideal approach to aggregating multiple commodities for a given country and year would be to multiply a vector of base-year local commodity prices expressed in dollars by a vector of quantities of individual commodities. In particular, they specify that the best price weights would be those most specific to the economic activity and agents in question. Yet, even in the absence of data constraints, there is no perfect way to implement this ideal. The key dimensions of the problem, in practice, lie in choosing appropriate deflator's for comparisons over time, and in choosing appropriate exchange rates for comparisons across countries. Severe constraints on the availability of commodity-specific price data over time for each country in sub-Saharan Africa add to these challenges of constructing internationally and intertemporally comparable agricultural output aggregates.

Given the availability of commodity-specific local currency-denominated prices over time, the standard approach for converting aggregate output in a given year into internationally comparable units of measure is to select a numeraire currency, and to use purchasing power parity (PPP) exchange rates for conversion.[1] For its global agricultural data set, the FAO has calculated "agricultural exchange rates," or agricultural PPPs, that it applies in creating internationally comparable aggregates of agricultural output. In practice, virtually every study of international agricultural productivity (whether global or region specific) simply uses these FAO data, based on PPP prices calculated from the global data set. In theory, however, as noted above, the best price weights to use in aggregating output are those that are most specific to the particular setting of concern.

The present study thus departs from standard practice by calculating a unique set of international commodity prices and PPP exchange rates specific to African agriculture.

In order to calculate the Africa-specific international prices and PPP exchange rates used to construct the data set for this study, I applied the

---

1. Craig, Pardey, and Roseboom (1991) provide an extensive discussion of the trade-offs involved in first deflating and then converting each year aggregate output versus first converting in any deflating.

Geary-Khamis method summarized by Rao (1993). This method requires calculating both a reference set of international commodity prices based on relevant PPP exchange rates and calculating the PPP exchange rates based on the reference set of international commodity prices. This problem is described by a system of two simultaneous equations. In the first equation, the international reference price for commodity i is calculated as a function of its local currency price in each country $j = 1, \ldots, m$ converted by the PPP exchange rate for country j. In the second equation, the PPP exchange rate for country j is calculated as a function of the quantities and international reference prices for each commodity $i = 1, \ldots, n$ in country j. This is done for a given base year. These two equations can be solved iteratively, ultimately converging on a unique set of reference prices and PPP exchange rates for the specific countries and commodities to be studied. For purposes of this study, I calculated international prices and PPP exchange rates using prices and quantities for the $n = 35$ commodities in the $m = 27$ sub-Saharan African countries for which data were available from the FAO.[2] I then applied these reference prices in aggregating output across these commodities for the full set of forty-four sub-Saharan African countries for which commodity-specific output data were available. Output data for each commodity are net of quantities used for seed and feed.

The base year for these reference prices was 2006. I then created a Paasche-type output index, applying the 2006 prices to aggregate the commodity output data in each country for each year going back to 1961. The rationale for applying the Paasche approach was that the range and, in particular, the quality of the price data has tended to improve over time, and that the best data would thus be the most recent.[3]

Data for the other standard inputs to be used in estimating the agricultural production function are also drawn from the FAO database. The land measure is hectares of permanent and arable cropland, the labor measure is the number of economically active males and females in agriculture, capital is represented by the number of tractors, fertilizer is measured in tons of inorganic plant nutrient, and livestock is measured as the number of "cattle equivalents" held on farms for productive use.[4]

Each of these indicators of agricultural inputs falls short of the ideal data for measuring agricultural productivity. In discussing the measurement problems generically associated productivity analysis, Griliches (1960, 1987) has noted that proper estimation of production functions should be based on the flow of services of capital (accounting for vintage) in constant prices,

---

2. Appendix table 1A.1 presents the list of commodities and countries used in calculating the Africa-specific international prices. Resulting output data for each country-year are available on request from the author.

3. I am grateful to Philip Pardey for suggesting this approach.

4. Craig, Pardey, and Roseboom (1997) note, for example, that up to 70 percent of total horsepower traction in African agriculture is provided by livestock.

as well as on the flow of labor services (e.g., hours worked) weighting different types of labor by their marginal prices. Clearly, the input data available for African agriculture, consisting of counts of the number of tractors and the number of agricultural workers (issues of data quality aside), fall far short of this ideal. In particular, the assumption in the data that all of what is counted as agricultural labor is specifically on-farm labor contradicts microbased evidence of significant nonfarm rural activity (Liedholm, McPherson, and Chuta 1994). Overcounting labor in this way may impose a downward bias on estimated TFP growth. There must also be substantial measurement error in fertilizer data that capture only inorganic fertilizer in a setting where manure is the primary source of added soil nutrients.

In short, the methodological trade-offs and measurement errors inevitably associated with constructing both the output and the input data for African agriculture are substantial, and suggest the potential for significant noise and bias in estimates of total factor productivity. Yet, as demonstrated in the seminal work of Jorgenson and Griliches (1967), it is possible to mitigate these problems by introducing explicit controls for the quality of inputs.

As described below, the quality of inputs differs across countries and over time within countries. To the limited extent possible, it is important to control for these differences by including input quality adjustments in productivity estimates. Data used here to adjust for variations in land quality include the proportion of permanent and arable cropland that is irrigated, and annual rainfall. The former are drawn from data compiled by Sebastian (2007). The annual rainfall data used in this study are drawn from Mitchell et al. (2003) and Jefferson and O'Connell (forthcoming), based on the crop-weighting scheme of Ramankutty and Foley (1998).[5] Quality adjustments to the agricultural labor force generally rely on literacy rates. This study takes advantage of newly released data on average years of schooling from Barro and Lee (2010). Additional data used in trying to decompose the productivity residual are described below.

1.4 Partial Productivity Ratios

Partial productivity ratios (output per worker and output per hectare) provide a useful initial overview of both the level and growth rate of agricultural productivity. While these ratios share the analytical limitation of not controlling for changes in other inputs, they have the virtue of reflecting the general nature of technical change and agriculture as being predominantly either land or labor saving. The simplicity of partial productivity ratios may also be a benefit in a preliminary analysis of noisy and often low-quality data.

5. These rainfall data, along with detailed explanations of their construction, are available at: http://acadweb.swarthmore.edu/acad/rain-econ/Framesets/CountryAggregated.htm.

Hayami and Ruttan (1985) present a useful and intuitive conceptual approach for analyzing joint trends in partial productivity ratios, based on the simple identity

(1)
$$\frac{Y}{L} \equiv \frac{A}{L} \times \frac{Y}{A},$$

where Y is output, A is area, and L is labor. Taking logarithms of this identity facilitates thinking in terms of relative changes, as in

(2)
$$\log\left(\frac{Y}{L}\right) \equiv \log\left(\frac{A}{L}\right) + \log\left(\frac{Y}{A}\right).$$

The welfare of Africa's agricultural labor force ultimately depends on increasing output per worker. Equation (2) illustrates the challenge to that process in an environment characterized by rapid population growth and limited land area. To the extent that population growth outpaces the rate of expansion of agricultural area, area per worker (A/L) declines, thus increasing the challenge of raising average labor productivity (Y/L) by means of increasing average yield (Y/A). This dynamic has been a major obstacle to agricultural development in sub-Saharan Africa.

Table 1.1 presents the growth rates of partial productivity ratios for sub-Saharan Africa and its subregions by decade from 1961 to 2007. For the region as a whole over this entire period the average annual growth rate of output per worker has been only 0.41 percent, despite an average annual growth rate of 1.24 percent in output per hectare. As suggested by equation (2), the limited ability of yield growth in African agriculture to drive growth in average labor productivity has been driven by the increasing population density of rural Africa, where the annual growth of the agricultural labor force has outpaced area expansion by 0.83 percent per year from 1961 to 2007. Yet, recent years demonstrate a more optimistic trend. For the period 2001 to 2007, the growth rate of average labor productivity in African agriculture has increased dramatically (to over 2 percent per year) relative to previous periods—an advance aided by a reversal of the historical trend toward declining area per worker.

In their seminal study of agricultural development, Hayami and Ruttan (1985) also developed a useful and intuitive graphical presentation of partial productivity ratios. Their graphical representation of equation (2) simultaneously relates changes over time in average land and labor productivity by measuring average land productivity along the vertical axis and average labor productivity along the horizontal axis. Changes in output per hectare and output per worker over a given period can be illustrated by drawing an arrow between the relevant beginning and ending coordinates in that space. Scaling the axes in logarithms conveniently implies that movements along any 45° line represent equal rates of change in both land and labor productivity. From equation (2), it follows that such equal rates of change imply a

Table 1.1   **Partial productivity ratio growth rates by region**

Region	1961–70	1971–80	1981–90	1991–2000	2001–07	1961–2007
East						
Output/worker	1.06	−0.73	1.3	−0.03	1.16	0.26
Output/ha	1.81	1.22	2.56	1.38	1.16	1.59
Ha/worker	−0.75	−1.95	−1.26	−1.41	0	−1.33
Central						
Output/worker	0.97	−0.76	−0.58	1.2	1.67	−0.09
Output/ha	0.55	−1.43	1.09	2.3	2.19	0.65
Ha/worker	0.42	0.67	−1.67	−1.1	−0.52	−0.74
Southern						
Output/worker	3.14	1.98	3.72	2.68	1.09	1.24
Output/ha	3	1.87	3.32	3.39	1.74	1.14
Ha/worker	0.14	0.11	0.4	−0.71	−0.65	0.1
Western						
Output/worker	0.4	1.31	3.16	2.77	4.67	1.05
Output/ha	1.14	1.46	3.61	2.14	2.69	1.27
Ha/worker	−0.74	−0.15	−0.45	0.63	1.98	−0.22
Sahel						
Output/worker	−0.99	−0.95	1.92	0.96	2.34	−0.05
Output/ha	0.38	0.24	0.23	0.42	1.71	0.56
Ha/worker	−1.37	−1.19	1.69	0.54	0.63	−0.61
SSA						
Output/worker	0.81	−0.02	1.79	1.12	2.18	0.41
Output/ha	1.38	0.78	1.79	1.79	1.65	1.24
Ha/worker	−0.57	−0.8	0	−0.67	0.53	−0.83

Source: The FAO and author's calculations.

constant level of area per worker. Thus, each 45° line in this space represents a unique and constant level of A/L. Partial productivity paths steeper than 45° reflect increased rural population density over time.

Timmer (1988) provides various interpretations of movements over time in this space. He notes, for example, that a movement due north (indicating growth in yield with no growth in average output per worker) may indicate population growth matched by increased yields through higher labor inputs and technical change, but no improvement in rural living standards. Movements to the northwest might suggest population growth faster than technical change in raising yields, with a consequent deterioration in rural living standards. In contrast, movements due east in this space might reflect a declining agricultural workforce with no changes in yields, but with new mechanical technologies needed to maintain output with fewer workers, hence increasing average labor productivity and rural welfare.

Figure 1.1 implements this framework, placing African agriculture in a global context. The partial productivity paths depicted in figure 1.1 illustrate changes from 1961/65 (period average) to 2001/05, distinguishing the coordinates also at 1981/85 for sub-Saharan Africa and other middle-income and

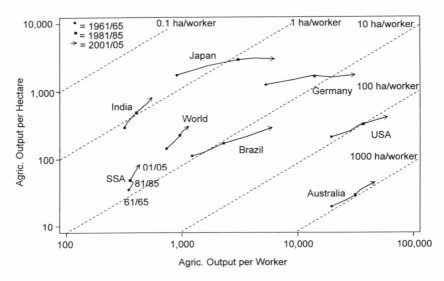

Fig. 1.1   Partial productivity ratios for Africa and global comparisons in agriculture, 1961/65–2001/05

advanced economies. The positions of these paths reflect different levels of land and labor productivity, while their lengths indicate rates of change. It is clear from figure 1.1 that Africa begins and ends this period with levels of land and labor productivity that are quite low in comparison with those found in more advanced economies, as well as in comparison with the world averages. Stated differently, African agriculture falls well within the meta-production frontier defined here by Japan, Germany, the United States of America, and Australia. Productivity growth in African agriculture, as reflected in these partial productivity ratios, has been driven almost entirely by increased yields per hectare, with little growth of output per worker. This results in a path substantially steeper than the 45° line, indicating that rural Africa has grown increasingly crowded.

While during the second half of this period sub-Saharan Africa reflects a slightly increased rate of growth in average labor productivity, that progress remains quite small by comparison with the other countries illustrated in figure 1.1. Note as well that those countries with the most rapid increases in agricultural labor productivity have followed paths shallower than the 45° lines, indicating increases in area per worker over time.

Figure 1.2 intensifies the focus on partial productivity ratios in Africa, disaggregating by five subregions and the averages of successive five-year periods.[6] Consistent with the data presented in table 1.1, no region of sub-

6. For purposes of global comparison, output in figure 1.1 was measured in constant agricultural value added. Beginning with figure 1.2, as discussed in the text, output is measured as aggregate crop output calculated for this study.

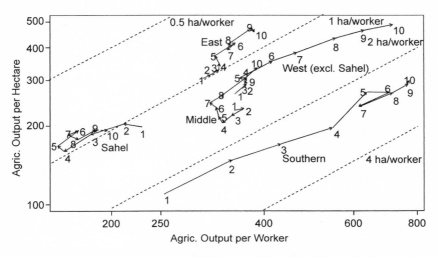

Fig. 1.2   Regional disaggregation of African partial productivity ratios (crop output) 1961/65–2006/07

Note: Output units: SSA intl. $; 1 = 61/65; 2 = 66/70; 3 = 71/75; 4 = 76/80; 5 = 81/85; 6 = 86/90/ 7 = 91/95; 8 = 96/00; 9 = 01/05; and 10 = 06/07.

Saharan Africa experienced continuous growth in both land and labor productivity, though some regions were clearly more successful than others. Southern Africa, for example, began in the early 1960s at a relatively low level of output per worker, yet experienced the fastest rate of subsequent growth (averaging 1.24 percent per year, per table 1.1), though with a significant setback between 1986/90 and 1991/95. West Africa, too, made substantial progress in increasing agricultural labor productivity beginning in the early 1980s. In contrast, Sahelian countries began with the lowest level of average labor productivity in 1961/65, and saw that level decline consistently (along with yields) until at least the early 1980s. Similarly, countries in middle Africa experienced slow declines in agricultural labor productivity until the early 1990s, while countries in eastern Africa experienced consistent but relatively slow increases in both land and labor productivity over most of the period.[7] These contrasting experiences, even at the regional level, illustrate the great heterogeneity of African agriculture. This heterogeneity pertains both to conditions and to rates of progress over time. (Note, for example, the substantially greater level of average area per worker in southern Africa as compared with eastern Africa.)

Figure 1.3 (panels a, b, c, and d) underscores this country-level heterogeneity. Figure 1.3, panel (a), presents country-level partial productivity

7. Note here that the East African countries begin with relatively high levels of rural population density (reflected in their position along a higher 45° line) and follow a relatively steep path over time, indicating a tendency toward land-saving technical change. This is consistent with the Induced Innovation Hypothesis, associated with Hayami and Ruttan (1985).

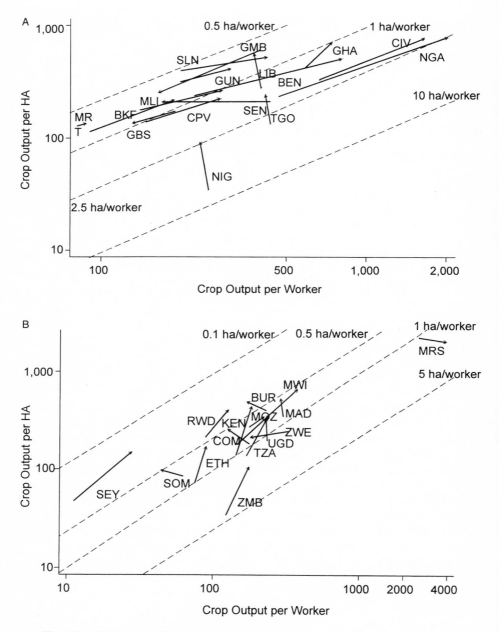

Fig. 1.3 Country-specific partial productivity ratios

Note: Panel (a) = west, panel (b) = east, panel (c) = middle, and panel (d) = southern.

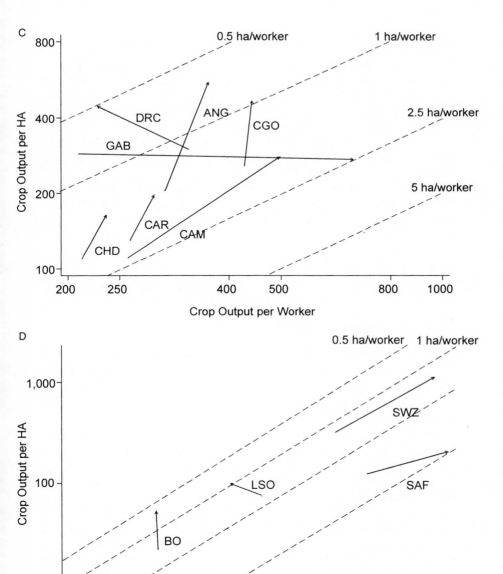

Fig. 1.3 (cont.)

paths for western Africa over the period 1961/65 to 2001/05. Some countries, such as Nigeria, Côte d'Ivoire, and Benin experienced significant growth in average labor productivity accompanied by moderate growth in crop yield, while other countries, such as Togo, Niger, and Liberia experienced gains in crop yield accompanied by small reductions in average labor productivity. At the same time, figure 1.3, panel (a) depicts rapid declines in agricultural labor productivity in Senegal, Gambia, and Guinea-Bissau. Among countries in eastern Africa (figure 1.3, panel [b]), there was the predominant tendency toward moderate gains in crop yield accompanied by slow growth in output per worker. Figure 1.3, panel (c) and 1.3, panel (d) depicts a similar heterogeneity of experience among the countries of middle and southern Africa, respectively. Table 1.2 presents partial productivity growth rates by country, and ranks countries in order of their growth rates of both land and labor productivity.

In general, these patterns (particularly at the level of regional disaggregation) conform to what is known of events on the ground. Gabre-Madhin and Haggblade (2004) provide an interesting perspective on successes in African agriculture. They conducted a survey of over 100 experts working in various areas related to African agriculture (two-thirds of whom were Africans), asking them to identify the most important factors in advancing African agriculture. The majority (62 percent) pointed to successes tied to specific commodities, 21 percent identified activities such as policy reform and enhancement of soil fertility, and 16 percent cited successful institution-building efforts as the primary drivers of African agriculture. Maize breeding (followed by cassava breeding) was the most widely cited contributor. Byerlee and Jewell (1997) report that most of the successes in breeding, releasing, and in adopting improved maize varieties was in east and southern Africa. Between 1966 and 1990, Byerlee and Jewell note the release of over 300 improved varieties and hybrids by national maize research programs.

The release of hybrid maize in Africa dates back to the early 1930s in Zimbabwe (then Southern Rhodesia), though there were no major successes until the release in Zimbabwe of the variety SR52 in 1960. Successful hybrid maize releases followed shortly thereafter in Kenya. Byerlee and Jewell (1997) report widely varying results for the adoption of maize hybrids and improved open-pollinated varieties. By 1990, nearly all of Zimbabwe's maize area was planted to hybrids, as was 70 percent of Kenya's maize area, and 77 percent of Zambia's maize area. At the same time, however, Malawian farmers had planted only 14 percent of maize area to improve varieties, similar to the 18 percent of Mozambique's maize area, and 13–29 percent of Ethiopia's maize area to improve varieties. Byerlee and Jewell also note that even in countries with substantial areas devoted to improved maize varieties, yield gains were often moderated by declining soil fertility combined with extremely limited application of chemical fertilizer. Kumwenda et al. (1997) cite declining soil fertility as the most widespread limitation on both yield

Table 1.2   **Growth rates of partial productivity ratios by country**

1961–2007	Growth rate of:		Ranked by:	
	Output/worker	Output/ha	Output/worker	Output/ha
Angola	–0.98	1.25	Nigeria	Nigeria
Benin	3.03	2.09	Benin	Seychelles
Botswana	–.625	1.52	Gabon	Swaziland
Burkina Faso	1.74	1.65	Swaziland	Malawi
Burundi	–0.47	0.79	South Africa	Zambia
Cameroon	1.09	1.81	Seychelles	Namibia
Cape Verde	1.91	1.51	Cape Verde	Ethiopia
Cent. Afr. Rep.	–.107	0.684	Côte d'Ivoire	Kenya
Chad	0.35	1.43	Namibia	Benin
Comoros	–0.62	0.803	Burkina Faso	Niger
Congo	–0.29	1.19	Mali	Côte d'Ivoire
Congo, Dem. Rep.	–0.63	1.15	Malawi	Cameroon
Côte d'Ivoire	1.88	1.82	Mauritania	Tanzania
Djibouti	6.17	10.61	Cameroon	Burkina Faso
Equatorial Guinea	–2.75	–2.01	Mauritius	Botswana
Eritrea	–3.99	–3.78	Guinea	Cape Verde
Ethiopia	–0.18	2.25	Sierra Leone	Chad
Gabon	3.02	0.47	Ghana	Ghana
Gambia	–2.86	–2.09	Rwanda	Angola
Ghana	0.6	1.41	Zambia	Rwanda
Guinea	0.78	0.81	Chad	Congo
Guinea-Bissau	–0.65	–0.44	Tanzania	Congo, Dem. Rep.
Kenya	0.15	2.17	Kenya	Lesotho
Lesotho	–0.54	1.12	Central African Rep	Togo
Liberia	–0.79	0.9	Mozambique	South Africa
Madagascar	–0.41	0.62	Ethiopia	Liberia
Malawi	1.46	2.62	Congo	Uganda
Mali	1.73	0.67	Togo	Guinea
Mauritania	1.12	0.17	Madagascar	Comoros
Mauritius	1.06	–0.09	Burundi	Burundi
Mozambique	–0.15	0.2	Uganda	Central African Republic
Namibia	1.87	2.39	Niger	Mali
Niger	–0.52	1.87	Lesotho	Madagascar
Nigeria	3.43	3.16	Zimbabwe	Zimbabwe
Rwanda	0.56	1.19	Comoros	Gabon
Senegal	–1.93	0.33	Botswana	Sierra Leone
Seychelles	2.54	2.78	Congo, Dem. Rep.	Senegal
Sierra Leone	0.65	0.42	Guinea-Bissau	Mozambique
Somalia	–1.1	–0.02	Liberia	Mauritania
South Africa	2.6	1.01	Angola	Somalia
Swaziland	2.91	2.63	Somalia	Mauritius
Tanzania	0.28	1.73	Senegal	Guinea-Bissau
Togo	–0.35	1.05	Equatorial Guinea	Equatorial Guinea
Uganda	–0.48	0.83	Gambia	Gambia
Zambia	0.36	2.46	Eritrea	Eritrea
Zimbabwe	–0.6	0.48	(excluding Djibouti, as too small and an outlier)	
AVERAGE (excl. Djibouti)	0.441	1.21		

Source: The FAO and author's calculations.

improvement in the sustainability of the maize-based production systems in southern and eastern Africa.

Gabre-Madhin and Haggblade's (2004) survey reinforces the specific success of maize breeding programs in East and southern Africa, where by the turn of the century, they reported that 58 percent of maize area planted to improved hybrids with yields gains of about 40 percent over local varieties. In contrast, only about 20 percent of total maize area in West and Central Africa were planted to improve varieties. Those regions were more dominated by improved open-pollinating varieties, with output gains of 15–45 percent over local varieties.

Evenson and Gollin (2003) track the annual rate of varietal releases for all improved crop varieties. While not disaggregating by regions within Africa, they do report a near doubling of the number of average annual releases between 1976–1980 and 1981–1985, from 23 to 43.2 (and to 50 per year by the early 1990s). This accelerated release of improved crop varieties coincides with the acceleration in the growth of both partial productivity ratios reported in table 1.1.

Other important sources of success in African agriculture cited in the survey included breeding to combat mosaic virus in cassava, as well as improvements in the yield and drought resistance of that crop (which is particularly important in West and Central Africa); expansion of horticultural and flower exports from East and southern Africa; rapid growth of cotton production and exports from West Africa (the Sahelian countries in particular); and, improved breeding of bananas in Central Africa. Among activity-led successes, Gabre-Madhin and Haggblade's survey noted soil fertility enhancement, such as alley cropping in West Africa and improved water management techniques in southern Africa. Respondents also noted the positive effects of market reforms, currency devaluation, and improved institutions as contributors to Africa's improved agricultural performance.

Partial productivity ratios, while indicative of broad trends in the rate and nature of productivity growth, are limited by their lack of control for potentially confounding changes in other inputs. The remaining sections of this chapter thus turn to the estimation of total factor productivity growth in African agriculture.

1.5   Measuring Total Factor Productivity Growth in Agriculture: Methodology

The rate of growth of total factor productivity (TFP) is conventionally defined as the difference between the rate of growth of real product and the rate of growth of real factor input. Assuming, as in Solow (1957), competitive factor markets and constant returns to scale in the aggregate production function, a change in total factor productivity can be measured as a vertical shift in the production function. A variety of methodological approaches have evolved for estimating total factor productivity growth, including the construction of TFP indices (such as the Tornquist-Theil), data envelopment analysis (based on the nonparametric Malmquist index), and stochastic frontier analysis, in addition to the econometric estimation of the aggregate production function. The TFP estimation in the present study is based on the latter approach of estimating the aggregate agricultural production function for a panel of African countries.[8] One key benefit of a parametric approach is that it helps to impose order in an otherwise noisy data set.

Specifying the aggregate agricultural production function requires numerous choices, beginning with functional form. I adopt the Cobb-Douglas functional form, which has been repeatedly validated in agricultural studies (Griliches 1964; Hayami and Ruttan 1985), as has been the assumption of constant returns to scale (Hayami and Ruttan 1985). The "traditional" inputs included in virtually every cross-country study of agricultural productivity include: land, labor, fertilizer, tractors, and livestock. As noted above, available data for each of these inputs almost certainly include significant measurement error. In addition, as emphasized in the early studies of US agriculture by Griliches (1963, 1964), and for the US economy as a whole by Jorgenson and Griliches (1967), much of what might mistakenly be attributed to TFP growth may in reality be changes over time in the *quality* of inputs.

Whether one puts such adjustments for input quality in the production function or in the residual is an interesting question. Griliches (1960, 1411) takes an agnostic approach, suggesting "Whether or not we want the input measures to cover all possible quality changes is a semantic rather than a substantive issue. Hybrid seed corn can be viewed either as improvement in the quality of seed or as 'technical change.' Since we are interested in explaining the growth of agricultural output, it does not matter much whether we put it into the 'input change' category or the 'productivity change' category as long as we put it somewhere and know where it is."

1.5.1   Specification

The dependent variable in my aggregate production function is crop output aggregated (as described above) based on the Africa-specific international commodity prices and PPP exchange rates calculated for this study.

---

8. Tornquist-Theil indices require detailed factor price data that are unavailable for African agriculture. Stochastic frontier approaches derive their results entirely by imposing very strong conditions on the error structure of the estimated production function—an approach that seems particularly ill suited to the present setting, which is characterized by low quality and quite noisy data. The data envelopment analysis approach, while often used in recent studies of agricultural productivity (Lusigi and Thirtle 1997; Fulginiti, Perrin, and Yu 2004; Nin-Pratt and Yu 2008; and Alene 2010, among others), is also problematic. Heady, Alauddin, and Prasada Rao (2010), along with Nin-Pratt, Arndt, and Preckel (2003), note that DEA studies of agricultural TFP often produce anomalous and implausible results. The DEA approach measures countries' progress relative to a productivity frontier, which depends arbitrarily on the number and selection of countries included in the sample, and which is poorly suited to distinguish between TFP growth, noisy data, and measurement error. Coelli et al. (2005) discuss the relative merits of these approaches.

The resulting TFP estimates are thus limited to crop agriculture. This, too, reflects a departure from most of the literature, which typically includes both crop and livestock output (summed) for aggregate output. The median share by value of livestock output in total agricultural output over the entire sample is 0.21, though this share varies by region and country. The mean livestock share in total agricultural output is highest in the five countries included from southern Africa (0.48) and lowest among the ten included (non-Sahelian) countries of western Africa (0.17). For certain countries, including Botswana, Sudan, Mali, Mauritania, and Namibia, livestock output accounts for greater than half of the value of total agricultural output. For such countries, excluding livestock is a potentially significant omission. Yet, that omission brings with it the broader benefit of more accurate aggregation of output (based on Africa-specific data, which are not available for livestock output). On average this omission is relatively small. (Appendix B demonstrates the robustness of my main results compared against those derived from using a broader output aggregate that includes livestock.)

There is also a more theoretical reason for excluding livestock from the output aggregate, arising largely from the construction and interpretation of the production function itself. As typically specified, with inputs including tractors, fertilizer, livestock (used both for traction and as a source of manure), the production function conceptually describes specifically crop output. The estimated coefficients on these inputs are interpreted as production elasticities and serve as input weights for productivity measurement. This interpretation of estimated coefficients for tractors and fertilizer, in particular, is clouded by the inclusion of livestock in the dependent variable. Indeed, by comparison with crop agriculture, livestock production is less labor intensive and more land intensive, thus blurring the interpretation of those coefficients as well. Yet, excluding livestock from the dependent variable does come at the cost of underemphasizing integrated crop-livestock production systems that have become increasingly common in Africa. Available cross-country data on inputs and output in agriculture provide no perfect match between what is included on the left- and right-hand sides of the production function. For instance, while I can (and do) eliminate permanent pasture from my measure of land, the labor variable still includes labor applied to livestock production.[9]

Prior to specifying and estimating the cross-country production function, it is useful to present the growth rates of output and inputs. Table 1.3 presents these growth rates, distinguishing the periods before and after 1985. Crop output for the entire period 1961 to 2007 grew at an average rate of just over 2 percent per year, accelerating post-1985. Growth of the agricultural

---

9. Even if the FAO labor data were to distinguish between crop and livestock labor, they would likely grow at the same rate in any given country and year. As it is ultimately the growth rate of inputs that matters for TFP estimation, overstating the level of labor may have little effect on estimated TFP growth.

Table 1.3   **Annual growth rates of crop output and conventional inputs**

	1961–1984	1985–2007	1961–2007
Crop output	1.66	2.22	2.09
Labor	1.60	1.64	1.63
Land	0.84	0.90	0.85
Livestock	2.28	1.67	1.88
Tractors	7.14	−0.5	3.47
Fertilizer	6.28	−0.5	3.35

Source: The FAO and author's calculations.

labor force was also stable at about 1.65 percent per year. Agricultural area also expanded at a relatively stable 0.85 percent per year. What is striking, however, is the dramatic reversal in the growth rates of the number of tractors and tons of chemical fertilizers pre- and post-1985, a breakpoint that may reflect the widespread onset of structural adjustment and related reforms. From 1961 to 1984, the average growth rates for tractors and fertilizer were just over 7 percent and 6 percent, respectively; yet, post-1985, consumption of both *fell* at an average rate of 0.5 percent per year.

Loosely borrowing notations from Craig, Pardey, and Roseboom (1997), I specify the initial production function for country i at time t with k conventional inputs $X_{ij}^*(t)$, and a country-invariant temporal shift of variable $A(t)$ as:

$$(3) \qquad Y_i(t) = A(t) \prod_{j=1}^{k} X_{ij}^*(t)^{\beta_j}.$$

The presence of both quality change and measurement error in the inputs creates a divergence between observed inputs and effective inputs. We can separate out measurable country-specific (but time-varying) quality shifters in input j, $Z_{ij}(t)$, and country-specific but time-invariant measurement error in input j, α_{ij}. In this case, Craig, Pardey, and Roseboom (1997) note that the relationship between observed input $X_{ij}(t)$ and effective input $A(t)$ is given by

$$(4) \qquad X_{ij}^*(t) = \alpha_{ij} Z_{ij}(t) X_{ij}(t).$$

Substituting equation (4) into equation (3) and scaling the production function by dividing by input $X_{i1}(t)$ yields

$$(5) \qquad \frac{Y_i(t)}{X_{i1}(t)} = A(t) \prod_{j=2}^{k} \left[\frac{X_{ij}(t)}{X_{i1}(t)} \right]^{\beta_j} \prod_{j=1}^{k} \left[\alpha_{ij} Z_{ij}(t) \right]^{\lambda_j}.$$

This production function imposes constant returns to scale across the conventional inputs. The production elasticity for variable X_1 can be recovered in estimation as $\hat{\beta}_1 = 1 - \sum_{i=2}^{k} \hat{\beta}_j$. In practice, the scaling variable will be labor.[10] Equation (5) provides the basic production function to be estimated in measuring TFP growth, where TFP growth is captured by the intertemporal shifts in the production function measured by $A(t)$. Once having estimated the rate of TFP growth, the second stage of the analysis will be to explain that growth. Toward that end, I add to the production function in equation (5) a vector of m potential explanations, $P_{ij}(t)$, for the observed productivity growth in African agriculture.

The final production function can thus be written as

$$(6) \qquad \frac{Y_i(t)}{X_{i1}(t)} = A(t)\prod_{j=2}^{k}\left[\frac{X_{ij}(t)}{X_{i1}(t)}\right]^{\beta_j}\prod_{j=1}^{k}\left[\alpha_{ij}Z_{ij}(t)\right]^{\lambda_j}\prod_{j=1}^{m}P_{ij}(t)^{\gamma_j}.$$

Following Craig, Pardey, and Roseboom (1997), in the empirical representation of equation (6) I replace $A(t)$ with time-period dummies, $TD(s)$. These time dummies track vertical shifts of the production function over time, and thus provide a basis for estimating the rate of TFP growth. I also aggregate the input- and country-specific measurement error into composite time-invariant, country-specific dummies, CD_h. Expressing all but the dummy variables in natural logs (as lower-case letters) in per worker terms leads to the estimating equation:

$$(7) \qquad y_i(t) = c + \sum_{j=2}^{k}\beta_j x_{ij}(t) + \sum_{j=1}^{k}\lambda_j z_{ij}(t) + \sum_{j=1}^{m}\gamma_j p_{ij}(t) + \sum_{s=2}^{T}\alpha_s TD(s)$$
$$+ \sum_{h}^{n-1}\varphi_h CD_h + \varepsilon_i(t).$$

In practice, data constraints limit the number of input quality-adjusting variables to fewer than the number of inputs. Thus, the Z variables to be used include two adjustments for land quality (annual rainfall and percentage of land equipped for irrigation), and one variable to adjust for the quality of the labor force (average years of schooling, from Barro and Lee [2010]).

1.5.2   Estimation Strategy

I implement two different econometric approaches to deriving the rate of TFP growth from the estimation of equation (7).[11] The strategy will be first to estimate the production function including only conventional inputs and the country and period dummy variables (that is, imposing the constraints $\lambda_j = \gamma_j = 0$). I then derive the input quality-adjusted estimates of TFP growth

---

10. Scaling the production function substantially eliminates the heteroskedasticity that would otherwise result from combining countries of greatly differing size.

11. In theory there is some risk of endogeneity in estimating production functions if, for example, farmers choose observed inputs as a function of unobserved inputs. Estimating fixed effects models, such as that proposed here, helps to the extent that these unobserved effects are constant over time. Fuglie (2010) estimates a cross-country agricultural production function both with and without instrumental variables, but finds little difference between the two approaches.

by reestimating equation (7), this time including the Z variables (relaxing the constraint that $\lambda_j = 0$). The resulting quality-adjusted TFP estimates provide the baseline against which I decompose this productivity residual into various explanations for productivity growth.

A key practical consideration in deriving TFP growth estimates from equation (7) is to distinguish trends in true productivity from the substantial noise inherent in these data. Productivity growth is ultimately measured as a reflection of the deeper process of technical change, which in principle does not fluctuate dramatically from year to year (Griliches 1987). Given the heavy reliance of African agriculture on rainfall in particular, some form of smoothing is essential. This study applies two alternative econometric approaches to address this problem.

The most common approach for addressing this problem, given the availability of panel data, has been to collapse the annual cross sections into successive five-year averages. While somewhat ad hoc and potentially sensitive to the starting and ending years chosen, this approach is effective in smoothing out annual fluctuations. In deriving TFP measures from the estimation of equation (7), I begin with this approach. Having annual data from 1961–2007 permits the creation of nine full cross sections of five-year averages. I then introduce a novel approach to deriving TFP estimates from annual data, based on semiparametric estimation of the production function. The core idea shared by both approaches is that one can estimate the rate of TFP growth directly from vertical shifts in the production function.

The first approach applies seemingly unrelated regression (SURE) to a panel data set consisting of sequential five-year averages of the annual data. The strategy here is to specify the same production function for each cross section in the panel, using the SURE estimator to apply appropriate cross-equation constraints on the parameter estimates for conventional agricultural inputs, leaving the intercept terms unconstrained. Constraining similar slope terms to be equal across pairs of adjacent production functions ensures that the change in the intercepts of the production functions between periods reflects vertical shifts of the same production function over time.[12] In this case, we can derive estimates of TFP growth directly from changes in the intercept terms of adjacent production functions. My SURE system of production functions thus takes the form:

$$y_{i,61/65} = \alpha_{61/65} + \beta_{1,61/65}a_{i,61/65} + \beta_{2,61/65}tr_{i,61/65} + \beta_{3,61/65}f_{i,61/65} + \beta_{4,61/65}lv_{i,61/65} + \varepsilon_{i,61/65}$$

$$y_{i,66/70} = \alpha_{66/70} + \beta_{1,66/70}a_{i,66/70} + \beta_{2,66/70}tr_{i,66/70} + \beta_{3,66/70}f_{i,66/70} + \beta_{4,66/70}lv_{i,66/70} + \varepsilon_{i,66/70}$$

$$\vdots \qquad\qquad \vdots \qquad\qquad \vdots$$

$$y_{i,01/07} = \alpha_{01/07} + \beta_{1,01/07}a_{i,01/07} + \beta_{2,01/07}tr_{i,01/07} + \beta_{3,01/07}f_{i,01/07} + \beta_{4,01/07}lv_{i,01/07} + \varepsilon_{i,01/07}$$

12. Pair-wise equality constraints of the slope terms in adjacent production functions (e.g., the first two five-year periods out of nine, then the second and third periods, etc.) is the minimal requirement for this approach. The maximal approach would be to constrain the slope coefficients for a given input to be equal across all time periods simultaneously. Wald tests reject this maximal constraint, yet, as reported in the text, tend not to reject pair-wise constraints across adjacent periods.

where (in logs) y is crop output per worker, a is area per worker, tr is tractors per worker, f is fertilizer per worker, and lv is livestock per worker.

Estimating the rate of TFP growth between 1961/65 and 1966/70 first requires imposing (and testing) the constraint $\beta_{k,61/65} = \beta_{k,66/70}$ jointly for all of the conventional inputs. The rate of TFP growth between these periods can then be calculated as

(8)   Annual TFP growth rate $= T^{-1}exp\{\alpha_{66/70} - \alpha_{61/65}\}$,

where (given this panel structure) $T = 5$. This econometric approach is not common in the literature, but was used in Block (1994, 1995).

I also introduce in this chapter a novel approach to estimating TFP growth from annual panel data. As noted above, a key concern in estimating TFP growth is to distinguish productivity trends from noise. For this purpose, I propose a semiparametric approach to estimating the production function in equation (7). This approach controls linearly for the conventional inputs while allowing the residual relationship between output and time to take an undefined functional form. This revised production function is thus

$$(9) \qquad y_i(t) = c + \sum_{j=2}^{k}\beta_j x_{ij}(t) + \sum_{j=1}^{k}\lambda_j z_{ij}(t) + \sum_{j=1}^{m}\gamma_{j+}p_{ij}(t) + g(TD(s))$$

$$+ \sum_{h=1}^{n-1}\varphi_h CD_h + \varepsilon_i(t)$$

The difference between equation (7) and equation (9) lies in the specified functional relationship between output, $y_i(t)$, and the year dummies, $TD(s)$. Equation (7) is fully parametric and thus imposes a linear relationship between output and time, the estimation of which would provide a basis for calculating a single average rate of TFP growth for the period. In contrast, equation (9) retains the linear parametric relationship between output and all other variables included in the production function with the exception of the year dummies. Rather than imposing linearity on the relationship between output and the year dummies, the semiparametric specification of equation (9) allows this relationship to take an undefined functional form $g(\cdot)$.[13] This approach allows the estimated rate of TFP growth to vary freely over time, as defined by the data themselves, rather than imposing linearity (or any other predefined parametric specification).

To clarify the estimation procedure, combine all the linear arguments in equation (9) into the matrix x, and write the semiparametric regression as,

$$(10) \qquad\qquad y_i = g(z_i) + x_i\beta + \varepsilon_i.$$

Yatchew (2003) describes that when the data are sorted by z in increasing order of size (and assuming that g is a smooth function), then first differencing the data tends to eliminate the nonparametric term, $g(z_i)$, since the first

---

13. Yatchew (2003) provides comprehensive detail on semiparametric regeression.

difference, $g[z_{i(n)}] - g[z_{i(n-1)}] \to 0$ as the sample size increases.[14] In this case, after first differencing, one can consistently estimate $\hat{\beta}_{diff}$ by ordinary least squares (OLS). Then, subtracting the estimated parametric portion of the model from both sides of equation (10) (as Lokshin [2006] shows), one is left with

(11) $$y_i - x_i\hat{\beta}_{diff} = x_i\left(\beta - \hat{\beta}_{diff}\right) + g(z_i) + \varepsilon_i \cong g(z_i) + \varepsilon_i,$$

since $\hat{\beta}_{diff}$ converges to β. What remains is a two-dimensional, purely non-parametric relationship between y_i and z_i, which is estimated by a locally weighted kernel density smoother (using Stata's *lowess* command).

Thus, estimation of equation (9) effectively partials out the linear effects of the conventional inputs and country dummies, leaving a nonparametric kernel regression of output on the annual time dummies. The resulting estimated function, $\hat{g}(TD(s))$, is a smoothed nonparametric representation of annual shifts in the production function, controlling linearly for all other variables in equation (9).

Transforming this continuous function into estimates of the instantaneous rate of TFP growth requires a calculation analogous to that described by equation (8). Equation (8) converts discrete shifts over time in the intercept of the production function into a rate of change—an estimate of the average rate of TFP growth during the period of estimation. In the semiparametric case, the analogous task is to convert the estimated nonparametric effect of time on output into rates of change (or estimates of the growth rate of TFP). In this case, $\hat{g}(TD(s))$ is a nonparametrically smoothed representation of the annual shifts of the production function, estimated from the year dummies. For arbitrarily small changes in time, the analogy to equation (8) is implemented by differentiating $\hat{g}(TD(s))$ with respect to time:

(12) $$\text{Instantaneous rate of TFP growth} = \frac{\partial \hat{g}(TD(s))}{\partial s}.$$

That is, the slope of $\hat{g}(TD(s))$ with respect to time provides a point estimate of the instantaneous rate of TFP growth. Taking this derivative at every point of $\hat{g}(TD(s))$ thus results in a smoothed nonparametric path that describes the rate of TFP growth as a continuous function of time.

The following section presents estimates of TFP growth rates derived from both the SURE and semiparametric approaches described above.

1.6   Measuring Total Factor Productivity Growth in Agriculture: Results

An African success emerges from figure 1.4, which presents the rates of TFP growth in African crop agriculture, averaged over successive five-year periods from 1961/65 to 2001/06.

---

14. Also see M. Lokshin (2006) for a detailed exposition of the *plreg* Stata command commonly used to implement this estimator.

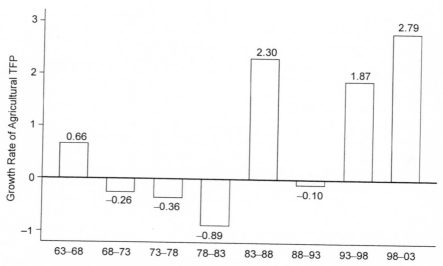

Fig. 1.4 Baseline TFP growth estimates for five-year periods (from SURE approach). Agricultural TFP growth rates, SSA, SURE estimates, excluding country effects and input quality adjustments

Note: Each year represents the middle of a five-year average.

These results reflect vertical shifts in the successive production functions based on five-year averages of annual panel data, estimated by the SURE regression procedure described above.[15] Thus, for example, the first bar in figure 1.4, marked 63–68 describes the average rate of TFP growth between 1963 (designating data averaged over the period 1961–1965) and 1968 (designating data averaged over the period 1966–1970). These baseline results control only for the conventional inputs, unadjusted for quality.

These preliminary results are encouraging in their reflection of a broad recovery of productivity growth in African crop agriculture beginning in the mid-1980s, reconfirming the results by Block (1994). Figure 1.4 depicts a history in which the early years of independence were characterized, on average, by a slow yet positive rate of productivity growth in African crop agriculture. This relatively auspicious start, however, was followed by fifteen years of stagnation and decline, as TFP growth rates became increasingly negative on average from the late 1960s through the early 1980s. In contrast,

15. Estimating TFP growth based on vertical shifts of the production function, as noted above, requires equality of the production elasticities for given conventional inputs across the production functions for the beginning and ending of the period being measured. Joint tests of the quality of the estimated coefficients on conventional inputs, implemented pair-wise for each of the eight sets of adjacent production functions failed to reject the equality of the production functions for all but one period (1968–1973), and in that case the rejection was only at the .10 level. These tests are thus highly supportive of this SURE approach to TFP estimation.

TFP growth rates since the mid-1980s, at least in this preliminary view, reflect a substantial turnaround, approaching 2.8 percent per year on average between the five-year periods centered around 1998 and 2003. The challenge, then, is to explain this reversal of fortune for African agriculture. I begin by examining the effect of changes in the quality of inputs, in particular land and labor. First, however, it is useful to review estimates of the underlying production function.

Table 1.4 presents estimates of the basic production function for African crop agriculture described by equation (7). The estimates in column (1) include only the conventional inputs. Column (2) adds controls for annual rainfall and the share of land equipped for irrigation to adjust for differences in land quality, and column (3) adds average years of schooling to control for changes in the quality of labor. In keeping with the inclusion of country dummies in equation (7) to control for, among other things, time-invariant measurement error, the production functions in table 1.4 are estimated as fixed-effects models.

The coefficient estimates in column (1) are all statistically significant and have the expected signs. By comparison with estimates in other studies of

Table 1.4   **Production function estimates (with country fixed effects), 1961–2000**

	(1)	(2)	(3)
Log land per worker	0.821***	0.822***	0.923***
	(17.07)	(17.22)	(18.12)
Log tractors per worker	0.025*	0.028**	0.031**
	(1.81)	(2.08)	(2.34)
Log livestock per worker	0.149***	0.106***	0.009
	(3.96)	(2.90)	(0.22)
Log fertilizer per worker	0.033***	0.034***	0.034***
	(4.05)	(4.30)	(4.37)
Log irrigated land share		0.050***	0.067***
		(3.09)	(4.10)
Log rainfall		0.365***	0.366***
		(8.67)	(8.80)
Avg. years schooling			0.058***
			(5.21)
Constant	5.123***	2.813***	2.774***
	(95.55)	(10.03)	(9.48)
Includes year dummies	Yes	Yes	Yes
Observations	1,038	1,038	1,038
Number of countries	30	30	30
R-squared	0.40	0.45	0.46

Note: Dependent variable: aggregate crop output. Absolute value of t statistics in parentheses.
***Significant at the 1 percent level.
**Significant at the 5 percent level.
*Significant at the 10 percent level.

African agriculture (such as Fuglie 2010), the production elasticity of land is quite high (and by implication, that of labor, quite low). The higher estimate for land in the present study may reflect in part the exclusion of livestock production from the output aggregate (described above). Historically, much of the increase in African crop output has been the result of land extensification. The implication that a 10 percent increase in land area per worker would result in a roughly 8 percent increase in crop output is thus plausible. Rainfall and share of land equipped for irrigation (which often differs from the share of land actually irrigated in any given year due to water constraints) both present significant positive effects on per capita output (column [2]). In addition, column (3) demonstrates the significant positive effect of average years of schooling of the labor force on agricultural output, suggesting that improvements in the quality of the labor force has been an important positive factor for African agriculture.

Figure 1.5 illustrates the nonparametric pattern of TFP growth rates over time, estimated from annual data and controlling linearly for (only) the five conventional inputs. These smoothed continuous results are consistent with the initial results presented in figure 1.4 in suggesting that the stagnation and decline of African crop productivity of the late 1960s through the early 1980s has been followed by two decades of substantial recovery and progress. While that progress appears to have stalled during the early and mid-1990s, average TFP growth rates for African crop agriculture have trended

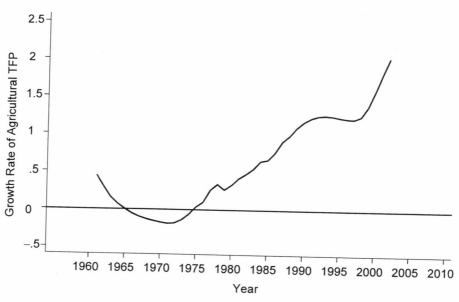

Fig 1.5   Baseline TFP growth rates (from semiparametric regression), SSA crops, excluding country effects and input quality adjustments

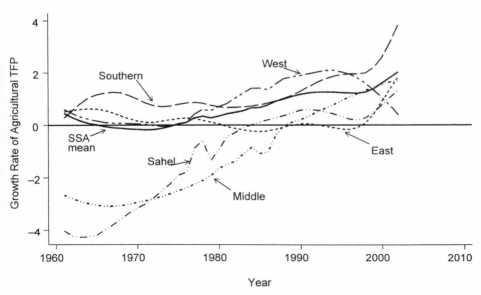

Fig. 1.6   Regional disaggregation of TFP growth rates, unadjusted for input quality, semiparametric regression

Note: Includes country fixed effects.

steeply upward since the late 1990s. By 2005, this growth rate exceeded 2 percent per year.

The average TFP growth rate of the path illustrated in figure 1.5 is 0.97 percent per year. This measurement is based on the period 1961–2000 for twenty-nine countries in sub-Saharan Africa. It is not adjusted for differences in the quality of inputs. Over this same period and set of countries, crop output grew at the average rate of 1.68 percent per year. As a first cut, then, TFP appears to explain 58 percent of the growth in Africa's crop output (though this estimate will be revised downward with the incorporation of adjustments for input quality).

Is interesting, as well, to disaggregate this average SSA result to the regional level (as presented above in figure 1.3, panels [a–d] for the partial productivity analysis). Here too, figure 1.6 demonstrates substantial heterogeneity across the regions of sub-Saharan Africa, though with a trend toward convergence in growth rates. Southern Africa has maintained a consistently high rate of TFP growth throughout this period, though the TFP growth rate for West Africa (excluding the Sahel) turned positive around 1975 and surpassed the growth rate for southern Africa between 1980 and 1995. On the low end, Sahelian and middle African countries began the postindependence period with negative rates of TFP growth, which turned positive only in the early and late 1980s, respectively. These results, sum-

Table 1.5   Regional TFP growth rates (unadjusted for input quality)

Region:	1960–1984	1985–2002	1960–2002
East	0.23	0.19	0.21
Southern	0.84	1.80	1.25
Middle	−2.43	0.61	−1.13
West	0.37	1.61	0.90
Sahel	−2.41	0.48	−1.17
SSA	0.14	1.24	0.61

marized in table 1.5, are consistent with those of the partial productivity analysis presented above. Comparing, in table 1.5, the regional average TFP growth rates for the periods 1961–1984 and 1985–2002, it is clear that every region except East Africa enjoyed a substantially greater rate of TFP growth in the later period.

Returning to the SSA average, the next step is to measure the contributions of changes in input quality to these initial estimates of TFP growth. Figure 1.7 repeats the semiparametric procedure underlying figure 1.5, adjusting first for changes in land quality, and then adjusting for labor quality as well.[16] Changes in the quality of land and labor emerge as significant contributors to TFP growth.

Table 1.6 quantifies these contributions by calculating the percentage change in the mean TFP growth rate over the entire period resulting from the inclusion of these additional explanatory variables. The mean TFP growth rate for the baseline estimates illustrated in figure 1.5 (and in the highest path in figure 1.7) for the period 1961 to 2000 was 0.97 percent per year.[17] After adjusting for land quality, this estimate falls to 0.87 percent per year. (This difference is significant at the .10 level in a one-sided t-test.) That is, adjustments for land quality explain just over 10 percent of the baseline growth rate of agricultural TFP. The nonparametric approach reveals that most of this difference has occurred since the mid-1980s, reflecting, in part, expansion of irrigation. Controlling in addition for improvements in the quality of the agricultural labor force reduces the mean TFP residual to 0.59 percent per year. Together, adjusting for changes in the quality of land and labor inputs thus account for 0.38 percentage points difference in, or 39 percent of, the baseline growth rate of agricultural TFP.

In terms of the broader growth accounting, this adjusted baseline TFP

16. Note that the baseline (unadjusted) TFP growth path depicted in figure 1.7 is shifted up relative to the baseline growth TFP path depicted in figure 1.5. This difference results from the loss of observations, given the availability of data for the adjustments to land and labor. Figures 1.4 and 1.5 use the same set of all available observations, whereas the three TFP growth paths presented in figure 1.7 all use the same, but more limited, sample of observations.

17. Note that this growth is greater than the unadjusted growth rate reported in table 1.5. This higher rate was estimated over a sample that was limited by the availability of data for land and labor quality adjustments, while the rate reported in table 1.5 was for the largest possible sample.

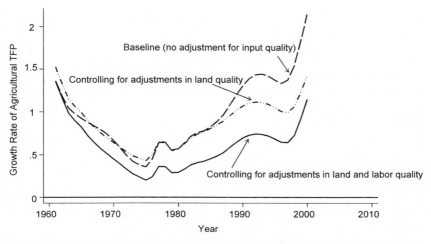

Fig. 1.7 Agricultural TFP growth rates adjusted for input quality, SSA crops, semiparametric regressions

Table 1.6   Accounting for changes in land and labor quality

	(1) Baseline TFP	(2) Adjusting for land quality	(3) Adjusting for land and labor quality
Mean growth rate	0.97	0.87	0.59
Percent change relative to baseline		10	39
t-test (*P*-value)		vs. (1): 0.103[a]*	vs. (2): 0.000***

[a]One-sided test.
***Significant at the 1 percent level.
**Significant at the 5 percent level.
*Significant at the 10 percent level.

growth rate estimate of 0.59 percent per year accounts for 36 percent of the 1.68 percent per year growth rate of aggregate crop output.

Even net of these adjustments, however, it is clear from figure 1.7 that TFP growth in African crop agriculture has generally accelerated since reaching its nadir in the late 1970s. Despite a modest deceleration in TFP growth during the early and mid-1990s, aggregate TFP growth for African crop agriculture in 2000 was four to five times greater than it had been twenty-five years earlier.

The following section continues the task of decomposing and explaining the TFP residual measured here, expanding that task to consider a wider range of potential explanations. My starting point for these additional decompositions is the TFP residual estimated net of adjustments for input quality.

1.7 Explanations for Total Factor Productivity Growth in Agriculture

This section considers several potential explanations for productivity growth in African crop agriculture, including: expenditures on agricultural research and development, infrastructure (roads), the effects of civil war, and incentives (agricultural and macroeconomic policy distortions). Severe data constraints, however, preclude a complete decomposition in which all of these potential explanations are considered together. The best one can do, then, is to compare the baseline TFP residual (net of adjustments for input quality) individually against each of these potential explanations. In each case, it is necessary to reestimate the "baseline" TFP growth rate based on the sample of observations available for each potential explanation of productivity growth. This approach provides estimates of the share of TFP growth explained by each of these factors; yet, these results will not be strictly additive across the potential explanations (as the explanatory variables are not orthogonal to one another), and the generalizability of these results must be qualified (as each decomposition must be estimated over a slightly different subsample of the full data set). It may be reasonable, then, to think of the following results as reflecting upper bounds on the role of any individual explanation for productivity growth.

As in my previous accounting for input quality adjustments, my approach to measuring the contribution of a given explanatory variable to TFP growth is first to estimate the quality-adjusted production function with and without the additional variable, and then to calculate the percentage difference in the means of the resulting nonparametric TFP growth paths as the contribution of that variable to TFP growth.

1.7.1 Agricultural R&D

Ultimately, measured productivity growth is intended to reflect a deeper process of technological change. Expenditures on agricultural R&D are thus a potentially important driver of productivity growth, as numerous studies have shown for Africa and for other developing and developed regions (most recently for Africa, Alene [2010]). Data on agricultural research expenditures for twenty-seven sub-Saharan African countries since 1971 have been collected by the Agricultural Science and Technology Indicators (ASTI) Initiative, housed at the International Food Policy Research Institute.[18] Beintema and Stads (2006) describe the rapid postindependence growth in funding for agricultural R&D in Africa, followed by slower growth in research expenditures during the 1980s, and near stagnation during the 1990s. Table 1.7, from Beintema and Stads (2006, 4), disaggregates agricultural R&D expenditures in Africa by region and decade. By region, the average growth rate of R&D expenditures from 1971 to 2000 has been greatest in East Africa—exceeding

---

18. The ASTI data are available for download at http://www.asti.cgiar.org/data/.

Table 1.7   Trends in agricultural research spending by subregion, 1971–2000

Subregion	Total spending (million 1993 international dollars)				Annual growth rate (percent)[a]			
	1971	1981	1991	2000[b]	1971–81	1981–91	1991–2000	1971–2000[b]
East Africa (7)	136.5	185.6	292.7	341.4	2.21	5.07	0.88	3.17
Southern Africa (6)	371.3	370.2	398.2	427.9	-0.19	0.30	1.20	1.25
West Africa (14)	224.0	358.2	345.5	315.3	4.62	0.14	0.06	0.39
Total (27)	731.8	914.0	1,036.4	1,084.7	2.02	1.32	0.77	1.43
Nigeria	62.5	127.9	68.3	106.0	5.64	-6.71	6.27	-1.84
South Africa	287.5	300.3	313.3	365.6	0.11	0.14	1.85	1.65
Total excluding Nigeria and South Africa (25)	381.8	485.8	654.8	613.1	2.46	3.31	-0.30	1.89

Source: Appendix table C.1 in Beintema and Stads (2006).

Notes: Figures in parentheses indicate the number of countries in each category. The seven East African countries are Burundi, Eritrea, Ethiopia, Kenya, Sudan, Tanzania, and Uganda; the six southern African countries are Botswana, Madagascar, Malawi, Mauritius, South Africa, and Zambia; the fourteen West African countries are Benin, Burkina Faso, Republic of Congo, Côte d'Ivoire, Gabon, Gambia, Ghana, Guinea, Mali, Mauritania, Niger, Nigeria, Senegal, and Togo. Data were not available prior to 1991 for six, mainly small, countries. Hence, they were estimated using trends for the other countries in the respective subregions.

[a] Annual growth rates are calculated using the least-squares regression method, which takes into account all observations in a period.

[b] For West Africa, total spending data are for 2001 and the growth rate is for 1991–2001.

the growth rate of expenditures in West Africa by a factor of nearly eight. These are annual expenditures by governments in each country. They thus reflect a flow of inputs into R&D. While much of the national funding for agricultural R&D in Africa is donor funded, these data do not include the benefits for any given country of expenditures by the international agricultural research centers. Thus, to the extent that national funding and the benefits of international research are correlated, the present estimates may be biased upward.

Substantial lags exist between the time expenditures on R&D occur and the time they affect productivity. Alene (2010) examines alternative lag structures on R&D expenditures, with lags ranging from two to sixteen years. His finding that the maximum effect of agricultural R&D occurs around lag 10 leads him to conclude that the slowdown in agricultural TFP growth during the 1990s is partially explained by the reduced growth rate of agricultural R&D expenditures in the 1980s. This is consistent with the prediction by Block (1995), which also found that agricultural research expenditures, lagged by ten years, were significant in explaining the recovery of African agricultural productivity during the 1980s (but which expressed concern for the future impact of reduced R&D expenditures by the late 1980s).

Adding the ten-year lag of log agricultural R&D expenditures to the production function estimated above (net of input quality adjustments) results in a production elasticity of approximately 0.2 ($P = 0.000$), suggesting that doubling the level of agricultural R&D expenditures at time t would boost agricultural output per worker by 20 percent at time $t + 10$—a substantial effect, and one that is consistent with studies that find high rates of return to agricultural research expenditures in Africa (Alene 2010).[19] Including the ten-year lag of R&D expenditures limits the estimation period to 1981–2000. For that period, the ten-year lag of R&D expenditures explains 75 percent of estimated TFP growth. Extending the estimation period back to 1976–2000 by including only the five-year lag of R&D expenditures results in only a small reduction in the estimated production elasticity (to 0.18). In this case, agricultural R&D expenditures still explain 45 percent of estimated TFP growth.

1.7.2   Roads

The potential benefits of increased road density for agricultural productivity have been explored in a variety of developing-country settings. These benefits, according to Zhang and Fan (2004) include: increased profitability of farming resulting from reduced transportation costs, greater purchases of inputs and marketing of output resulting from reduced transportation

---

19. Including R&D expenditures in the production function required, excluding the country dummies, as virtually all of the variation in R&D expenditure is in the cross-section dimension of the data (rendering the "within" estimator impractical).

costs, and the potential to shift land from low-value cereals to higher-value horticulture with reduced risks of perishability. Zhang and Fan (2004) demonstrate significant contributions of roads to crop TFP in rural India, as do Mendes, Teixeira, and Salvato (2009) for Brazil, and Suphannachart and Warr (2009) for Thailand, among many others. In a simulation model of Uganda, Gollin, and Rogerson (2010) also find significant complementarities between road density and agricultural TFP. Most recently, Dorosh et al. (2010) provide evidence from sub-Saharan Africa that agricultural production is higher in areas with lower travel times to urban markets, and that adoption of modern technologies is negatively correlated with travel time to urban centers.

Such findings are consistent with both intuition and with the broadly held presumption that roads are a critical ingredient for growth in agricultural productivity in Africa. For instance, in its Framework for African Agricultural Productivity, the Comprehensive African Agriculture Development Program (CAADP 2006, 16) presents it as a given that, "investment in infrastructure, particularly rural feeder roads, can also lead to large productivity growth and poverty reduction efforts." It is difficult, however, to demonstrate this contribution with available cross-country country data.

To account for the potential contributions of roads to agricultural TFP in Africa, I reestimate my baseline semiparametric production function to include countries' share of paved roads as a proportion of total roads. These roads data, drawn from the World Bank's World Development Indicators, are quite limited in their country coverage and only begin in 1990. The median paved road share for 1990–2007 was 16 percent. Perhaps owing to either the small sample size or to the general lack of paved roads, the estimated production elasticity for paved road share is effectively zero, and its inclusion makes virtually no difference to the estimated rate of TFP growth. Replacing the paved road share of total roads with the ratio of road kilometers to arable land does not change this result. One cannot conclude from this that the broad intuition regarding roads' potential contribution to agricultural TFP is wrong. Rather, available cross-country data and historical experience in Africa do not yet provide the expected statistical support for that intuition.

1.7.3   Civil War

Civil conflict has been endemic in much of sub-Saharan Africa in the postindependence period. Sambanis and Elbadawi (2000) report that between 1960 and 2000, 40 percent of sub-Saharan African countries had experienced at least one period of civil war, and that in the year 2000 alone 20 percent of sub-Saharan Africa's population lived in countries that were formally at war (with endemic low-intensity conflict in many other countries). They attributed this problem to high levels of poverty, failed political institutions, and economic dependence on natural resources. It is reasonable to suppose that endemic civil war (and perhaps even the expectation of civil war) could negatively affect agricultural productivity. Physical destruction of crops, damaged infrastructure inhibiting both the purchase of inputs and the marketing of outputs, the diversion and destruction of human capital, and the potential reticence of households to invest in agricultural improvement given the threat of these disruptions, could all lead to reductions in agricultural productivity. I test this hypothesis by including in the production function data on the incidence of civil wars, carefully constructed by Sambanis and Doyle (2006).[20]

A dummy variable equal to one during years of civil war enters the production function negatively, with a coefficient equal to −.04 ($P = 0.11$), suggesting that average crop output across the sample falls by 4 percent during years of civil war. Its effect on productivity is greater. Comparing the averages of the nonparametric TFP growth paths with and without the incidence of civil wars suggest that average TFP growth in African crop agriculture for the period 1960 to 2000 would have been over 11 percent greater in the absence of civil wars. This is the average effect based on the occurrence of civil war in 13 percent of the country-year observations included in the regression. A cautious interpretation of this result might consider the possibility that the incidence of civil war acts as a proxy for broader (and excluded) institutional failures.

Given this qualification, one can gain additional insight into the effect of civil war on agricultural productivity in Africa by dividing the sample into observations with and without civil war, observing their distinct experiences over time as opposed to the average effect of civil war across the entire sample. This approach reveals that the average rate of agricultural TFP growth was 0.74 percentage points lower (and negative on average) in the presence of civil war. Figure 1.8 illustrates these differences, which (given the inclusion of country fixed effects) are identified by countries moving in or out of the state of civil war.[21]

1.7.4   Macroeconomic Policy Distortions (Black-Market Premium)

It is well documented that African economies have historically experienced high degrees of distortion in macroeconomic policy. It has also been documented, first by Krueger, Schiff, and Valdes (1988), that macroeconomic distortions in developing countries have often imposed indirect taxes on agricultural producers in excess of their rates of direct taxation. That story

---

20. I am grateful to Nicholas Sambanis and to Robert Bates for making these civil war data available.

21. It is possible that this overestimates the difference between settings with and without civil war if TFP is underestimated during civil wars. This could be the case if the data simply count the number of workers in the sector, some of whom are prevented from working by war. The author is grateful to Keith Fuglie for noting this.

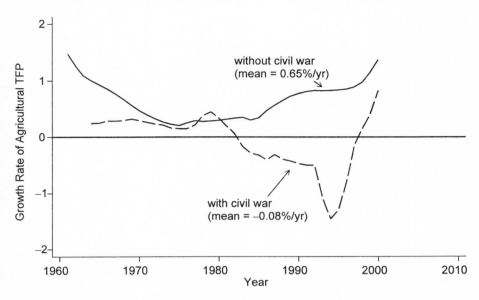

Fig. 1.8   Effect of civil war on agricultural TFP, semiparametric regression

highlighted the role of real exchange rates, which were often overvalued to the detriment of African farmers (who tended to produce import-competing tradables or exportables). By undermining agricultural incentives, macroeconomic policy distortions might also have affected agricultural productivity. To test that hypothesis, I use data on the black-market premium for foreign currency, often employed as a proxy for such distortions. Over the period 1961–2004, the mean black-market premium for sub-Saharan Africa was approximately 66 percent (though this mean falls to 30 percent if one excludes as outliers observations with black-market premia greater than 500 percent).

The estimated coefficient on the log black-market premium in the production function is not statistically different from zero, indicating that this proxy for macroeconomic distortions did not affect crop output, per se.[22] Yet, including the log black-market premium in the specification accounts for 29 percent of measured TFP growth. Figure 1.9 illustrates this result. It is interesting to note that the productivity cost of this macroeconomic distortion diminishes over time relative to the baseline TFP growth path, given that black-market currency premia in Africa over this period fell on average by 12 percent per year (and was half the level post-1990 that had pertained to pre-1990).

22. This regression excludes outliers on black-market premia (over 500 percent).

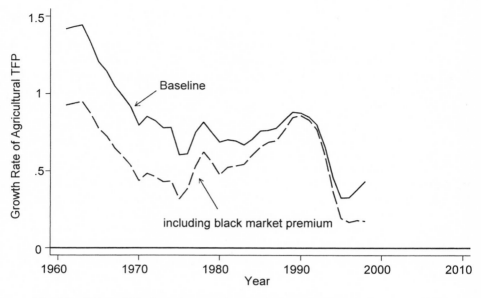

Fig. 1.9   Effect of black-market premium on TFP growth rates, semi-parametric regression

1.7.5   Agricultural Policy Distortions (Relative Rate of Assistance)

Producer incentives might also exert a substantial effect on agricultural productivity, particularly as it regards farmers' choices on production intensity, crop mix, and input use. In a recent and major update to the earlier work by Krueger, Schiff, and Valdes (1988), the World Bank has released an extensive data set on trade-based agricultural price distortions (Anderson and Valenzuela 2008). This data set provides commodity-specific indicators of the policy-induced divergence between domestic and international prices, covering thirty different commodities in sixty-eight countries (including thirteen countries from sub-Saharan Africa) since 1955. The key analytical building block of this data set is the nominal rate of assistance (NRA) for each commodity-year observation, essentially measuring the rate of tax or subsidy at the border. Anderson and Valenzuela (2008) also aggregate these nominal rates of assistance into agricultural and nonagricultural categories. By calculating the ratio of the rate of assistance to agricultural versus nonagricultural commodities, they create a relative rate of assistance (RRA) indicator, which measures the extent to which agriculture is either favored or disfavored by trade policy.[23] Historically, African governments

23. An RRA less than zero indicates relative discrimination against agriculture; an RRA greater than zero indicates a relative discrimination in favor of agriculture.

have discriminated heavily against their agricultural sectors (Bates 1981). This discrimination peaked around 1980, and though reduced during the subsequent years of structural adjustment, was still present in 2005 (Masters and Garcia 2010; Bates and Block 2010).

Figure 1.10 juxtaposes the TFP growth paths (with and without controlling for RRA) with the nonparametric time path of the RRA itself. The similarity of these patterns is striking. The RRA is negative throughout this period. The fact that TFP growth rates and the RRA decline and then rise together suggests the possibility that it is the first difference (rather than the level) of the RRA that drives TFP growth. With this motivation, I include the first difference of RRA in the semiparametric production function. The RRA, however, is a policy choice and thus potentially vulnerable to reverse causation. This would require that governments choose to discriminate more heavily against sectors that perform worse over time, and discriminate less heavily against sectors as their performance improves. Such a perspective runs contrary to the logic found in much of the political economy literature on this subject (Bates 1981), and ignores the external pressures for reform that characterized much of the 1980s and 1990s in Africa. Nonetheless, to provide at least some degree of protection against the potential for reverse causation, I specify the production function to include the lagged first difference of the RRA. The point estimate (as expected) is positive, yet not statistically different from zero (0.037, $P = .62$).

The effect of RRA on TFP growth, however, is statistically significant

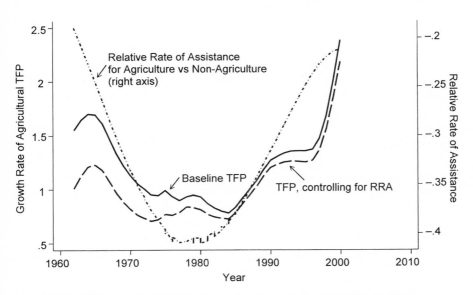

Fig. 1.10   Effect of agricultural price policy distortions on agricultural TFP, semiparametric regression

Table 1.8   **Pair-wise decompositions of agricultural TFP**

	Percent change vs. baseline TFP[a]	T-test vs. baseline	Sample size of regression[c]	No. of years included	No. of countries included
R&D ($t - 10$)	75	P = .044	219	11	11
R&D ($t - 5$)	45	P = .06[b]	274	16	11
Paved road share	3	P = .47	237	11	28
Civil war	11	P = .13[b]	1,037	37	28
Black-mkt. prem.	29	P = 0.00	737	37	28
ΔRRA($t - 1$)	16	P = .016	387	38	10

[a]Baseline net of input quality adjustments.

[b]One-sided t-test.

[c]Refers to underlying estimation of production function from which TFP growth path is derived.

($P = .016$), as the lagged first difference of RRA explains 16 percent of TFP growth over this period (as illustrated in figure 1.10).[24]

Table 1.8 summarizes the results described in this section. This list of potential explanations for agricultural productivity growth in Africa is far from comprehensive, yet it represents the broad categories that have been addressed in the literature. Ideally, one would incorporate all of these potential explanations into a single decomposition. In practice, data constraints preclude such a comprehensive approach, requiring instead the pair-wise comparisons presented above. I take at least a small step toward that ideal by estimating the contributions of each potential explanation for productivity growth against baseline estimates that are adjusted for variations in the quality of land and labor. Nonetheless, this approach supports only broad statements regarding the relative importance of various explanations for productivity growth. As table 1.8 reflects, expenditures on agricultural R&D, albeit with substantial lags, play the largest role in explaining agricultural TFP growth. Policy distortions, both at the macroeconomic and sectoral level, have also played an important, though smaller, role. Africa's agricultural TFP growth, on average, would have been 11 percent faster in the absence of civil wars (though the difference is much greater in the specific comparison of country-year observations with and without civil wars). And, contrary to expectations, available data suggest that infrastructure as

24. Headey, Alauddin, and Prasada Rao (2010) find positive contributions to agricultural TFP growth with the same RRA indicator in a broader sample of mostly non-African-developing countries. This is consistent, as well, with earlier evidence based on the use of the nominal protection coefficient in a small sample of non-African-developing countries by Fulginiti and Perrin (1999). The black-market premium and the first difference of the RRA are only loosely correlated ($\rho = -0.11$). While this negative correlation suggests that countries with distorted currency regimes also tended to discriminate against agriculture, the small magnitude of this correlation suggests that these two indicators do indeed reflect different impacts on agricultural productivity.

represented by paved roads has contributed little to Africa's agricultural TFP growth.

Ghana, in many ways, reflects the experience of sub-Saharan Africa over this period. The following section draws on the broader cross-country analysis to highlight key aspects and determinants of Ghana's agricultural productivity.

1.8   The Case of Ghana

This brief review is not intended to be a comprehensive analysis of Ghana's agricultural productivity experience. Rather, the primary objective is to explore in greater detail key findings from the cross-country analysis regarding the drivers of productivity growth. A secondary objective of this brief review of Ghana is to highlight some of the issues that arise in country-level analysis—issues that are generally invisible at the cross-country level, but which may suggest caution in interpreting cross-country findings.

1.8.1   Partial and Total Factor Productivity in Ghana

Ghana typifies the decline and rise pattern of agricultural productivity seen in the broader African sample. Figure 1.11 summarizes Ghana's experience as reflected in the time path of its partial productivity ratios. The first decade of independence saw small gains in crop yield combined with declining output per worker. The country's decline into economic chaos during the 1970s is reflected in the rapid deterioration of both land and

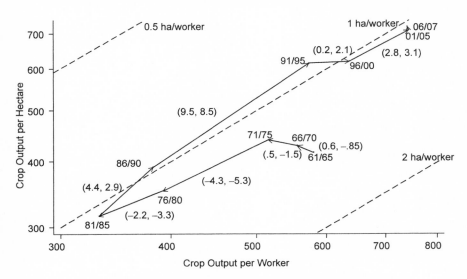

Fig. 1.11   Partial productivity ratios for Ghana, 1961/65–2006/07

Note: Annual growth rates for each period: (output/ha, output/worker).

labor productivity depicted in figure 1.11. For agriculture, the country's economic nadir in 1983 was exacerbated by severe drought (starting in 1981), widespread bushfires, and the forced repatriation of one million Ghanaians from Nigeria.

These negative trends were strikingly reversed in the early 1980s, leading to a sustained (and continuing) period of growth in the productivity of both land and labor. Clearly, looking only at a path connecting the first and last periods (from which we would conclude that the annual growth rates of average land and labor productivity were 1.35 percent and 0.6 percent, respectively) would obscure the dramatic decline and resurgence seen by tracing out successive five-year period averages. The narrative of Ghana's agricultural productivity is thus much more complex than would be implied by the moderate rates of growth in land and labor productivity observed on average over the period 1961–2007. The challenge is to explain the decline and rise.

The semiparametric estimation approach developed above is not well applied to a single-country time series of only forty observations. The estimated (input quality-adjusted) production elasticities are not statistically significant. Yet, controlling linearly for the conventional inputs results in a TFP growth path, depicted in figure 1.12, which is statistically different from zero and suggests an average rate of crop TFP growth of 1.03 percent per year from 1961–2000. This pattern of TFP growth rates is also consistent with the pattern of partial productivity ratios for Ghana shown in figure 1.11.

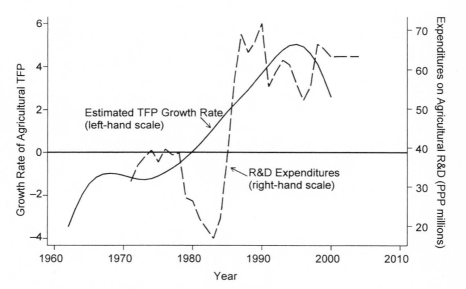

Fig. 1.12   Agricultural TFP growth and R&D expenditures, Ghana

For the period 1961–2000, aggregate crop output in Ghana grew at the average annual rate of 2.37 percent. Growth accounting thus suggests that a TFP growth rate of 1.03 percent accounts for approximately 43 percent of the growth in crop output.

One way to summarize the current levels of crop productivity is to compare current yields against potential yields. Such analysis by Ghana's Ministry of Agriculture (2007) suggests that the yields gaps remain substantial. For example, average maize yield of 1.5 MT/Ha is reported to be 40 percent short of the achievable yield. Yield gaps calculated for other staple grains are reported on the same order of magnitude, while the yield gap for cassava in Ghana is reported to be 57.5 percent (Breisinger et al. 2008). The challenge is to identify the constraints to reducing these yield gaps.

One critical constraint to reducing the yield gap is the great heterogeneity of conditions that characterize agriculture in Ghana (and virtually every other country in sub-Saharan Africa). Figure 1.13 shows that Ghanaian agriculture is spread across six distinct agroecological zones, each listed here with its mean annual rainfall in millimeters: rain forest (2,200), deciduous forest (1,500), transitional (1,300), coastal (800), Guinea savanna (1,100), and Sudan savanna (1,000). These zones differ in their average annual rainfall by a factor of nearly four (figure 1.14); unlike the first four zones, which have two growing seasons, the two savanna zones have only one. Ghana's agroecological zones also differ in their soil types and in the length of their growing seasons; as a result, they also differ widely in the mix of crops produced. In addition, the productivity levels and growth rates for individual crops also vary widely across agroecological zones.

Figure 1.15 illustrates this diversity for maize, cassava, sorghum, and plantains. Maize is grown widely across Ghana, yet maize yields also vary widely across agroecological zones. The greatest concentration of relatively high-yield maize production is in the southern Guinea savanna in transitional zones, while the greatest concentration of relatively low-yield maize production lies just south of there in the forest zone. Average yields in the former are approximately twice those of the latter. Cassava production is similarly widespread (with the exception of the northernmost savanna areas), with a spatial distribution of yields similar to that of maize. In contrast, sorghum is grown exclusively in the Guinea and Sudan savanna zones, and districts with vastly different yields border one another, while plantain is grown exclusively in the forest and coastal zones, with somewhat less spatial variation in yields.

1.8.2   R&D

The cross-country analysis identified expenditure on agricultural R&D as a key determinant of productivity growth. The diversity of agricultural conditions within Ghana multiplies the technical challenges to increasing agricultural productivity. Broadly, however, the relationship between R&D

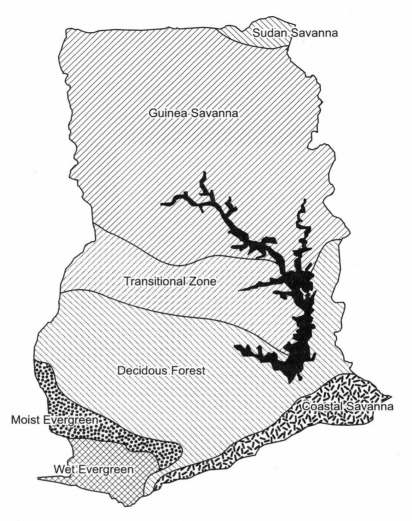

Fig. 1.13   Agroecological zones of Ghana

expenditures and TFP growth in Ghana is consistent with the cross-country evidence.

While the poor estimation of the underlying production function renders the estimated TFP growth rates for Ghana as merely suggestive, their conformity with a ten-year lag of expenditures on agricultural R&D is striking.[25] Figure 1.12 juxtaposes the growth path of crop TFP with R&D expendi-

25. The TFP growth path for Ghana is not statistically different from zero when lagged R&D expenditures are included in the production function (though the sample falls to nineteen years).

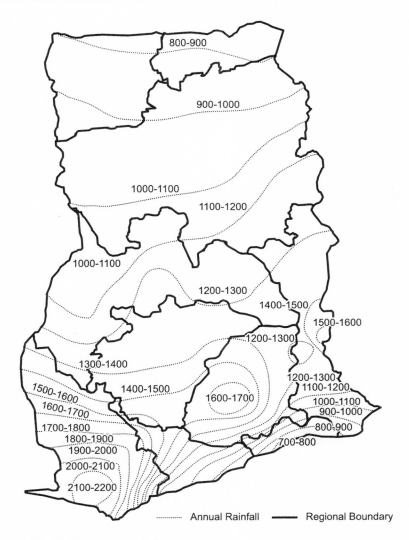

Fig. 1.14   Rainfall patterns in Ghana

tures. The transition to positive rates of TFP growth in the early 1980s follows by roughly ten years the increased expenditures on agricultural R&D of the early 1970s; the peak in TFP growth rates seen in the mid-1990s similarly follows the peak of R&D expenditures of the mid-1980s; and the decline in TFP growth rates in the late 1990s also lags by approximately ten years the reduced R&D expenditures of the late 1980s. The main anomaly to this pattern is that the reduced expenditures of the late 1970s and early 1980s are not reflected in the estimated TFP growth path.

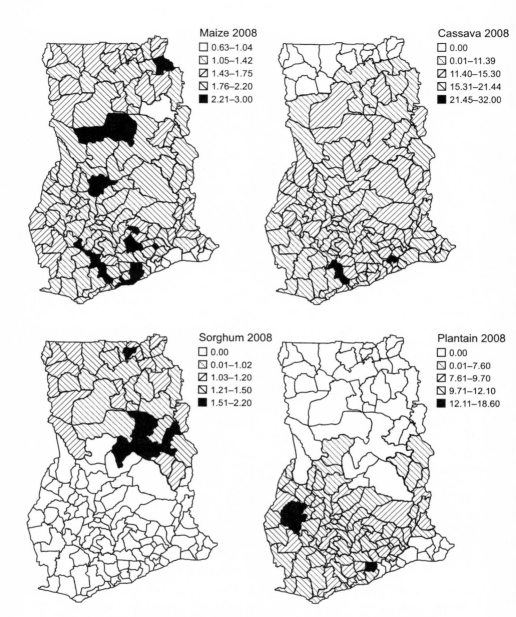

Fig. 1.15   Yield by district for maize, cassava, sorghum, and plantain (2008)

The R&D expenditure is a blunt proxy for specific research outputs. The main research output of interest here is improved varieties of staple grains. As figure 1.15 demonstrates, maize is grown in all of Ghana's agroecological zones. The diversity of growing conditions, however, implies that improved maize varieties must be adapted to specific settings. Ghana's Crop Research Institute takes the lead in developing and releasing improved varieties. During the critical period of reversal in crop productivity trends, the Crop Research Institute, in collaboration with the International Maize and Wheat Improvement Center (CIMMYT), the International Institute of Tropical Agriculture (IITA), and the Canadian International Development Agency (CIDA) implemented the Ghana Grains Development Project. Between 1984 and 1996, this project developed and released twelve improved varieties of maize (Morris, Tripp, and Dankyi 1999). The project also promoted use of chemical fertilizers to complement these improved varieties and recommended new planting strategies.

While these research advances created the potential for improved maize productivity, the real benefits came only with their widespread adoption. By 1997, a nation-wide survey found that 54 percent of farmers planted modern varieties of maize, though adoption rates varied widely across agroecological zones (the highest adoption rate, 69 percent, was in the coastal savanna, while the lowest rate, 38 percent, was in the forest zone). Adoption of recommended planting strategies followed a similar pattern. Yet, only 21 percent of farmers adopted the recommended fertilizers (ranging from 36 percent in the Guinea savanna to 9 percent in the forest zone), and only 26 percent of the national maize crop (by area) received fertilizer (Morris, Tripp, and Dankyi 1999). In 1997, approximately half of Ghana's maize area was planted to modern varieties (ranging from 75 percent in the coastal savanna to 33 percent in the forest).[26]

Adoption of improved maize was thus reasonably widespread, if unevenly so, across the country. On the supply side, one constraint to more widespread adoption of improved maize varieties was an inability of the Ghana Seed Company (a government entity) to multiply the improved seeds in sufficient quantity (Morris, Tripp, and Dankyi 1999). On the demand side, Doss and Morris (2001) found that the key constraints to adoption were lack of access to land, labor, and credit. Jatoe, Al-Hassan, and Abatania (2005) found similar constraints to the adoption of improved sorghum varieties in northern Ghana, where 40 percent of farmers had adopted improved sorghum, but only 0.1 percent of total sorghum area was planted to modern varieties.

More recently, Kwadzo et al. (2010) surveyed farmers in Ghana's eastern

26. The survey also found that 9 percent of farmers who adopted modern varieties subsequently "disadopted" them, along with nearly one-third of those who had tried fertilizer, and 13 percent of those who had adopted recommended management techniques.

region. They found that 83 percent of farmers had adopted improved maize, which covered 78 percent of maize area planted in the region. Yet, they also found that the yield potential of this adoption was not maximized because only 34 percent of farmers had also adopted nitrogen fertilizer, and that only 30 percent of maize area received fertilizer. They also found that the likelihood of adoption of improved maize was a positive function of both road access by farmers and the number of visits by extension agents.

1.8.3   Policy Interventions

Policy interventions—both macroeconomic and sectoral—were also found to play important roles in shaping agricultural productivity patterns in the African cross section. In this regard, too, Ghana is representative.

Ghana's postindependence economic and policy experience is divided into two distinct periods. Following its auspicious emergence into independence in 1957 as an essentially middle-income country, Ghana's economy spiraled gradually downward into chaos, reaching its nadir in the crisis of 1983. With the adoption of its well-known Economic Recovery Program in that year, the country entered an extended (and continuing) period of stable growth. The macroeconomic environment that ended in crisis was characterized by high inflation, large fiscal deficits, declining exports, and a black-market premium on its currency that grew from 35 percent in the early 1970s to 367 percent in the late 1970s, to nearly 1,300 percent in the early 1980s (World Bank data cited in Brooks, Croppenstedt, and Aggrey-Fynn [2009]).

This history coincides cleanly with the sharp reversal of the partial productivity path depicted in figure 1.11, as well as with the transition to positive rates of TFP growth depicted in figure 1.15. The potential connections between macroeconomic distortions and agricultural productivity are direct. The dramatically overvalued exchange rates that characterized the late 1970s and early 1980s in Ghana directly undermined incentives for domestic producers of import-competing crops (such as maize and rice), as well as for export-crop producers (cocoa). The 90 percent real depreciation of the cedi between 1983 and 1987 helped to relieve prior macroeconomic discrimination against agriculture, improving incentive on the output side, yet also increasing the cost of imported inputs. In addition, economic reform included the elimination of numerous input subsidies that had contributed to the unsustainable fiscal deficits. Thus, for example, the removal of fertilizer subsidies in 1990 led to a 36 percent increase in the real price of fertilizer, while the prices of insecticides and fungicides tripled in real terms with the removal of their subsidies (Seini 2002).

Policy reforms at the sectoral level were less ambiguous in their benefits for Ghana's farmers. The period from independence to 1983 was characterized by high rates of agricultural taxation—both indirect (arising largely from the overvalued exchange rate) and direct. Subsequent to the liberalization of Ghana's foreign exchange market and the devaluation of the cedi in 1984, agricultural taxation was primarily direct taxation. The example of cocoa taxation is notorious. The combination of an overvalued exchange rate and direct taxation in the form of low producer prices paid by the monopsonistic Ghana Cocoa Board was such that by 1983, farmers received about one-fifth of the free on board (FOB) price of cocoa (Seini 2002). With the subsequent devaluation and the reform of agricultural policies that accompanied the Economic Reform Program, cocoa farmers' share of the FOB price had increased to 40 percent by 1995, and to 50 percent by 2001 (Brooks, Croppenstedt, and Aggrey-Fynn 2009).

The nominal and relative rates of assistance (described above) provide a more general indicator of agricultural policy in Ghana. Average rates of taxation (measured relative to international prices) for agricultural tradables increased from approximately 17 percent in the early 1960s to 50 percent by the late 1970s. With the period of reform, these rates of taxation fell back to 17 percent by the late 1980s, and averaged just over 3 percent for 2000–2004 (Brooks, Croppenstedt, and Aggrey-Fynn 2009). Comparing this indicator to similar measures for nonagriculture provides an indicator of price discrimination of agriculture relative to nonagriculture (the "relative rate of assistance"). From this broader perspective, as well, one finds substantial and increasing discrimination against agriculture in the prereform period, with declining but persistent discrimination against agriculture in the postreform period. Relative discrimination against agriculture averaged just over 6 percent in the early 1960s, increasing to approximately 25 percent in the late 1970s. While falling substantially during the period of economic reform, this indicator of relative discrimination was still 8 percent for 2000–2004.

Figure 1.16 highlights the close association between the TFP growth path for Ghana's crop agriculture with the (nonparametrically smoothed) path of the relative rate of assistance for agriculture versus nonagriculture in Ghana. As in the broader cross section, the RRA remains negative throughout the period (indicating relative discrimination against agriculture); yet, it is clear from figure 1.16 that reductions in this rate of discrimination were associated with increases in the rate of TFP growth. The potential for this association to be explained by reverse causation, in which improved TFP growth led to reduced discrimination against agriculture, is strongly limited by the fact that the severity of Ghana's economic crisis (and its multiple sectoral and macroeconomic adjustment agreements with the International Monetary Fund [IMF] and World Bank) left the government no choice but to implement its broad program of economic reforms.

This brief review demonstrates that agricultural productivity growth in Ghana broadly reflects the cross-country experience of sub-Saharan Africa. The general pattern of postindependence decline followed by renewed productivity growth since the 1980s is clear in Ghana. The important roles of

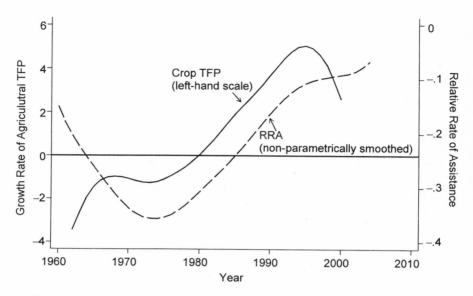

Fig. 1.16   **TFP and relative rate of assistance to agriculture versus nonagriculture in Ghana**

agricultural R&D expenditure and policy interventions seen in the broader cross section are also clear in Ghana.

1.8.4   Cautionary Note

Even a brief country case study can serve the purpose of providing a cautionary note for the interpretation of cross-country findings. In particular, Ghana's agroecological diversity is common in sub-Saharan Africa. From a technological perspective, this diversity greatly complicates current efforts to promote a new green revolution for Africa. As seen in figure 1.15, different crops are specific to different agroecological zones, and for ubiquitous crops such as maize, an improved variety that thrives in humid evergreen zones of southwestern Ghana may be inappropriate for planting in the arid zones of the northern savanna. An analysis that explains aggregate agricultural productivity at the country level based on total expenditures on agricultural R&D inevitably obscures the fact that both expenditures and productivity growth are likely to be quite unevenly distributed across the country.[27] This diversity is even more obscured when that aggregate country-level analysis is merely part of a broader cross-country panel data set.

Looking within a particular country also enables a closer examination of

27. Indeed, regional disparities between Ghana's northern and southern zones are a source of considerable tension.

the sources and quality of agricultural data. In the case of Ghana, Obirih-Opareh (2004) provides a critical examination of the methods applied by the Ministry of Food and Agriculture in compiling its national area and production data. He notes, for example, that most Ghanaian farmers do not keep their own records of area and production. In addition, Obirih-Opareh notes that most farmers mix numerous crops in a single field, further complicating the calculation of area and yield of individual crops, and that many farms are not accessible by road. As a result, production and area surveys must rely on limited and potentially poorly measured samples. For export crops, such as cocoa, the situation is better. Similarly, consumption data for imported inputs such as chemical fertilizer are also more reliable. Yet Obirih-Opareh finds, in general, that the limited ability of the government to undertake annual nation-wide surveys of complex and remote production systems often leads to statistical anomalies in the published data. He also notes that different international and national sources of published data on agricultural area and production in Ghana provide conflicting information. In this respect, too, Ghana is undoubtedly not unique in sub-Saharan Africa.

1.9   Conclusions

Agricultural productivity growth in sub-Saharan Africa has been a qualified success. Total factor productivity growth has increased rapidly since the early 1980s. By early in the twenty-first century, average annual TFP growth was roughly four times faster than it had been twenty-five years earlier. This period of accelerated growth, however, followed nearly twenty years of declining rates of TFP growth subsequent to independence in the early 1960s. Average agricultural TFP growth for sub-Saharan Africa was 0.14 percent per year during 1960–1984, and increased to 1.24 percent per year from 1985–2002. The average over this period was approximately 0.6 percent per year, which accounts for 36 percent of the increase in total crop output over this period.

These highly aggregated results conceal substantial regional and country-level variation. While regional TFP growth rates have tended to converge over time, the most rapid rate of TFP agricultural growth over the entire period 1960–2002 was in southern Africa (1.25 percent per year), while the slowest rate was in the Sahel (–1.17 percent). With the exception of East Africa, every region's TFP growth rate was higher between the years 1985–2002 than it had been during 1960–1984.

From among the long list of potential explanations for these trends, this chapter considers several leading contenders. Data constraints on individual explanations preclude a unified and comprehensive decomposition of the productivity residual. It is clear, however, that expenditures on agricultural R&D, along with the reform of macroeconomic and sectoral policies shaping agricultural incentives have played a substantial role in explaining both the decline and the rise in agricultural productivity found in this paper. The case study of Ghana clearly reflects these broader findings, and permits a more nuanced view of their effects. The case study also provides a brief window into the vast complexity of agricultural development in any single country, and in doing so, provides a cautionary note for the interpretation of aggregate cross-country results.

Appendix A

Table 1A.1   **Commodities and international prices included in aggregate crop output**

Commodity	Price ($I)*
Wheat	157.0241
Rice_paddy	274.6291
Barley	146.3894
Maize	98.85061
Oats	129.3321
Millet	227.9305
Sorghum	183.9405
Potatoes	183.828
Sweet_potatoes	147.4281
Cassava	170.8198
Yams	348.0107
Sugar_cane	39.34161
Cow_peas_dry	253.0388
Pulses_nes	233.8105
Nuts_nes	2,186.915
Soybeans	207.6962
Groundnuts_with_shell	509.03
Oil_palm_fruit	57.23346
Sunflower_seed	290.227
Sesame_seed	485.4894
Seed_cotton	315.2179
Lettuce_chicory	363.9961
Tomatoes	816.665
Beans_green	557.1413
Leguminous_vegetables_nes	342.7727
Carrots_turnips	393.2994
Bananas	208.0983
Citrus_fruit_nes	337.675
Avocados	1,002.395
Dates	879.3388
Coffee_green	1,179.314
Cocoa_beans	1,421.738
Tea	1,500.892
Tobacco	2,541.928
Natural_rubber	1,197.116

*Base year = 2006.

Appendix B

Comparison of Baseline TFP Growth Rates with Alternative Output Aggregates

The main results presented in the chapter are based on an output aggregate that includes only crops, and that uses international prices that were calculated specifically for this African sample to aggregate those crops. This appendix compares the baseline TFP growth rate estimates derived from that crop aggregate output with two alternative output aggregates—one using only crop output but using the FAOs global international prices for aggregation, and another using total agricultural output (from FAO)—the sum of crop and livestock output—aggregated with global FAO international prices. In the latter case, I include permanent pasture land in the measure of land input.

As figure 1B.1 illustrates, the resulting sets of TFP growth paths tell a broadly similar story, though with different average TFP growth over the period.

Mean TFP growth-rate estimates:

- crop output with African international prices = 0.61 percent/year,
- crop output with FAO global international prices = 0.52 percent/year, and
- total agricultural output with FAO global international prices = 0.74 percent/year.

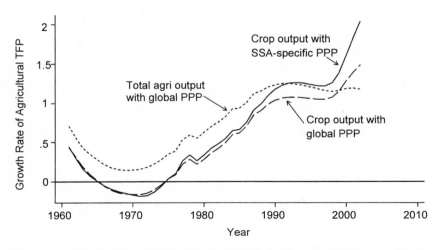

Fig. 1B.1   Comparison of TFP estimates with alternative output aggregates, semi-parametric regression

Note: Unadjusted for input quality; total agri = crops + livestock, land input for total agri includes pasture.

References

Alene, A. 2010. "Productivity Growth and the Effects of R&D in African Agriculture." *Agricultural Economics* 41 (3–4): 223–38.

Anderson, K., and E. Valenzuela. 2008. *Estimates of Distortions to Agricultural Incentives, 1955 to 2007.* Core database at www.worldbank.org/agdistortions.

Barro, R., and J-W Lee. 2010. "A New Data Set of Educational Attainment in the World, 1950–2010." NBER Working Paper no. 15902, Cambridge, MA.

Bates, R. 1981. *Markets and States in Tropical Africa.* Berkeley: University of California Press.

Bates, R., and S. Block. 2010. "The Political Economy of Agricultural Trade Interventions in Africa." In *The Political Economy of Agricultural Price Distortions*, edited by K. Anderson. Cambridge: Cambridge University Press.

Beintema, N., and G-J. Stads. 2006. "Agricultural Research and Development in sub-Saharan Africa: An Era of Stagnation." Background Paper, ASTI Initiative, Washington, DC, International Food Policy Research Institute.

Block, S. 1994. "A New View of Agricultural Productivity in Sub-Saharan Africa." *American Journal of Agricultural Economics* 76 (3): 619–24.

———. 1995. "The Recovery of Agricultural Productivity in Sub-Saharan Africa." *Food Policy* 20 (5): 385–405.

Breisinger, C., X. Diao, J. Thurlow, and R. Al-Hassan. 2008. "Agriculture for Development in Ghana: New Opportunities and Challenges." Discussion Paper no. 784, Washington, DC, International Food Policy Research Institute.

Brooks, J., A. Croppenstedt, and E. Aggrey-Fynn. 2009. "Ghana." In *Distortions to Agricultural Incentives in Africa*, edited by K. Anderson and W. Masters. Washington, DC: World Bank.

Byerlee, D., and D. Jewell. 1997. "The Technological Foundation of the Revolution." In *Africa's Emerging Maize Revolution*, edited by D. Byerlee and C. Eicher. Boulder, CO: Lynne Rienner Publishers.

CAADP. 2006. "Framework for African Agricultural Productivity." Comprehensive African Agriculture Development Program.

Chan-Kang, C., P. Pardey, S. Wood, J. Roseboom, and M. Cremers. 1999. "Reassessing Productivity Growth in African Agriculture." Selected paper for the annual meeting of the American Agricultural Economics Association, Nashville, Tennessee, August 8–11.

Coelli, T., D. S. Prasada Rao, C. O'Donnell, and G. Battese. 2005. *An Introduction to Efficiency and Productivity Analysis.* New York: Springer Press.

Craig, B., P. Pardey, and J. Roseboom. 1991. "Patterns of Agricultural Growth and Economic Development." In *Agricultural Research Policy: International Quantitative Perspectives*, edited by P. Pardey, J. Roseboom, and J. Anderson. Cambridge: Cambridge University Press.

———. 1997. "International Productivity Patterns: Accounting for Input Quality, Infrastructure, and Research." *American Journal of Agricultural Economics* 79:1064–76.

Dorosh, P., H-G Wang, L. You, and E. Schmidt. 2010. "Crop Production and Road Connectivity in Sub-Saharan Africa, A Spatial Analysis." Policy Research Working Paper no. 5385, Washington, DC, World Bank.

Doss, C., and M. Morris. 2001. "How Does Gender Affect the Adoption of Agricultural Innovations? The Case of Improved Maize Technology in Ghana." *Agricultural Economics* 25:27–39.

Evenson, R., and D. Gollin. 2003. "Assessing the Impact of the Green Revolution, 1960 to 2000." *Science* 300 (2 May): 758–62.

Frisvold, G., and K. Ingram. 1995. "Sources of Agricultural Productivity Growth and Stagnation in Sub-Saharan Africa." *Agricultural Economics* 4:169–80.

Fuglie, K. 2010. "Agricultural Productivity in Sub-Saharan Africa." Unpublished Manuscript, Washington, DC, Economic Research Service, US Department of Agriculture.

Fulginiti, L., and R. Perrin. 1999. "Have Price Policies Damaged LDC Agricultural Productivity?" *Contemporary Economic Policy* 17 (4): 469–75.

Fulginiti, L., R. Perrin, and B. Yu. 2004. "Institutions and Agricultural Productivity in Sub-Saharan Africa." *Agricultural Economics* 4:169–80.

Gabre-Madhin, E., and S. Haggblade. 2004. "Successes in African Agriculture: Results of an Expert Survey." *World Development* 32 (5): 745–66.

Gollin, D., and R. Rogerson. 2010. "Agriculture, Roads, and Economic Development in Uganda." NBER Working Paper no. 15863, Cambridge, MA.

Griliches, Zvi. 1960. "Measuring Inputs in Agriculture: A Critical Survey." *Journal of Farm Economics* 42 (5): 1411–27.

———. 1963. "The Sources of Measured Productivity Growth: United States Agriculture, 1940–1960." *Journal of Political Economy* 71 (4): 331.

———. 1964. "Research Expenditures, Education, and the Aggregate Agricultural Production Function." *American Economic Review* 54 (6): 961–74.

———. 1987. "Productivity: Measurement Problems." *The New Palgrave: A Dictionary of Economics* 4:1010–13.

Hayami, Y., and V. Ruttan. 1985. *International Development: An International Perspective.* Baltimore: Johns Hopkins University Press.

Headey, D., M. Alauddin, and D. S. Prasada Rao. 2010. "Explaining Agricultural Productivity Growth: An International Perspective." *Agricultural Economics* 41:1–14.

Jatoe, J. B., R. Al-Hassan, and L. Abatania. 2005. "Factors Affecting the Adoption of Improved Sorghum Varieties among Farm Households in Northwest Ghana: A Probit Analysis." *Ghana Journal of Development Studies* 2 (1): 37–50.

Jefferson, Philip N., and Stephen A. O'Connell. Forthcoming. "Rainfall Shocks and Economic Performance in Four African Countries."

Jorgenson, D., and Z. Griliches. 1967. "The Explanation of Productivity Change." *Review of Economic Studies* 34 (3): 249–83.

Krueger, A., M. Schiff, and A. Valdes. 1988. "Agricultural Incentives in Developing Countries: Measuring the Effect of Sectoral and Economywide Policies." *World Bank Economic Review* 2 (3): 255–71.

Kumwenda, J., S. Waddington, S. Snapp, R. Jones, and M. Blackie. 1997. "Soil Fertility Management in Southern Africa." In *Africa's Emerging Maize Revolution*, edited by D. Byerlee and C. Eicher. Boulder, CO: Lynne Rienner Publishers.

Kwadzo, G. T-M., W. Ansah, J. M. K. Kuwornu, and D. P. K. Amegashie. 2010. "Technology Package Adoption by Smallholder Maize Farmers: Acceptability Index and Logit Model Analysis." Unpublished Manuscript, Department of Agricultural Economics, University of Ghana.

Liedholm, C., M. McPherson, and E. Chuta. 1994. "Small Enterprise Employment Growth in Rural Africa." *American Journal of Agricultural Economics* 76:1177–82.

Lokshin, M. 2006. "Difference-Based Semiparametric Estimation of Partial Linear Regression Models." *Stata Journal* 6 (3): 377–83.

Lusigi, A., and C. Thirtle. 1997. "Total Factor Productivity and the Effects of R&D in African Agriculture." *Journal of International Development* 2:529–38.

Masters, W., and A. Garcia. 2010. "Agricultural Price Distortions and Stabilization." In *The Political Economy of Agricultural Price Distortions*, edited by K. Anderson. Cambridge: Cambridge University Press.

Mendes, S., E. Teixeira, and M. Salvato. 2009. "Effect of Infrastructure Investments on Total Factor Productivity (TFP) in Brazilian Agriculture." Contributed paper prepared for presentation at the International Association of Agricultural Economists Conference, Beijing, China, August 16–22.

Ministry of Food and Agriculture. 2007. "District-Level Agricultural Production and Price Data." Accra: Government of Ghana.

Mitchell, T. D., et al. 2003. "A Comprehensive Set of Climate Scenarios for Europe and the Globe." www. tyndall.ac.uk.

Morris, M., R. Tripp, and A. A. Dankyi. 1999. "Adaptation and Impacts of Improved Maize Production Technology: A Case Study of the Ghana Grains Development Project." Economics Program Paper no. 99–01, Mexico, D. F., International Maize and Wheat Improvement Center.

Nin-Pratt, C., Arndt, and P. V. Preckel. 2003. "Is Agricultural Productivity in Developing Countries Really Shrinking? New Evidence Using a Modified Nonparametric Approach." *Journal of Development Economics* 71 (2): 395–415.

Nin-Pratt, A., and B. Yu. 2008. "An Updated Look at the Recovery of Agricultural Productivity in Sub-Saharan Africa." Discussion Paper no. 00787, Washington, DC, International Food Policy Research Institute.

Obirih-Opareh, N. 2004. "Quality Agricultural Statistical Analysis for Better Policy Planning and Analysis in Ghana." *Empirical Economic Letters* 3 (6): 299–310.

Ramankutty, N., and J. A. Foley. 1998. "Characterizing Patterns of Global Land Use: An Analysis of Global Croplands Data." *Global Biogeochemical Cycles* 12:667–85.

Rao, D. S. P. 1993. "Inter-Country Comparisons of Agricultural Output and Productivity." Social and Economic Development Paper no. 112, Rome, Food and Agriculture Organisation.

Sahn, D., P. Dorosh, and S. Younger. 1997. *Structural Adjustment Reconsidered–Economic Policy and Poverty in Africa*. Cambridge: Cambridge University Press.

Sambanis, N., and M. Doyle. 2006. *Making War and Building Peace: United Nations Peace Operations*. Princeton, NJ: Princeton University Press.

Sambanis, N., and I. Elbadawi. 2000. "Why Are There So Many Civil Wars in Africa? Understanding and Preventing Violent Conflict." *Journal of African Economies* 9 (3): 244–69.

Sebastian, K. 2007. "GIS/Spatial Analysis Contribution to 2008 WDR: Technical Notes on Data & Methodologies." Background Paper for the World Development Report 2008, Washington, DC, World Bank.

Seini, A. W. 2002. "Agricultural Growth and Competitiveness under Policy Reforms in Ghana." Technical Publication no. 61, Institute of Statistical, Social and Economic Research, University of Ghana.

Solow, R. 1957. "Technological Change in the Aggregate Production Function." *Review of Economics and Statistics* 39 (3): 312–20.

Suphannachart, W., and P. Warr. 2009. "Research and Productivity in Thai Agriculture." Unpublished Manuscript, Kasetsart University, Bangkok, Thailand.

Thirtle, C., D. Hadley, and R. Townsend. 1995. "Policy Induced Innovation in Sub-Saharan African Agriculture: A Multilateral Malmquist Productivity Index Approach." *Development Policy Review* 13 (4): 323–42.

Timmer, C. P. 1988. "The Agricultural Transformation." In *Handbook of Development Economics*, vol. 1, edited by H. Chenery and T. N. Srinivasan. Amsterdam: North Holland Press.

World Bank. 2000. *Can Africa Claim the 21st Century?* Washington, DC: World Bank.

————. 2010. "African Development Indicators." Washington, DC, World Bank.

Yatchew, A. 2003. *Semiparametric Regression for the Applied Econometrician.* Cambridge: Cambridge University Press.

Zhang, X., and S. Fan. 2004. "How Productive is Infrastructure? A New Approach and Evidence from Rural India." *American Journal of Agricultural Economics* 86 (2): 492–501.

Agriculture, Roads, and Economic Development in Uganda

Douglas Gollin and Richard Rogerson

2.1 Introduction

In many developing countries, agriculture is the dominant economic activity, accounting for large shares of employment and output. This chapter considers the case of Uganda, a country in East Africa in which the

Douglas Gollin is professor of development economics at Oxford University. Richard Rogerson is professor of economics and public affairs at Princeton University and a research associate of the National Bureau of Economic Research.

Research for this chapter was funded by the NBER Program on African Successes. In Uganda, we were hosted and supported by the Makerere Institute of Social Research at Makerere University. We gratefully acknowledge the support of both institutions, while noting that the results and conclusions of our research do not reflect the official views of either NBER or MISR. We particularly appreciate the intellectual support and encouragement of Sebastian Edwards, Simon Johnson, and David Weil, the joint organizers of the African Successes Program, and we also appreciate the helpful comments of conference participants in the program workshops in February 2009 and December 2009, including especially Diego Comin, our discussant. Elisa Pepe has provided exceptional support as coordinator of the program.

We have benefited from comments on previous versions of this chapter made by seminar participants at Williams College, the University of Connecticut, the North American Summer Meetings of the Econometric Society 2009 in Boston, the Society for Economic Dynamics Summer Meetings 2009 in Istanbul, and the International Food Policy Research Institute (IFPRI) in Washington, DC.

We owe many intellectual debts, as well, particularly to Stephen Parente, with whom we have worked closely on previous papers that address related topics. We have also benefited from conversations with Cheryl Doss, Berthold Herrendorf, Jim Schmitz, and Anand Swamy. In Uganda, we received extraordinary help and intellectual contributions from Dr. Wilberforce Kisamba-Mugerwa, who took a great interest in our work in his official capacity as Chair of the National Planning Authority—but who also contributed his insights as a scholar, a policy practitioner, and a farmer. We gratefully acknowledge his help and support, without holding him accountable for any of the conclusions of our research.

We also acknowledge help from the following individuals in Uganda who took time to talk with us about our research: Mwendya Augustine, Uganda National Farmers Federation; Godfrey Bahiigwa, Plan for Modernisation of Agriculture; J. Ddumba-Ssentamu, Makerere economy is heavily dependent on agriculture. Over 80 percent of Uganda's households (and 85 percent of the people) live in rural areas, and most of these depend on agriculture for their primary source of income.[1]

By any measure, rural and agricultural households are overwhelmingly and disproportionately poor. The poverty rate in rural areas was estimated at 34.2 percent in 2005/06, compared to an urban poverty rate of 13.7 percent. Other measures of living standards tend to support this estimate; rural households spend far larger fractions of their incomes on food and have significantly fewer clothes, shoes, and other possessions than do urban households.

This chapter asks a series of questions about the agricultural sector's role in economic development in Uganda. To begin with, why do so many people live and work in rural areas, when material living conditions are relatively much worse than in cities? In particular, why are so many people dependent for their livelihood on semisubsistence agriculture? The government estimates that in some regions of the country, 85–90 percent of households receive their main source of income from subsistence agriculture.

The literature notes several possible reasons why so many individuals are involved in subsistence agriculture, including such things as various barriers that impede the growth of the nonagricultural sector or a variety of factors that lead to low productivity in the agricultural sector. While our analysis will include an evaluation of these explanations, our primary focus is to assess the role that lack of transportation infrastructure plays in promoting such a large subsistence agriculture sector. While the idea that poor trans-

---

University; Mbadhwe John, Ministry of Works and Transport; Angela Katama, Ministry of Finance, Planning, and Economic Development (Competitiveness and Investment Climate Strategy Secretariat); Boaz Blackie Keizire, Ministry of Agriculture, Animal Industry, and Fisheries; Lawrence Kiiza, Ministry of Finance, Planning, and Economic Development (Economic Affairs); Nicholas Kilimani, Economic Policy Research Center; John Bosco Kintu, National Planning Authority; Amos Lugoloobi, National Planning Authority; J. B. Magezi-Apuuli, Uganda Bureau of Statistics; Seth Mayinza, Uganda Bureau of Statistics (Census of Agriculture); Rwakakamba Morrison, Uganda National Farmers Federation; Leonard Msemakweli, Uganda Co-Operative Alliance Ltd.; Moses Ogwapus, Ministry of Finance, Planning, and Economic Development (Tax Policy Department); Charles Opio Owalu, Ministry of Works, Housing, and Communication; Abel Rwendeire, NPA; Sarah Ssewanyana, Economic Policy Research Center; Leena Tripathi, International Institute for Tropical Agriculture; and Everest Twimukye, Economic Policy Research Center.

Finally, we gratefully acknowledge the support of FEWS NET (the Famine Early Warning System Network) who provided us with a lengthy time series of data on agricultural prices in Uganda. The FEWS NET is a project of the US Agency for International Development. We particularly appreciate additional information and thoughtful comments provided by Mildred Magut and Patricia Bonnard of FEWS while absolving them of any responsibility for our interpretation of the data. For acknowledgments, sources of research support, and disclosure of the authors' material financial relationships, if any, please see http://www.nber.org/chapters /c13433.ack.

1. To be precise, nationally representative household surveys estimate that 78.8 percent of households in Uganda were rural in 2005/06, accounting for 84.6 percent of the population and 93.2 percent of those living below the poverty line.

portation infrastructure might play a key role in the development process does feature prominently in many policy discussions, there is relatively little systematic work to explore the economic mechanisms through which it operates. A key objective of this work is to take a first step toward articulating these economic mechanisms.

To pursue this, our chapter uses a static general equilibrium model that reflects key features of the Ugandan economy. We use a two-sector model in which there is an agricultural sector and a nonagricultural sector. This model is similar in spirit to earlier papers by Gollin, Parente, and Rogerson (2002, 2007) that focus on the structural transformation that accompanies development—in which economies move labor and other resources out of agriculture into other sectors and activities. We extend this basic model to reflect one of the realities of the Ugandan economy, namely, the fact that in much of the country, roads and other transportation infrastructure are very poor. This means that rural markets in Uganda are characterized by high transportation and transaction costs. Our model correspondingly includes an iceberg cost of moving goods from rural areas to urban areas (and vice versa). We examine the extent to which high transport costs can partly account for the large fraction of people living in rural areas in Uganda.

The underlying economics are intuitive. Individuals require food, implying that sufficient food must be produced in rural areas and transported to urban areas to support the nonagricultural workforce. If transport costs are very high, food becomes very expensive in urban areas relative to rural areas, creating an incentive for individuals to locate in rural areas to economize on transportation costs. In a poor country where food accounts for a large share of overall expenditure, this force is potentially very large.

Next, our chapter asks how specific interventions would affect the allocation of labor and inputs across economic activities, and how these interventions would alter the welfare of people in the Ugandan economy. To assess the impact of these interventions, we first calibrate the model to replicate certain features of the Ugandan data. By altering parameters in the model, we can conduct some simple and straightforward simulations of various policies and interventions.

First, we ask how the economy would benefit from improvements in agricultural productivity. Would increased agricultural total factor productivity (TFP) push workers out of the agricultural sector, or would it draw more workers in? How much would TFP increases affect welfare in an economy where agricultural goods account for a large fraction of consumption? Second, we ask how the economy would respond to increases in nonagricultural productivity. How would these affect the fraction of the population living in urban areas and working in nonagriculture? How would nonagricultural TFP growth affect welfare? Third, we consider the impact of a reduction in transportation costs, such as might result from improvements in roads or other transportation infrastructure. How would the allocation of workers across sectors be affected by changes in the transportation cost structure? What would be the effects on welfare? What would be the joint effect of reducing transport costs simultaneous with an increase in agricultural TFP? Finally, we consider the effect of population growth on a fixed land base. Although this is not explicitly a policy question, we believe it offers useful insights on an economy that currently features one of the highest population growth rates in the world.

To briefly summarize the findings of the chapter, we find that agricultural productivity improvements have a relatively large impact on the economy. Because the nonagricultural sector is initially small, and because the economy faces a subsistence constraint that limits the expansion of the nonagricultural sector, improvements in nonagricultural TFP have relatively small positive impacts on the economy. Reductions in transportation costs generate sizable benefits for the economy and trigger substantial reallocations of labor across sectors. When agricultural TFP improves at the same time that transportation costs are reduced, the welfare gains exceed those achieved from the two interventions separately, suggesting a kind of interaction effect.

The remainder of the chapter is organized as follows. Section 2.2 presents some background information on Uganda's development, with a particular focus on agriculture and on transportation costs and infrastructure. In section 2.3, we review related literature. Section 2.4 presents a two-region model that will provide the backbone for our analysis. Section 2.5 discusses the calibration of this model and shows results. In section 2.6, we offer an expanded model with three regions, which allows us to focus in more detail on the quasi-subsistence agricultural sector. Section 2.7 draws out some conclusions and implications for policy.

2.2   Background

Uganda is among the poorest countries in the world, with real per capita income of just over $1,100 in 2003, according to the Penn World Tables (version 6.2; Heston, Summers, and Aten [2006]). This level of income places the country firmly in the bottom quintile of the cross-country income distribution. As noted above, Uganda also ranks among the countries most heavily dependent on agriculture. In many ways, Uganda is fairly typical of many sub-Saharan countries with large rural populations. However, in some respects, Uganda offers a distinct set of challenges and characteristics.

2.2.1   Agriculture in Uganda

Because it is landlocked, Uganda produces essentially all of its own food, and most of its agriculture is oriented toward production of food for domestic consumption. Clearly there is a significant amount of agricultural production for export—chiefly in coffee and a few other crops. Our model economy will be closed, so we will essentially ignore export agriculture. In the paragraphs that follow, we will explain why we think this is a reasonable depiction of agriculture in Uganda. We will also explain why we are specifically interested in the quasi-subsistence agriculture sector, which is a large fraction of the total in Uganda.

Almost all agricultural production in Uganda takes place on smallholder plots, with mixed cropping systems predominating. Two-thirds of agricultural households had between one and four plots in 2002, and about 40 percent of the plots were themselves mixed stands, where multiple crops are grown together (Uganda Bureau of Statistics 2004, 5–6). Most plots are close to the household (less than one kilometer), but 37 percent are more than one kilometer away from the homestead (Uganda Bureau of Statistics 2007b, 36). Few purchased inputs are used on smallholder plots, with only 1.0 percent of plots using chemical fertilizer and 6.3 percent reporting the use of improved seeds (Uganda Bureau of Statistics 2007b, 86). Fewer than 1.0 percent are irrigated (Uganda Bureau of Statistics 2007b, 86).

Ten crops account for over 90 percent of the plots under cultivation: matoke (a kind of cooking banana), beans, cassava, sweet potatoes, coffee, groundnuts, maize, millet, sorghum, and sesame. With the exception of coffee, all are food crops that are produced primarily for domestic consumption.[2] Although there is some disagreement in the data, one estimate from household survey data (Uganda Bureau of Statistics 2007b, 46) suggests that very large fractions of agricultural households in Uganda were growing bananas (73.1 percent), maize (85.8 percent), cassava (74.3 percent), and beans (80.8 percent). Presumably many households were growing several of these crops.[3]

Farms also typically include livestock. About 20 percent of farm households reported owning at least one cow, 30 percent reported keeping goats, and 46 percent of households reported keeping chickens, mostly on a very small scale (Uganda Bureau of Statistics 2004).

Most small farms market some fraction of their output, with the fraction varying by crop, by region, and by distance from markets. For example, households in 2005/06 reported selling 80 percent of the soybeans that they produced and about half the maize, but only 32 percent of matoke, 23 percent of cassava, and 16 percent of beans. There is significant variation across regions in the fraction of agricultural households that are primarily in subsistence, with government figures showing some regions—primarily those

2. The bananas produced in Uganda are largely—though not exclusively—cooking bananas that differ from the dessert bananas that represent a major global export commodity. Uganda is a nearly negligible exporter of bananas, ranking outside the top thirty countries of the world in net exports.

3. An earlier survey (Uganda Bureau of Statistics 2004, 7) suggested that 40 percent of households grew cassava and beans, with 30 percent growing maize, sweet potato, and banana. These data were drawn from an agricultural module added to the census. We prefer the data taken from the Uganda National Household Survey, which appears to have done a thorough job of documenting plot-level characteristics of agriculture.

near Kampala and with good market access to the city—having fewer than 70 percent of households in subsistence agriculture. In the more remote regions of the country, over 80 percent of households are reported as deriving their livelihoods from subsistence farming (Uganda Bureau of Statistics 2007a, 82).

There is size heterogeneity among smallholder farms. This is presumably linked to differences in the fraction of output marketed. In household survey data, about 20 percent of households farm more than five acres of land, with about 7 percent farming more than ten acres.

A small but active commercial agricultural sector also operates in Uganda. One portion of the commercial sector consists of large farms that are typically privately held. In 2006/07, the Uganda Bureau of Statistics reported nearly 400 officially registered commercial farms, employing 28,000 workers (Uganda Bureau of Statistics 2008, 142). Most of these businesses were quite small, with half employing five to nine workers, but about sixty were large farms employing fifty or more workers, and clearly a number were far larger, given a mean size of seventy workers. Most of the large farms specialized in animal agriculture, but of the very large farms, most were in crop agriculture, producing horticultural crops and grain, including tea, sugar, and cotton. One study in 1999 noted that the largest maize farm that could be identified by experts at the time was 150 acres (60 ha) (Robbins and Ferris 1999).

The principal food crops are not traded much on international markets: matoke, maize, cassava, yams, and other root crops. Of these, only maize is traded to any significant degree. The country does produce large amounts of coffee for export markets (along with smaller amounts of sugar and cotton), but the fraction of land devoted to export commodities is relatively modest, and some of these crops are produced on a scale comparable to that of basic food crops.

The major export crops—coffee, tea, cotton, and sugar—together account for under 8 percent of cropped area (FAOSTAT 2009). Of these, the most important is coffee, which is grown on over 3.5 million plots with an average plot size of 0.16 hectares. Even quasi-subsistence farmers often produce a little coffee for sale to the market. But across the country, the bulk of agricultural activity is devoted to producing food staples.

Another way of measuring the fraction of Ugandan agriculture that is devoted to domestic food production is to look at consumption. Imports of grain account for about 2.1 percent of Uganda's total food energy. Since Uganda is a net exporter of pulses, fish, and some other commodities that are domestically consumed, in a net sense, only 1.7 percent of total calorie consumption depends on imported foods.

Taking all these facts together, we will argue below that it is reasonable to model Uganda's food economy using a closed economy representation. Even though the country has a number of important agricultural exports, most of the resources devoted to agriculture in Uganda are applied to the production of food crops for domestic consumption, and by the same token, most of domestic consumption needs are met from domestic production.

2.2.2 Rural Income and Poverty

About three-quarters of Uganda's population live in rural areas, and most make their livings from subsistence agriculture (Uganda Bureau of Statistics 2007a, 16–17). By most estimates, rural households in Uganda are very poor. In 2005/06, 93.2 percent of Uganda's poor households (using a headcount measure) were rural, somewhat higher than the 84.6 percent of households in rural areas. The poverty rate for rural households, using a headcount measure, was 34.2 percent, which was almost triple the rate for urban households (Uganda Bureau of Statistics 2006, 60). Also, median nominal wages in rural areas are only one-third of the urban level (Uganda Bureau of Statistics 2007a, 19).[4]

Rural households allocated about 50 percent of their total expenditure to food, drink, and tobacco—although the pricing of these goods is complicated, since much of consumption is home produced (Uganda Bureau of Statistics 2006, 56–59). About 15 percent of rural households had fewer than two sets of clothes per household member, and only 43 percent reported that each member of the household had a pair of shoes in good condition. Most households outside Kampala owned their own homes and furnishings, including a radio or other electronic device. About 40 percent of rural households owned a bicycle, but very few owned any other mode of transportation (Uganda Bureau of Statistics 2006, 94–95).

Rural households primarily earn their livings from agriculture—but other activities are also important. Almost 40 percent of rural households reported operating informal noncrop enterprises in 2005/06, with most of these enterprises concentrated in trade (both wholesale and retail) and manufacturing (Uganda Bureau of Statistics 2007a, 26).

2.2.3 Transaction Costs and Access to Markets

Our chapter will focus in part on the high transaction costs faced by rural households in Uganda. In particular, we explore the hypothesis that high rural-to-urban transportation costs implicitly create incentives for poor people to live close to their food sources—effectively reducing the real price of food, which is their largest single expenditure category. This section of the chapter seeks to document and quantify the transportation costs involved in moving goods from Uganda's rural areas to its cities.

Like most countries in sub-Saharan Africa, Uganda has very low levels of physical infrastructure and public services. All forms of physical infrastructure are underdeveloped, and this is widely cited as one of the country's main

---

4. Of course, the median wages may reflect differences in skill levels, hours worked, costs of living, and other factors.

constraints to development. The lack of infrastructure is particularly acute in rural areas. Existing road networks leave many communities inaccessible by vehicles, and very few rural residents have access to electricity or piped water. (For example, less than 1 percent of rural households were estimated to have access to grid-supplied electricity in 2000. A large number—perhaps a majority—of towns and market centers also lacked electrical access.)

The government of Uganda has highlighted the need for infrastructure development in a series of planning documents, including a series of Poverty Eradication Action Plans and its most recent National Development Plan. In addition, a consortium of donors, including the World Bank, the African Development Bank, and several key national aid agencies, issued a Joint Assistance Strategy for Uganda in 2006. This document identified the most pressing needs for development investments in Uganda and agreed on a coordinated set of programs, with rural transportation infrastructure featuring high on the list of priorities.

Spatial data suggest that more than three-quarters of Uganda's population (78 percent) live two or more hours from a market center, and 25 percent live five or more hours from a market.[5] In the most remote regions of the country, transportation consists primarily of foot traffic. People walk long distances to markets and other services. For example, for the country as a whole (including urban areas), the average distance to a government health clinic was about 7 km, and 77 percent of people reported that they walked to these clinics. In less remote areas, people make effective use of bicycles and motorcycles. Cars, trucks, and buses traverse the limited network of major roads.

Measures of road length support the notion that Uganda's road network is far behind those of developed countries. In 2003, Uganda reported a network of paved roads consisting of 16,300 km in a land area of 200,000 km^2 (CIA Factbook 2009).[6] For a startling benchmark, we note that this was not much greater than the paved road density found in Britain in AD 350, when the retreating Roman Empire left a network of 12–15,000 km of paved roads in a land area of 242,000 km^2 (Lay 1992, 55). In this specific sense, then, Uganda lags Britain by almost two thousand years in the development of its road infrastructure.

Measures of roads and remoteness offer only an indirect view of trans-

5. Roads are not the only form of infrastructure lacking from rural areas; in 2005/06, only 9 percent of rural communities had any access to electricity.

6. It is only fair to note—as any traveler in Africa can attest—that paved roads are not necessarily better than unpaved roads; particularly when maintenance is poor, pavement may actually provide a worse surface than dirt or gravel. In this sense, we hesitate to use paved roads as a measure of transportation quality; nevertheless, we believe that this is a useful proxy for a more general measure of transportation infrastructure.

portation and transaction costs. To get a more detailed look, we turn to two types of data: price dispersion data and direct evidence on transportation costs and marketing margins.

Price Dispersion Data

The poor quality of Uganda's road network corresponds directly to an environment of high transaction costs that contributes to high dispersion of prices at a moment in time across geographic space. Although there are many possible reasons for the spatial dispersion of prices (including various forms of market power and collusion), these price wedges must, in some sense, reflect underlying transportation costs, or else the pressure would be great to arbitrage away the price differences.

Most of the available data on price dispersion are at the level of wholesale or retail markets. Table 2.1 shows price dispersion across wholesale markets for a number of crops at a single moment in time (the week of March 10–14, 2008). Each column of this table refers to a different wholesale market. Most are in agricultural regions. The one exception is the Kalerwe market, just north of Kampala, which is one of the major markets serving the capital city. Several features of the data are immediately striking. First, the spatial dispersion of prices is high. For matoke, the lowest wholesale price is in Mbarara, in the southwest of the country, at 180 USh/kg; the highest price is at Lira, in the north central part of the country, where the same commodity sold for 600 USh/kg. The straight line distance between the two markets is about 400 km; the estimated road distance is about 500 km. By contrast, the prices in nearby Kisenyi (about 35 km distance) is much closer to the Mbarara price, at 230 USh/kg.

Table 2.2 shows the full set of pairwise distances and price differentials for matoke between Mbarara and other markets. In general, distance from the center of cultivation is closely linked to price level. A similar picture comes from the market for potatoes—a crop for which there is a primary area of production in southwestern Uganda near Kabale and Kasese and a secondary area near Tororo in the east. As shown in table 2.3, this leads to a generally rising pattern of prices with distance from Kasese, although Tororo itself has prices that reflect the production in nearby Mbale and Kapchorwa districts.

The same general patterns hold in the price data for other moments in time. Figure 2.1 shows monthly prices of matoke and sweet potatoes at six major markets in Uganda from 1997 to 2006. It is apparent from the figure that prices of matoke move together across markets over time, and the same is true for sweet potatoes. (It also appears that the prices of the two starch foods are themselves correlated.) At any given moment in time, however, the price spreads across markets for a given commodity are substantial. For matoke, the major growing areas are in Mbarara, in the southwest, and

Table 2.1   Price dispersion in wholesale markets for agricultural crops, Uganda (March 10–14, 2008)

Crop	Kisenyi	Kalerwe	Arua	Kabale	Kasese	Kiboga	Lira	Masaka	Mbarara	Soroti	Tororo
Matoke	230	230	750	240	250	230	600	200	180	567	300
Fresh cassava	195	180	600		90			80			
Sweet potatoes			450		120			200			
Irish potatoes	265	275	1,000	220	180	400	900	300	400	700	400
Beans (K132)	1,000	1,050	1,300	900	930	1,500	1,050	900	1,050	1,100	1,200
Beans rosecoco	1,000	1,150		900	950	1,500	1,150	900	1,050		1,200
Cassava chips	200			370	320	200	350		280	250	200
Cassava flour	300	400	300	550	350	450	700	450	500	480	230
Groundnuts	1,400	1,600	350	1,800	1,400		1,400	1,600	1,600	1,400	1,600
Maize grain	338	375	310	380	250	240	320	170	380	300	350
Maize flour	550	620	750	700	400	550	700	600	700	600	550
Millet grain	580	600	530	580	750		500	400	700	750	800
Millet flour	650	750	550	700	950	850	900	600	900	1,150	1,000
Rice (super)	1,100	1,100	1,700	1,100	1,000	1,300	1,100	1,300	1,500	1,200	1,250
Sesame	1,650	1,700	1,500				1,500		2,200	1,800	1,800
Sorghum grain	270	400	350	500	750		350		300	300	350
Sorghum flour	450	500	650		900		600		700	700	400
Soybeans	930	1,000	550	1,000	480		750	800	900	1,000	1,100

Source: The ASPS/Danida/CIAT Market Information Service, Kawanda Agricultural Research Complex.
Note: All prices in Ugandan shillings per kg.

Table 2.2   **Distances from Mbarara and matoke price dispersion (March 10–14, 2008)**

Market	Distance from Mbarara		Matoke price difference	Price difference as percent of Mbarara price
	Linear	Road		
Kisenyi	32	38	50	27.8
Kabale	105	126	60	33.3
Masaka	122	145	20	11.1
Kasese	125	150	70	38.9
Kiboga	213	255	50	27.8
Kalerwe	236	278	50	27.8
Masindi	284	343	120	66.7
Arua	410	492	570	316.7
Lira	400	500	420	66.7
Tororo	417	500	120	233.3
Soroti	418	501	387	215.0

Table 2.3   **Distance from Kasese and potato price dispersion (March 10–14, 2008)**

Market	Linear	Road	Potato price difference	Price difference as percent of Kasese price
Kisenyi	101	121	85	47.2
Mbarara	125	150	220	122.2
Kabale	173	207	40	22.2
Masaka	201	241	120	66.7
Kiboga	213	256	220	122.2
Masindi	250	300	220	122.2
Kalerwe	287	343	95	52.8
Arua	327	392	820	455.6
Lira	394	473	720	400.0
Soroti	435	522	520	288.9
Tororo	469	563	220	122.2

Mbale, in the southeast. These two markets typically have the lowest prices, and the remote northwestern market of Gulu invariably has the highest prices. The relative ordering of other markets is fairly stable and the price bands separating different markets appear to remain relatively constant over time. Even leaving aside the prices from Gulu, the width of the price band appears to be consistently about 50–100 USh/kg, meaning that the prices in Kampala, Jinja, and Mbale are often 60–70 percent higher than the prices in Mbarara. For sweet potato, price spreads are similarly large.

Table 2.4 provides information on the price bands across markets, based on monthly price observations across the six major wholesale markets during the year July 2005 to June 2006. The table shows the lowest of the six prices, the ratio of the highest price to the lowest price, the average (across

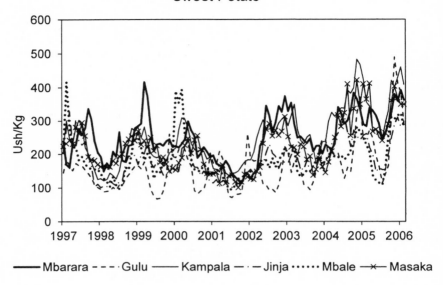

Fig. 2.1   Monthly wholesale prices for matoke and sweet potato, major Ugandan markets, June 1997 to July 2006

Table 2.4   **Price dispersion across six wholesale markets, average of monthly data for July 2005–June 2006**

Commodity	Min. price (USh/Kg) Max./min.	Max.-Min. (USh/kg)	2nd highest price– 2nd lowest(USh/kg)	
Cassava flour*	565	1.84	472	83
Dry beans, Kanyewba*	714	1.36	260	69
Dry beans, Nambale**	708	1.35	253	91
Fresh cassava**	144	2.44	205	121
Groundnuts, unpounded	1,509	1.25	390	202
Irish potato	321	2.15	346	95
Maize flour	593	1.37	206	110
Matoke	210	2.55	315	81
Millet flour	785	1.37	289	134
Rice	1,084	1.21	225	106
Sweet potato	193	2.00	169	107

Source: Uganda Bureau of Statistics, CPI data on food prices.

Note: Data are for six wholesale markets: Mbarara, Gulu, Kampala, Jinja, Mbale, and Masaka.

*Data available for four markets only.

**Data available for five markets only.

twelve monthly observations) of the absolute gap in prices between the highest and lowest, and the average of the absolute gap between the second highest and second lowest prices. These gaps are large, in general. Averaging across crops and across the whole year, nearly 300 USh/kg separated the most expensive price from the least expensive price, and on average over 100 USh/kg separated the second highest price from the second lowest.

The examples given here illustrate the point that prices of agricultural commodities are related to the distances over which the goods need to move—as well as to road quality and other factors that are not observed precisely. For the purposes of this chapter, we do not need to argue that all of the price differences across markets are due to actual transportation costs; we acknowledge that there are many other factors causing dispersion of prices across space. For instance, spatial dispersion of prices may reflect policy barriers, market power, and other factors. In Uganda's case, however, distance and road conditions are immediate and clear features of reality.

Transport Cost Data

As an alternative to looking at geographic dispersion of prices, we can try to measure transport costs directly. In principle, shipping costs should be observed directly without much difficulty. In practice, however, the costs of shipping agricultural goods are closely associated with the costs of grading, bagging, storing, and milling, among others. These costs can also contribute to the price wedges between different market locations. All of these constitute distribution costs associated with moving food from rural to urban areas. From our perspective, however, we will focus most closely on the transportation costs, since these will play an explicit role in our model.

The best source of data on shipping costs are agricultural marketing studies, which have been done by a number of agencies—often with a view to project interventions that aim to reduce marketing wedges between farmers and consumers. A major 2002 study undertaken as part of the government of Uganda's Plan for the Modernization of Agriculture documented transaction costs in the marketing process for six agricultural commodities: coffee, cotton, fish, maize, cassava, and dairy (Plan for Modernization of Agriculture 2002). We focus on the marketing costs of the three domestically consumed commodities.

For maize, the study considers four rural districts, where farm gate prices of maize ranged from 50 USh/kg (near Kapchorwa) to 65 USh/kg (near Mbale). As shown in table 2.5, transport from farm gate to primary market centers was estimated at 10 USh/kg. Further transport to secondary market centers (i.e., district markets) cost an additional 5–10 USh/kg; other handling costs—including labor charges for loading and unloading, bagging, storage, and losses—added up to around 10 USh/kg of additional transport-related cost. The price of maize at the secondary markets ranged from 90 USh/kg to 105 USh/kg, implying a 60–85 percent increase relative to farm gate prices. The study estimates that the total margins earned by traders and middlemen accounted for close to 10 USh/kg in all cases; essentially all of the remaining price wedges can be attributed to transportation and transaction costs. From the secondary markets, maize moved to major wholesale markets in cities like Mbale, Tororo, and Kampala. Wholesale prices in these markets were 115–20 USh/kg, with all of the price wedges between secondary and tertiary markets attributed to transportation costs (PMA 2002, 119–21). Eventual retail prices for milled maize flour were 210–400 USh/kg, depending on quality.

Summarizing, the farm gate prices of maize were 40–55 percent of urban wholesale prices for unmilled maize. By far the largest part of the price gap was attributed to explicit transport costs. Across the four rural districts, pure transport costs of moving maize to wholesale markets were approximately 55 USh/kg—meaning that the farm gate price and the transport cost were approximately the same.

For cassava, marketing takes place in several forms. Cassava is sold to market fresh, but it is also marketed as cassava chips (for subsequent milling into flour) and as flour. In all these forms, there are large price wedges between farmers and markets, with transportation costs accounting for a large fraction of the total. Table 2.6 reports data on the prices of cassava chips at various points in the distribution and marketing chain. Farm gate prices for cassava chips are 40–50 USh/kg, compared to wholesale prices

Table 2.5   **Maize marketing margins and transport costs: Farm gate to wholesale, 2002**

	Kapchorwa	Mbale	Iganga	Masindi
Farm gate price	**50**	**65**	**60**	**60**
Bagging materials	1	1	2	5
Labor costs (loading, sorting)				3
Weighing costs				
Transport (farm gate to primary market)	10	10	10	10
Market dues/local tax			2	2
Margins	4	9	6	5
Primary market price	**65**	**85**	**80**	**85**
Bagging materials	—	2	2	2
Labor costs (loading, sorting, unloading/weighing costs)	4	5	5	4
Transport (rural to urban market)	10	5	5	10
Storage	0.5	1	1	1
Losses	2	2	2	2
Market dues/local tax	1	1	1	1
Trading license & security	—	0.5	0.5	0.5
Margin	5	3.5	5	4.5
Total	22.5	20	21.5	25
Secondary market price	**90**	**105**	**101.5**	**110**
Labor costs (loading, sorting)				
Weighing costs				
Transport				
Mbale	20			
Kampala	45		20	25
Tororo			20	40
Kenya	25			
Market dues/local tax				
Total				
Tertiary market prices				
Mbale	**115**	**115**	**115**	**115**
Kampala	**120**	**120**	**120**	**120**
Kenya	**120**	**120**	**120**	**120**

Source: Plan for Modernization of Agriculture (2002, 119–21).

of 110–20 USh/kg, implying that farmers receive 33 to 45 percent of the wholesale price.

Similar figures can be found in the market for dried cassava, in which farmers receive something less than one-third of the wholesale price, and in which pure transport costs account for slightly more (4,500 USh/100 kg) than the farm gate price (4,000 USh/100 kg). Table 2.7 shows the other components of the price wedge between farm gate and wholesale. Although gross margins are large, net margins appear to be modest.

Table 2.6   **Cassava chip prices, January–February 2002**

Prices received by:	USh/kg	Source of information
Traveling traders, Kampala	120–40	Kampala wholesalers, who use custom mills and sell flour
Village dealers in Kumi district	50–55	Wholesalers in Jinja
Village dealers in Soroti district	60	Wholesalers in Jinja
Farmers in villages of Pallisa, Kumi, or Soroti districts	40–50	DAO Pallisa, farmers, wholesalers in Jinja, Kumi, and Soroti, AO Kumi
Farmers delivering chips at roadside markets in Kumi district	50–60	Farmers, trader
Farmers in Lira district	50–60	Wholesalers in Lira Town
Village dealers in Lira district	70–80	Wholesalers in Lira Town
Wholesale price in Lira Town	110–20	Wholesalers in Lira Town
Arua Mmarket	Approx. 200	Farmers in Bweyale

Source: Plan for Modernization of Agriculture (2002, 131).

Table 2.7   **Dried cassava marketing margins and transportation costs, 2002**

	Kampala-based traders Paidha, Kumi, Pallisa USh/100 kg
Farm gate price	**4,000**
Transport (farm gate to primary market)	1,000
Market dues/local tax	200
Estimated capital cost	36
Margins	764
Primary market price	**6,000**
Bagging materials	500
Labor costs (loading, sorting, unloading /weighing costs)	700
Transport (rural to urban market)	3,500
Estimated capital cost	162
Market dues/local tax	500
Trading license & security	200
Margin	1,438
Wholesale market price	**13,000**

Source: Plan for Modernization of Agriculture (2002, 140–41).

For fresh cassava, too, transport costs may easily exceed farm gate prices. By the time additional labor costs are added for loading, unloading, and bagging, along with market fees and similar charges, the gap between farm gate prices and wholesale prices may be large. In some cases, farmers may sell cassava standing in the field. The purchaser provides the labor to dig up the cassava and to market it. In these cases, the revenues received by farmers for cassava in the field are estimated to be just over 20 percent of the wholesale price.

Taken together, the evidence for maize and cassava suggests that transport costs and marketing margins are very high. Farm gate prices are often significantly less than half of wholesale prices, across many crops and regions. Although these data are only suggestive, a similar conclusion emerges from recent work by Svensson and Yanagizawa (2009) who calculate farm gate prices for maize from the nationally representative Uganda National Household Survey 2005. They find that for the period July 2004–June 2005, the average farm gate price of maize for households in a subset of maize-growing districts was 188 USh/kg, compared to a district market price of 291 USh/kg. The implied ratio of farm gate price to secondary market price is very similar to the data included in table 2.5.

A Benchmark for Costs: Grain Shipping in US Markets

To put the Ugandan data into perspective, it is useful to make a comparison to data from the United States. First, consider the data on US corn prices at major wholesale markets across the United States, presented in table 2.8. In this table, we consider several of the same measures used in table 2.4, including the ratio of the maximum price to the minimum. It is striking that other than the "gulf ports," all the other major markets have prices for each year that fall within a very narrow band. The average ratio of the highest price to the lowest price, across the seven years of data, was 1.25. By comparison, for maize in Uganda, the average ratio of the higest price to the lowest price across six wholesale markets was 1.61, even though the geographic distance between markets was much smaller in Uganda. The gap between the second highest price and the second lowest price averaged 10 percent of the minimum price in the United States, compared with 27 percent of the minimum price for Uganda.

Next, consider the unit costs of transporting 100 kg of maize a distance of

Table 2.8   US corn prices, major wholesale markets: Annual average prices for yellow corn no. 2

Market	2002	2003	2004	2005	2006	2007	2008
Central Illinois	2.34	2.52	1.93	2.00	3.33	4.79	3.68
Gulf ports	2.70	2.94	2.48	2.69	3.94	5.53	4.39
St. Louis	2.49	2.73	2.13	2.19	3.60	5.05	3.92
Omaha	2.29	2.50	1.82	1.88	3.33	4.84	3.80
Chicago	2.46	2.66	2.08	2.10	3.46	4.98	3.89
Kansas City	2.43	2.55	1.90	1.98	3.42	4.95	3.81
Toledo	2.47	2.58	1.97	2.00	3.41	4.92	3.86
Memphis	2.46	2.67	2.12	2.23	3.57	5.01	3.78
Minneapolis	2.26	2.50	1.88	1.85	3.16	4.70	3.62
Minimum Price	2.26	2.50	1.82	1.85	3.16	4.70	3.62
Max./min.	1.19	1.18	1.36	1.45	1.25	1.18	1.21
Max.–min.	0.44	0.44	0.66	0.84	0.78	0.83	0.77
2nd max.–2nd min.	0.20	0.23	0.25	0.35	0.27	0.26	0.23

100 km from farm to market. For the United States, as of 2009, a standard calculation used for farm-to-market transportation costs was $0.285/bushel per 100 miles. This is equivalent to $0.65 per 100 kg/100 km. For Uganda, by contrast, the cost associated with moving maize from the farm gate to a secondary market was about 20 USh/kg in 2002. At the prevailing exchange rate of 1,738 USh/$US, and assuming that on average farms were 50 km from the relevant market center, this corresponds to a unit transport cost of $2.30 per 100 kg/100 km. This is approximately four times the unit cost in the United States. If we assume instead that an average farm was only 25 km from the market center—which is perhaps a more reasonable estimate—the unit transport cost rises to $4.60 per 100 kg/100 km, which is about seven times the cost in the United States.

Similar results emerge from comparisons of shipping costs between wholesale markets (as opposed to farm-to-market transport). To ship maize from Minneapolis to St. Louis, a distance of 560 miles, cost an average of about $0.305/bushel in 2002–2008. This corresponds to a total cost of about $0.125 per 100 kg/100 km. To ship maize from Gulu to Jinja, by comparison, is a distance of 426 km by road. The implied cost per 100 kg/100 km is $15.74, about two orders of magnitude greater than the bulk transport rate in the United States.[7]

A conclusion from this analysis is that transport costs at all levels are high in Uganda. Transport costs, along with related storage and handling charges, appear to account for large fractions of the price wedges between farm and market, as well as the price wedges between markets. We make no judgment here as to the extent of market power in this sector. Some analyses suggest that traders behave noncompetitively, especially on long-distance routes, but the reported net margins in trading do not appear to be unreasonable, and there is robust (though not free) entry and exit from the markets.

2.3   Related Literature

This chapter has roots in several strands of economic literature. Our theoretical framework is most closely related to recent work on structural transformation and economic growth. We also draw on a large body of previous literature that deals with the issue of transportation and transaction costs.

2.3.1   Structural Transformation and the Movement out of Subsistence Agriculture

Modern economic growth is accompanied by a number of changes in the structural characteristics of production—including changes in the types of

---

7. The comparison is perhaps somewhat unfair; in the United States, barge transport helps to reduce the costs of moving grain along this route. But to some extent, the problem in Uganda is precisely the lack of alternatives to (low quality) roads.

goods produced, the size and organization of establishments, and the role of home production (Buera and Kaboski 2008). Changes in the sectoral composition of output are perhaps the most visible feature of the structural transformation. As economies grow, they move out of agriculture into industry and services. This empirical regularity was documented by Kuznets (1966), Chenery and Syrquin (1975), and others (e.g., Syrquin 1988). In fact, much early writing viewed development as essentially identical with the movement of people out of quasi-subsistence agriculture and into "modern" economic activities (e.g., Rosenstein-Rodan 1943; Rostow 1960; Lewis 1966; Fei and Ranis 1964).

What role does agricultural productivity play in this process? Some early development economist argued that growth depends on an economy's ability to generate an agricultural surplus—in other words, to reach a level of labor productivity such that farmers can produce substantial quantities in excess of their own food needs and can thereby support urban populations. T. W. Schultz (1953) characterized this challenge as the "food problem" facing poor countries. Schultz's view was later echoed in writings by many economists who argued that agricultural productivity increases drive the structural transformation (e.g., Johnston and Mellor 1961; Schultz 1964, 1968; Johnston 1970; Johnston and Kilby 1975; Timmer 1988; Johnson 1997). The same theme figures prominently in the later works of Mellor (1995, 1996) and the analyses of many other scholars (e.g., Eswaran and Kotwal 1993; Mundlak 2000).

In recent years, a number of papers have used two-sector growth models to examine this process in greater detail. A number of papers have sought to show how a growth model can generate changes in the sectoral composition of output (e.g., Echevarria 1995, 1997; Kogel and Prskawetz 2001; Irz and Roe 2005; Kongsamut, Rebelo, and Xie 2001). A related set of papers sought to model the structural transformation in a one-sector economy, focusing on the transition from a low-growth or no-growth traditional economy to a modern "Solow" economy. Among these papers are King and Rebelo (1993), Goodfriend and McDermott (1998), Laitner (2000), Hansen and Prescott (2002), Ngai (2004), and Ngai and Pissarides (2007).

Although these models can generate structural transformations, they have some difficulty in explaining the coexistence of a rich ("modern") sector and a poor ("traditional") agricultural sector. The "dualism" of developing economies is puzzling. Why do labor and capital not move more rapidly across sectors? As argued by Buera and Kaboski (2008), theories of dualistic economies may need to assume sector-specific distortions or more general market failures. For example, Temple (2004, 2005) and Vollrath (2009a, 2009b), among others, have explored multisector models in which unemployment or underemployment is possible. In these papers, there may be fixed urban wages or other rigidities that prevent the urban labor market from clearing. Caselli and Coleman (2001) use a framework in which transaction cost wedges prevent the labor market from equalizing marginal products across sectors. Dekle and Vandenbroucke (2006) similarly focus on distortions in labor markets. A slightly different approach is found in Restuccia, Yang, and Zhu (2008) and Herrendorf and Teixeira (2008), who consider the impact of distortions in the cost of farm inputs. These papers have the feature that the allocation of resources across sectors is inefficient; the social planner would allocate labor and capital differently.

Gollin, Parente, and Rogerson (2002, 2007) use models in which the allocation is efficient. They follow Schultz in assuming that many poor countries need to tie down large amounts of labor and other resources in food production. Countries that have low agricultural productivity—which could be due to poor technology, geography, or institutions—may sustain large differences in average productivity across sectors.

2.3.2   Transportation and Transaction Costs

Within the recent literature on structural transformation, few papers have addressed the role of transportation or the costs of moving goods between rural and urban areas. By contrast, transport cost has been a major topic in the international trade literature, as well as in the empirical literature on development economics. In the development policy literature, too, many donor organizations have directed attention and resources to the issue of rural transportation infrastructure. Transport costs also figure prominently in the agricultural economics literature, where there is a long tradition of studying marketing margins and farm-to-market value chains, in which transportation costs are prominent.

In the growth literature, our chapter is related to recent work by Herrendorf, Schmitz, and Teixeira (2006) and Herrendorf and Teixeira (2011). It is also somewhat related to Adamopoulos (2006), who uses a model with transportation costs to conduct a development accounting exercise.

In the development literature, many papers have looked at the impact of roads and infrastructure on development in Africa and other regions of the developing world. This includes theoretical papers, along with a number of recent policy and empirical papers, such as Platteau (1996), Limão and Venables (1999), Fan and Hazell (2001), Fan and Chan-Kang (2004), Torero and Chowdhury (2005), Renkow, Hallstrom, and Karahja (2004), Zhang and Fan (2004), Calderón (2009), Dorosh et al. (2008), and Minten and Stifel (2008). Many of these papers rely on cross-section regressions at the country or district level. There are obviously difficult identification problems with this approach.

Most analyses conclude that Africa suffers from a substantial deficit in transportation infrastructure, and studies along these lines have been used to advocate increases in spending on road construction and road maintenance. A consortium of donors have consequently established the African Infrastructure Country Diagnostic (AICD) to share knowledge and mobilize funding for further investments in infrastructure. One AICD document calls for an additional $31 billion annually on infrastructure spending in Africa, and another paper calls for $20 billion annually in spending on transportation infrastructure, including both capital improvements and maintenance of existing stocks.

Some observers have argued that transportation infrastructure is less of an issue in Africa than market imperfections and collusion in the transport sector. Raballand and Macchi (2008) have argued that trucking companies do not face particularly high costs of vehicle operation (and in fact, face very low labor costs), but that the prices they charge to customers reflect substantial markups that reflect cartelization in transport. Related work by Gachassin, Najman, and Raballand (2010) questions the likely impact of road investments on rural poverty, noting that in a study from Cameroon, rural infrastructure investments were not linked to increases in consumption expenditure. The authors argue that road improvements are most likely to have value in areas where they can support nonagricultural activities rather than in areas of smallholder farming.

Transportation and Agricultural Marketing in Uganda

Concerns over high transportation costs and marketing margins date back many decades in Uganda. Colonial governments viewed road construction as one of the priorities for the expansion of markets, and for an extended period, the colonial government required communities to provide forced labor for road construction and maintenance. Roads remain a concern of today's Ugandan government. As noted above, the existing road network is poor, but expansion is likely to be expensive. Road construction is expensive. Carruthers, Krishnamani, and Murray (2008) calculate that a program of road construction and maintenance that would expand Uganda's network of all-weather roads so that 75 percent of the population would be able to access such a road within a distance of 2 km would require spending of 3.6 percent of gross domestic product (GDP) annually for a period of ten years. Even a more modest goal (50 percent of the population, with lower-quality roads) would require 2.2 percent of GDP annually.

Our chapter relates to an issue raised by Raballand et al. (2009), who have argued that improvements in rural roads in Uganda would have little impact because productivity levels are too low to justify more frequent or heavier traffic. Their paper takes productivity levels as fixed; ours considers the connections between improvements in transportation, changes in input and output prices, and the resulting changes in yield and production.

2.4   Model

In this section we lay out a sequence of models that serve to highlight several forces that influence the allocation of workers to agriculture. We start with a simple version of the model in Gollin, Parente, and Rogerson. (2002) and then extend this model along several dimensions. We believe that developing these models sequentially serves to highlight the underlying economic forces in a more transparent and intuitive fashion. We note here that our analysis will exclusively focus on models of closed economies. The essence of this assumption is that an economy needs to be able to produce sufficient food to feed its population. As described previously in section 2.2.1, this assumption seems reasonable for an economy like Uganda, which is the focus of our analysis. Uganda imports relatively little of the basic food items that serves to sustain the vast majority of its population.

Looking ahead, some of the specifications that we analyze implicitly create an incentive for Uganda to import basic foodstuffs from abroad. Understanding why this does not occur is an important issue. Consistent with our general focus on transportation infrastructure, we believe that an important element of the explanation has to do with the difficult logistics of importing food into a landlocked country with very poor transportation infrastructure. Nonetheless, in our models we simply rule out trade and focus on allocations within a closed economy.

2.4.1   A Benchmark Model

We begin with a static version of the model in Gollin, Parente, and Rogerson. (2002). The basic setup is as follows: There is a measure one of identical agents. Each individual has preferences over two goods, which we label as agriculture (a) and manufacturing (m), given by:[8]

$$(1) \qquad u(a - \bar{a}) + v(m + \bar{m})$$

where u and v are both increasing, strictly concave functions and $\bar{a}$ and $\bar{m}$ are both strictly positive. The key feature of these preferences is the presence of the $\bar{a}$ and $\bar{m}$ terms, which serve to make the income elasticity of the agricultural good less than one and that of the manufactured good greater than one.[9] Gollin, Parente, and Rogerson (2002) consider the special case where the function u has the property that it is minus infinity if $a - \bar{a}$ is negative and equal to a constant for all nonnegative values of $a - \bar{a}$. The implication of this specification is that individuals will consume exactly $\bar{a}$ units of food. While not essential, this simplifies the analytics and increases the transparency of the key economic forces. In our quantitative work we will consider a more general specification in which individuals also value consumption of the agricultural good beyond $\bar{a}$.

The economy is endowed with one unit of land and each individual is

8. While we follow the tradition of referring to the nonagricultural good as the manufacturing good, it should be interpreted as representing both the manufacturing and the service sectors.
9. It is sufficient that at least one of $\bar{a}$ or $\bar{m}$ be greater than zero for this property to hold. Having both positive allows for the possibility of a corner solution in which $m = 0$

endowed with one unit of time. We assume that land ownership is equally distributed across the population. The technology for producing the manufactured good is given by:

$$(2) \qquad m = A_m n_m$$

where n_m is the number of workers that work in the manufacturing sector, and the technology for producing the agricultural good is given by:

$$(3) \qquad a = A_a L^{\theta} n_a^{1-\theta}$$

where n_a is the number of workers that work in the agricultural sector and l is land. We assume that the economy is able to produce sufficient amounts of a so as to provide all individuals with at least $\bar{a}$ units of the agricultural good. A sufficient condition for this is that $A_a > \bar{a}$.

We study the competitive equilibrium allocation for this economy, which can be obtained by solving the social planner's problem in which the utility of a representative household is maximized subject to the feasibility constraints. This turns out to be somewhat trivial given the extreme form of preferences that we have assumed. In particular, given that everyone needs to consume exactly $\bar{a}$ units of the agricultural good, but receives no benefit from consuming any additional amount, the optimal allocation is to allocate enough workers to the agricultural sector so as to produce $\bar{a}$ for each individual in the economy, and then to allocate all remaining workers to the manufacturing sector. It follows that the optimal value for n_a is given by:

$$(4) \qquad n_a = \left[\frac{\bar{a}}{A_a} \right]^{1/(1-\theta)}.$$

The key implication of this model is that in an economy in which food is a necessity, there is a powerful negative relationship between agricultural TFP and employment in agriculture. In particular, a 1 percent decrease in agricultural TFP A_a will lead to an even larger percentage increase in employment in agriculture, equal to $1/(1-\theta)$.

We next extend this simple model in order to illustrate two additional economic mechanisms that are potentially important determinants of the allocation of labor to agriculture.

2.4.2   Intermediate Goods In Agriculture

We modify the previous model by assuming that the output of the manufacturing sector can be used either for consumption or as an input in the production of the agricultural good. Let x denote the input of the manufactured good used in the agricultural sector. To simplify the exposition we again restrict attention to an agricultural production function that is Cobb-Douglas:

(5)
$$a = A_a l^{(1-\theta_x-\theta_n)} x^{\theta_x} n_a^{\theta_n}.$$

The social planner's problem for this economy is not as trivial as in the previous model, since there is now a decision about the input mix that is used to produce the required amount of agricultural output. Specifically, the social planner now seeks to solve:

$$\max_{n_a, x} v\left(A_m(1-n_a) - x + \bar{m}\right)$$

subject to:

$$\bar{a} = A_a x^{\theta_x} n_a^{\theta_n}.$$

This problem amounts to maximizing the consumption of the nonagricultural good subject to making sure that food requirements are met. Given our assumption of a Cobb-Douglas production function the solution for x will necessarily be interior. Letting λ_a be the Lagrange multiplier on the constraint, the first-order conditions for an interior solution are given by:

(6)
$$v'\left(A_m(1-n_a) - x + \bar{m}\right) A_m = \lambda_a \theta_n A_a x^{\theta_x} n_a^{\theta_n-1}$$

(7)
$$v'\left(A_m(1-n_a) - x + \bar{m}\right) = \lambda_a \theta_x A_a x^{\theta_x-1} n_a^{\theta_n}.$$

Dividing the two equations by each other yields:

(8)
$$A_m = \frac{\theta_n}{\theta_x} \frac{x}{n_a},$$

which implies that the optimal choice of x for a given choice of n_a satisfies:

(9)
$$x = A_m \frac{\theta_x}{\theta_n} n_a.$$

It follows that we can rewrite the social planner's problem as:

$$\max_{n_a} v\left(A_m(1-n_a) - A_m \frac{\theta_x}{\theta_n} n_a + \bar{m}\right)$$

subject to:

$$\bar{a} = A_a A_m^{\theta_x} (\theta_x / \theta_n)^{\theta_x} n_a^{\theta_n+\theta_x}.$$

Because n_a is the only choice variable it follows that the constraint effectively determines the value of n_a, just as in the previous model, with the solution given by:

(10)
$$n_a = B\left[\frac{1}{A_a A_m^{\theta_x}}\right]^{1/(\theta_n+\theta_x)}$$

where $B = [\bar{a}\theta_n/\theta_x]^{1/(\theta_n+\theta_x)}$. The key result is that in this extended model, low productivity in either the agricultural or the manufacturing sector can give rise to increased employment in the agricultural sector. However, it is important to note that the elasticity of n_a with respect to A_m is smaller than the elasticity of n_a with respect to A_a by a factor of θ_x.

The above analysis has focused on optimal allocations taking as given the productivity of the economy in each of the two sectors. It is important to note that while the above argument stressed low productivity in the manufacturing sector as a factor leading to high employment in agriculture, the exact same logic shows that policies that increase the relative price of the intermediate good used in the agricultural sector would have the same effects.

2.4.3   Transportation Costs

In this subsection we abstract from intermediate inputs in agricultural production, but consider a different extension of the basic model described above. In particular, we consider a model in which production of agriculture and manufacturing goods takes place in different locations and it is costly to transport these goods between locations. Specifically, the two production technologies are as in the simple model that we described initially:

$$(11) \qquad\qquad a = A_a l^\theta n_a^{1-\theta}$$

$$(12) \qquad\qquad m = A_m n_m.$$

Workers reside in the location in which they work, and must consume goods delivered to that location. For simplicity, we assume that transportation costs take the form of iceberg costs and are symmetric, that is, the cost of transporting m from one region to the other is the same as transporting a from one region to the other. We denote this cost by q. We abstract from moving costs for individuals and hence do not need to specify the initial location of workers. We discuss this in more detail below. Letting a_m and a_a denote the consumption of agricultural goods of workers in region m and a respectively, and similarly for m_a and m_m, feasibility now requires the following:

$$(13) \qquad\qquad n_a a_a + \left(1 - n_a\right)\frac{a_m}{\left(1 - q\right)} = A_a l^\theta n_a^{1-\theta}$$

$$(14) \qquad\qquad \left(1 - n_a\right)m_m + n_a \frac{m_a}{\left(1 - q\right)} = A_m n_m.$$

We again consider the social planner's problem for this economy. The presence of the location decision gives rise to a nonconvexity in this economy, which means that optimal allocations will not necessarily equate utilities across individuals in different locations. We assume that the transfers across individuals that are implicitly part of supporting such an allocation as an equilibrium are taken care of within the family, so that we are viewing the economy as consisting of many families, each of which has many members.

In equilibrium, each family behaves the same way. This assumption serves to simplify the analysis by allowing us to better focus on the role of transportation costs for goods, and is not critical for our results. Our main result is that transportation costs also have the effect of inducing a larger allocation of workers to the agricultural sector. If we were to assume that all individuals begin in the agricultural location and it is costly for an individual to move to the other location, this would simply reinforce this result.

It remains true that the social planner needs to allocate workers so that each worker obtains $\bar{a}$ units of the agricultural good. From the feasibility condition for the agricultural good it follows that there is a unique value of n_a that is consistent with this outcome. Specifically, setting a_a and a_m equal to $\bar{a}$ in this expression yields:

$$(15) \qquad n_a \bar{a} \frac{q}{1-q} = \frac{\bar{a}}{1-q} - A_a n_a^{1-\theta}.$$

It follows that decreases in A_a and increases in q both lead to increases in n_a. Considering the case in which $\theta = 0$ provides some additional insight. In this case we obtain:

$$(16) \qquad n_a = \frac{\bar{a}}{\bar{a}q + (1-q)A_a}.$$

From this expression there are three results of interest. First, as in the initial model model, a decrease in A_a leads to an increase in n_a. Second, whereas in the case of no transportation costs (i.e., $q = 0$) this elasticity is equal to negative one, when $q > 0$ the elasticity is less than one in absolute value. Third, an increase in transportation costs leads to an increase in n_a, since our maintained assumption for an interior solution for n_a is that $A_a > \bar{a}$. The elasticity of n_a with respect to q is given by $(A_a - \bar{a})/(\bar{a}n_a)$. The intuition for these results is straightforward. Transportation costs imply that it takes agricultural production in excess of $\bar{a}$ in order to support an individual who resides in the manufacturing sector. It follows that if transportation costs increase, then holding the labor allocation fixed will result in a shortage of agricultural production, thereby necessitating an increase in labor allocated to agricultural production. It follows that holding all else constant, an economy with greater transportation costs will have a greater fraction of its employment in the agricultural sector. The effect of changes in A_a are also muted by the presence of transportation costs. When $\theta = 0$ and there are no transportation costs, a 1 percent increase in A_a leads to a 1 percent decrease in n_a since the same amount of food can now be produced by 1 percent fewer workers. In an economy with transportation costs it remains true that the same amount of output can be produced by 1 percent fewer workers, but when more individuals move from the agricultural sector to the manufacturing sector, it is necessary to transport more food, and therefore the decrease in n_a is necessarily less.

2.4.4   The Interaction of Intermediate Inputs and Transportation Costs

To simplify exposition we have thus far considered intermediate inputs and transportation costs in isolation from each other. However, there is an interaction between the two that is important to point out. In our analysis of the intermediate input case we showed that low productivity in the production of intermediates acted in a similar fashion (though with a smaller magnitude) to low productivity in agriculture in terms of how it influences the allocation of labor. We commented at the end of that section that a policy distortion that serves to increase the relative price of the intermediate good would have the same effects. In this section we show that the introduction of transportation costs into a model with intermediate inputs in agriculture necessarily creates this same effect. The intuition is simple: if intermediate goods need to be transported to the agricultural region, then increases in transportation costs serve to decrease use of intermediates, thereby reducing labor productivity in that sector. In this section we quickly show this formally, in the simplest setting possible. Specifically, our starting point will be the intermediate good model studied in the previous subsection, extended to assume that there is a cost associated with transporting intermediate goods for use in agriculture. To facilitate exposition, we abstract from transportation costs associated with moving the final goods between locations. Given there is no cost associated with moving final goods between locations, the social planner will allocate the same final consumption allocation to all individuals.

The social planner now seeks to solve:

$$\max_{n_a, x} v\left(A_m(1 - n_a) - \frac{x}{1 - q} + \bar{m} \right)$$

subject to:

$$\bar{a} = A_a x^{\theta_x} n_a^{\theta_n}.$$

The presence of transportation costs for the intermediate input in agriculture implies that using one more unit of x in the agricultural sector implies a greater than one-unit sacrifice in terms of final consumption of the non-agricultural good. Proceeding just as before, and letting λ_a be the Lagrange multiplier on the constraint, the first-order conditions for an interior solution are given by:

(17)
$$v'\left(A_m(1 - n_a) - \frac{x}{1 - q} + \bar{m} \right) A_m = \lambda_a \theta_n A_a x^{\theta_x} n_a^{\theta_n - 1}$$

(18)
$$v'\left(A_m(1 - n_a) - \frac{x}{1 - q} + \bar{m} \right) = (1 - q)\lambda_a \theta_x A_a x^{\theta_x - 1} n_a^{\theta_n}.$$

Dividing the two equations by each other yields:

$$A_m = \frac{1}{(1-q)} \frac{\theta_n}{\theta_x} \frac{x}{n_a},$$

which implies that the optimal choice of x for a given choice of n_a satisfies:

$$x = (1-q) A_m \frac{\theta_x}{\theta_n} n_a.$$

Relative to our earlier derivations, we see the intuitive result that a higher value of q reduces the ratio intermediate input use relative to labor. Proceeding just as before, it follows that we can rewrite the social planner's problem as:

$$\max_{n_a} v\left(A_m(1-n_a) - (1-q) A_m \frac{\theta_x}{\theta_n} n_a + \bar{m} \right)$$

subject to:

$$\bar{a} = A_a (1-q)^{\theta_x} A_m^{\theta_x} (\theta_x / \theta_n)^{\theta_x} n_a^{\theta_n + \theta_x}.$$

Because n_a is the only choice variable it follows that the constraint effectively determines the value of n_a, just as in the previous model, with the solution given by:

$$\text{(21)} \qquad n_a = B\left[\frac{1}{A_a A_m^{\theta_x} (1-q)^{\theta_x}} \right]^{1/(\theta_n + \theta_x)}$$

where $B = [\bar{a}\theta_n/\theta_x]^{1/(\theta_n + \theta_x)}$. The key result is that in this extended model, a lower value for $(1-q)$ operates just like a decrease in A_m.

2.4.5   Summary

The key message from the above analysis is to note three channels that can lead to greater allocation of labor to the agricultural sector. The first channel is low TFP in agriculture. The second channel is low TFP in the production of an intermediate good used in the agricultural sector (or equivalently, a policy that raises the relative price of this input). The third channel is higher transportation costs. Two results of interest emerge from the above analysis concerning the size of these effects. First, in a model without transportation costs, the magnitude of the second channel is likely to be much smaller than the first channel, since the second channel is reduced relative to the first by a factor equal to the factor share of the intermediate good. Second, the presence of transportation costs tends to decrease the magnitude of the first channel and increase the magnitude of the second channel.

2.5   Quantitative Analysis

The previous analysis has formally demonstrated three different channels that influence the allocation of labor to the agricultural sector in a setting in which some minimal amount of food is required. The goal of this section is to carry out a quantitative analysis to provide some information regarding the relative magnitudes of these effects, as well as to measure the welfare effects associated with these three channels. In this section we consider a two-sector model along the lines of the ones considered in the previous section, allowing for both intermediate goods as inputs into the agricultural sector, as well as symmetric transport costs q that apply to movement of both final and intermediate goods across locations. For our quantitative analysis we generalize preferences so that food consumption is not necessarily equal to $\bar{a}$:

$$(22) \qquad \alpha \log(a - \bar{a}) + (1 - \alpha)\log(m + \bar{m}).$$

We continue to assume a Cobb-Douglas production function for agriculture, defined over land (l), intermediates (x) and labor (n_a):

$$(23) \qquad a = A_a F(l, x, n_a) = A_a l^{1-\theta_x-\theta_n} x^{\theta_x} n^{\theta_n}.$$

Assuming that the land endowment is normalized to one, feasibility is determined by the two constraints:

$$(24) \qquad n_a a_a + (1 - n_a)\frac{a_m}{(1-q)} = A_a F(1, x, n_a)$$

$$(25) \qquad (1 - n_a)m_m + n_a \frac{m_a}{(1-q)} + \frac{x}{(1-q)} = A_m(1 - n_a).$$

We solve a social planner's problem for this economy, which as noted earlier, can be understood as the competitive equilibrium allocation that would emerge if we interpret our model as consisting of a large number of households, each with a large number of members, where households maximize the average utility of their members. As noted earlier, the presence of the nonconvexity associated with the discrete location choice coupled with transportation costs implies that not all household members will end up with the same utility. This implies that households are implicitly making transfers across family members.

Many of the results that we derived in the previous section continue to hold in this model that features a more general utility function. In particular, given an allocation of labor across the two locations and a choice of x that is feasible given the choice of n_a, we can derive closed form solutions for the consumption allocations. In particular, we have:

$$(26) \qquad a_a = A_a F(1,x,n_a) - (1-n_a)\bar{a}\frac{q}{1-q}$$

$$(27) \qquad a_m = (1-q)A_a F(1,x,n_a) + n_a q\bar{a}.$$

As noted earlier, when $\bar{m} > 0$, it is possible that the solution for m_a will be zero even when there is positive production of the manufacturing good net of inputs into the agricultural sector. This is easily incorporated into the analysis. Specifically, we have:

$$(28) \qquad m_a = \max\left\{(1-q)\left[A_m(1-n_a) - \frac{x}{1-q}\right] - (1-n_a)\bar{m}q, 0\right\}$$

$$(29) \qquad m_m = \max\left\{A_m(1-n_a) - \frac{x}{1-q} + n_a\bar{m}\frac{q}{1-q}, A_m - \frac{x}{(1-n_a)(1-q)}\right\}.$$

It follows that consumption in each location is biased toward consumption of the good produced in that location.

For a given value of n_a, and using the above allocation rules, increasing x shifts the overall consumption bundle, as well as production from the manufactured good, toward the agricultural good. The optimal choice of x will equate the marginal rate of substitution between consumption of agriculture and manufacturing to the marginal rate of transformation between the two, taking into account transportation costs and the rule for allocating consumption within the family. A simple calculation shows that if all solutions are interior, then the choice of x should be such that the following holds:

$$(30) \qquad \frac{(1-\alpha)}{\alpha}\frac{(a_a - \bar{a})}{(m_a + \bar{m})} = A_a F_2$$

where the solutions for a_a and m_a are those derived above.

We now turn to the quantitative analysis. We choose parameters so that the model captures some features of the Ugandan economy. The technology parameters A_a and A_m can be set to one without loss of generality, as this simply amounts to a choice of units. We also normalize the size of the population to equal one. For our benchmark results we set $\theta_x = .2$ and $\theta_n = .4$, implying a share for land that is also equal to .4. The preference parameter α is set to .20.

If $\bar{a}$ and $\bar{m}$ were zero, then expenditure shares would provide information on α. The parameters $\bar{a}$ and $\bar{m}$ become less relevant as a country becomes richer, so looking at expenditure shares for rich countries does provide information about α if we assume that preferences are the same across countries. If we were interpreting the agricultural sector output exclusively as food, then expenditure shares in a rich country such as the United States would suggest that our value of α is somewhat on the high side, but we think it is reasonable to have a broader notion of agricultural output that also includes clothing, for example, thereby motivating the somewhat higher value for α.

In terms of how they influence labor allocations, the parameters $\bar{a}$ and $\bar{m}$ have the same effect, which is to lead to a greater allocation of labor to agriculture holding all else constant. In view of this we set $\bar{m} = 0$ in our benchmark specification and rely on $\bar{a}$ to achieve the desired allocation of labor. In particular, we will choose $\bar{a}$ so that roughly 80 percent of the population works in the agricultural sector, consistent with the allocation of labor in Uganda. The final parameter to be set is the transportation cost parameter q. For our benchmark results we set $q = .5$. In the decentralized equilibrium, this would imply that prices of agricultural goods in the urban region are twice as high as in the rural area. This dispersion is consistent with the evidence for Uganda presented in section 2.2. Table 2.9 displays the equilibrium allocation that results from our calibrated economy.

We now consider the effects of changes in several of the model's parameters for the equilibrium allocations and welfare. Our measure of welfare is standard. Specifically, let the benchmark equilibrium have n_a^* workers in the agricultural sector and a consumption allocation to be $(a_a^*, m_a^*, a_m^*, m_m^*)$ and suppose that the new allocation that emerges from a particular change in the economy is given by $n_a', a_a', m_a', a_m', m_m'$. We then ask what proportional change in the consumption bundle $(a_a^*, m_a^*, a_m^*, m_m^*)$ holding the labor allocation n_a fixed, would yield the same average utility as generated by the new allocation.

In our qualitative analysis we considered three key driving forces for the allocation of labor to agriculture: TFP in agriculture, TFP in manufacturing, and transportation costs. We begin by exploring the impact of a 10 percent improvement in each of these variables in isolation. Table 2.10 presents the results.

Several points are worth noting. First, consistent with our theoretical analysis, all three changes result in a decline in the fraction of the population in the agricultural sector. Moreover, the ratio of θ_x to $\theta_x + \theta_n$ is one-third and the effect of a 10 percent increase in manufacturing TFP on labor allocated

Table 2.9   **Benchmark equilibrium allocation**

n_a/Pop	a_m	a_a	m_m	m_a	x
.800	.454	.458	.045	.023	.077

Table 2.10   **Comparison of the three channels**

	n_a/Pop	a_m	a_a	m_m	m_a	x	Δ
Benchmark	.800	.454	.458	.045	.023	.077	—
$A_a = 1.1$	.736	.460	.469	.103	.052	.081	.33
$A_m = 1.1$	.787	.455	.460	.063	.031	.086	.045
$q = .45$	.747	.457	.463	.080	.044	.095	.173
$A_a = 1.1, q = .45$	.681	.463	.474	.143	.079	.097	.769

to agriculture is roughly one-third the size of the effect from a 10 percent increase in A_a. The effect of a 10 percent improvement in transportation has an impact on labor allocated to agriculture that is roughly 80 percent as large as the 10 percent increase in agricultural TFP. At least in this parameterization, the effects of improvements in transportation technology seem to be of roughly similar importance to equivalent improvements in agricultural TFP, and are more important than improvements in the TFP for producing intermediate goods. This last result was predicted by our theoretical analysis, since we saw in the previous section that one of the effects of a 10 percent improvement in transportation is to mimic a 10 percent improvement in the TFP for producing intermediates, but that there are additional effects as well.

The welfare effects associated with these changes are very large—for example, a 10 percent increase in A_a leads to a welfare increase of more than 30 percent. From a mechanical perspective, note that the source of this large increase is mostly attributable to the fact that although the increase in the consumption levels is small, it represents a large percentage change in m. Specifically, for the case of the increase in A_a, the value of m more than doubles for workers in both locations. To understand why a 10 percent improvement in technology in only one sector can have such a large effect, it is important to note that the welfare effect is highly nonlinear due to the presence of the $\bar{a}$ term. For example, if we considered the welfare increase associated with changing A_a by 10 percent starting from a value of $A_a = 2$ instead of $A_a = 1$, and holding all other parameters fixed, then the welfare increase is only about half as large. Aside from noting the large welfare increases associated with small improvements in technology at low levels of development, it is also worth noting that the welfare effects associated with the increase in A_a are the largest in this economy, but that the welfare gain from a decrease in q is also very substantial. Given that the economy devotes 80 percent of its labor to the agricultural sector, it should not be surprising that the welfare effect of a change in A_m is substantially lower than that associated with a change in A_a.

There are two different channels through which changes in q influence welfare. One effect is that fewer resources are used in transportation. A second effect is that consumption allocations are smoother across locations. It is of interest to know what the relative importance of these two effects is. It turns out that the second effect is extremely small: if we compute the utility gain associated with smoothing consumption across locations, keeping total consumption constant, then the welfare gain is only .003.

It is also instructive to notice how the consumption allocation changes to better appreciate the different mechanisms at work. Table 2.10 shows that in each case the consumption allocation increases along all dimensions, with the increase in consumption being the greatest for the increase in A_a. However, the increase in intermediates used in agriculture is actually smallest for this case. As noted earlier, the cases of increases in A_m and decreases in q both

Table 2.11   **The effects of population growth**

	n_a/Pop	a_a	a_m	m_a	m_m	x	Δ
Benchmark	.800	.454	.458	.045	.023	.077	—
Pop = 1.1	.826	.452	.454	.023	.011	.084	−.009
Pop =1.1, A_a = 1.038	.800	.454	.458	.045	.023	.085	.000

serve to decrease the relative price of intermediates, and therefore lead to a larger increase in intermediate usage relative to the case of an increase in A_a.

The last row of table 2.10 reports the effects of having two of the changes occur simultaneously. The effect on the allocation of labor is roughly the sum of the two individual effects, but the improvement in welfare is much larger than the sum of the effects. This indicates a significant interaction effect between the two types of changes.

We next consider the effects of an increase in population size. It turns out that in a model with a fixed factor and food requirements, an increase in population pushes not only more people into agriculture but also a greater fraction of the population into this sector. This suggests that population increases (relative to available land) are also potentially an important factor in understanding the dynamics of labor allocation and productivity. Table 2.11 reports the results.

The first row of table 2.11 reports the results for a 10 percent increase in population. We note that not only does this lead to a lower fraction of people in the manufacturing sector, but also that the absolute size of the population in this sector also decreases. There is also a modest decrease in welfare associated with a 10 percent increase in population. Note that although fewer workers are working in the manufacturing sector, use of intermediate inputs in agriculture actually increases as a result of the population increase. The next row asks what increase in productivity in the agricultural sector would be required in order to offset the change in the fraction of the population in agriculture due to the 10 percent population increase. The answer turns out to be an increase of 3.8 percent. As this row shows, in this case the rest of the consumption allocation is also identical to that in the benchmark specification so that there is no net change in welfare, either. But this table illustrates an important finding, which is that in the presence of a fixed amount of land, population increases require fairly substantial improvements in agricultural productivity just to maintain a constant share of the workforce devoted to agriculture.

The next issue we examine is how improvements in transportation (or lack thereof) influence a develop path. Table 2.12 reports the results.

The second row shows the consequences of a doubling of TFP in both of the productive sectors. As the table shows, this had dramatic effects on the allocation of labor, the level of consumption, and on welfare. In par-

Table 2.12   Development paths

	n_a/Pop	a_a	a_m	m_a	m_m	x	Δ
Benchmark	.800	.454	.458	.045	.023	.077	—
$A_a = A_m = 2$	.344	.525	.599	1.01	.50	.15	10.45
$A_a = A_m = 2, q = .25$	.229	.614	.668	1.31	.980	.176	17.14

ticular, the share of labor devoted to agriculture is more than cut in half, and the welfare increase is roughly a factor of ten. As in standard models, large improvements in TFP lead to large improvements in welfare. The third row shows how the development path is altered if we assume that the large improvements in TFP in the two productive sectors are accompanied by an equivalent improvement in the transportation technology. The results are quite dramatic. In addition to producing an additional decline in the agricultural share of the workforce by roughly one-third, we see that the welfare gain is almost doubled. Comparing the second and third rows, one can conclude that the consequences for development of neglecting transportation are very substantial. A simple calculation that serves to quantify this is the following: Taking the third row of table 2.12 as a benchmark, we can ask how large would the improvements in the TFP parameters A_a and A_m need to be in order to achieve the same movement of labor out of agriculture if there were no associated improvements in transportation. The answer is that they would have to increase to 2.8 in order to achieve this same outcome.

2.6   Three-Region Analysis

A distinctive feature of agriculture in Uganda is its heterogeneity. As documented earlier, while a high percentage of individuals do subsistence agriculture using very low productivity methods, there is also a small segment of the agricultural sector that appears to be very modern. In this section we develop an extension of our model that can address this heterogeneity. There are three reasons why this extension is of interest. First, we think this heterogeneity is additional evidence for the importance of transportation costs relative to other factors, such as low productivity in producing intermediates. Second, it allows us to address the issue of subsistence agriculture. Third, while the basic messages from this extension are similar to those in the previous section, we think that it provides a richer structure for thinking about policy choices.

The extension that we consider is to assume that there are two rural regions instead of just one. Each rural region has a production function identical to that in the previous model, and each has a fraction of the total endowment of land. The distinguishing feature of the two regions is the cost associated with moving goods into and out of the region. We will refer to the region with lower transportation costs as region 1 and the region with higher transportation costs as region 2. We will refer to the urban area as region 0. We assume an iceberg cost of q_1 associated with moving goods between the urban area and the region 1, and an iceberg cost of q_2 associated with moving goods from region 1 to the region 2. The only way in which goods can be moved between the urban area and the region 2 is to pass through region 1. Note that if we set $q_2 = 0$ then this model reduces to that of the previous section.

We do not provide a detailed analysis of the analytics for the three-region case. It is straightforward to show that food is never transported from region 1 to region 2. This allows one to express feasibility in terms of the following two equations:

$$n_0 m_0 + n_1 \frac{m_1 + x_1}{1 - q_1} + n_2 \frac{m_2 + x_2}{(1 - q_1)(1 - q_2)} = A_m n_0$$

$$n_0 \frac{a_0}{(1 - q_1)} + n_1 a_1 + n_2 (1 - q_2) a_2 = A_a l_1^{1-\theta_x-\theta_n} x_1^{\theta_x} n_1^{\theta_n}$$

$$+ (1 - q_2) A_a l_2^{1-\theta_x-\theta_n} x_2^{\theta_x} n_2^{\theta_n}.$$

Assuming interior solutions, and similar to the two-region case, one can show that consumption allocations will satisfy:

$$m_0 + \bar{m} = \frac{m_1 + \bar{m}}{(1 - q_1)} = \frac{m_2 + \bar{m}}{(1 - q_1)(1 - q_2)}$$

$$\frac{a_0 - \bar{a}}{(1 - q_1)} = a_1 - \bar{a} = (1 - q_2)(a_2 - \bar{a}).$$

This implies that allocations become increasingly skewed toward agriculture and away from manufacturing as we move from region 0 to region 1 to region 2.

We now move to presentation of some illustrative quantitative results. We choose the same technology parameters as in the previous section: $\theta_x = .2$ and $\theta_n = .4$, and again set $\alpha = .2$. We allocate land between the two regions according to $l_1 = .1$ and $l_2 = .9$. Transportation costs are set according to $q_1 = .1$ and $q_2 = .6$. As in the previous section we set $\bar{m} = 0$ and choose the value of $\bar{a}$ so that in the equilibrium we have 80 percent of the population in agriculture. In the equilibrium it turns out that $n_1 = .096$ and $n_2 = .707$. Table 2.13 shows the consumption allocations.

Consistent with the above analysis, we see that individuals in region 2 have much lower consumption of manufacturing goods than do individuals in the other two regions. In terms of consumption allocations, individuals in region 2 very much capture the notion of subsistence agriculture. It is also of interest to examine the nature of agricultural production in the two regions. Table 2.14 provides some summary statistics.

Table 2.13   Consumption allocations: Three-region model

n_1	n_2	a_0	a_1	a_2	m_0	m_1	m_2
.096	.707	.409	.410	.425	.0516	.0464	.0186

Table 2.14   Agriculture production: Three-region model

l_1/n_1	l_2/n_2	x_1/n_1	x_2/n_2	y_{a1}/n_1	y_{a2}/n_2	y_{a1}/l_1	y_{a2}/l_2
1.04	1.27	.187	.066	.73	.64	.70	.50

The statistics reported are the land per worker (l/n), intermediates per worker (x/n), average labor productivity (y_a/n), and yield (y_a/l). Contrasting the two regions, we see that production in region 1 is relatively intensive in intermediate inputs, whereas production in region 2 is relatively intensive in land. The difference in relative use of intermediates is very large: region 1 has almost three times as much use of intermediate goods per worker. These factor intensities have opposing effects in terms of average labor productivity, but reinforcing effects in terms of yields. Nonetheless, we see that in the benchmark equilibrium, not only is yield higher in region 1, but that average labor productivity is also. However, perhaps somewhat surprisingly, despite the much more intensive use of intermediates in region 1, the yield in region 1 is only about 40 percent higher than in region 2.

We now carry out some counterfactual experiments similar to those conducted in the two-region model. Results for consumer allocations are presented in table 2.15, and results for agricultural production are in table 2.16. For completeness we include the results of the benchmark equilibrium in each table. The welfare measure is the same one that we used earlier.

We begin by discussing the results on allocations. The effects here are very similar to those from the two-region case. Of particular interest is that the welfare effects of TFP improvements are very similar in this model, while the effects of improvements in transportation are somewhat larger. Once again there are very large interaction effects between changes in agricultural TFP and changes in transportation costs. And as before, population increases have the effect of not only changing the share of the population in agriculture, but also reducing the absolute size of the population in the urban region. Moreover, the increase in the size of the population in subsistence is larger than the increase in the size of the overall population, so increases in population lead to an increase in the size of the subsistence farmer population.

The three-region model allows us to consider a new experiment relative to the two-region case. In particular, we can contrast the effect of improving overall transportation with that of expanding the size of region 1. Loosely

Table 2.15   **Experiments in the three-region model: Consumption allocations**

	n_1	n_2	a_0	a_1	a_2	m_0	m_1	m_2	Δ
Benchmark	.096	.707	.409	.410	.425	.052	.046	.019	—
$A_a = 1.1$	.115	.625	.415	.417	.442	.096	.087	.035	.32
$A_m = 1.1$	.105	.685	.411	.412	.429	.065	.059	.024	.06
$q = .9q$	.098	.643	.413	.414	.431	.085	.077	.036	.26
A_a, A_m, q	.124	.536	.420	.422	.448	.16	.15	.068	1.07
A_a and q	.114	.566	.420	.421	.447	.14	.13	.057	.82
$l_1 = 2$	.216	.504	.414	.415	.438	.095	.085	.034	.35
Pop = 1.1	.099	.812	.407	.407	.418	.036	.032	.013	−.02

Table 2.16   **Experiments in the three-region model: Agricultural production**

	l_1/n_1	l_2/n_2	x_1/n_1	x_2/n_2	y_{a1}/n_1	y_{a2}/n_2	y_{a1}/l_1	y_{a2}/l_2
Benchmark	1.04	1.27	.187	.066	.73	.64	.70	.50
$A_a = 1.1$	.87	1.44	.196	.080	.75	.77	.86	.53
$A_m = 1.1$	.95	1.31	.200	.075	.71	.66	.75	.51
$q = .9q$	1.02	1.40	.221	.097	.75	.72	.73	.51
A_a, A_m, q	.81	1.68	.254	.137	.77	.91	.95	.54
A_a and q	.88	1.59	.225	.115	.77	.86	.88	.54
$l_1 = 2$	.92	1.59	.226	.094	.72	.75	.78	.47
Pop = 1.1	1.02	1.11	.176	.058	.71	.59	.70	.53

speaking, if we think of region 1 as the well-connected region and region 2 as the remote region, we can contrast the effects of a general reduction in transport costs with the effects of increasing the size of the region that is well connected. This corresponds to the row in which l_1 is increased from .1 to .2. This corresponds to increasing the share of total land that is well connected by 10 percentage points. It is striking that this results in a substantially higher welfare effect than a uniform 10 percent reduction in transportation costs. It is important to keep in mind that we do not offer any metric in terms of the relative costs of these two types of changes, but we think it is definitely of interest that these policies have very quantitative effects in terms of welfare.

Next we consider the impact on the nature of agricultural production. Here there are some interesting patterns. Consider the case of a 10 percent increase in agricultural TFP. We know that this leads to fewer people in agriculture. But whereas the land per worker ratio does increase in region 2, somewhat surprisingly, this ratio actually decreases in region 1. This is because the flow of workers out of agriculture leads to greater production of manufacturing goods and hence greater use of intermediates in agriculture. This greater use of intermediates increases labor productivity and hence allows the economy to use even more workers in region 1, helping them to economize on transportation costs. A similar pattern is found for improvements in manufacturing TFP and reductions in transportation costs. The fact that these improvements lead to fewer workers per unit of land in region 2 but more workers per unit of land in region 1 lead to opposing effects on labor productivity, but amplify the differences in yields. In some cases, output per worker even becomes greater in region 2 than in region 1. The fact that we do not have capital as a factor of production may help explain this seemingly anomalous prediction. It may also be that the Cobb-Douglas production function also plays a role. For example, it could be that subsistence farming involves a constraint on how much land one individual can use productively. More generally, richer specifications of agricultural technology and technology choice are interesting extensions to explore.

An interesting finding is that crop yields (output per unit of land) in region 2 vary little across the experiments shown in table 2.16. In particular, these yields vary far less than the yields of the more intensively farmed region 1. Where some of the experiments lead to yield increases of 35 percent or more in region 1, relative to the benchmark, the largest increase in region 2 is 8 percent. A reason for this seems to be that rising agricultural TFP tends to lead to a movement of workers out of region 2 into the more productive region 1, with the reduction in labor offsetting the productivity benefits of increased TFP. A possible implication is that it may be somewhat difficult for policymakers to increase yields in the quasi-subsistence sector—even though it may be possible to increase welfare.

2.7   Conclusion

A key feature of the Ugandan economy is the large fraction of individuals engaged in farming at the same time that productivity of the agricultural sector is low relative to the nonagricultural sector. Earlier work has emphasized that this pattern obtains when low productivity in the agricultural sector is coupled with minimum food requirements and food is not easily imported. Our goal in this chapter has been to explore the possibility that high transportation costs associated with low infrastructure spending might also reinforce this pattern of labor allocation.

We first present evidence showing that regional price dispersion associated with transportation costs is very high in Uganda and then incorporate this feature into an otherwise standard two-sector model. We calibrate this model to resemble key features of the Ugandan economy and then perform several exercises aimed at uncovering the potential significance of transportation costs in accounting for the pattern of labor allocation in Uganda. We find that high transportation costs represent an important force in shaping the allocation of labor. Moreover, we find that improvements in transportation have an important interaction with improvements in agricultural productivity.

The underlying economics are intuitive: high transportation costs create an incentive for individuals to locate so as to minimize transportation costs for those goods that are most important to them. Since agricultural goods are relatively more important in poor economies, this leads to a greater fraction of the population in agriculture. Moreover, we argue that the predominance of subsistence agriculture can also be explained by this, since people who locate in remote areas in order to be close to their source of food will necessarily engage in little trade for other goods precisely because of the high transport costs. While our model has been simple and stylized, we believe it captures some important economic forces. Nonetheless, we want to emphasize three important directions for future research. The first is to gather more systematic data on the nature of transport costs. The second is to develop richer versions of our model that can provide better estimates of the quantitative effects of transportation infrastructure. Third, it is important to incorporate the costs associated with transportation infrastructure in order to provide better guidance regarding optimal policy.

References

Adamopoulos, Tasso. 2006. *Transportation Costs, Agricultural Productivity and Cross-Country Income Differences.* Unpublished Manuscript, Department of Economics, York University.

Buera, Francisco J., and Joseph Kaboski. 2008. "Scale and the Origins of Structural Change." Working Paper Series no. WP-08–06, Federal Reserve Bank of Chicago.

Calderón, César. 2009. "Infrastructure and Growth in Africa." Policy Research Working Paper Series no. 4914, Washington, DC, World Bank.

Carruthers, Robin, Ranga R. Krishnamani, and Siobhan Murray. 2008. "Improving Connectivity: Investing in Transport Infrastructure in Sub-Saharan Africa." AICD Background Paper, Washington, DC, World Bank.

Caselli, Francesco, and Wilbur John Coleman II. 2001. "The US Structural Transformation and Regional Convergence: A Reinterpretation." *Journal of Political Economy* 109 (3): 584–616.

Chenery, Hollis B., and Moshe Syrquin. 1975. *Patterns of Development, 1950–1970.* London: Oxford University Press.

Central Intelligence Agency (CIA). 2009. *World Factbook 2009.* Accessed March 12, 2010. https://www.cia.gov/library/ publications/the-world-factbook/geos/ug.html.

Dekle, Robert, and Guillaume Vandenbroucke. 2006. "A Quantitative Analysis of China's Structural Transformation." IEPR Working Paper no. 06.51, Institute of Economic Policy Research.

Dorosh, P., H. Wang, L. You, and E. Schmidt. 2008. "Crop Production and Road Connectivity in Sub-Saharan Africa: A Spatial Analysis." AICD Working Paper, Washington, DC, World Bank.

Echevarria, Cristina. 1995. "Agricultural Development vs. Industrialization: Effects of Trade." *Canadian Journal of Economics* 28 (3): 631–47.

———. 1997. "Changes in Sectoral Composition Associated with Economic Growth." *International Economic Review* 38 (2): 431–52.

Eswaran, Mukesh, and Ashok Kotwal. 1993. "A Theory of Real Wage Growth in LDCs." *Journal of Development Economics* 42 (2): 243–69.

Fan, Shenggen, and Connie Chan-Kang. 2004. "Road Development, Economic Growth, and Poverty Reduction in China." IFPRI Research Report, International Food Policy Research Institute. http://www.ifpri.org/publication/road-development-economic-growth-and-poverty-reduction-china-1.

Fan, Shenggen, and Peter Hazell. 2001. "Returns to Public Investment in the Less-Favored Areas of India and China." *American Journal of Agricultural Economics* 83 (5): 1217–22.

Food and Agriculture Organization of the United Nations (FAOSTAT). 2009. Online database. Last accessed March 2010. http://www.fao.org/home/en/.

Fei, John C. H., and Gustav Ranis. 1964. *Development of the Labor Surplus Economy: Theory and Policy.* Homewood, IL: Richard D. Irwin for the Economic Growth Center, Yale University Press.

Gachassin, Marie, Boris Najman, and Gaël Raballand. 2010. "The Impact of Roads on Poverty Reduction: A Case Study of Cameroon." Policy Research Working Paper Series no. 5209, Washington, DC, World Bank.

Gollin, Douglas, Stephen L. Parente, and Richard Rogerson. 2002. "The Role of Agriculture in Development." *American Economic Review Papers and Proceedings* 92 (2): 160–64.

———. 2007. "The Food Problem and the Evolution of International Income Levels." *Journal of Monetary Economics* 54 (4): 1230–55.

Goodfriend, Marvin, and John McDermott. 1998. "Industrial Development and the Convergence Question." *American Economic Review* 88 (5): 1277–89.

Hansen, G., and E. C. Prescott. 2002. "Malthus to Solow." *American Economic Review* 92 (4): 1205–17.

Herrendorf, Berthold, James A. Schmitz, and Arilton Teixeira. 2006. "How Important was the 19th Century Transportation Revolution for US Development?" Unpublished Manuscript, Department of Economics, Arizona State University.

Herrendorf, Berthold, and Arilton Teixeira. 2011. "Barriers to Entry and Development." *International Economic Review* 52 (2): 573–602.

Heston, Alan, Robert Summers, and Bettina Aten. 2006. Penn World Table (version 6.2). Center for International Comparisons of Production, Income and Prices, University of Pennsylvania.

Irz, Xavier, and Terry Roe. 2005. "Seeds of Growth? Agricultural Productivity and the Transitional Dynamics of the Ramsey Model." *European Review of Agricultural Economics* 32 (2): 143–65.

Johnson, D. Gale. 1997. "Agriculture and the Wealth of Nations." *American Economic Review* 87 (2): 1–12.

Johnston, Bruce F. 1970. "Agriculture and Structural Transformation in Developing Countries: A Survey of Research." *Journal of Economic Literature* 8 (2): 369–404.

Johnston, Bruce F., and Peter Kilby. 1975. *Agriculture and Structural Transformation: Economic Strategies in Late-Developing Countries.* New York: Oxford University Press.

Johnston, Bruce F., and John W. Mellor. 1961. "The Role of Agriculture in Economic Development." *American Economic Review* 51 (4): 566–93.

King, Robert G., and Sergio T. Rebelo. 1993. "Transitional Dynamics and Economic Growth in the Neoclassical Model." *American Economic Review* 83 (4): 908–31.

Kogel, T., and A. Prskawetz. 2001. "Agricultural Productivity Growth and Escape from the Malthusian Trap." *Journal of Economic Growth* 6:337–57.

Kongsamut, Piyabha, Sergio Rebelo, and Danyang Xie. 2001. "Beyond Balanced Growth." *Review of Economic Studies* 68 (4): 869–82.

Kuznets, Simon. 1966. *Modern Economic Growth.* New Haven: Yale University Press.

Laitner, John. 2000. "Structural Change and Economic Growth." *Review of Economic Studies* 67:545–61.

Lay, M. G. 1992. *Ways of the World: A History of the World's Roads and the Vehicles That Used Them.* New Brunswick, NJ: Rutgers University Press.

Lewis, W. Arthur. 1966. *Development Planning: The Essentials of Economic Policy.* London: George Allen & Unwin.

Limão, Nuno, and Anthony J. Venables. 1999. "Infrastructure, Geographical Disadvantage, and Transport Costs." Policy Research Working Paper Series no. 2257, Washington, DC, World Bank.

Mellor, John W. 1995. "Introduction." In *Agriculture on the Road to Industrialization,* edited by John W. Mellor. Baltimore: Johns Hopkins University Press for the International Food Policy Research Institute (IFPRI).

———. 1996. "Agriculture on the Road to Industrialization." In *Development Strategies Reconsidered,* edited by John P. Lewis and Valeriana Kallab. New Brunswick, NJ: Transaction Books for the Overseas Development Council.

Minten, Bart, and David C. Stifel. 2008. "Isolation and Agricultural Productivity." *Agricultural Economics* 39 (1): 1–15.

Mundlak, Yair. 2000. *Agriculture and Economic Growth: Theory and Measurement.* Cambridge, MA: Harvard University Press.

Ngai, Rachel. 2004. "Barriers and the Transition to Modern Growth." *Journal of Monetary Economics* 51 (7): 1353–83.

Ngai, L. Rachel, and Christopher A. Pissarides. 2007. "Structural Change in a Multi-Sector Model of Growth." *American Economic Review* 97 (1): 429–43.

Plan for Modernization of Agriculture, Government of Uganda. 2002. *Transaction Cost Analysis: Final Report.* Prepared by The Natural Resources Institute (C. D. Collinson, U. Kleih, and D. G. Burnett) and The International Institute of Tropical Agriculture, FOODNET, (R. S. B. Ferris, J. N. Jagwe, and A. K. Muganga). Kampala: PMA.

Platteau, Jean-Philippe. 1996. "Physical Infrastructure as a Constraint on Agricultural Growth: The Case of Sub-Saharan Africa." *Oxford Development Studies* 24 (3): 189–219.

Raballand, Gaël, and Patricia Macchi. 2008. "Transport Prices and Costs: The Need to Revisit Donors' Policies in Transport in Africa." BREAD Working Paper no. 190, Bureau for Research and Economic Analysis of Development.

Raballand, Gaël, Patricia Macchi, Dino Merotto, and Carly Petracco. 2009. "Revising the Roads Investment Strategy in Rural Areas: An Application for Uganda." Policy Research Working Paper Series no. 5036, Washington, DC, World Bank.

Renkow, M., D. J. Hallstrom, and D. D. Karahja. 2004. "Rural Infrastructure, Transactions Costs, and Market Participation in Kenya." *Journal of Development Economics* 73 (1): 349–67.

Restuccia, Diego, Dennis Tao Yang, and Xiadong Zhu. 2008. "Agriculture and Aggregate Productivity: A Quantitative Cross-Country Analysis." *Journal of Monetary Economics* 55 (2): 234–50.

Robbins, Peter, and Shawn Ferris. 1999. "A Preliminary Study of the Maize Marketing System in Uganda and the Design of a Market Information System." Preliminary Study Report, Foodnet Commodity Marketing Information Services.

Rosenstein-Rodan, P. N. 1943. "Problems of Industrialization of Eastern and South-Eastern Europe." *Economic Journal* 53 (June-September): 204–07.

Rostow, W. W. 1960. *The Stages of Economic Growth.* Cambridge: Cambridge University Press.

Schultz, T. W. 1953. *The Economic Organization of Agriculture*. New York: McGraw-Hill.
———. 1964. *Transforming Traditional Agriculture*. New Haven: Yale University Press.
———. 1968. *Economic Growth and Agriculture*. New York: McGraw-Hill.
Svensson, Jakob, and David Yanagizawa. 2009. "Getting Prices Right: The Impact of the Market Information Service in Uganda." *Journal of the European Economic Association* 7 (2–3): 435–45.
Syrquin, Moshe. 1988. "Patterns of Structural Change." In *Handbook of Development Economics*, vol. I, edited by H. Chenery and T. N. Srinivasan. Amsterdam: Elsevier Science Publishers.
Temple, J. R. W. 2004. "Dualism and Aggregate Productivity." CEPR Discussion Paper No. 4387, Center for Economic and Policy Research.
———. 2005. "Dual Economy Models: A Primer for Growth Economists." *The Manchester School* 73 (4): 435–78.
Timmer, C. Peter. 1988. "The Agricultural Transformation." In *Handbook of Development Economics*, vol. I, edited by H. Chenery and T. N. Srinivasan. Amsterdam: Elsevier Science Publishers.
Torero, Maximo, and Shyamal Chowdhury. 2005. "Increasing Access to Infrastructure for Africa's Rural Poor." IFPRI 2020 Vision Briefs no. 32, Washington, DC, International Food Policy Research Institute. http://ebrary.ifpri.org/cdm/ref/collection/p15738coll2/id/73031.
Uganda Bureau of Statistics. 2004. *Report on the Agricultural Module, Piggy-Backed onto the Population and Housing Census (PHC), 2002: Household Based Agricultural Activities; Crop, Livestock, and Poultry Characteristics*. Kampala: UBOS.
———. 2006. *Uganda National Household Survey 2005/2006: Report on the Socio-Economic Module*. Kampala: UBOS.
———. 2007a. *Report on the Labour Market Conditions in Uganda*. Kampala: UBOS.
———. 2007b. *Uganda National Household Survey 2005/2006: Report on the Agricultural Module*. Kampala: UBOS.
———. 2008. *2008 Statistical Abstract*. Kampala: UBOS.
Vollrath, Dietrich. 2009a. "The Dual Economy in Long-Run Development." *Journal of Economic Growth* 14 (4): 287–312.
———. 2009b. "How Important Are Dual Economy Effects for Aggregate Productivity?" *Journal of Development Economics* 88 (2): 325–34.
Zhang, Xiaobo, and Shenggen Fan. 2004. "How Productive is Infrastructure? A New Approach and Evidence from Rural India." *American Journal of Agricultural Economics* 86 (2): 494–501.

The Sahel's Silent Maize Revolution
Analyzing Maize Productivity in Mali at the Farm Level

Jeremy Foltz, Ursula Aldana, and Paul Laris

N'i ti kaba séné, e ti balo
If you are not growing maize, you cannot feed your family.
—Malian Farmer (2010)

3.1 Introduction

According to aggregate data, since 1961 total maize production in Mali has increased more than tenfold, bringing maize from being a minor crop to one on par with traditional Sahelian crops of millet and sorghum (see figure 3.1). This tenfold increase in production has come about through both a major increase in acreage and impressive improvements in yields. Maize yields in Mali have doubled in this period while those in Burkina Faso have tripled; in contrast, yields in Senegal, Mauritania, and Niger have barely increased. The maize revolution in the Sahel has gone relatively unnoticed in research circles. Recent work on productivity growth of agriculture in Africa has indeed identified significant increases in productivity in the last decade after some decades of stagnation (Block 1994, 2010) and increases in maize production have led the way in many parts of Africa (Smale, Byerlee, and Jayne 2011). But commentators such as Smale, Byerlee, and Jayne (2011) point out a number of disappointing results in maize production across the continent and suggest a key role of fertilizer in determining yield increases and the potential for maize to jump-start a green revolution.

While the current yields in Mali of around two tons per hectare are still

Jeremy Foltz is professor of agricultural and applied economics at the University of Wisconsin–Madison. Ursula Aldana is an economist at the Institute for Peruvian Studies. Paul Laris is professor and Chair of Geography at California State University, Long Beach.

This work was funded by a grant from the NBER Africa Project. The authors would like to thank without implicating: Ntji Coulibaly, Mamadou Coulibaly, Urbain Dembele, Hamady Djouara, Steven Block, the CRRA-Sikasso, IER-Bamako, and participants in the University of Wisconsin development seminar and the NBER Africa Project conference in Zanzibar. For acknowledgments, sources of research support, and disclosure of the authors' material financial relationships, if any, please see http://www.nber.org/chapters/c13436.ack.

low by world standards, the rate of yield increase over the last forty-five years (~2 percent) is equal or better than that of maize production in Iowa, Wisconsin, and India. The maize yield increases in the Midwest of the United States have been the work of hundreds of scientists and garnered many laurels, and yet similar yield increases in the Sahel have gone mostly unnoticed and unexplained. In addition, these great increases in yields go in the opposite direction of most of the rest of sub-Saharan Africa where maize yields have stagnated since the mid-1970s.

Such a success suggests Mali has succeeded in at least partially solving exactly the issues that most bedevil agricultural development projects in the Sahel and most of Africa: farmers bought inputs such as fertilizer, farmers changed their agronomic techniques, farmers paid for new seeds, farmers found markets for their production, and farmers responded to price signals. The large increases in yields in Mali would also not have been possible without research, extension, and marketing. It is evidence of successful extension work that brought to farmers information that induced them to add more fertilizer, invest in new plowing techniques (i.e., animal traction), purchase improved quality seeds, and change their eating habits.

What has pushed the great expansion of maize production in Mali? How much is due to expanded use of inputs such as fertilizer versus technical

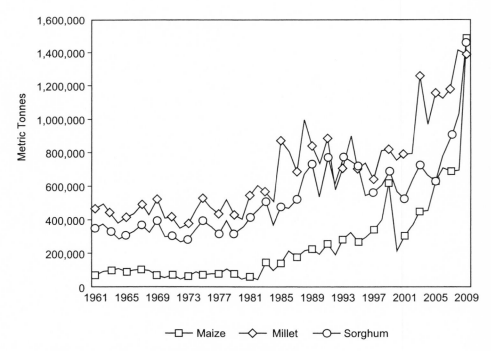

Fig. 3.1   The growth of maize production 1961–2009

changes in seeds and management? What are the key elements of this technical change? This work analyzes these questions by documenting and analyzing the growth of maize production in southern Mali using a novel panel data set that spans the last twenty years. In order to disentangle the different factors behind the increase in maize production, we focus our efforts on generating a consistent and nonbiased estimate of the impact of fertilizer use on yields.

Generally the economics literature shows estimates of high returns to fertilizer in Africa, but that farmers do not adopt fertilizer or they use too little of it (Crawford, Jayne, and Kelly 2006). Standard estimates of the average fertilizer use in Africa is one-tenth of the levels used in the rest of the world. The literature has explained this puzzle through the presence of high levels of heterogeneity in the returns to fertilizer use.

Duflo, Kremer, and Robinson (2008) use a randomized controlled trial (RCT) to find high but heterogeneous returns to fertilizer in maize production in Kenya. They find that the optimal fertilizer use is less than recommended levels, and that the heterogeneity in returns seems related to length of use (i.e., knowledge in how to use fertilizer). Duflo, Kremer, and Robinson (2011) find that helping farmers save for fertilizer can nudge them into using more on their maize. Marenya and Barrett (2009) show that returns to fertilizer in Kenya are a function of soil qualities, in particular the amount of organic matter in the soil. Xu et al. (2009) find substantial variability in the yield response of fertilizer based on a number of observable agronomic (timelines of application) and household factors (access to complementary production factors). In the scientific literature Sileshi et al. (2010) find similar variability in maize yields across the African continent.

In the work closest in spirit to our work, Suri (2011) also finds high but heterogeneous returns to fertilizer and hybrid corn in Kenya. Suri's methodology accounts for unobserved heterogeneity in choice of fertilizer and hybrid econometrically through a control function approach where farmer choice of fertilizer/hybrid is a function of future and past period's fertilizer/hybrid use. While robust to some heterogeneity, the Suri methodology does not allow for unobserved heterogeneity to change through time, nor does it adequately address potential dynamics in soil fertility. Suri concludes that farmers do not use fertilizer where it is not available or expensive, even though returns are high. Overall these studies identify a large amount of heterogeneity in returns to fertilizer and that the sources of heterogeneity are both observable (price of and experience with fertilizer) and unobservable to most econometric efforts (soil organic matter, knowledge).

The presence of heterogeneity in the impact of fertilizer use poses a problem for the estimation of this impact. While Suri's method allows for control of unobserved heterogeneity, her assumption that heterogeneity does not change through time is not applicable to our data set and context. During the years covered by our data set, new seeds where continuously appearing in the market, changing the impact of fertilizer use. Since we do not observe the seeds used by the farmers, this technological innovation could generate a time-varying unobserved heterogeneity.

The current work estimates the impact of fertilizer use and explores the heterogeneity in these returns for the Sikasso region in Mali. It focuses on analyzing technological change as both a disembodied technological change and one due to observed as well as unobserved heterogeneity in the returns to fertilizer use. With regard to observed heterogeneity, we test whether the impact of fertilizer use on yields varies with literacy levels and with the use of organic fertilizer. In order to address unobserved heterogeneity, we apply a control function method first presented by Garen (1984). He developed the method to test for unobserved heterogeneity and control for the bias that it brings. Such a control-function method allows us to control also for the endogeneity that might exist even in the absence of unobserved heterogeneity in the impact of fertilizer use. This last type of endogeneity is the more classic one and it is related to the potential bias that could come from the correlation between unobserved determinants of yields and fertilizer use. All of these efforts allow us to consistently estimate the impact of fertilizer use and, consequently, to analyze the importance of increases in fertilizer use versus generalized technological change in the yield increases in Mali.

The work proceeds as follows: Section 3.2 describes the data and farmer interviews that form the basis for the analysis presented in this work and provides a descriptive analysis of the success in maize production in Mali. Section 3.3 develops a theoretical and econometric model to estimate the determinants of maize yields with a focus on farmer heterogeneity and the returns to fertilizer. Specifically, it develops a model of fertilizer choice based on farm profit functions with heterogeneity in farm returns and builds an econometric technique based on control functions to account for farmer heterogeneity in fertilizer responsiveness. Section 3.4 estimates and provides results for fertilizer-demand functions and then maize-yield functions that account for farmer heterogeneity. Section 3.5 concludes and points to open questions for future research.

3.2   Description of the Data

We use a twelve-year-panel data set (1994–2006) for over 100 farm households from nine villages located in Mali's southern maize belt. The Malian agricultural research organization Institut d'Economie Rurale (IER) started collecting these data in 1988 from 149 farmers spread across twelve villages in three different communes in the Sikasso region. The data set starts with 149 farmers in 1988 and ends with 84 in 2008 due to sample attrition. The IER researchers chose the villages to represent different agroecological zones within the Sikasso region and the farmers to represent different types of farms stratified by farm assets.[1]

The IER researchers collected the data primarily for agronomic studies and they most closely resemble the kind of data one might get from farm trials, except that they come from individual farmers. With their level of agronomic detail and long time series, these microlevel panel data can answer questions that aggregate and cross-sectional data are unable to tackle. They have details such as daily rainfall data that can solve a number of the econometric problems that cause difficulties for many productivity studies. The data set contains disaggregated fertilizer and chemical input data by input type and by crop.

3.2.1   Sikasso Region Context

The Sikasso region is the best-watered region of Mali (800–1,200 mm of rainfall) and the zone best adapted to maize and cotton cultivation. Yet the Sikasso region is reputed to be the location of the greatest poverty in the country (Delarue et al. 2008).[2] The data comes from three of the primary ecological zones within the region (see figure 3.2). Koutiala is where the farmers are the most sophisticated and have a long tradition of growing cotton. Kadiolo subregion is the traditional maize growing area, but with less progressive farmers. Bougouni started the 1990s as the least developed of these regions with farmers least touched by extension services among the subregions, but has developed in the last twenty years into a major maize and cotton growing area through a combination of extensification along with improved techniques (intensification).

In terms of the agronomy of maize production in Mali, there are significant dynamics between years since soil quality can change from one year to the next. That change in soil quality can be a function of the previous year's crop, especially because maize is typically grown in rotation on a field that had cotton the previous year. In addition, maize varieties in Mali have proliferated from one or two to eight to ten in the decade of the data set and seed varieties are unobserved in this data set. The main differences between varieties are related to their suitability to soils and weed conditions, not maximum yield potential. Thus we expect there to be significant unobserved heterogeneity in the impact of fertilizer use in this data set.

Figure 3.3 shows the increases in maize productivity in the sample and across the three surveyed regions. Overall it shows a 17 percent increase in maize yields, but that hides a near flat change in yields in Bougouni to a nearly 35 percent increase in yields in Kadiolo. The figure is suggestive

1. Most of the analysis is conducted using data from 1994–2006 because of problems matching the data from 1988–1993 with later years.

2. Many scholars knowledgeable in the economics of Mali dispute this finding in private conversations, but no refutation of the data has yet appeared in the literature.

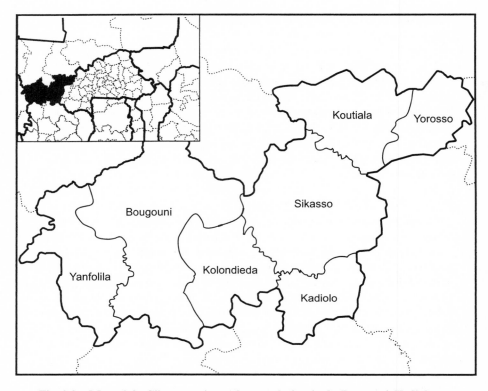

Fig. 3.2   Map of the Sikasso region and research sites in the Bougouni, Kadiolo, and Koutiala districts

of reasonably high levels of technological change that could be either in the form of better seeds, management, or more use of inputs, in particular fertilizer.

Figure 3.4 shows the relationship between fertilizer use, its price, and the price of maize. What is obvious is the great increase in fertilizer use (left axis) of about 25 percent at the same time that its price increased 175 percent (right axis) and maize prices increased only marginally in the same period. This suggests that there has been a secular increase in fertilizer use that is more akin to the adoption of a new technology rather than to marginal calculations of the price/cost margins that would drive the use of a well-known variable input.

This pattern of adoption of fertilizer in maize production is well demonstrated by the regional fertilizer data in figure 3.5. There one sees that Koutiala, the region with the most progressive and informed farmers, has fairly consistent fertilizer use across time and in a pattern reminiscent of a variable input that obeys price signals. Meanwhile, both Bougouni and

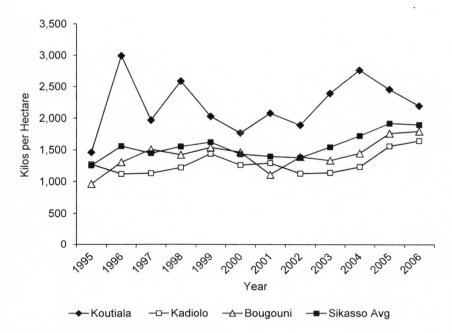

Fig. 3.3   Maize yields by Sikasso region zone

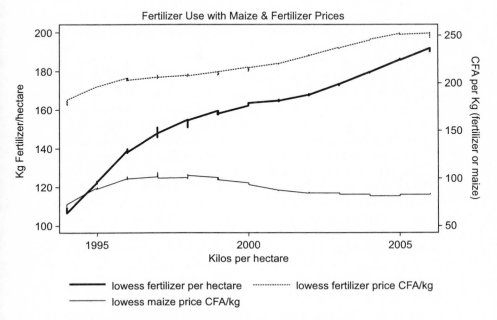

Fig. 3.4   Fertilizer use with maize and fertilizer prices, Lowess curves

Kadiolo exhibit a pattern of fertilizer use increase that mimics the S-curves of standard technology adoption models.

Fok et al. (2000) argue that maize is a risky crop and that the farmers' widespread adoption of maize could be related to a change in their risk aversion. They argue that maize is risky due to the use of expensive inputs such as fertilizers and herbicides. Nevertheless, as explained in Laris and Foltz (2014), maize also reduces risk because it matures quickly, providing a good harvest in years with a short rainfall season. In addition, as shown in figure 3.6, the distribution of yield outcomes of maize production has changed over the last twenty years, reducing the risk farmers face in growing maize. Figure 3.6 shows the distribution of yields in the Sikasso farm data over different time periods. The distributions show a distinct pattern of technological change with the distribution on average moving up in a steady fashion over the twelve years of the data. The mean of the distribution increases and one sees for almost all quantiles of the distribution that yields increase close to 500 kg per hectare, which is suggestive of broad-based participation in the benefits of maize yield increases. In addition, the downside risk of maize production in terms of yields is greatly reduced, with many fewer farmers below 500 kg/ha.

Laris and Foltz (2014) argue that an important factor behind the increase in fertilizer use is the provision of credit for fertilizer. As the authors point out, in the area that corresponds to the data we use, the credit for fertilizer is obtained through the parastatal CMDT (Compagnie Malienne pour le Developpment des Textiles). This company provides fertilizer at the beginning of the season in exchange for the cotton that this company will receive at the time of the harvest. In some cases, the farmers use, in their maize plots, some of the fertilizer they claim that will be used for growing cotton.

Laris and Foltz (2014) provide evidence of this link between cotton and the access to fertilizer for maize. Their interview and quantitative evidence shows, for example, that farmers who grow cotton get higher yields in their other field crops. The estimations that we present below support the idea presented in Laris and Foltz, as they show that the percentage of land under cotton is positively associated with the amount of fertilizer used for growing maize, which contrasts somewhat with Benjaminsen, Aune, and Sidibé's (2010) finding of declining soil fertility in cotton growing areas.

Taken together, the graphical data in figures 3.3, 3.4, 3.5, and 3.6 show increases in maize yield at the same time that there are major increases in fertilizer use. Below we test whether the increase in maize yield is solely attributable to the increased use of fertilizer or whether there is an element of disembodied technological change such as improvements in seeds and or management.

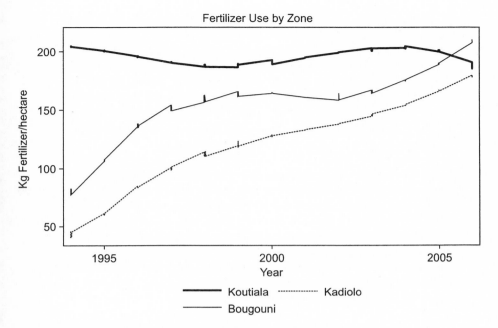

Fig. 3.5   Fertilizer use by Sikasso region zone, Lowess curves

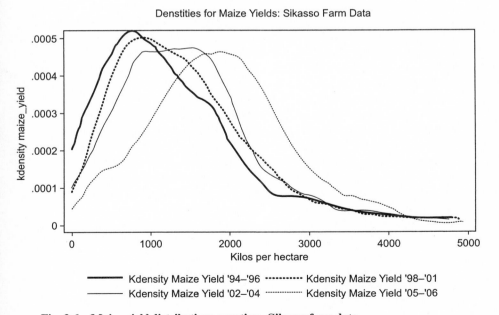

Fig. 3.6   Maize yield distributions over time, Sikasso farm data

3.3   Conceptual Framework

The conceptual framework for analyzing the determinants of maize yields starts with a farmer maximizing profits on his farm: $\Pi = \pi T$ where T represents total land area and π is per hectare profits. Assuming that land is fixed or that the production function exhibits constant returns to scale the farmer can maximize per hectare profits, which setting the price of output to 1, can be described as:

$$(1) \qquad \pi = g(\alpha, f, x, r) - p_f f - p_x x,$$

where $g(.)$ reflects the yield function, α represents the level of technology, f reflects the amount of fertilizer per hectare, x reflects other variables that affect yields, r reflects those unobserved variables, such as soil quality that affect yields, and the relative input prices are p_f and p_x. The first-order conditions to maximize profits with respect to fertilizer will produce the following first-order condition for optimality: $\delta\pi/\delta f = \partial g/\partial f - p_f = 0$, which when solved for fertilizer will give the following fertilizer demand function for the optimizing farmer:

$$(2) \qquad f = h(\alpha, f, x, r, p_f).$$

Note if the unobserved component, r, is additive in equation (1), then it does not enter into equation (2). But if heterogeneity and the observed differences, x, enter the production function $g(.)$ in a nonadditive way, as they would in a Cobb-Douglas, generalized quadratic, or translog production function, then they will appear in the fertilizer demand function $h(.)$. We use a Cobb-Douglas and allow unobserved variables to appear not only as factors of production (multiplying fertilizer use), but also in the exponent associated to fertilizer use.

This simple maximization problem has a number of immediate implications for the observability of different levels of fertilizer use in real-world data. First, assuming that r is not additive, optimal levels of fertilizer chosen by farmers will be a function of both observable, x, and unobservable, r, differences between farms. Second, the returns to fertilizer will be a function of both observable and unobservable variables. The dependence of fertilizer use and of fertilizer's impact on unobservable variables poses an econometric problem in that these unobservables could bias our estimates of the returns to fertilizer.

3.3.1   Econometric Framework

This section presents the econometric framework that will be used to estimate technological change in maize yields (the Solow residual) and the impact of fertilizer use on yields. While the level of technological change is a straightforward parameter estimation, that of the impact of fertilizer is more complex due to the maximization problem outlined above. The estimation method we use is based on a fixed effect estimation that allows the demeaned error to be correlated with the demeaned fertilizer variable and that also allows for heterogeneity in the impact of fertilizer use. Specifically, the marginal effect of fertilizer on yields can change according to both observables and unobservables that can be different for observations across time and farms.[3]

Our basic yield specification is a standard one, where the impact of fertilizer on yields is the same for all the households in all the periods.

$$(3) \qquad y_{it} = \alpha A_t + \beta_x x_{it} + \beta_f f_{it} + \mu_{it},$$

where y_{it} is the log of yield per hectare, A_t is a time variable whose coefficient, α, is the standard Solow residual measuring disembodied technological change, f_{it} is log of fertilizer per hectare, and x_{it} is a vector that contains other variables that determine yields. We are interested in estimating both the rate of disembodied technical change and the marginal product of fertilizer, α and β_f. The estimate of α is straightforward, while that of β_f requires careful attention to both observable and unobservable determinants, whose econometric properties are delineated below.

In a panel data context it is useful to decompose the unobservable component, μ_{it}, into a time invariant and a time variant component. That is:

$$\mu_{it} = \eta_i + \varepsilon_{it}.$$

As it is well known, access to a panel data allows for a fixed effect estimation, which controls for the potential correlation between the independent variables and the farm or plot specific error term, η_i. Nevertheless, it is likely that a fixed effect will not fully capture or control for the farm-level heterogeneity we seek to measure. Specifically, we expect the effects of fertilizer use to be nonuniform across time, since it can change with seeds used and time-varying differences in soil and other agronomic conditions. We therefore use a modified fixed effect estimation that allows the impact of fertilizer to change for different individuals and at different periods. The heterogeneity in marginal returns to fertilizer is likely to have both observable and unobservable (to the econometrician) elements.[4] Thus, we specify β_{fit} as:

$$\beta_{fit} = \gamma + \gamma_0 x_{it}^0 + \gamma_{it},$$

where x_{it}^0 is a vector of observable variables that affect the impact of fertilizer use on yields and γ_{it} reflects unobservable heterogeneity on the impact of fertilizer on yields. The parameter γ_{it} can be considered as an element from

3. Note this focus on unobservables that affect the marginal returns to a factor of production differs from the methods proposed by Levinsohn and Petrin (2003) for capturing unobservables in a measurement of overall productivity.
4. We assume that farmers know, observe, and act on the elements that are unobservable to the econometrician.

r, the unobserved variables in the production function. We assume that the unobservable element, γ_{it}, has an expected value of zero: $E(\gamma_{it}) = 0$.

Taking into account this specification of β_{fit}, and ignoring A_t to simplify the exposition, the new yield equation will be given by:

$$(4) \qquad y_{it} = \beta_x x_{it} + \gamma f_{it} + \gamma_0 x_{it}^0 f_{it} + \gamma_{it} f_{it} + \mu_{it}.$$

Equation (4) provides a less restrictive specification of the impact of fertilizer on yields.

The presence of unobserved heterogeneity will bring a bias in the estimation of the average impact of fertilizer use (γ). In the current work, we apply Garen's (1984) control function method to account for unobserved heterogeneity in an estimation based on fixed effects, which is to our knowledge the first application of control functions to a panel data setting.[5]

A fixed effects estimation controls for the potential correlation between f_{it} and μ_{it}, through η_i. This method estimates the demeaned dependent variable as a function of the demeaned independent variables:

$$(5) \quad y_{it} - \overline{y_i} = \beta_x\left(x_{it} - \overline{x_i}\right) + \gamma\left(f_{it} - \overline{f_i}\right) + \gamma_0 x_{it}^0\left(f_{it} - \overline{f_i}\right) + \gamma_{it} f_{it} - \overline{\gamma_{it} f_{it}}.$$
$$+ \left(\mu_{it} - \overline{\mu_i}\right)$$

Given that γ_{it} is not observable, the new error of the estimation, μ_{it} will include the terms related to this unobserved heterogeneity. That is:

$$u_{it} = \gamma_{it} f_{it} - \overline{\gamma_{it} f_{it}} + \left(\mu_{it} - \overline{\mu_i}\right).$$

The first two terms of this compounded error come from the unobserved heterogeneity γ_{it}. These two terms are likely to be correlated with $f_{it} - \overline{f_i}$, creating a bias in the estimation of γ. Assuming that $\left(\mu_{it} - \overline{\mu_i}\right)$ is not correlated with $\left(f_{it} - \overline{f_i}\right)$, the linear projection of the error μ_{it} over $\left(f_{it} - \overline{f_i}\right)$ will be given by:

$$u_{it} = \theta\left(f_{it} - \overline{f_{it}}\right) + r_{it},$$

where $\theta = \mathrm{cov}((f_{it} - \overline{f_i})(\gamma_{it} f_{it} - \overline{\gamma_{it} f_{it}})) / Var((f_{it} - \overline{f_i}))$. Thus the estimated coefficient γ^{hat} will be given by: $\gamma^{hat} = \gamma + \theta$. Theta is expected to be positive given that an increase in γ_{it} is likely to be correlated with an increase in f_{it}.[6]

As argued by Garen (1984), one can recover γ_{it} from the residual of an estimation where the dependent variable is f_{it}. The idea, which comes from the first-order conditions of a firm profit function that produces the fertilizer factor demand function, equation (2), is that if the impact of fertilizer use

---

5. The control function used here is similar in spirit to Suri's (2011) method for controlling for heterogeneous returns, but avoids the problem of using past choices to identify current choices, which could be biased in a situation with crop rotations across years on a single plot. In general, panel data should obviate the need for a control function approach with its multiple years of data to account for individual heterogeneity. In this case the heterogeneity is independent-variable specific and changes through time, which means a simple fixed effect cannot fully control for the heterogeneity.

6. This implies a positive correlation between $\left(f_{it} - \overline{f_i}\right)$ and $\gamma_{it} f_{it} - \overline{\gamma_{it} f_{it}}$.

on yields is higher, farmers will respond by using more fertilizer. Thus, the error from estimation of f_{it} will be positively correlated with γ_{it}.

A second potential problem of the fixed effects estimator is that even after eliminating the time invariant component from the error, the demeaned error, $(\mu_{it} - \overline{\mu}_i)$, might still be correlated with the dependent variable, $(f_{it} - \overline{f}_i)$. This might happen if, for example, the use of fertilizer responds to conditions that change over time, and, simultaneously, these changing conditions affect yields. For example, if the use of fertilizer responds to unobservable changes in the fertility of the soil, there will be a correlation between $(\mu_{it} - \overline{\mu}_i)$ and $(f_{it} - \overline{f}_i)$. We consider the presence of unobservables in the exponent of fertilizer, and also as an additional production factor that multiplies fertilizer use. The presence of unobservables as an additional production factor imply a correlation between $(\mu_{it} - \overline{\mu}_i)$ and $(f_{it} - \overline{f}_i)$. This correlation will further bias the estimates of the impact of fertilizer on yields. The control function method that we deploy allows us to overcome these two potential problems.

The coefficient γ_{it} has two components, one component that is observed by the farmer before deciding how much fertilizer to use (γ_{it}^0) and another that is not observed early enough in the growing season (γ_{it}^u) and, consequently, does not affect the farmer's choice of the amount of fertilizer. If we assume a standard production function, the factor demand equation for fertilizer in equation (2), which describes the optimal amount of fertilizer per hectare (in logs), will depend negatively on the price of fertilizer, positively on the log of the other inputs used in production (per hectare), and positively on the observable component of γ_{it}. Using a first-order approximation of the fertilizer demand equation, we have:

$$(6) \qquad f_{it} = \Omega_f x_{it} + \Omega_{p_f} m_{it} + \Omega_{x^0} x_{it}^0 + z_{it}$$

where m_{it} includes variables that determine the price of fertilizer and z_{it} is equal to the derivative of f_{it} with respect to γ_{it}^0 multiplied by γ_{it}^0. If we estimate equation (6) including the relevant production inputs that determine fertilizer demand and an exhaustive list of the variables that determine the price of fertilizer, z_{it} can be recovered by estimating equation (4) and capturing the residuals of such estimation.

Expressing individual heterogeneity γ_{it} as well as the error of equation (4) as functions of z_{it}, we have:

$$(7) \qquad \gamma_{it} = \lambda_\gamma z_{it} + v_{it}$$

$$\mu_{it} = \lambda_\mu z_{it} + w_{it}$$

where v_{it} is equal to γ_{it}^u.

Plugging equation (7) in equation (5), we have:

$$(8) \qquad y_{it} - \overline{y}_i = \beta_x \left(x_{it} - \overline{x}_i \right) + \gamma \left(f_{it} - \overline{f}_i \right) + \gamma_0 x_{it}^0 \left(f_{it} - \overline{f}_i \right)$$
$$+ \lambda_\gamma \left(z_{it} f_{it} - \overline{z_{it} f_{it}} \right) + \lambda_\mu \left(z_{it} - \overline{z_{it}} \right) + \omega_{it}$$

where $\omega_{it} = (v_{it}f_{it} - \overline{v_{it}f_{it}}) + w_{it} - \overline{w_i}$.

The term $\lambda_\gamma(z_{it}f_{it} - \overline{z_{it}f_{it}})$ controls for unobserved heterogeneity, or the presence of unobservables in the exponent associated with fertilizer use. The term $\lambda_\mu(z_{it} - \overline{z_{it}})$ controls for the more classical endogeneity, that will be brought about by the presence of unobservables as additional inputs. Under the assumption that $E(v_{it}|z_{i1},z_{i2},z_{iT},x_{it}) = 0$ (assumption 1), we will have that $E(\omega_{it}(f_{it} - \overline{f_{it}})) = 0$, which will allow us to consistently estimate γ.[7]

For ASSUMPTION 1 to hold, we need to include the relevant other factors of production that determine fertilizer demand and all potential determinants of the price of fertilizer. If this is not the case, v_{it} will include not only γ_{it}^u, but also the determinants of fertilizer use that have been excluded from the estimation. If ASSUMPTION 1 holds, including the interaction of the log of fertilizer and the residual will take care of unobserved heterogeneity. At the same time, the inclusion of the residual, by itself, will take care of the potential time-varying correlation that might exist between fertilizer use and the error, even after controlling for unobserved heterogeneity.

3.4   Econometric Estimations and Results

3.4.1   Specification of the Equations

The current section estimates the impact of fertilizer use on yields at the plot level where each observation is a specific plot in a particular year. We will use the control function method described above, which uses the residuals from the estimation of the fertilizer demand equation in order to account for two potential biases. The first one originates in unobserved heterogeneity while the second one comes from the potential correlation between the demeaned fertilizer variable and unobservables, a correlation that might exist even after controlling for unobserved heterogeneity.

As shown in the previous section, the use of fertilizer can be estimated as a function of the other factors of production, the factors linked to observed heterogeneity, and the price of fertilizer. We consider as potential factors linked to observed heterogeneity: organic fertilizer and the percentage of adult members (members with more than sixteen years old) who are literate.[8]

---

7. If $E(v_{it}|z_{i1},z_{i2},...z_{iT},x_{it}) = 0$ then $E(v_{it}|f_{i1},f_{i2},...f_{iT},x_{it}) = 0$ given that f_{it} and z_{it} are one-to-one functions of each other given x_{it}. Using the law of iterated expectations it can be shown that: $E((v_{it}f_{it} - \overline{\gamma_{it}f_{it}})|f_{i1},f_{i2},..f_{iT},x_{it}) = 0$. Since $(f_{it} - \overline{f_i})$ is a function of $f_{i1},f_{i2},..f_{iT}$, we can say that $E((v_{it}f_{it} - \overline{v_{it}f_{it}})|f_{i1},f_{i2} - \overline{f_i},x_{it}) = 0$. Using the law of iterated expectations, then: $E((v_{it}f_{it} - \overline{v_{it}f_{it}})(f_{it} - \overline{f_i})) = 0$.

Additionally, if the observable determinants of fertilizer use are not correlated with the error and since $z_{it} - \overline{z_i}$ is, by construction, not correlated with $f_{it} - \overline{f_i}$, we can conclude that $E((w_{it} - \overline{w_i})(f_{it} - \overline{f_i})) = 0$.

Thus, we can conclude that $E((\omega_{it} - \overline{\omega_i})(f_{it} - \overline{f_i})) = 0$.

8. Literacy of household members is likely to improve the productivity of fertilizer in two important ways. First it can help farmers understand the instructions in how to use fertilizer,

We use two types of measures for the price of fertilizer, one for the relative price and the other for the availability of capital to finance fertilizer purchases. For the relative price we use the log of the price of fertilizer divided by the average price for maize in the household's village. To measure capital availability we measure with proxy variables the two main ways villagers access capital: remittances and cotton-based loans. Households that have higher remittances face a more relaxed budget constraint, which should affect fertilizer demand and use. As a proxy for remittances, we use the number of permanent migrants from the household. In the Sikasso region, producers can acquire fertilizer on credit from CMDT, the cotton parastatal, under the promise of paying for it with cotton after the harvest. We therefore use the percentage of land under cotton in the current year as a determinant of access to credit to buy fertilizer.

In addition to the variables describing heterogeneity and costs/access to fertilizer, we include key determinants of production from the yield equation: adult family labor per hectare, a dummy for having grown cotton last year on the plot, and a time trend. We expect that maize grown on fields that in the previous year grew cotton are likely to require more fertilizer and have lower yields because cotton is well known for depleting the soil. Table 3.1 shows the descriptive statistics of the variables used in the estimations of fertilizer use and of yields.

In order to capture z_{it} from the estimation of equation (6), we need the coefficients of the determinants of fertilizer use to be estimated consistently. Nevertheless, some of the independent variables included in equation (6) are likely to be correlated with z_{it}. To avoid a potential inconsistency in the estimation of these coefficients, we exploit the panel structure of the data and estimate the coefficients of the variables that are not constant through time, through a fixed effects method. Thus, we run the following estimations:

$$(9.1) \qquad f_{it} - \overline{f}_i = \Omega^1 \left(\kappa_{it}^1 - \overline{\kappa_{it}^1} \right) + \xi_{it}$$

$$(9.2) \qquad f_{it} - \Omega^{\text{1hat}} \kappa_{it}^1 = \Omega^2 \kappa_{it}^2 + z_{it}.$$

where κ_{it}^1 denotes the subset of variables included in equation (4) that change through time, Ω^1 denotes the coefficients associated with these variables, Ω^{1hat} denotes the estimated coefficients of Ω^1, κ_{it}^2 denotes the subset of variables that do not change through time, and Ω^2 the coefficients of these variables. That is, we first run a fixed effects estimation of the use of fertilizer, including only those variables that change through time. Afterward, we run

and second it likely increases farmers' ability to learn from extension agents and other knowledgeable outsiders. Interviews in the study villages identified the latter effect as quite important, in that literate farmers were much more likely to have the local extension agents and school teachers as part of their social networks. One can also think of the literacy variable in the context of a target input model (e.g., Foster and Rosenzweig 1995, 2010) in which higher levels of literacy improves farmer accuracy in hitting the optimal level of fertilizer.

Table 3.1   **Descriptive statistics**

Variable	Measurement unit	Mean	Std. dev.
Yield estimation variables			
Log (maize yields)	log (kg per ha)	7.11	0.69
Maize yields	kg per ha	1,494.5	942.38
Log (area of the plot)	log (hectares)	−0.07	0.95
Area of the plot	hectares	1.33	1.04
Time trend (1995 = 1)	year (1995 = 1)	6.65	3.07
Previous yr. cotton dummy	0–1	0.23	0.42
Number of adults per cultivated hectare		0.66	0.27
Log (number of adults/ha)		−0.498	0.44
Log (rain in June)		5.00	0.33
Rain in June	millimeters	157.24	53.74
Log (rain August)		5.74	0.34
Rain in August	millimeters	328.83	111.81
Log (organic fert. per ha)	log (150 kg per ha)	−6.14	2.70
Organic fert. per hectare (150 kg)	150 kg per ha	4.55	37.72
Log (fertilizer per ha)	log (kg per ha)	3.39	3.94
Percent lit members * log (fertilizer per ha)		0.35	0.73
Log (fertilizer per ha) * log (organic fert. per ha)		−20.52	28.24
Fertilizer demand additional variables			
Percent of land under cotton	(from 0 to 1)	0.29	0.13
Relative per kg price of fertilizer/price of maize		2.53	0.88
Number of migrants in the household		4.14	4.18
Percent of adult members that are literate	(from 0 to 1)	0.10	0.12

a standard estimation of the error of the first estimation against the variables that do not change through time. The residuals of this last estimation will be used in the estimation of yields as shown in equation (8).

The fertilizer (6) and maize yield equations (8) are estimated as fixed effect models at the plot level with robust standard errors clustered at the farm household level. There are up to eight observations per plot with an average just below three observations per plot across 120 households in twelve years. The panel is unbalanced and the number of observations varies between 733 and 675 depending on the variables included in the model. In all models the fixed effects are tested to be significant.

Yield estimates will have log maize yields as a function of key production variables, a time trend to capture disembodied technological change and observable and unobservable determinants of fertilizer returns. For key production variables we include adult labor in the household, rainfall in June during planting, rainfall in August during maize flowering, and the area of the plot. Labor inputs are only available at the household, rather than the plot level, and only measures household adult labor available to farm, rather than actual labor inputs. Because farmer interviews identified hired labor as being rare in the survey villages and representing only a small proportion of labor inputs, this measure is likely reasonably well correlated with total labor use. We measure labor in per hectare terms. We chose the two key periods of rainfall for maize production, planting and harvesting, rather than total rainfall, which includes rainfall outside of the growing season, in order to get a more precise estimate. Lack of June rainfall often leads to plants not sprouting and farmers having to replant maize, while lack of August rainfall can affect whether the maize will pollinate and is the most common reason for crop failures. We include the area of the plot to control for any potential increasing or decreasing returns to scale as is sometimes found in peasant agriculture (e.g., Chayanov 1986; Benjamin 1995), although yield estimations implicitly assumes constant returns to scale.

We estimate the yield model two ways to measure the returns to soil fertility both observed and unobserved. The first basic model includes an observable related to knowledge acquisition, the percent literate household members as an interaction with fertilizer. Following the findings of Marenya and Barrett (2009) as well as many agronomic studies (e.g., Chikowo et al. 2010; Sileshi et al. 2010; Wopereis, Vanlauwe, and Mando 2008) that higher levels of soil organic matter improves the efficiency of chemical fertilizer use, the second model includes measures of the amount of organic fertilizer (cow manure) applied to the fields. Soils in Mali are particularly low in organic matter and cow manure is the primary method available, aside from long-term fallowing, that Malian farmers can use to improve soil organic matter. Organic fertilizer is measured as the log of 150 kg donkey cartloads. The first version of model 2 includes organic fertilizer alone, while the second also includes the interaction of organic fertilizer with chemical fertilizer.

In addition, as a robustness check we provide estimates of the yield function in both model 1 and 2 versions without controlling for endogeneity through the residuals of the control function. These estimates provide the baseline from which we can understand the importance of controlling for the endogeneity of chosen inputs in yield functions.

3.4.2   Fertilizer Function Estimates

Table 3.2 shows the estimation of the fertilizer equation in two specifications. The difference between the specifications is the inclusion of the use of organic fertilizer as an independent variable for model 2. The model is a fixed-effects estimation with robust standard errors to correct for the correlation of the error across plots that belong to the same household.

The estimations show no time trend in fertilizer demand once one controls for other factors that influence fertilizer demand. There is a strong association between previous cotton production on a plot and the following year's fertilizer use, with an 82–86 percent higher rate of application on plots that previously grew cotton. In addition, the model 2 specification shows farmers applying lower levels of chemical fertilizer to plots that received higher

Table 3.2   **Estimation for fertilizer demand**

Dep. variable: log (fertilizer per ha)	Model 1 coefficient	S. E.	Model 2 coefficient	S. E.
Time trend	0.087	0.06	0.067	0.07
1 if cotton plant previous year	0.861***	0.24	0.821***	0.25
Log(organic fert. per ha)			−0.116*	0.06
Log fert. price/maize price	−1.074*	0.6	−0.788	0.56
Number of migrants in the household	0.222	0.19	0.286	0.18
Percent land under cotton	3.832***	1.41	4.426***	1.41
Log (number of adults/ha)	0.176	0.66	0.479	0.64
Percent of adults that are literate in hh	2.5793**	1.21	2.622**	1.34
Constant	1.782**	0.82	0.597	0.77
Number of observations	733		675	

***Significant at the 1 percent level.
**Significant at the 5 percent level.
*Significant at the 10 percent level.

levels of organic fertilizer, suggesting farmers see these as at least partial substitutes. These two results suggest that Malian farmers apply chemical fertilizer to improve fields with lower natural or applied fertility, which implies that a naïve regression of the effects of fertilizer that did not control for the endogeneity of its use would produce biased estimates.

We do not find a statistically significant effect of labor availability, but see a strong effect in terms of labor quality in our measure of the number of literate adults in the household. As seen below in the yield equations, levels of household literacy increase the productivity of fertilizer (likely through learning and management effects) and it stands to reason that this would also increase fertilizer demand.

In terms of price variables, the estimates show a weakly significant but negative effect of fertilizer prices on fertilizer demand. We find much stronger effects on fertilizer demand from our proxies for access to capital. While the number of migrants is not significant, the percentage of land devoted to cotton in the household shows a large and significant effect on the ability of farmers to purchase chemical fertilizer for their maize fields.

3.4.3   Yield Function Estimates

Table 3.3 presents the fixed-effects yield estimations for the baseline model and model 1. Both estimates include a time trend to capture disembodied technical change and a set of yield determinants including land, labor, rainfall, and fertilizer. The baseline estimation does not include the terms associated with the residuals of the fertilizer estimation, while the second includes the residuals and their interaction with the log of fertilizer as specified in equation (8).

The baseline estimation demonstrates a number of the pitfalls of not addressing farm and farmer heterogeneity in the demand for fertilizer. It shows a negative and statistically nonsignificant impact of the use of chemical fertilizer on yields. The only positive relation between fertilizers and maize yields is through the interaction with the percentage of adult members that are literate in the household. In addition the baseline estimation shows a strong time trend, suggesting a nearly 4 percent per year level of technical change in maize yields.

In contrast the model 1 estimates, which control for the potential endogeneity of fertilizer use, show much stronger effects of chemical fertilizer on yields and a much more modest and marginally significant level of technical change of ~2 percent. The model 1 estimate of a yield elasticity of 0.2 for fertilizer when combined with the literacy premium of 0.36, yields a substantial effect of fertilizer on yields especially for the most educated households. The positive impact of the interaction between literacy and the use of fertilizer is consistent with the importance of adequate management in fertilizer application. At the same time, this coefficient might reflect other variables such as a higher presence of extension agents in areas that are more developed and that consequently present a more educated population.

The model 1 estimates show significant effects of farmer heterogeneity in their optimal fertilizer application and that this heterogeneity does effect yields. This second specification shows a negative and statistically significant relationship between the demeaned residuals of fertilizer use and the demeaned yields: our estimate of λ_μ (in equation [7]) is negative. At the same time, the estimation shows a positive and statistically significant impact of

Table 3.3   **Maize yield estimations: Model 1**

Dep. variable: Log (maize per ha)	Baseline coefficient	S. E.	Model 1 coefficient	S. E.
Time trend	0.039***	0.01	0.019*	0.01
Log(area of the plot)	−0.006	0.05	0.038	0.06
One if cotton plant prev. year	−0.031	0.07	−0.173*	0.09
Log (number of adults/ha)	−0.077	0.15	−0.115	0.16
Log (rain in June)	−0.048	0.10	−0.02	0.10
Log (rain August)	0.005	0.13	0.014	0.13
Log (fertilizer per ha)	−0.015	0.01	0.232***	0.05
Percent lit members * log (fertilizer/ha)	0.343**	0.14	0.364***	0.12
Residuals of fert. demand equation			−0.208***	0.05
Residuals * (log [fertilizer per ha])			0.010***	0.001
Constant	6.971***	0.56	5.941***	0.61
N	733		733	

***Significant at the 1 percent level.
**Significant at the 5 percent level.
*Significant at the 10 percent level.

the interaction between fertilizer use and the residuals of the fertilizer equation: our estimate of λ_γ (in equation [7]) is positive.

A positive and statistically significant estimation of λ_γ implies that households that use more fertilizer are households that benefit more from the using it. These results confirm the presence of unobserved heterogeneity in the sample under analysis. On the other hand, the negative and statistically significant estimate of λ_μ, implying a negative correlation between the residuals of the fertilizer equation and yields, suggests that fertilizers might compensate for the declining soil fertility. The residuals alone having a significant and negative coefficient suggest that the unobservables in the fertilizer equation that tend to increase fertilizer demand have a negative effect on maize yields (for example, unobserved low soil fertility). Meanwhile, the interaction of the unobservables with fertilizer use suggests that those unobservables increase the marginal productivity of fertilizer. If one takes the unobservables from the fertilizer equation to be related to soil fertility, one sees that it reduces maize yields but produces a higher marginal return to fertilizer application as one would expect across low ranges of soil fertility common in West African soils.

We find no effect of either rainfall or household labor on maize yields. The lack of a rainfall result may be due to farmer's ability to do ex post farm management of the crops in which they can make up for poor rain in June by replanting, and poor rain in August by extra effort in other farm tasks such as weeding. The household labor variable is likely not measured accurately enough to demonstrate an effect on yields.

A second factor that might influence yields, as well as the impact of fertilizer on yields, is the use of organic fertilizer, which we control for in our model 2 estimates. The next set of estimations includes the use of organic fertilizer as an additional determinant of yields as well as a determinant of the use of chemical fertilizer. Table 3.4 shows yield estimations that include the use of organic fertilizer. The first specification shows the baseline model, which has a positive and statistically significant impact of organic fertilizer use on yields. The second specification corrects for the residuals of the fertilizer use equation, where this equation includes the use of organic fertilizer as an independent variable. The results for either fertilizer, its residual, or other variables do not change much from the results shown in table 3.3. The third specification includes the interaction between the use of organic fertilizer and the use of chemical fertilizers. The estimated coefficient on this interaction is not statistically significant, suggesting no significant complementary interaction between organic and chemical fertilizer. While this result contrasts with that of Marenya and Barrett (2009), this lack of significant complementarity matches well with the fertilizer demand equation, which shows chemical and organic fertilizer to be substitutes rather than complements.

Table 3.4   **Maize yield estimates: Model 2 with organic fertilizer**

Dep. variable: Log (maize per ha)	Baseline coeff.	S. E.	Model 2A coeff.	S. E.	Model 2B coeff.	S. E.
Time trend	0.036***	0.01	0.009	0.01	0.008	0.01
Log(area of the plot)	−0.006	0.05	0.025	0.05	0.029	0.05
One if cotton plant prev. year	−0.052	0.08	−0.227**	0.10	−0.228**	0.10
Log (number of adults/ha)	−0.111	0.16	−0.22	0.16	−0.22	0.16
Log (rain in June)	−0.038	0.10	−0.026	0.10	−0.024	0.10
Log (rain August)	0.059	0.12	0.064	0.12	0.062	0.12
Log(organic fert. per ha)	0.027**	0.01	0.054***	0.01	0.061***	0.02
Log (fertilizer per ha)	−0.014	0.01	0.255***	0.05	0.247***	0.05
Percent lit members * log (fertilizer/ha)	0.377***	0.13	0.397***	0.12	0.407***	0.12
Log (fert./ha).*.log (organic fert./ha)					−0.002	0.003
Residuals of fert. use equation			−0.238***	0.05	−0.243***	0.05
Residuals * l(og [fertilizer/ha])			0.009**	0.004	0.009**	0.004
Constant	6.775***	0.55	5.977***	0.59	5.998***	0.59
N	675		675		675	

***Significant at the 1 percent level.
**Significant at the 5 percent level.
*Significant at the 10 percent level.

3.4.4   Econometric Results Discussion

The estimations presented here have demonstrated the importance of controlling for the endogeneity of fertilizer use. The results indicate that in the absence of controlling for endogeneity, the impact of fertilizer use on yields would not be consistently estimated due to the correlation between the unobservables and the use of chemical fertilizer. In addition, we find that there is evidence of heterogeneity in the impact of fertilizer on yields. First, this impact is higher for households with a higher percentage of members in the household that are literate. Secondly, we find strong evidence of unobserved heterogeneity, which affects both the choice of fertilizer amounts and the marginal returns to fertilizers.

The estimations show much stronger evidence for the growth in maize yields having been driven by farmer adoption of higher levels of fertilizer use rather than improvements in seeds and management, disembodied technical change. This is not to say that farmers did not adopt new technologies, but rather the maize revolution came as a sequential adoption process (e.g., Aldana et al. 2010) in which farmers adopted parts of a package in succession: seed first, appropriate levels of organic and chemical fertilizer later.

The importance of controlling for endogeneity in fertilizer use goes beyond a correct decomposition of the determinants of corn yields. The naïve model ignoring this endogeneity would have decided that most of the technical change was in seeds and management and seriously underestimated the return to fertilizer. Such an underestimate of the returns to fertilizer could seriously call into question public policies such as the Malian government's current program to subsidize fertilizer. Once one controls for both observed and unobserved heterogeneity in the returns to fertilizer, one sees yield elasticities of about 0.2–0.3 for fertilizer. In addition, farmers seem to respond to reduced fertility of their soils, as happens with cotton cultivation (Benjaminsen, Aune, and Sidibé 2010), with increased applications of fertilizer. This suggests a sophistication in African farmer knowledge that goes beyond that commonly suggested in the economics literature. Malian farmers are using fertilizer application rates to make both temporally and dynamically rational decisions about the fertility of their soils.

3.5   Conclusions

The success of Mali's farmers in adopting technologies and intensifying their maize production has created a green revolution in maize production in the region. In part through the adoption of improved maize seeds, farming techniques, and the growing use of fertilizer on maize fields, farmers in southern Mali have helped turn Mali from being a food-deficit country to a regional bread basket. This success has been fostered by a combination of research efforts, extension and diffusion of ideas especially by the cotton parastatal CMDT, and a farmer willingness to adopt new seeds and inputs. The success is not unique, as Alene et al. (2009) show that a number of other countries have had similar improvements in maize production.

Adoption of improved maize varieties in Mali in the late 1980s to early 1990s led first to a growth in maize production, which was followed by a sharp growth in the use of fertilizer in maize production from the late 1990s to early in the twenty-first century. This later growth in fertilizer use (adoption of fertilizer for maize cultivation) is primarily responsible for the growth in maize yields one sees in the last decade, as opposed to better management or seeds. Counter to the situation one sees in many African countries, Malian farmers adopted fertilizer for maize in growing numbers despite an increasing price for fertilizer relative to the flat price of maize. This suggests that recent efforts to subsidize fertilizer for maize production could have an increasing knock-on effect.

It is important to highlight that the high estimates of the impact of fertilizer do not mean that the adoption of new seed varieties has had no impact on yields. Based on our results, we can assert that the adoption of new seed varieties needs to be complemented by increased use of fertilizers. This finding is aligned with Smale, Byerlee, and Jayne (2011) who assert that yields in many African countries have remained stagnated, in spite of the generalized adoption of new seeds, due to the low levels of fertilizer use.

The results presented in this chapter also highlight the importance of cash and credit constraints in the adoption and use of fertilizer. The results show that an important determinant of fertilizer use is given by the percentage of land under cotton. Since the fertilizer used in corn plots is financed with the promise of delivering cotton to the parastatal textile company CMDT, our results confirm the argument presented in Laris and Foltz (2014) and in Tefft (2010) that cotton production contributes to food security through the credit it provides for fertilizer use.

There remains room for a great deal of improvement in maize yields in Mali and the West African region in the future. Most of the last decade's growth in yields is due to improved use of inputs, but higher performing varieties of maize seed, including hybrids, are already available on the market in Mali and could lead to a next jump in maize yields and production. In addition, new maize varieties that are drought resistant have the potential to spread maize production into lower rainfall regions of Mali and give those farmers the potential to access the higher fertilizer responsiveness of maize compared to sorghum or millet. There is also room for more work on the silent green revolution in maize in Mali. First, Mali is not alone in experiencing this growth, and work that compared and analyzed the similarly large growth of maize in Burkina Faso would provide a comparative perspective that might help identify key institutional factors that promoted this revolution. Expanding the analysis to the whole region could be particularly important in identifying institutional factors, since other neighboring countries such as Senegal, Gambia, Guinea, and Niger have been left out of the growth in maize.

Appendix

Table 3A.1 Available maize varieties in Mali, 2008

Maize variety	Maximum farmer yields	Origin	Type	Minimum rainfall	Date of intro.	Other quality
Kogoni B	2–3 T/HA	Mali IER	OPV	800 mm/yr.	1970	90-day variety, resists leaf disease
Tzersw	2–3 T/HA	Mali IER	OPV	800 mm/yr.	1983	90-day variety, resists leaf disease
Tiémantié	3.5–4 T/HA	Mali IER	OPV	800 mm/yr.	1983	100–120 day, sensitive to leaf disease
SR22 (EV8422SR)	4–5 T/HA	Mali IER	OPV	800 mm/yr.	1984	100–120 day, resists leaf disease
Sotubaka	4–5 T/HA	Mali IER	OPV	800 mm/yr.	1985	100–120 day, resists leaf disease
Niéléni	3 T/HA	Mali IER	OPV	600 mm/yr.	1996	90-day variety, resists leaf disease
Appolo	2 T/HA	Mali IER	OPV	500 mm/yr.	1996	70-day variety, resists leaf disease
Dembanyuman	4–5 T/HA	Ghana	OPV	800 mm/yr.	1998	100–120 day, resists leaf disease
Jorobana	2–3 T/HA	Mali IER	OPV	600 mm/yr.	2008	80-day variety, resists leaf disease
Mali Hybride 7	6–7 T/HA	Mali IER	Hybrid	800 mm/yr.	2008	100–120 day, resists leaf disease

Source: Coulibaly (2008). "Fiche Technique sur Les Variétés de Maïs au Mali" IER-Mali.

References

Aldana, U., J. Foltz, B. Barham, and P. Useche. 2010. "Sequential Adoption of Package Technologies: The Dynamics of Stacked Corn Adoption." *American Journal of Agricultural Economics* 93 (1): 130–43.

Alene, A. D., A. Menkir, S. O. Ajala, B. Badu-Apraku, A. S. Olanrewaju, V. M. Manyong, and Abdou Ndiaye. 2009. "The Economic and Poverty Impacts of Maize Research in West and Central Africa." *Agricultural Economics* 40:535–50.

Benjamin, D. 1995. "Can Unobserved Land Quality Explain the Inverse Productivity Relationship?" *Journal of Development Economics* 46 (1): 51–84.

Benjaminsen, Tor A., Jens B. Aune, and Daouda Sidibé. 2010. "A Critical Political Ecology of Cotton and Soil Fertility in Mali." *Geoforum* 41 (1): 647–56.

Block, S. 1994. "A New View of Agricultural Productivity in Sub-Saharan Africa." *American Journal of Agricultural Economics* (76) 3: 619–24.

———. 2010. "The Decline and Rise of Agricultural Productivity in Sub-Saharan Africa since 1961." NBER Working Paper no. 16481, Cambridge, MA.

Chayanov, A. V. 1986. *Theory of the Peasant Economy*. Madison: University of Wisconsin Press.

Chikowo, R., B. Vanlauwe, K. E. Giller, P. Tittonell, M. Corbeels, and P. Mapfumo. 2010. "Nitrogen and Phosphorus Capture and Recovery Efficiencies, and Crop Responses to a Range of Soil Fertility Management Strategies in Sub-Saharan Africa." *Nutrient Cycling in Agroecosystems* 88 (1): 59–77.

Coulibaly, Ntji. 2008. "Fiche Technique sur Les Variétés de Mais au Mali." Bamako, Mali: Institut d'Economie Rural.

Crawford, C., T. Jayne, and V. Kelly. 2006. "Alternative Approaches for Promoting Fertilizer Use in Africa." Agriculture and Rural Development Discussion Paper no. 22, Washington, DC, World Bank.

Delarue, Jocelyne, Sandrine Mesplé-Somps, Jean-David Naudet, Denis Cogneau, and Anne-Sophie Robilliard. 2008. "The Sikasso Paradox: Does Cotton Reduce Poverty?" Paper presented at PEGnet conference 2008: Assessing Development Impact—Learning from Experience, Accra, Ghana, September 11–12.

Duflo, E., M. Kremer, and J. Robinson. 2008. "How High are Rates of Return to Fertilizer? Evidence from Field Experiments in Kenya." *American Economic Review* 98 (2): 482–88.

———. 2011. "Nudging Farmers to Use Fertilizer: Evidence from Kenya." *American Economic Review* 101 (6): 2350–90.

Fok, M., M. Kone, H. Djouara, and A. Dolo. 2000. "Combined and Changing Effects of Market Incentives, Technical Innovations and Support on Maize Production in Southern Mali." Communication associated to a poster presented to the IAAE 24th International Conference, Berlin, Germany.

Foster, A., and M. R. Rosenzweig. 1995. "Learning by Doing and Learning from Others: Human Capital and Technical Change in Agriculture." *Journal of Political Economy* 103 (6): 1176–209.

———. 2010. "Microeconomics of Technology Adoption." Center Discussion Paper no. 984, Economic Growth Center, Yale University.

Garen, John. 1984. "The Returns to Schooling: A Selectivity Bias Approach with a Continuous Choice Variable." *Econometrica* 52 (5): 1199–218.

Laris, Paul, and Jeremy Foltz. 2014. "Cotton as Catalyst: The Shifting Role of Fertilizer in Mali's Silent Maize Revolution." *Human Ecology* 42 (6): 857–72.

Levinsohn, J., and A. Petrin. 2003. "Estimating Production Functions Using Inputs to Control for Unobservables." *Review of Economic Studies* 70:317–42.

Marenya, P., and C. Barrett. 2009. "Soil Quality and Fertilizer Use Rates among Smallholder Farmers in Western Kenya." *Agricultural Economics* 40:561–72.

Sileshi, Gudeta, Oluyede C. Ajayi, Simon Mong'omba, Tracy Beedy, Festus K. Akinnifesi, and Legesse K. Debusho. 2010. "Variation in Maize Yield Gaps with Plant Nutrient Inputs, Soil Type and Climate across Sub-Saharan Africa." *Field Crops Research* 116 (1–2): 1–13.

Smale, M., D. Byerlee, and T. Jayne. 2011. "Maize Revolutions in Sub-Saharan Africa." Policy Research Working Paper no. 5659, Washington, DC, World Bank Development Group.

Suri, Tavneet. 2011. "Selection and Comparative Advantage in Technology Adoption." *Econometrica* 79 (1): 159–209.

Tefft, James. 2010. "Mali's White Revolution: Smallholder Cotton, 1960–2007." In *Successes in African Agriculture: Lessons for the Future*, edited by Steven Haggblade and Peter B. R. Hazell. Baltimore: Johns Hopkins University Press.

Wopereis, M., B. Vanlauwe, and A. Mando. 2008. "Agroecological Principles of Integrated Soil Fertility Management: A Guide with Special Reference to Sub-Saharan Africa." International Center for Soil Fertility and Agricultural Development. Muscle Shoals, Ala.: International Center for Soil Fertility and Agricultural Development.

Xu, Z., Z. Guan, T. S. Jayne, and R. Black. 2009. "Factors Influencing the Profitability of Fertilizer Use on Maize in Zambia." *Agricultural Economics* 40:437–46.

4

Contract Farming and Agricultural Productivity in Western Kenya

Lorenzo Casaburi, Michael Kremer, and
Sendhil Mullainathan

4.1 Introduction

The shift from subsistence to cash crops and from sales on spot markets to more complex contractual arrangements is often considered an important driver of structural transformation and growth. In the developing world, including sub-Saharan Africa, contract farming[1] is often considered one of the most successful examples of this pattern, both from the producers' and particularly from the buyers' perspectives.[2]

In contract farming, the buyer and the producer commit in advance to exchange the product. In addition, in most cases, the buyer provides credit,

Lorenzo Casaburi is a postdoctoral fellow at the Stanford Institute for Economic Policy Research. Michael Kremer is the Gates Professor of Developing Societies in the department of economics at Harvard University and a research associate of the National Bureau of Economic Research. Sendhil Mullainathan is professor of economics at Harvard University and a research associate of the National Bureau of Economic Research.

We thank Jeremy Foltz, Andrew Foster, Jon Robinson, and seminar audiences at the Harvard University Development Lunch and the NBER Africa Successes Conference for helpful comments. Helene Ba, Gretchen Carrigan, Sayon Deb, Owen Ozier, Ravindra Ramrattan, and Ian Tomb provided excellent research assistance. We acknowledge support from the National Bureau of Economic Research Africa Project and from the Sustainability Science Program at the Harvard University, with the support of Italy's Ministry for Environment, Land and Sea (project "The Impact of Rainfall Shocks on Cooperation and in Contract Farming: Evidence from Kenya"). Innovations for Poverty Action Kenya provided administrative support. The usual disclaimer applies. For acknowledgments, sources of research support, and disclosure of the authors' material financial relationships, if any, please see http://www.nber.org/chapters/c13437.ack.

1. Throughout the chapter, we use the terms "contract farming" and "outgrower scheme" interchangeably. Yet some authors (Glover 1990) define the former as purely private and stress the state role in the latter.

2. Importantly, some scholars (see, for example, Singh [2002] and Little and Watts [1994]) present a more negative view, highlighting for instance that smaller farmers are often excluded by the schemes.

monitoring, or is directly involved in part of the production process. The need for a steady supply of raw material, the scope for the buyer to provide in-kind loans, and the presence of increasing returns in some of the cultivation or postharvesting tasks are among the major factors thought to affect the emergence and the success of contract-farming schemes.

In many cases, the state had an important role in setting up contract-farming schemes. Thereafter, structural adjustment programs led both to the establishment of new private schemes and to a reduction in state ownership among existing ones. Contract-farming schemes play a disproportionate role in agricultural exports and in the provision of foreign exchange.

In this chapter we focus our attention on sugarcane outgrower schemes in western Kenya, one of the crops with the highest contract farming production share, along with tea and horticulture. In the first part of the chapter we present a brief overview of the literature on contract farming. There is a large body of work that studies the conditions determining the emergence and success of contract-farming schemes and their impact on smallholders. We apply some of the basic lessons from this literature to the specific case under study. In addition, we provide some institutional background for the Mumias Sugar Company, the largest cane outgrower scheme in Kenya.

In the second part of the chapter, we use administrative data to provide evidence on some of the questions emphasized by the above literature. We were granted access to a subset of the administrative records of the company, covering about 14,000 contracting accounts over an eighteen-year time span (1988–2006). The database contains information on production levels, yields, and net revenues (defined as the difference between cane revenues and company-provided input charges).

First, we look at patterns of entry and exit into the scheme, account splitting, and cane plot sizes. We document expansion of the scheme in areas farther away from the mill. In addition, consistent with findings from earlier periods (Ayako et al. 1989), we find relatively low levels of exits from the scheme during the sample period. However, we find clear evidence of both a reduction in cane plot sizes and of an increase in the number of contracted accounts in a given land parcel, resulting from the subdivision of the original larger plot.

Second, we focus on yields and net revenues (using the World Bank gross domestic product [GDP] deflator to deflate monetary values). We find evidence of decreasing yields and net revenues per hectare over time. In addition, our data suggest that smaller plots have, on average, both higher yields and higher net revenues per hectare. In related work in progress (Casaburi, Kremer, and Mullainathan 2012), we delve into this latter result, looking at its robustness to alternative econometric methodologies and assessing its implications for aggregate levels of output per hectare. Finally, we argue that the inverse relation between plot size and yields magnifies the potential benefits of contract farming relative to more vertically integrated organizational forms, such as plantation estates. Labor market imperfections are likely to lead to higher labor intensity in smaller plots, a result that is found throughout the developing world. By preserving the existence of small plots within the existing property rights institutions, contract-farming schemes generate higher yields while still enabling the buying company to take advantage of economies of scale in other tasks such as land preparation, transport, and processing.

The remainder of the chapter is organized as follows: Section 4.2 briefly summarizes the literature on contract farming in sub-Saharan Africa. Section 4.3 focuses on the case of sugarcane outgrower schemes in western Kenya. Section 4.4 presents relevant details of the contract-farming schemes and introduces the database. Section 4.5 looks at patterns of entry, exit, and trends in plot sizes. Section 4.6 focuses on trends and determinants of yields and net revenues per hectare. Section 4.7 concludes.

4.2 Contract Farming in Sub-Saharan Africa: An Overview

Contract farming is defined as "an agreement between farmers and processing and/or marketing firms for the production and supply of agricultural products under forward agreements, frequently at predetermined prices" (Eaton and Shepherd 2001, 2). In addition, the large majority of these schemes include the provision of inputs and some form of production monitoring. Eaton and Shepherd also identify five main typologies of contract farming, primarily based on the number of contractors. Another important distinction across schemes is based on the price-setting mechanism. In "fixed-price contracts," the contracts specify in advance the price producers will receive at harvest. In "formula-price contracts," a predetermined formula determines the price received by farmers' using the current market price as a starting point, and factoring in the costs and the interest on the inputs provided by the buyer during the production process.

With the dismantling of marketing boards and the liberalization of agricultural markets, the prevalence of contract-farming schemes has been steadily increasing throughout the developing world, including Africa (Porter and Phillips-Howard 1997). In Kenya, the country we focus on in this chapter, Grosh (1994) reports an increase in the share of contracted crops over the total value of marketed crops from 22 percent in 1964 to 45–50 percent in the mid-1980s. Following the increase in the prevalence of such schemes, the body of social science research addressing the topic has expanded, too. Research typically focused on one of the following questions: Which market failures does contract farming address? What are the conditions under which contract-farming schemes succeed? What is their impact on farmers' income and welfare? While a comprehensive review of the findings of this literature is beyond the scope of this contribution, we provide a brief overview of a few important lessons. In the next section, we will then look at the case of sugarcane farming in Kenya in light of those guidelines.

Grosh (1994) argues that contract-farming schemes typically arise in response to one or more of the following market or coordination failures: (a) imperfections in capital markets, which limit small farmers' potentially profitable investments (particularly lumpy ones); (b) imperfections in labor markets, such as moral hazard and high monitoring costs, which make plantation cultivation unfeasible; (c) coordination problems between suppliers and processors/buyers, especially when the buyers require a steady supply of raw material in order to break even; and (d) imperfections in the insurance markets, which, in the presence of risk-averse producers, might prevent farmers from undertaking investments with positive expected return.[3]

The relevance of the above problems varies across crops and buyers. In a recent review, Bijman (2008) argues that heterogeneity in quality, perishability of the agricultural products, and technical difficulty of production make the contracting option more likely. In particular, he observes that the need for immediate processing following harvesting favors the establishment of centralized mills, which coordinate harvesting, transporting, and processing, exploiting potential increasing returns to scale in each of these tasks. In addition, Minot (2007), among others, argues that the above coordination problems are more likely to arise with large-scale processors or supermarket chains rather than with traditional wholesalers. Finally, Deb and Suri (2012), among others, propose that contract-farming schemes are more likely to succeed in areas where the contract-farming buyer is the only one who can offer high prices, as the outside option for farmers is limited. Grosh (1994) argues that this is particularly true for sub-Saharan Africa, where the cost of enforcing contracts is particularly high and, in most cases, discontinuation of the contract is the only real threat the buyer can exert. In summary, the contract-farming framework makes it possible to exploit technical increasing returns to scale in settings where contracting inefficiencies would otherwise push toward small-scale farming. In the next section, we delve into the specific contracting problems and sources of economies of scale for the case of sugarcane.

Finally, the literature that studies the impact of contract-farming schemes presents the following results. First, farmers who enter contracting almost unambiguously achieve higher yields, incomes, and input usage (Little and Watts 1994; Porter and Phillips-Howard 1997; Singh 2002).[4] For the Kenya case, Jaffee (1987) shows that income per hectare in contracted crops is much higher than noncontracted ones. Similarly, Ayako et al. (1989) argue that establishment of contract-farming schemes has led to socioeconomic ben-

---

3. Grosh (1994) also argues that contract farming reduces the risk buyers face because of potential expropriation relative to vertical integration options.
4. See also Barrett et al. (2012) for a recent meta-analysis.

efits for five of the six crops reviewed in the Kenya experience. However, Little (1994) provides evidence that the degree of the returns varies significantly within schemes (across farmers) and across schemes. In several case studies, income from contract farming needed to be complemented with other sources in order to achieve subsistence levels.

Second, another set of studies looks at determinants of participation of smallholders to the scheme, focusing on issues of exclusion and dualism in agricultural development. Guo et al. (2007) argue that, at least in some schemes, small producers are less likely to participate. This is consistent with the evidence reported by Grosh (1994), who argues that, to prevent the damages arising from monocropping, some contract-farming schemes limit participation to farmers that have a large plot to devote to subsistence crops.[5] Some authors then argue that contract farming might have a negative effect on nonparticipating households, for instance, by raising food crop prices. Finally, Bijman (2008) argues that, by fostering monocropping, contract farming might lead to overexploitation of natural resources.

In the next sections, we investigate whether and how the above lessons, concerning relevant market failures, determinants of success of the schemes, and impact on smallholders apply to the case of sugarcane contract farming in Kenya.

4.3 Sugarcane Contract Farming in Western Kenya

Over the last few decades, the establishment of sugarcane contract farming has radically changed the agricultural sector and farmers' livelihood in western Kenya. Following the establishment of five outgrower schemes between 1968 and 1981, sugarcane has become the most common cash crop in the area. In spite of important caveats, the establishment and expansion of these cane contract-farming schemes is generally considered a major success story in the transition toward commercial agriculture in East Africa.

Milling capacity expanded rapidly postindependence in response to targeted government investments. The construction of the parastatal mills in Nyanza and Western provinces was the driving factor of this growth. Following the establishment of the mills, there has been a significant growth in production. In Kenya, there has been an expansion of total sugar production from 369,000t in 1984 to 520,000t in 2008 as smallholder farmers have increasingly diversified away from food crops (Kenya Sugar Board 2011).

The government played a central role in the development of the sector. First, the government willingness to achieve self-sufficiency in sugar consumption was a major determinant in the establishment of the mills. Second, the schemes were initially developed as parastatals. In the Mumias Sugar

---

5. However, this finding does not hold in other case studies, such as the one in Senegal by Warning and Key (2002).

Company case, the state held 70 percent of the shares at the beginning of operations (Buch-Hansen and Markusen 1982). While the first two factories were organized in cooperatives, subsequent establishments, including Mumias, followed the "nucleus estate model," which include both a plantation estate (typically surrounding the mill) and an outgrowing scheme. The creation of the nucleus estate implied the eviction of thousands of farming households and was obviously a major source of concern for both politicians and processors.[6] The sector undertook substantial reforms in the nineties, with privatization of the government-owned mills (with the government often retaining majority shares).

How does the sugarcane contract-farming experience in Kenya, and particularly the Mumias one, fit into the broad questions described above? First, all of the aforementioned market failures appear to be relevant in the scheme under study. Formal credit markets and insurance markets are still severely underdeveloped (Dupas et al. 2016; Allen et al. 2016). The importance of monitoring, one of the major sources of labor market imperfections, is lower in sugarcane than in other crops since, for instance, there is no need for daily assessment of the harvesting potential of a given plot (Grosh 1994). Yet, residual-claimant outgrowers still have much stronger incentives in properly performing basic activities than hired workers in a plantation estate. Consistent with this statement, several reports show that yields in the outgrowing scheme are higher than in the nucleus. A report produced by the Kenya Sugar Board (2005) shows that the difference amounts to about 16 percent.

Sugar production processing also requires high coordination between harvesting, transporting, and processing. The contract-farming system relies on the steady supply of sugarcane, which leads to a staggering of the growing cycles across plots. Finally, transporting is relatively costly (high bulk/value ratio) and thus better suited to a large buyer who can exploit economies of scale in this task. To summarize, plantations relying on hired labor may not attain first best in the presence of monitoring costs. Yet, high fixed costs of factory processing and high transport costs imply that ex post spot markets with bargaining over the price of cane will not in general yield efficiency.

Second, while sugarcane does not present a high level of quality heterogeneity relative to other crops, it presents a high level of perishability (Sartorius, Kirsten, and Masuku 2003). Processing needs to occur shortly after harvesting as sugar content starts declining after the cane is cut. Finally, the contract-farming scheme allows the company to undertake soil tests to make an informed choice concerning some of the most "technically difficult" decisions, such as cane variety choice and fertilizer usage.

Third, when looking at the impact on smallholders' welfare, the develop-

6. For an early account of the nucleus estate establishment, see Holtham and Hazlewood (1976) and Barclay (1977).

ment of sugarcane contract farming is generally considered to have produced overall positive effects. The establishment of contract-farming schemes in the area represented a major turning point in the regional economy, leading to increased incomes, services, input usage, and nonagricultural employment (in the factory). In addition, taxation of sugarcane production is an important source of tax revenues (Ayako et al. 1989). With regard to the targeting of contracted farmers, the factory has tried to enforce both a floor on cane plot size and a minimum requirement concerning the amount of land devoted to subsistence crops. Yet, the gradual account splitting and the development of the practice of "joint farming" across years has in fact relaxed these constraints, thus potentially enabling very small holders to join. Buch-Hansen and Markusen (1982) already reported that a substantial share of smallholders already had too little land allocated to food crop production. In the presence of population growth, land scarcity, and partial inheritance, this share is likely to have increased over the last three decades. Finally, the persistence of monocropping, mentioned by Grosh (1994) as one of the potential factors reducing welfare in the long run, is likely to be one of the major sources in the decline in yields we discuss in the next section.

In the rest of the chapter, we use newly collected data to provide rigorous evidence on a subset of the questions discussed so far. This first requires that we provide some administrative detail on the functioning of the specific sugarcane contract-farming scheme we target for our analysis.

4.4   The Mumias Outgrowing Scheme: Background and Data Description

In the contract-farming scheme under study, the company and the contracting farmer sign a contract that typically spans for one replant cycle, made up of one planting and several ratoon harvests. Ratooning leaves the root and lower parts of the plant uncut at the time of harvesting. The main benefit of ratooning is that the crop matures earlier. However, the yield of the ratoon crop decreases after each cycle. The contract typically includes the initial planting harvest and two ratoon harvests, for a total of five to six years. Formally, the company decides whether to enter another ratoon cycle versus replanting, based on yields from the last harvest agronomic analysis. However, farmers' opinion, which can certainly differ from the company's best interests, can have an important role in shaping extensions to the original contract.

The duration of each harvest cycle spans between eighteen and twenty-four months, though early or late harvesting can occur following specific raw material demand from the mill. Planting and harvesting occur in a staggered fashion throughout most of the year, in order to provide a constant supply of cane to the processing mill. The length of the harvest cycle is a major difference from the other major crop in the area, maize, which is harvested twice a year. The difference in harvest durations is an important factor in shaping the farmer's decision to allocate land to one of the two crops.

Farmers are paid based on the tonnage of cane provided at harvest time. The cane prices are based on the current sugar price, via a formula that includes the conversion rate between cane and final sugar output and taxes on sugar production. The Kenya Sugar Board provides a recommended sugar price. Fluctuations in the international sugar prices affect this recommended price and the one the company uses. However, case studies and discussions with both company management and Kenya Sugar Board officials suggest that other factors affect sugar prices. For instance, politicians often advocate higher prices for farmers, especially around election times. In addition, the intensity of competition with other contract-farming schemes also impacts the company prices. As a result of the pricing formula, the company is expected to make a profit on each unit of cane purchased from the outgrowers. In turn, this shapes the company incentives to achieve higher output.

Cane prices are homogeneous for all the farmers that harvest at the same time. Price changes are typically announced a few weeks before their implementation. Timing of the changes are plausibly orthogonal to the characteristics of the farmers who are approaching harvest in that specific period. The relevant price for a given farmer is the one set at the harvest time, not the one in place at the beginning of the cycle. Thus, following the terminology used by Grosh (1994) the scheme sets formula price contracts, not fixed price ones.

The company provides several inputs on credit. These include land preparation (ploughing, harrowing) in the replant cycles, fertilizer (DAP and UREA), harvesting, and transport to the mill. The unit cost of transport per ton of cane varies according to discrete transport zones. The farmer's main duties include weeding (several times during the harvest cycle) and fertilizer application, both of which are important determinants of the final yield level and, particularly for the latter, would require costly monitoring if undertaken by hired workers. The company extension workers occasionally monitor the weeding activity of the farmers. If a farmer fails to weed, the company issues a warning and eventually hires an external contractor to perform the task, charging the cost of the inputs to the farmer's account. In 1996, the company outgrowing scheme spanned across sixty-six sublocations. The scheme included about 65,000 smallholder farmers. The administrative unit used by the company, and thus the unit used for our analysis, is the "account." At any point in time an account is held by one or more contracting farmers.

The contracting farmer recorded on a given account can vary over time. First, the changes can reflect transmission of plot management across members of the same household or inheritance episodes. Second, land rental markets are quite developed in the area. Following a formal rental agreement, the tenant can then replace the landlord on the contract.

Each account is typically matched to one (sub)parcel as defined by the Kenyan land registry. Different accounts can share the same parcel in cases where a parcel gets split into two parts, for instance, between two brothers or between a landlord and a tenant. In addition, accounts are aggregated into fields, sets of plots that are usually treated homogeneously for input provision, in order to exploit economies of scale.

The target population for the database included of all the accounts that had processed at least one payment between 1997 and mid-2006 in sixteen target sublocations. Administrative paper records had to be located in the company register, scanned, and entered. Among the target accounts, approximately 92 percent were located. About two-thirds of the attrition comes from three sublocations. The final sample is comprised of 14,516 accounts, close to a full census of the population of accounts in the target sublocations. In addition, we estimate that in about 5 percent of the cases a certain harvest document is missing from our database. This can occur if the form is missing from the account folder in the registry or if its quality makes it unfit for data entry (image deteriorated, blurred printing, waning ink).

The database is based on the forms the company records at each harvest. This includes information spanning between 1988 and mid-2006. The staggered fashion in which harvesting occurs implies that we have a continuous flow of observations across months and years. We have information on cane production tonnage and net amount paid to the farmer (which can also be negative). The data also include information on plot sizes registered by the account at each harvest. These can change from harvest to harvest, due to the outcome of the maize versus cane allocation choice or the subdivision of the plot across different household members.[7]

Using the information contained in our database, we attempt to provide evidence on two broad questions. First, we focus on participation in the scheme, looking at patterns of entry, exit, and cane plot sizes. Second, we study yields and value added. For each of these variables, we focus on: (a) the moments of their distribution, (b) their evolution over time, and (c) their observable determinants. Finally, we interpret these results on the basis of the conclusions of the literature we reviewed in previous sections.

4.5   Participation in the Scheme: Entry, Exit, and Plot Size

Over the time span of the sample, the Mumias outgrowing scheme grew substantially. Grosh (1994) reports that the scheme more than doubled, from 30,000 to about 65,000 accounts, between 1984 and the mid-1990s. Figure 4.1 shows the number of account-harvest observations in our database across harvest years, by plant cycle (i.e., plant vs. ratoon).

---

7. Plot sizes are typically approximated to one-tenth of a hectare.

Our database enables us to look at the patterns of entry and exit into the scheme in the target zones. As we discussed above, we target accounts that harvested at least once between 1997 and 2006. Yet, we have information on these accounts for the previous decade, too. First, this allows us to look at patterns of entry across years, conditional on surviving until 1997. More precisely, we define the "entry" year as the first harvest year in which a given account appears in the database. Obviously, a substantial share of accounts had been operating pre-1988. Thus, our entry variable spikes in the first couple of years of the sample. However, figure 4.2 shows that a substantial share of accounts appears for the first time in the database after 1990, suggesting real entry (or reentry) into the scheme, rather than merely first occurrence in the data. More specifically, we find that about 50 percent of the targeted accounts entered between 1991 and 2006 and about 26 percent entered after 1997.

The establishment of new accounts can arise either from the splitting of land from old accounts or from the entry of new land into the scheme. In order to partially address this difference, we look at the entry of land registry parcels (as opposed to accounts) into our database. We find that approximately 70 percent of land parcels entered the scheme by 1990, and 87 percent by 1997. When compared to the 50 percent entry of accounts post-1991, these figures suggest that splitting of cane plots across multiple accounts played an important role in the increase in the number of accounts, a fact that we further document below. Nevertheless, we still detect a general

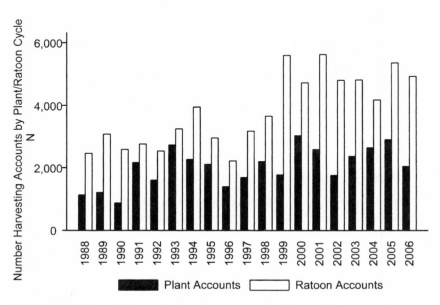

Fig. 4.1   **Number of observations per harvest year by plant cycle**

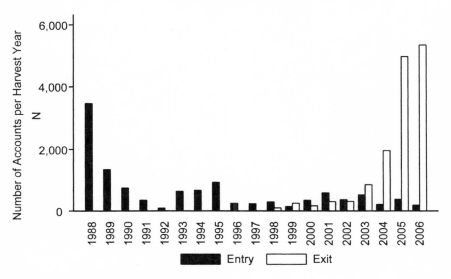

Fig. 4.2   Entry and exit by harvest year

positive trend in the amount of land harvested on a yearly basis in the targeted sublocations, although the increase is not constant across years (for instance, some years present substantial decreases relative to the previous one). Finally, it must be noted that, over the years, the company expanded its catchment area to locations farther away from the mill. However, our database is focused on zones that were already included in the scheme by 1988 and thus does not capture this pattern.

Given that we targeted accounts with at least one harvest between 1997 and 2006, we cannot observe patterns of exit before 1997, but can only look at exit after that. In figure 4.2, an account is defined as an "exit" in a given harvest year if we observe it for the last time in that year. This variable is highly clustered in the last three years of our sample. We find that 85 percent of the accounts appear lastly in 2004 or later, and 90 perent in 2003 or later. Thus, 10 percent of accounts are observed for the last time between 1997 and 2002, probably because of real exit from the scheme. For the remaining 90 percent, we cannot disentangle leaving the scheme from just final observation in the data. Assuming an equal likelihood of exit across years of the sample, we can estimate that about 16 percent of the accounts left the scheme between 1997 and 2006. Using administrative data for other sublocations in the scheme, for which we lack other variables we use in the subsequent analysis, we obtain very similar figures on the rate of exit, suggesting that the low exit rates in the above sample are not driven by the attrition described above.

Another important margin of adjustment is account plot size. Accounts could decrease their plot size to reallocate part of the plot to other crops. In

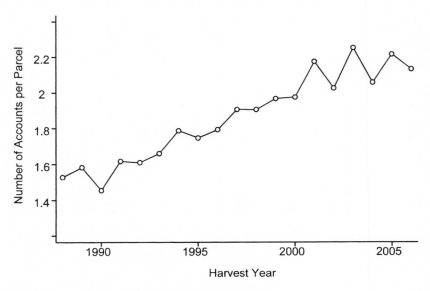

Fig. 4.3   Number of accounts per land registry parcel

addition, accounts could gradually be split across different family members. This could lead both to an increase in the number of accounts and to an increase in the prevalence of "joint accounts," accounts where two or more farmers cultivate the plot, often two separate subplots. Below, we provide evidence for both these patterns.

We have information about the specific (sub)parcel in the land registry a given account is located in. Partial inheritance, which implies that land is split across male heirs, is one of the factors potentially driving subdivision of one original account into multiple smaller accounts, thus leading to an increase in the number of accounts per land parcel. Figure 4.3 presents strong evidence of this pattern. The number of accounts per land registry parcel increases from 1.23 in 1988 to 1.48 in 2006, a 20 percent increase. The increase between 1988 and 1997, the first half of our sample time span, was 13 percent instead. Given the rates of population growth, this pattern is likely to continue. More and more plots will hit the floors the company sets for cane plot accounts. While this varies across years, company staff report the floor to be at 1 acre (0.4 ha). However, we find evidence that a growing share of plots falls below this figure. We provide more evidence on these patterns below.

In order to comply with the company-imposed guidelines on minimum cane plot size, another response to demographic pressure is having more than one farmer contracting over the same account. Throughout our sample, approximately 30 percent of the account/harvest observations include more than one contracting farmer. According to our discussions with the company extension staff, joint contracting instances can arise for several reasons. First, two members of the same family can decide to share a plot of land if its size is too small to enable contracting under two different accounts (throughout the span of the sample the company discouraged contracting of extremely small plots). Typically, in this case, each of the two (or more) farmers is in charge of a well-defined subplot. At harvest, the company is then able to track the amount of cane coming from each subplot in the revenue computation. Second, the presence of more than one contracted farmer can in other cases arise from standard renting or sharecropping arrangements, with the landowner renting out the plot (or a portion of it) but keeping her name on the contract.

In response to increased demographic pressure and partial inheritance, we expect the prevalence of joint accounts to rise across years. Figure 4.4 clearly shows that this is indeed the case. We observe a steady increase in the prevalence of joint plot contracting over the years of our sample, with a share of about 40 percent toward the end of the period. In more recent years, the company has discouraged the establishment of joint plots, which might explain part of the substantial increase in the number of accounts across the sample years.

So far, we have found basic evidence consistent with the hypothesis that demographic pressure, which increased over time, has led to account splitting and to an increase of the prevalence of joint plots. What is the trend in the other adjustment margin, the size of cane plots? Figure 4.5 provides

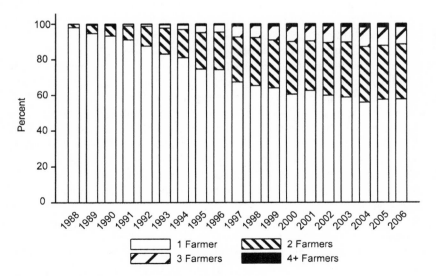

Fig. 4.4   Number of contracting farmers per account

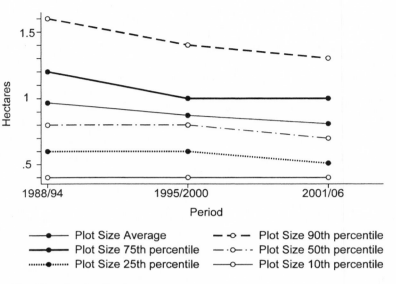

Fig. 4.5   Plot-size distribution

some evidence with regard to this question. The graph shows the 10th, 25th, 50th (median), 75th, and 90th percentile of the distribution, as well as the average, for three different periods: 1988/94, 1995/2000, and 2001/06. With the exception of the 10th percentile, which stays at the floor of 0.4 hectares throughout the sample period, all the other percentiles and the average plot size fall by 15 to 20 percent over the sample period. Consistent with the account-splitting findings, the highest percentiles experience the largest drops in absolute terms.

We then attempt to shed more light on the relation between initial plot size and subsequent plot-size growth rates. Large plots have more margin for adjustment. On the contrary, very small plots cannot further decrease their size without reaching the company-imposed limits on plot size. We focus on the growth rates (logarithmic difference) in plot sizes between two subsequent replant cycles and we correlate these with the plot size in the first of the two cycles. Figure 4.6 provides a kernel-weighted local polynomial smoothing of this relation, including also the 95 percent confidence intervals. There is strong evidence of a negative relationship between initial plot size and subsequent growth. One potential concern with the above results is the presence of transitory measurement error leading to mechanical regression to the mean (Romer 1989). In order to partially address these concerns, we first adapt the strategy adopted by Barro (1991) to deal with similar issues when looking at income per capita convergence across countries. Specifically, we run a linear regression of the growth in plot size between plant t and $t + 1$ on plot size in t instrumented with plot size in $t - 1$. This strategy

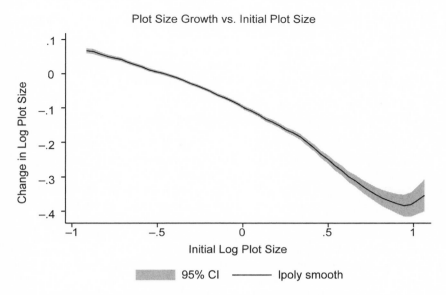

Fig. 4.6   Size last harvest/size first harvest versus size first harvest
Note: Kernel = epanechnikov, degree = 0, bandwidth = .16, and pwidth = .24.

deals with measurement error, as long as this is uncorrelated over time (on the other hand, if measurement error in plot sizes were strongly correlated across plant cycles, it would be less of a concern to start with). We find a coefficient of –0.021 (S. E.= 0.008). This estimate is comparable to the coefficient obtained in a simple ordinary least squares (OLS) regression (–0.024), suggesting that the above effect is not a regression artifact (the standard error in the OLS regression is about half of the IV one, because the sample size is larger).[8] In addition, we define a binary indicator that takes value one if the plot size fell by more than 30 percent between the first and the last observation for a given account. This discrete measure is likely to be less subject to measurement error than the continuous one since a large mismeasurement in the continuous variable is required to turn the value of the dummy to one. In addition, given that the measure is in relative terms, standard measurement error will mechanically lead to a higher number of "false positives" for initially small plots, thus pushing against a positive correlation between baseline plot size and nonzero values of the above binary indicator. Yet, we still find that the probability of such large cuts significantly grows with baseline plot size ($\beta = 0.25$, S. E. = 0.024).

We summarize the results of this section. First, we find that over the

---

8. We note that 90 percent of the plots of our sample have three or fewer plant cycles. As a consequence, we cannot apply more sophisticated GMM techniques that require longer lags.

observation period, there are low levels of exits. Second, we find substantial evidence of plot splitting, either via an increase in the number of accounts in a given land registry parcel or through an increased prevalence of joint contracts. Finally, we document a decreasing trend in plot size, concentrated primarily among plots with relatively large size initially.

4.6   Yields and Net Revenues: Trends and Determinants

In this section, we focus our attention on yields and net revenues per hectare. First, we describe the evolution of these indicators over time, focusing on different moments and quantiles of the distribution. Second we study to which extent differences in performance arise from systematic differences across accounts as opposed to transitory shocks. Finally, we look at the specific role of plot size in shaping yields and net revenues per hectare.

Figure 4.7 reports the trend in yields in the three "periods" previously defined for plant cycles (1988–1995, 1996–2000, 2001–2006). We find a clear negative trend. The average yield in the 2001–2006 period is about 75 percent of the average yield in 1988–1995. The decline is more pronounced in the lowest percentiles. For instance, the bottom decile of yields in the third period is 61 percent of the same decile in the first period. The reduction between the second and the last period is generally steeper than the one between the first and the second. We observe similar patterns when looking at ratoon yields (results not reported). Unsurprisingly, average yields are always higher in plant than in ratoon cycles.

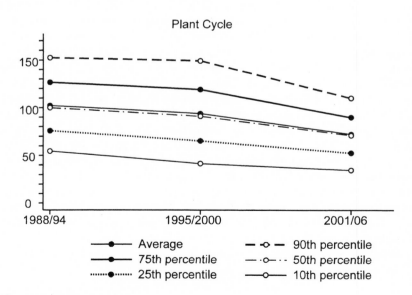

Fig. 4.7   Yields (tons/ha)

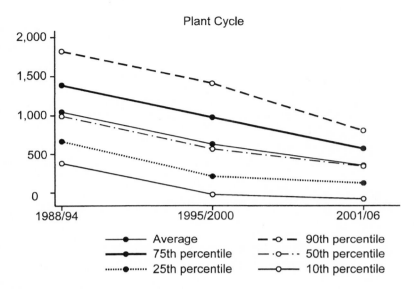

Fig. 4.8   Net revenues per hectare

The evidence of declining yields from our database is consistent with data reported in other sectoral publications (Kenya Sugar Board 2005), although the levels in our database are 10–15 percent lower than the aggregate levels reported there. Declining soil fertility and continuous sugarcane monoculture are often reported as primary causes of these trends. However, we do not have information on soil quality in our database. Thus, we cannot reach any conclusion of the role of soil fertility in shaping these patterns.

We also have data on net revenues realized at each harvest. This variable is defined as the difference between the payment the farmers receive from the company and the amount charged for company-provided inputs. We deflate monetary values using national GDP deflators from the World Bank World Development Index for the 1988–2006 period. We focus on net revenues per hectare. When looking at plant cycles, which include higher charges for company-provided inputs because of land preparation and seedcane distribution, we find evidence of a decline even starker than that of yields. Figure 4.8 summarizes the results. We find that the average of deflated net revenues in the last period is 34 percent of the value in the first period. The decline is steeper for lowest percentiles of the distribution. The 25th percentile falls by 81 percent between the first and the last period. The 75th percentile declines by 60 percent.

Figure 4.9 shows the trends for ratoon cycles. While still remarkable, the decline is less steep than the one in planting cycles. For instance, the average of deflated net revenues in the last period is 58 percent of the value in the first period. The change in net revenues can arise from three sources: a decline in

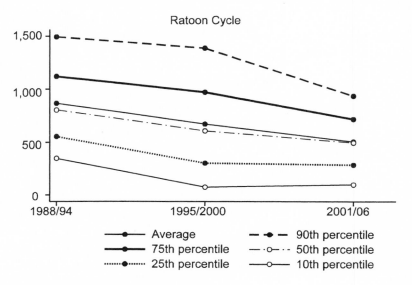

Fig. 4.9   Net revenues per hectare

tonnage per hectare, a decline in the ratio between cane revenues and input charges, and a decline in the price of cane in real terms. We documented the patterns in yields above. In addition, we find that the ratio between revenues and input charges decreases substantially for plant cycles (a decline of 25 percent on average) but is relatively stable for ratoon cycles (an average decline of 9 percent). Finally, the price of cane in real terms falls by 25 percent. However, it must be noted that the GDP deflator used to estimate this change does not necessarily capture the consumption bundle in the areas targeted by our study. This bias could potentially lead to an overestimation of the reduction in net revenues over time.

While the previous results show a clear declining pattern in yields and net revenues, another question concerns whether, over time, certain producers experience systematically higher returns from cane cultivation. To shed light on these issues, we exploit the panel structure of our data. We decompose the variance in yields into a "within" and a "between" component. The former is the portion of variance that captures the variability in the yields for a given account, possibly controlling for important determinants of production levels such as plant cycle. The latter captures systematic differences in the average levels of output per hectare across different accounts. The analysis provides several insights. First, the overall dispersion of the distribution of yields does not change systematically over time. The coefficient of variation takes values of 0.41, 0.49, and 0.45 in periods 1, 2, and 3, respectively. Second, using a basic fixed effect variance model, we find that permanent characteristics of the accounts over the sample period explain about 31.7 percent of the variance in logarithmic yields. The share rises to 43 percent once we include plant cycle and harvest year dummies in the model. In an alternative model, we allow a fixed effect for any account-period combination, thus capturing the portion of variance explained by fixed characteristics of an account in a given period (where the periods are again defined as 1988–1995, 1996–2000, and 2001–2006). We find that in this model, the between variance amounts to at least 45 percent of the total variance, with the fraction increasing to 61 percent if one includes other determinants of yields. Finally, we find that the between portion of the variance does not significantly change across periods.

These results point at an important role of permanent heterogeneity across accounts. Yet, our model cannot disentangle differences in land quality from differences in producers' ability and labor intensity. Lack of soil quality data prevents us from providing a definitive answer on this. Nevertheless, we use precise information on the geographical location of each account to make some progress in this direction. Specifically, we exploit the fact that, as we described above, accounts are grouped into "fields," macroplots containing on average eleven accounts across our sample. Accounts belonging to the same field receive similar land preparation and harvesting services from the company and, in a given harvest year, have comparable soil quality, rainfall exposure, and temperature. In order to assess the importance of permanent heterogeneity across producers in a given field, we residualize the raw yield data after taking into account the effect of plot size, plant cycle, and field-harvest year dummies. Permanent heterogeneity across accounts of a given field, as opposed to transitory shocks, still explains 32 percent of the variance in these residual yields. Even for a crop that is considered to have relatively low labor intensity and in a scheme where the buyer provides a substantial amount of inputs and supervision, we find that a substantial share of variance in yields is explained by unobserved time-invariant (or "period-invariant") characteristics across accounts. In addition, this does not seem to arise only from variation in soil quality, but rather points at the importance of permanent differences in productivity and labor intensity across producers.

Finally, we shed light on another potentially important determinant of productivity: plot size. The relation between plot size and output per hectare has spanned a huge literature covering a wide range of crops, countries, and time periods. While the literature still lacks a definitive answer (see Eastwood, Lipton, and Newell [2010] for a recent review), evidence of an inverse relationship has been found in many contexts. Here, we provide some basic evidence on the occurrence of the inverse relationship in our database. Figure 4.10 presents the results of a kernel-weighted local polynomial smoothing of log yields on log plot size. The graph shows that, throughout

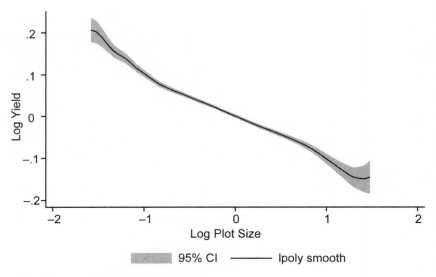

Fig. 4.10   Log yields versus plot size
Note: Variables demeaned by plant cycle * harvest year dummies.

the domain of observed plot sizes, there is a significant decreasing relation between plot size and plot yields.[9] Using parametric estimates, we find that an increase in 10 log points in plot size decreases yields by 2 to 5 log points. Casaburi, Kremer, and Mullainathan (2012) fully exploit the panel-data structure. The detailed information on the locations of the plots allows us to control for potential alternative explanations that might drive a spurious relation, such as unobserved heterogeneity in soil quality or contracting farmer characteristics. The above relation becomes even stronger when including those controls.

Figure 4.11 shows the results of a similar analysis focusing on net revenues per hectare. Given that this variable can take negative values, we choose to estimate a level-log model, rather than a log-log one. The graph shows a negative and significant relationship in this case, too. However, the magnitude of the relation is much weaker. In a simple linear level-log cross-sectional regression, we find that a 10 percent increase in plot size reduces net revenues per hectare by less than 1 percent of the mean value.[10]

The relation highlighted in figure 4.11 suggests that, for a given total amount of land allocated to cane in the company catchment area, the company profitability decreases with the average cane plot size. Two caveats

9. In figures 4.10 and 4.11 the variables are first demeaned by harvest year and plant cycle.
10. However, in Casaburi, Kremer, and Mullainathan (2012) we find that the magnitude of the coefficient rises significantly when including account fixed effects.

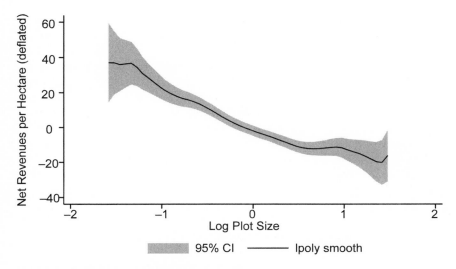

Fig. 4.11   Net revenues per hectare versus plot size
Note: Net revenues deflated by GDP deflator from World Bank World Development Indicators. Variables demeaned by plant cycle * harvest year dummies.

apply to this conclusion. First, transaction costs (for instance, the administrative cost of managing an account in terms of agricultural extension or payroll) could be higher for small plots. However, it is unlikely that administrative costs are large enough to offset the estimated yield differentials. Second, gradual subdivision of plots across family members might decrease total amount of land allocated to cane, for instance, if each subplot needs to allocate a minimum share to food-crop farming, and reduce profitability in the presence of economies of scale in the processing. We do not find evidence of these patterns in our data. The amount of land allocated to cane in a given land registry parcel is increasing in the number of active accounts that are matched to it. However, this result does not completely rule out the above concern as we cannot distinguish instances of splitting of an old account from entry into the scheme of new subparcels within the same parcel (i.e., cases where two or more producers were already sharing the land but only one was previously involved in cane).

4.7   Conclusion

The prevalence of contract-farming schemes in Africa has been growing over the last few decades. As a result, such schemes are attracting the interest of a growing number of scholars from different disciplines. Yet, there are few studies that use microdata to assess trends and productivity determinants in these contexts. In this chapter we have used administrative data for a large sample of Kenyan farmers over a two-decade time span in order to provide rigorous evidence on participation and productivity within one of the largest contract-farming schemes in East Africa.

After reviewing the scheme's origins and impact through the lens of the existing literature, our data analysis has highlighted several stylized facts. First, across our sample time span, there is a net entry of producers into the scheme. Second, average cane plot sizes decrease over time. Plot splits across family members seem to play an important role in this pattern. Third, yields and net revenues decrease over time. Fourth, unobserved producer-level characteristics explain a large share of the variance in yields. Fifth, yields are decreasing in plot size, consistent with the hypothesis that labor intensity is higher in small plots.

The latter finding provides important policy implications. While our database does not include labor data, evidence from fieldwork and interactions with the company extension staff suggests that the main hypothesis for the inverse relation is that labor intensity decreases with plot size. This is driven by monitoring costs, limited outside worker hiring, and a wedge between inside and outside workers. This provides strong empirical support to a key argument for contract farming. Outgrower schemes allow the processor to exploit key economies of scale in some of the production and processing tasks—for instance, by ensuring enforcement of farmers' obligations with regard to inputs provided on credit—but they also preserve existing property rights over the land. On the one hand, in the presence of monitoring costs and other labor market imperfections, a contractual form that preserves decentralized land holdings has key advantages over a plantation estate. On the other hand, the contract-farming arrangement prevents some of the failures that would likely arise in a fully decentralized market, such as underinvestment in inputs due to credit constraints or lack of commitment ability for a monopsonist buyer.

The experience of Kenyan sugarcane contract-farming schemes represents an important case study in the development of a formal market-oriented agricultural sector in sub-Saharan Africa. Analysis of new data for the coming years will contribute to shed light on how the sector responds to the increased challenges and opportunities arising from the economic integration that will follow the dismantling of sugar trade restrictions in Kenya in the coming years.

References

Allen, F., E. Carletti, R. Cull, J. Qian, L. Senbet, and P. Valenzuela. 2016. "Resolving the African Financial Development Gap: Cross-Country Comparisons and a Within-Country Study of Kenya." In *African Successes, Volume III: Moderniza-*

tion and Development, edited by S. Edwards, S. Johnson, and D. N. Weil, 13–62. Chicago: University of Chicago Press.

Ayako, A. B., D. M. Makanda, S. M. Mwabu, L. M. Awiti, and Okech-Owiti. 1989. "Contract Farming and Outgrower Schemes in Kenya: Case Studies." *Eastern Africa Economic Review* 5:4–14.

Barclay, A. H. 1977. "The Mumias Sugar Project: A Study of Rural Development in Western Kenya." PhD diss., Columbia University.

Barrett, C. B., M. E. Bachke, M. F. Bellemare, H. C. Michelson, S. Narayanan, and T. F. Walker. 2012. "Smallholder Participation in Contract Farming: Comparative Evidence from Five Countries." *World Development* 4 (4): 715–30.

Barro, R. J. 1991. "Economic Growth in a Cross Section of Countries." *Quarterly Journal of Economics* 106 (2): 407–43.

Bijman, J. 2008. "Contract Farming in Developing Countries." Working Paper, Wageningen University.

Buch-Hansen, M., and H. S. Markusen. 1982. "Contract Farming and the Peasantry: Cases from Western Kenya." *Review of African Political Economy* 23:9–36.

Casaburi, L., M. Kremer, and S. Mullainathan. 2012. "Contract Farming, Rainfall Shocks, and Agricultural Dynamics in Western Kenya." Working paper, Harvard University.

Deb, R., and T. Suri. 2013. "Endogenous Emergence of Credit Markets: Contracting in Response to a New Technology in Ghana." *Journal of Development Economics* 101 (2013): 268–83.

Dupas, P., S. Green, A. Keats, and J. Robinson. 2016. "Challenges in Banking the Rural Poor: Evidence from Kenya's Western Province." In *African Successes, Volume III: Modernization and Development*, edited by S. Edwards, S. Johnson, and D. N. Weil, 63–101. Chicago: University of Chicago Press.

Eastwood, R., M. Lipton, and A. Newell. 2010. "Farm Size." *Handbook of Agricultural Economics* 4 (2010): 3323–97.

Eaton, C., and A. Shepherd. 2001. *Contract Farming: Partnerships for Growth*. Rome: Food and Agriculture Organization of the UN (FAO).

Glover, D. J. 1990. "Contract Farming and Outgrowers Schemes in East and Southern Africa." *Journal of Agricultural Economics* 41 (3): 303–15.

Grosh, M. 1994. "Contract Farming in Africa: An Application of the New Institutional Economics." *Journal of African Economies* 3 (2): 231–61.

Guo, H., R. W. Jolly, and J. Zhu. 2007. "Contract Farming in China: Perspectives of Farm Households and Agribusiness Firms." *Comparative Economic Studies* 49 (2): 285–312.

Holtham, G., and A. Hazlewood. 1976. *Aid and Inequality in Kenya: British Development Assistance to Kenya*. Kent, UK: Croom Helm.

Jaffee, S. M. 1987. "Case Studies of Contract Farming in the Horticultural Sector of Kenya." IDA Working Paper no. 83, Institute for Development Anthropology.

Kenya Sugar Board. 2005. *Year Book of Sugar Statistics*. http://www.kenyasugar .co.ke/new/.

———. 2011. *Kenya Sugar Industry Strategic Plan, 2010–2014*. http://www.kenya sugar.co.ke/new/.

Little, P. D. 1994. "Contract Farming and the Development Question." In *Living under Contract: Contract Farming and Agrarian Transformation in Sub-Saharan Africa*, edited by P. D. Little and M. J. Watts, 216–47 Madison: University of Wisconsin Press.

Little, P. D., and M. J. Watts, eds. 1994. *Living under Contract: Contract Farming and Agrarian Transformation in Sub-Saharan Africa*. Madison: University of Wisconsin Press.

Minot, N. 2007. "Contract Farming in Developing Countries: Patterns, Impact, and Policy Implications." In *Food Policy for Developing Countries: Case Studies*, edited by Per Pintstrup-Andersen and Fuzhi Cheng. Ithica, NY: Cornell University. http://cip.cornell.edu/DPubS?verb=Display&version=1.0&service=UI&handle=dns.gfs/1200428173&page=record.

Porter, G., and K. Phillips-Howard. 1997. "Comparing Contracts: An Evaluation of Contract Farming Schemes in Africa." *World Development* 25 (2): 227–38.

Romer, P. M. 1989. "Human Capital and Growth: Theory and Evidence." NBER Working Paper no. 3173, Cambridge, MA.

Sartorius, K., J. Kirsten, and M. Masuku. 2003. "A New Institutional Economic Analysis of Small Farmer Contracts and Relations in the Sugar Supply Chains in South Africa and Swaziland." Department of Agricultural Economics, University of Pretoria.

Singh, S. 2002. "Contracting Out Solutions: Political Economy of Contract Farming in the Indian Punjab." *World Development* 30 (9): 1621–38.

Warning, M., and N. Key. 2002. "The Social Performance and Distributional Consequences of Contract Farming: An Equilibrium Analysis of the Arachide de Bouche Program in Senegal." *World Development* 30 (2): 255–63.

5

The Determinants of Food-Aid Provisions to Africa and the Developing World

Nathan Nunn and Nancy Qian

5.1 Introduction

Food aid has been one of the most important policies for economic development since World War II. During its peak in 1965, food aid accounted for 22 percent of all aid given to developing countries. It is meant to alleviate hunger by feeding the local population. Through monetization, it is also meant to help fund projects that the recipient governments deem helpful for general economic development. The effectiveness of food aid has been the subject of intense debate in recent years. In the academic realm, existing studies that empirically estimate the impacts of food aid have found mixed results. Some have found that food aid alleviates hunger (Levinsohn and McMillan 2007; Quisumbing 2003; Yamano, Alderman, and Christiaensen 2005), and by doing so can be an effective policy for reducing conflict (e.g., Bardhan 1997). Critics have observed that food aid is not always targeted or delivered to the most needy. Some have even argued that it could have the unintended and perverse effect of making the populations in recipient countries worse off. For example, there are many accounts of how food aid can increase conflict (Knack 2001). A companion study to this chapter confirms this fear and finds a positive relationship between food aid and the incidence of conflict (Nunn and Qian 2011).

This chapter addresses the important issue of food aid by focusing on the

Nathan Nunn is professor of economics at Harvard University and a research associate of the National Bureau of Economic Research. Nancy Qian is associate professor of economics at Yale University and a faculty research fellow of the National Bureau of Economic Research.

We gratefully acknowledge funding from the NBER Africa Project. We thank Eva Ng, Sayon Deb, and Katherine Wilson for valuable research assistance. For acknowledgments, sources of research support, and disclosure of the authors' material financial relationships, if any, please see http://www.nber.org/chapters/c13434.ack.

determinants (rather than the consequences) of food aid, and the different patterns of food aid across donors and recipients. We are particularly interested in the differences for African countries, as they are arguably the most reliant on food aid today.

The analysis begins by first providing a statistical overview of food-aid shipments to Africa and the rest of the developing world. Then we examine a number of specific determinants of annual bilateral shipments of cereal aid between 1971 and 2008.

We find that an important determinant of food aid is the recipient country's domestic production of food in the previous years. Less food production in period t is correlated with increased food aid received in the next two years. This relationship is much stronger for African recipients than for non-African recipients. In other words, food aid given to Africa appears much more responsive to recipient need than food aid given to the rest of the developing world.

For each donor country, we then estimate the responsiveness of its food-aid shipments to adverse production shocks in receiving countries. We find strong evidence that food aid from many of the largest cereal-producing countries, which are also some of the largest donors (e.g., Canada, the United States of America, India, and China), is the least responsive to variation in recipient cereal production.

We then turn to factors in the donor countries that affect food-aid shipments. We focus on two donor-country factors: domestic cereal production and former colonial ties. We show that US production of cereals—wheat in particular—is an important determinant of food-aid flows. If the United States experiences a positive production shock, the amount of food aid given increases in the subsequent two years. Interestingly, the correlation between donor domestic production and aid flows seems unique to the United States.

For Old World donors, we examine another potential determinant of food aid: former colonial ties. We find that only African countries are more likely to receive more food aid from former colonial masters, whereas all countries are more likely to receive food aid from countries that were colonized by the same colonizer. This is interesting because it suggests that foreign countries, especially former colonial masters, are a more important source of food aid for the economies of African countries. The greater importance of the colonizer-colony relationship for food-aid flows to Africa may be explained by the fact that African countries more recently gained independence relative to countries in Latin America and Asia.

Our last results examine the interaction between colonial history and the responsiveness of donors to recipient need, as measured by recipient cereal production. We find that for all countries, when the recipient and donor have the same former colonizer, food-aid shipments are less responsive to recipient need. For African countries this is also true when the donor is the former colonizer. This suggests that although colonial ties increase the total amount of aid flows between two countries, the increased flows appear to be much less responsive to need. These flows are not necessarily going to the locations that need it most. This is interesting and suggests that food aid from former colonial masters are intended for general development or other objectives rather than for the alleviation of acute hunger.

This chapter is organized as follows: In the following section, to help motivate our investigation of the determinants of food aid, we review the existing evidence on the consequences of food aid. Section 5.3 provides a statistical overview of food-aid flows to all developing countries. In section 5.4, we focus on the determinants of food aid to Africa and the rest of the world. Finally, we offer concluding remarks in section 5.5.

5.2 Consequences of Food Aid in Africa and the Rest of the World

Before presenting our analysis on the determinants of food-aid shipments to developing countries, we first provide a brief overview of the potential benefits and costs to the receiving countries. A more detailed description is provided in Nunn and Qian (2011).

The most prominent problems associated with food aid can be divided into three categories. The first problem is one that faces all foreign aid. Food aid can be a significant source of revenue for some recipient countries. It is also entirely fungible and can be monetized and spent at the discretion of the recipient government. This increase in resources could increase political competition, which can often lead to increased conflicts within the recipient countries.

Second, a closely related problem is that governments of poor countries often have little political incentive to deliver these additional resources appropriately, that is, to the most needy. For example, in his study of food aid in Rwanda during the early 1990s, Peter Uvin (1998) finds that aid was misused by the government and allocated to a few elites, generating discontent and conflict. He writes: "The development enterprise directly and actively contributes to inequality and humiliation. The material advantages accorded to a small group of people . . . living in Rwanda contribute to greater economic inequality and the devaluation of life of the majority" (Uvin 1998, 142). This is just one of many examples that one comes across in the accounts of aid workers. Another example is in Zimbabwe, where the government would only provide food aid to known political supporters (Thurow and Kilman 2009). Or, in Somalia, where food aid was often not at all used to alleviate the hunger of any population. During the early 1990s, many observed food aid being traded for arms or stolen goods and then sold for money, which was pocketed by the government (Perlez 1992). Or, in Rwanda during the early 1990s, where government stealing of food aid was so problematic that aid was canceled on several occasions (Uvin 1998, 90).

Finally, a commonly cited problem is that food aid increases the amount of cheap foods in recipient countries, and thus decreases the price of agricultural production and the income of farmers in those countries (Pedersen 1996; Kirwan and McMillan 2007). This not only decreases agricultural incomes but also increases income inequality between urban and rural workers.

In a companion paper, Nunn and Qian (2011), we examine the effect of food aid on the incidence of conflict, a potential negative impact of food aid that has been hypothesized in the literature but never formally tested. Identifying such a causal mechanism is fraught with difficulties. To overcome these, we focus specifically on wheat aid from the United States, which constitutes the vast majority of aid given by the largest donor of aid in the world (see below). We instrument for US wheat aid to donor countries using weather-induced wheat production shocks. Our estimates show that food aid causes increased civil war incidence in receiving countries. Although we find large effects for internal conflicts, we find no effects on interstate conflict. We find that the effects on receiving countries within Africa are not statistically different from other parts of the world. However, the regional estimates are very imprecise.

In summary, studies on the consequences of food aid thus far provide enough evidence on the negative effects of food aid to warrant great concern over its effectiveness. To understand why food aid does not have the impact it is meant to, we must first understand the determinants of food aid, which is the focus of this study.

5.3   A Statistical Overview of Food Aid to Africa and the Rest of the Developing World

This section provides a descriptive overview of the pattern of global food-aid shipments. It is important to keep a few facts in mind for the following discussion. First, over 90 percent of food aid is cereals. Therefore, food aid will be synonymous with cereals aid in this chapter. Second, when food aid is reported, the value of food aid typically includes shipping costs, which can constitute more than half of the total value of aid (Barrett and Maxwell 2005). Since data on the itemized value of food aid are not available and shipping companies are typically from the rich countries, we will report food aid in terms of volume of food rather than dollar value. This also sidesteps some difficulties in interpretation since it is not clear how exactly food aid is valued. Moreover, grain markets are thought to be segmented, and the price that the donor government values the food (or even the world grain price) may not reflect the value to the recipients of food aid.

We begin by examining the aggregate trend in food-aid shipments to Africa and to the rest of the world. The total volume of food aid shipped each year (measured in tonnes) between 1971 and 2008 is reported in figures 5.1 and 5.2 for African and for non-African countries, respectively. The data

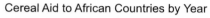

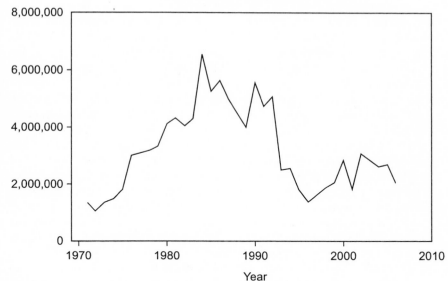

Fig. 5.1   Total cereal aid shipped each year to African countries

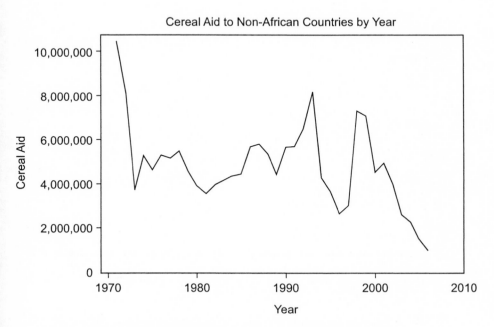

Fig. 5.2   Total cereal aid shipped each year to non-African countries

are from the Food and Agricultural Organization's (FAO) FAOSTAT Database. Cereals include wheat, rice, barley, maize, rye, oats, millets, sorghum, buckwheat, quinoa, and other grains, including mixed grains. Donor and recipient countries may ship and receive different types of cereals. Therefore, for the purposes of comparison, we often use this broad category of cereals rather than specific types of cereals. Where possible, we also consider specific cereals, such as wheat.

There are interesting differences in the aggregate patterns between African and non-African recipients. For Africa as a whole, food aid has increased steadily from 1971 to the mid-1980s, while for the rest of the developing world, after a sharp fall in the early 1970s, it remained remarkably stable during this time. In the late 1980s food aid to Africa fell noticeably, while it remained much more stable for the rest of the developing world. Even today, the amount of food aid shipped to African countries remains well below the levels that existed during the Cold War. Importantly, this decline in food aid does not correspond to a similar decline in poverty within Africa during the period, which suggests that other factors are responsible for the significant decline in food aid.

Figures 5.3 and 5.4 report the origins of food-aid shipments to African and non-African recipients. From the figures, it is clear that the vast major-

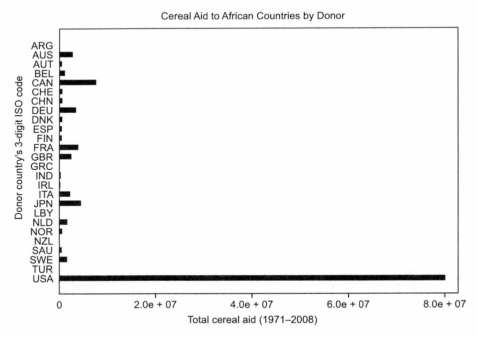

Fig. 5.3   **Total cereal aid shipped to African countries between 1971–2008, by donor**

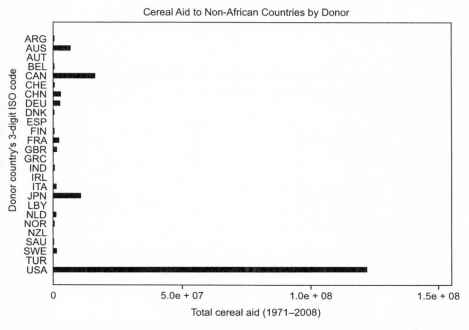

Fig. 5.4   Total cereal aid shipped to non-African countries between 1971–2008, by donor

ity of food aid is from the United States. Canada, Australia, and Japan are also significant suppliers of aid to both African and non-African countries.

Next, we turn to an overview of the recipient countries within Africa. The total amount of food aid received during our sample period by each African country is shown in figures 5.5 and 5.6. Figure 5.5 shows the countries with the largest food-aid receipts and figure 5.6 shows the countries with the smallest food-aid receipts. Note the difference in scales for the two figures.

From the figures, it is clear that Egypt has been by far the largest recipient of food aid. It is followed by Ethiopia, Sudan, Morocco, and Mozambique. The identity of recipient countries within Africa makes clear the fact that aid is often (or typically) not given to the most needy. Egypt, the largest beneficiary of food aid, has per capita income that is well above the average for the rest of Africa.

5.4   Determinants of Food Aid in Africa and the Rest of the World

We now turn to an examination of the determinants of food aid, focusing both on the supply side (donor-specific factors) as well as on the demand side (recipient-specific factors). We also consider historical bilateral determinants of food aid.

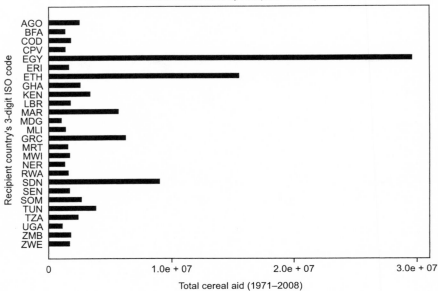

Fig. 5.5   The largest African recipients of total cereal aid (1971–2008)

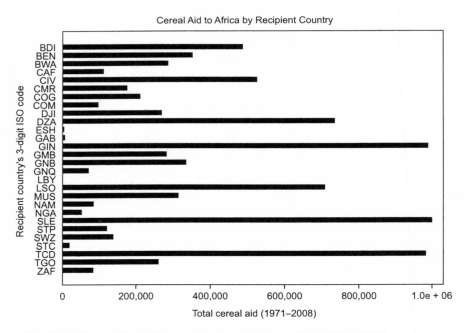

Fig. 5.6   The smallest African recipients of total cereal aid (1971–2008)

Our empirical analysis examines variation in cereal food-aid shipments from donor countries to recipient countries every year between 1971 and 2008. Let d denote donor countries, r recipient countries, and t years. Further, let $\ln y_{d,r,t}$ denote the natural log of the total amount of cereal aid (measured by weight) shipped from donor country d to receiving country r in year t. Our estimating equations take the following form:

$$(1) \qquad \ln y_{d,r,t} = \alpha_d + \alpha_r + \alpha_t + \beta_1 X_{d,r} + \beta_2 X_{r,t-1} + \beta_3 X_{d,t-1} + \varepsilon_{d,r,t}.$$

Our specification includes donor fixed effects α_d, recipient fixed effects α_r and time-period fixed effects $\alpha\alpha_t$. The equation includes the following determinants of food-aid shipments: lagged recipient production of cereals denoted $X_{r,t-1}$, lagged donor production of cereals $X_{d,t-1}$, and historical connections between donor and recipient countries $X_{d,r}$. In practice, when examining donor and recipient production, we will consider various lag structures.

Since the dependent variable in equation (1) is the natural log of food-aid shipments, countries with zero aid flows in a particular period are omitted from the sample. Therefore, our coefficients capture the correlation between the independent variables of interest and the amount of food aid shipped, conditional on food aid being shipped. In other words, our estimates capture the intensive margin only, and not the extensive margin. Our estimates do not provide any evidence on the determinants of whether donors ship any food aid to recipient countries in a particular year.

5.4.1   Recipient Country Cereal Production

The first determinant we examine is food production in recipient countries. Since the stated purpose of most food aid is for humanitarian relief, we expect that food-aid shipments will be greater to countries after they have a production shortage in their country. A priori, the expected delay between domestic production and food-aid receipts is not clear. For example, if food aid can respond immediately, then we would expect a contemporaneous relationship between domestic production and food aid. If instead food aid responds more slowly, then we would expect production to affect food-aid receipts with a one- or two-year lag.

We test for a contemporaneous effect and one-year and two-year lagged effects of domestic production on food aid. Domestic production is measured as the natural log of domestic production, measured in metric tons (MT). The data are from FAOSTAT.

Estimates are reported in table 5.1. The results in column (1) show that when countries have lower production in a period, then food-aid receipts increase that period and in the following period. There is also evidence of a response two years later, but this effect is not statistically significant. These results provide evidence that food aid does respond to recipient country production shocks. Looking at African and non-African recipients separately

Table 5.1   **Responsiveness of food aid to recipient production**

	Dependent variable: ln cereal aid		
	All recipient countries (1)	African recipient countries (2)	Non-African recipient countries (2)
ln recipient cereal production (*t*)	−0.187**	−0.221**	−0.064
	(0.080)	(0.111)	(0.131)
ln recipient cereal production (*t* − 1)	−0.151*	−0.161*	−0.163
	(0.083)	(0.09)	(0.135)
ln recipient cereal production (*t* − 2)	−0.082	−0.090	−0.106
	(0.076)	(0.090)	(0.138)
Recipient country fixed effects	Yes	Yes	Yes
Donor country fixed effects	Yes	Yes	Yes
Year fixed effects	Yes	Yes	Yes
Observations	11,692	6,886	4,805

Notes: The OLS estimates are reported with two-way clustered standard errors in brackets (by year and by recipient country). The unit of observation is a donor-recipient country pair in a year between 1971 and 2008. Recipient production is measured in metric tons and food-aid shipments are measured in tonnes Both variables are from FAOSTAT.
***Significant at the 1 percent level.
**Significant at the 5 percent level.
*Significant at the 10 percent level.

(columns [2] and [3]), we find some differences. Food aid appears to respond much more strongly to the adverse production shocks of African countries relative to non-African countries. One explanation for this is that negative production shocks are much more likely to result in loss of life in Africa, where a larger proportion of the population is at or near subsistence consumption. Therefore, the international community is much more responsive to these shocks.

The responsiveness of food aid to domestic production provides evidence that a portion of food aid is indeed driven by humanitarian motives. Because both production and food aid are measured in logs, the estimates provide the elasticity of food aid with respect to recipient production. The 0.22, 0.16, and 0.09 elasticities for African countries in the three years following a shock are large. They suggest that for African countries, food aid does provide some insurance against negative production shocks.

We examine how this responsiveness varies by donor country. Motivated by the finding in table 5.1 that contemporaneous and one-year lags of recipient production are important, we examine the responsiveness of food aid in period *t* to recipient production in periods *t* and *t* −1. We allow the estimated impact to differ by donor country. The estimation results are reported in table 5.2. Each row of the table reports the coefficient and standard error of the relationship between recipient cereal production and food-aid ship-

Table 5.2   **Responsiveness of food aid to recipient production by donor**

All countries			African countries			Non-African countries		
Country	Coefficient	SE	Country	Coefficient	SE	Country	Coefficient	SE
Libya	−0.408	0.262	Libya	−0.452	0.288	Greece	−0.553	0.159
Austria	−0.320	0.048	New Zealand	−0.383	0.145	Libya	−0.551	0.109
New Zealand	−0.285	0.084	Austria	−0.359	0.061	Saudi Arabia	−0.497	0.304
Belgium	−0.278	0.057	Argentina	−0.300	0.086	Turkey	−0.319	0.113
Saudi Arabia	−0.269	0.084	Turkey	−0.287	0.090	Italy	−0.306	0.079
Italy	−0.262	0.059	Belgium	−0.286	0.073	Switzerland	−0.253	0.072
Netherlands	−0.258	0.061	Spain	−0.281	0.089	Netherlands	−0.253	0.085
Turkey	−0.253	0.079	Switzerland	−0.280	0.069	Belgium	−0.249	0.076
Switzerland	−0.251	0.053	Italy	−0.263	0.078	Austria	−0.246	0.078
Spain	−0.245	0.067	Ireland	−0.261	0.080	Sweden	−0.242	0.067
Ireland	−0.242	0.060	Netherlands	−0.256	0.077	France	−0.226	0.074
Greece	−0.238	0.062	Greece	−0.250	0.078	Ireland	−0.220	0.108
Sweden	−0.228	0.056	Norway	−0.248	0.086	Argentina	−0.202	0.073
Norway	−0.224	0.062	Sweden	−0.244	0.077	Spain	−0.201	0.074
France	−0.218	0.052	Saudi Arabia	−0.243	0.077	Great Britain	−0.183	0.073
Germany	−0.217	0.052	Austria	−0.242	0.077	Germany	−0.178	0.066
Finland	−0.206	0.063	Finland	−0.239	0.080	Denmark	−0.174	0.103
Denmark	−0.201	0.058	Germany	−0.238	0.073	Finland	−0.165	0.081
Argentina	−0.200	0.061	Denmark	−0.232	0.078	Norway	−0.156	0.082
Great Britain	−0.189	0.055	France	−0.231	0.071	China	−0.149	0.132
Japan	−0.180	0.053	Japan	−0.229	0.075	USA	−0.133	0.063
Austria	−0.169	0.056	China	−0.208	0.089	Canada	−0.122	0.074
China	−0.154	0.079	India	−0.200	0.083	Japan	−0.113	0.061
India	−0.145	0.065	Great Britain	−0.182	0.069	Austria	−0.112	0.067
USA	−0.125	0.053	USA	−0.146	0.074	India	−0.106	0.095
Canada	−0.123	0.057	Canada	−0.125	0.080	New Zealand	−0.023	0.089

ments from a donor country. The reported country coefficients are ordered from the largest estimated impact to the smallest. The results are reported separately for all recipients, African recipients, and non-African recipients.

A clear pattern emerges. First, the coefficients are negative for all countries, which suggests that, in general, aid is more likely to go to countries soon after they experience adverse production shocks. Second, the results show that the food aid provided by large cereal-producing countries like Canada, China, and the United States respond most weakly to domestic production. This is consistent with the finding in Nunn and Qian (2011) that food-aid shipments—at least for the United States—are driven not only by need in receiving countries, but also by donor-country supply considerations. We consider this possibility explicitly later in this study.

Comparing the results for African and non-African aid recipients, several interesting patterns emerge. The overall ranking of the responsiveness of donor countries is broadly similar. For example, Libya is always among the most responsive and the United States of America, Canada, India, and China are always among the least responsive. However, there are some stark differences. For example, while aid from New Zealand and Austria is very responsive to African-recipient production shocks (coeff = –0.38 and –0.36), they are very unresponsive to non-African-recipient production shocks (coeff = –0.02 and –0.11).

5.4.2   Donor-Specific Determinants of Food Aid

One reason that may explain why for some countries aid is less responsive to the needs of recipient country production is that aid may also be driven by objectives of the donor country that are unrelated to recipient production. We investigate two such possible objectives.

Donor Cereal Production

First, we explore the role that production shocks in donor countries may play. Many of the rich donor countries implement policies that protect domestic agricultural prices. One way of doing this is to purchase "excess" domestic food production and give or sell it in faraway markets where it will not affect the prices of domestic producers. Barrett and Maxwell (2005) discuss such policies in his book on food-aid policy. Many of the largest food producers practice such policies.

The United States has perhaps been the most persistent practitioner of such policies under PL 480, which was established under the Eisenhower administration in 1954. President Kennedy renamed it the Food for Peace Program in 1962. It is comprised of three aid categories: Titles I, II, and III. Title I, which historically has been the most important component of food aid, is administered by the US Department of Agriculture (USDA) and provides low-interest loans to developing and transition countries for the purchases of US agricultural commodities. Title II aid is gifts of food from the US government for meeting emergency and nonemergency food needs. In recent years, emergency food needs have received much more resources than nonemergency food needs. The aid is often administered by non-governmental organizations (NGOs). Title III provides government-to-government grants to support long-term growth in developing countries and makes up a very small part of PL480 food aid (Kodras 1993).

We now examine whether domestic production shocks in the donor country are correlated with subsequent food-aid shipments. We continue to examine the year of the production shock and the two years that follow: t, $t + 1$, and $t + 2$. If domestic production shocks affect food-aid shipments, then this suggests that alternative factors—besides purely humanitarian considerations—also come into play when deciding food-aid shipments.

We begin by examining whether food-aid shipments from the United States are affected by US production shocks. This is motivated by the findings from Nunn and Qian (2011). Table 5.3 reports these estimates in columns (1)–(3). The unit of observation is a recipient country in a year. The estimates show that there is strong evidence of a positive cereal-production

Table 5.3   US production and US food aid

	In cereal aid			In wheat aid		
	All recipient countries	African recipient countries	Non-African recipient countries	All recipient countries	African recipient countries	Non-African recipient countries
	(1)	(2)	(3)	(4)	(5)	(6)
ln US production (t)	0.046	0.458	−0.381	−0.181	0.162	−0.419
	(0.024)	(0.156)	(0.378)	(0.303)	(0.434)	(0.431)
ln US production ($t-1$)	−0.059	0.188	−0.305	0.202	0.234	0.193
	(0.238)	(0.290)	(0.364)	(0.323)	(0.410)	(0.464)
ln US production ($t-2$)	0.534	1.000***	0.071	1.293***	1.300***	1.286***
	(0.270)	(0.341)	(0.361)	(0.302)	(0.353)	(0.440)
Recipient country fixed effects	Yes	Yes	Yes	Yes	Yes	Yes
Year trend	Yes	Yes	Yes	Yes	Yes	Yes
Observations	2,684	1,394	11,844	1,749	700	1,049

Notes: The OLS estimates are reported with two-way clustered standard errors in brackets (by year and by recipient country). The unit of observation is a donor-recipient country pair in a year between 1971 and 2008. US production is measured in metric tons and food-aid shipments are measured in tonnes (t). Both variables are from FAOSTAT.

***Significant at the 1 percent level.

**Significant at the 5 percent level.

*Significant at the 10 percent level.

shock increasing the supply of cereal aid two years later if the recipient country is African.

Columns (4)–(6) of table 5.3 report estimates looking specifically at wheat, which comprises the vast majority of US food aid (Nunn and Qian 2011). With wheat, a similar relationship is found. A positive wheat-production shock increases the amount of wheat aid given to African countries two years later. For wheat we also find an almost identical effect for non-African countries. For both, the elasticity is about 1.3. This suggests a very strong relationship between US production and food-aid shipments. Note that the estimates shown here illustrate that US food aid is driven by US production, consistent with the argument from Nunn and Qian (2011). However, the estimates from the two studies are not directly comparable because Nunn and Qian (2011) estimate a different specification; they exploit both time variation in US production and cross-sectional variation in the likelihood of receiving any US food aid.

Table 5.4 reports the same estimates, but for all other donor countries. The findings show that for non-US donors, there is no relationship between domestic cereal production and cereal-aid shipments. This is true whether or not the recipient country is African.

Taken together, the results of tables 5.3 and 5.4 provide evidence that the United States is the only donor that systematically determines its food aid amounts based on its own domestic production.

Table 5.4   **Production and food aid (non-US donors)**

	Dependent variable: ln cereal aid		
	All recipient countries (1)	African recipient countries (2)	Non-African recipient countries (3)
ln donor cereal production (t)	−0.016	0.016	−0.010
	(0.167)	(0.159)	(0.211)
ln donor cereal production ($t-1$)	−0.066	−0.091	−0.036
	(0.152)	(0.158)	(0.208)
ln donor cereal production ($t-2$)	0.047	0.016	0.080
	(0.145)	(0.168)	(0.172)
Recipient country fixed effects	Yes	Yes	Yes
Donor country fixed effects	Yes	Yes	Yes
Year fixed effects	Yes	Yes	Yes
Observations	12,018	7,001	5,017

Notes: The OLS estimates are reported with two-way clustered standard errors in brackets (by year and by recipient country). The unit of observation is a donor-recipient country pair in a year between 1971 and 2008. Donor cereal production is measured in metric tons and food-aid shipments are measured in tonnes (t). Both variables are from FAOSTAT.

***Significant at the 1 percent level.

**Significant at the 5 percent level.

*Significant at the 10 percent level.

Table 5.5   **The importance of colonial ties**

	Dependent variable: ln cereal aid		
	All recipient countries (1)	Africa recipient countries (2)	Non-African recipient countries (3)
Former colony indicator	0.245**	0.370***	−0.144
	(0.104)	(0.126)	(0.189)
Same colonizer indicator	0.489***	0.441***	0.558***
	(0.114)	(0.148)	(0.167)
Recipient country fixed effects	Yes	Yes	Yes
Donor country fixed effects	Yes	Yes	Yes
Year fixed effects	Yes	Yes	Yes
Observations	12,170	7,114	5,056

Notes: The OLS estimates are reported with two-way clustered standard errors in brackets (by year and by recipient country). The unit of observation is a donor-recipient country pair in a year between 1971 and 2008.

***Significant at the 1 percent level.
**Significant at the 5 percent level.
*Significant at the 10 percent level.

Donor-Recipient Colonial Ties

We also investigate the role of former colonial ties. The importance of colonial links through historical channels has been emphasized by recent influential studies such as Acemoglu, Johnson, and Robinson (2001). We argue that colonial history can continue to matter through contemporary channels if it affects the relationship between two countries today. We ask whether colonial heritage matters for the pattern of food-aid shipments. To test for this, we include in our estimating equation two indicator variables. The first equals 1 if the donor country is a former colonial "master" of the recipient country. An example is Britain and Ghana. The second equals 1 if the donor country and the recipient country are former colonial "brothers"—that is, both are former colonies of a European country. An example would be the United States and Nigeria, which were both colonies of Britain.

Estimation results are reported in table 5.5. As shown in column (1), colonial heritage matters. Food-aid shipments are greater if either the donor was a former colonizer of the recipient or if the two countries shared a similar colonizer. Interestingly, the latter effect is statistically larger in magnitude than the former effect.

We find stark differences between former colonies within and outside of Africa. The estimates in columns (2) and (3) show that both sets of countries are more likely to receive aid from a donor that was a colonial brother (relative to a country with no colonial ties). However, only African countries receive more aid from their former colonial masters. This is interesting because it suggests that former colonial ties are much more important in

African economies. This likely reflects the fact that African colonies more recently gained independence relative to other former colonies.

It is possible that colonial ties not only affect the level of food aid shipped from donor to recipient country, but also the responsiveness of aid to recipient needs. This would occur, for example, if colonial ties facilitated greater concern by the donor country for the recipient country or if ties resulted in better infrastructure that increase the flow of information regarding a production fall and/or the physical transportation of food aid in response to that fall. We test for such effects by returning to our examination of the responsiveness of food-aid shipments to recipient production, but allowing for the relationship between donor shipments and recipient production shocks to differ depending on the colonial history of the pair.

The results are reported in table 5.6. To simplify the exposition of the interpretation of the results, we examine the average of the natural log of production in periods $t-1$ and t instead of production in periods $t-2, t-1$, and t. (The conclusions from the estimates are qualitatively identical if one considers production in the three periods separately.) We then interact domestic production with the two colonial indicator variables to allow differential responsiveness by colonial history. We also include both indicator variables directly in the estimating equation.

Table 5.6   **Colonial ties and food-aid responsiveness**

	Dependent variable: ln cereal aid		
	All recipient countries (1)	African recipient countries (2)	Non-African recipient countries (3)
ln recipient production $(t,t+1)$	−0.404***	−0.451***	−0.312**
	(0.107)	(0.146)	(0.132)
ln recipient cereal production $(t,t+1)$ × former colony indicator	−0.003	0.047**	−0.047
	(0.044)	(0.022)	(0.109)
ln recipient cereal production $(t,t+1)$ × same colonizer indicator	0.165***	0.153**	0.147***
	(0.047)	(0.063)	(0.049)
Former colony, same colonizer indicators	Yes	Yes	Yes
Recipient country fixed effects	Yes	Yes	Yes
Donor country fixed effects	Yes	Yes	Yes
Year fixed effects	Yes	Yes	Yes
Observations	11,755	6,914	4,841

Notes: The OLS estimates are reported with two-way clustered standard errors in brackets (by year and by recipient country). The unit of observation is a donor-recipient country pair in a year between 1971 and 2008. Recipient production is measured in metric tons and food-aid shipments are measured in tonnes (t). Both variables are from FAOSTAT.

***Significant at the 1 percent level.

**Significant at the 5 percent level.

*Significant at the 10 percent level.

The results show that for all recipient countries, aid is less responsive to local production shocks when it comes from colonial brothers. For African countries, food-aid shipments are less responsive to recipient shocks from both former colonial masters and brothers. These results suggest that although former colonial ties result in more aid being given, that aid is not targeted to relieve the pressures from production shocks.

5.5   Conclusions

The determinants and consequences of foreign aid have come under significant amounts of scrutiny and criticism in recent years. For example, the first three articles in the *CATO Journal* in 2009 were about the fallibility of aid. Food aid is central to foreign aid, as it is obviously meant for humanitarian purposes and has historically been the most important component of foreign aid. Its humanitarian intent is explicit. For example, US president John F. Kenney named the US food-aid program *Food For Peace*. In this descriptive chapter, we provide evidence consistent with the observations of concerned policymakers: food aid is partly determined by humanitarian purposes and partly determined by objectives that are unrelated to the needs of the recipient countries, such as colonial ties and other policy objectives of the donor countries.

In addition, we show three striking new facts. First, food aid flows from the largest donors, such as the United States, are the least responsive to the production of recipients. Second, former colonial ties are an important determinant for food-aid receipt, but this increased aid is less responsive to donor need. It does not appear successful at reaching those that need it most or reaching them when it is needed. In addition, the importance of colonial ties appears to be different for African and non-African countries, reflecting perhaps the differences in time since independence of the two groups. All countries are more likely to get aid from their former colonial brothers. But only African countries are also more likely to get food aid from former colonial masters. Finally, aid due to former colonial ties is less responsive to food production falls in recipient countries than other aid, especially for African countries.

These findings strongly support the recent concerns of policymakers and observers that food aid is not being allocated to fulfill its primary purpose, which is to alleviate hunger. They also open up several questions. For example, what roles do former colonial links play in development through contemporary channels? And perhaps more importantly, what are the barriers to more effective targeting of aid? Is it a lack of intent (or the presence of other objectives) for donor countries—that is, is it political? Or are there other barriers such as the transmission of information, transport, or effective delivery within the recipient countries? These are all important avenues for future research.

References

Acemoglu, Daron, Simon Johnson, and James A. Robinson. 2001. "The Colonial Origins of Comparative Development: An Empirical Investigation." *American Economic Review* 91:1369–401.

Bardhan, Pranab. 1997. "Method in the Madness? A Political-Economy Analysis of the Ethnic Conflicts in Less Developed Countries." *World Development* 25:1381–98.

Barrett, Christopher B., and Daniel G. Maxwell. 2005. *Food Aid after Fifty Years: Recasting Its Role*. London: Routledge.

Kirwan, Barrett, and Margaret McMillan. 2007. "Food Aid and Poverty." *American Journal of Agricultural Economics* 89 (5): 1152–60.

Knack, Stephen. 2001. "Aid Dependence and the Quality of Governance: Cross-Country Empirical Tests." *Southern Economic Journal* 68:310–29.

Kodras, Janet. 1993. "Shifting Global Strategies of US Foreign Food Aid, 1955–1990." *Political Geography* 12 (3): 232–46.

Levinsohn, James, and Margaret McMillan. 2007. "Does Food Aid Harm the Poor? Household Evidence from Ethiopia." In *Globalization and Poverty*, edited by A. Harrison, 561–98. Chicago: University of Chicago Press.

Nunn, Nathan, and Nancy Qian. 2011. "Aiding Conflict: The Unintended Consequences of US Food Aid on Civil War." Working Paper, Harvard University and Yale University.

Pedersen, Karl. 1996. "Aid, Investment and Incentives." *Scandinavian Journal of Economics* 98 (3): 423–37.

Perlez, Jane. 1992. "Somalia Aid Workers Split on Troops." *New York Times*, November, p. A14.

Quisumbing, Agnes R. 2003. "Food Aid and Child Nutrition in Rural Ethiopia." FCND Discussion paper no. 158, International Food Policy Research Institute.

Thurow, Roger, and Scott Kilman. 2009. *Enough: Why the World's Poorest Starve in an Age of Plenty*. New York: Public Affairs.

Uvin, Peter. 1998. *Aiding Violence: The Development Enterprise in Rwanda*. West Hartford, CT: Kumarian Press.

Yamano, Takashi, Harold Alderman, and Luc Christiaensen. 2005. "Child Growth, Shocks, and Food Aid in Rural Ethiopia." *American Journal of Agricultural Economics* 87:273–88.

6

International and Intranational Market Segmentation and Integration in West Africa

Jenny C. Aker, Michael W. Klein, and
Stephen A. O'Connell

6.1 Introduction

What muffles, or amplifies, the voice of the Walrasian auctioneer? This question is of more than theoretical interest since a common policy goal is fostering market integration, especially across international borders. The welfare benefits of policies that succeed in integrating cross-border markets are likely to be greater in low-income countries, especially the landlocked countries of sub-Saharan Africa, than in industrial countries. But can government policies like tariff reductions actually increase market integration in the presence of political or social barriers that impede trade? Can regional investments in transport infrastructure help create unified markets in the face of corruption at the border? Put more simply, do borders pose a significant challenge to market integration in sub-Saharan Africa? Or does the Walrasian auctioneer have as clear and loud a voice across countries in sub-Saharan Africa as elsewhere?

Jenny C. Aker is associate professor of development economics at the Fletcher School at Tufts University. Michael W. Klein is the William L. Clayton Professor of International Economic Affairs at the Fletcher School at Tufts University and a research associate of the National Bureau of Economic Research. Stephen A. O'Connell is the Gil and Frank Mustin Professor of Economics at Swarthmore College.

A significantly revised and updated version of this chapter, using new data, new econometric techniques, and with a new coauthor (Muzhe Yang) was published in the *Journal of Development Economics* (March 2014: vol. 107, 1–16.). This research was partially funded by the National Bureau of Economic Research (NBER) Africa Project. We would like to thank participants at seminars at the Center for Global Development, National Bureau of Economic Research (NBER), Northeast Universities Development Economic Conference (NEUDC), Université de Clermont-Ferrand, and University of Gottingen for their helpful comments and suggestions. All errors are our own. For acknowledgments, sources of research support, and disclosure of the author's or authors' material financial relationships, if any, please see http://www.nber.org/chapters/c13438.ack.

Answers to these questions that are based on the volume of trade are mixed. Foroutan and Pritchett (1993) show that the level of trade among African countries is actually higher than that predicted by a gravity model. But other research suggests that intra-African trade is too low, due to internal political tensions and mismanagement of economic policies (Longo and Sekkat 2004). Oyejide, Elbadawi, and Collier (1997) observe that competing national priorities have repeatedly undermined formal attempts at regional integration in Africa, while Azam (2007) stresses the role of informal trade in arbitraging the cross-border price differences created by divergent national trade policies.

In this chapter, we address the impact of political borders on intra-African trade by focusing on prices rather than trade volumes.[1] We consider prices of two staple grains (millet and sorghum) and one cash crop (cowpeas) in markets in Niger and Nigeria. We look at price dispersion in cross-border markets as compared to price dispersions in different markets within the same country. This follows the strand of empirical literature that compares price dispersion in spatially separated markets in industrial countries. Results in that literature show that price dispersion is larger when, conditional on distance, two markets are on either side of an international border than when they are in the same country. The seminal contribution by Engel and Rogers (1996), and subsequent work on other industrialized countries, such as the United States and Japan (Parsley and Wei 2001) and EU countries (Crucini, Shintani, and Tsuruga 2010; Crucini, Telmer, and Zachariadis 2005), has consistently found a relatively large border effect.[2]

In this chapter, we show that there is a statistically significant border effect, that is, conditional price dispersion is higher between a market in Niger and Nigeria than between two markets in Niger, or two markets in Nigeria. But this border effect is much lower than what has been found for industrial countries. Furthermore, we also show that the border effect is lower if the cross-border markets share a common ethnic profile, while the effect of ethnicity is to raise conditional price dispersion between two ethnically distinct

1. Border effects in low-income countries have not been the subject of much research, partly due to the lack of high-frequency data on narrowly defined goods. Cross-border comparisons have typically been restricted to a small number of locations and over a limited time period. Daubrée (1995) compares the prices of a range of consumer goods between Niamey (the capital of Niger), Maradi (Niger), and Kano (Nigeria), and finds tighter comovements between Maradi and Kano than between Maradi and Niamey. Oyejide, Ogunkola, and Bankole et al. (2005) compare prices for markets within Nigeria with those in between the capitals of Niger, Togo, and Benin, and finds suggestive evidence of a border effect. Araujo-Bonjean, Aubert, and Egg (2008), use a vector autoregression model to estimate integration of millet prices between countries within the CFA zone (Niger, Mali, and Burkina Faso), and find a statistically significant border effect.

2. As discussed in more detail below, Gorodnichenko and Tesar (2009) have shown that these estimates overstate the border effect when they do not take into account underlying differences in price heterogeneity between countries.

markets in Niger. We also show that the presence of mobile phones mitigates the international border effect, which extends the intra-Niger results in Aker (2010) to an international setting.

The results presented here offer a positive message with regard to ongoing efforts to integrate West African economies. These countries have attempted to foster trade and economic integration through a system of monetary and trade unions such as the West African Economic and Monetary Union (or UEMOA), a customs and monetary union created in 1994 that shares a common currency (the CFA franc) and a common external tariff.[3] The UEMOA is also part of the Economic Community of West African States (ECOWAS), a regional integration initiative created in 2001 among all West African states. More specifically for the two countries studied in this chapter, the National Boundary Commission of Nigeria and a Nigeria–Niger Joint Commission (NNJC) have convened transborder workshops to address issues of cross-border trade. Our results with respect to the effect of the border on price dispersion suggest the positive potential of these efforts.

The rest of the chapter is structured as follows. Section 6.2 provides a context for our analysis by discussing some relevant characteristics of Niger, including the establishment of its international border with Nigeria and the geographic nature of its ethnic divisions. Section 6.3 describes the data we use and provides some preliminary statistics. Section 6.4 present an analysis of the international border effect based on conditional distributions, while section 6.5 analyzes the market-pair data using regressions. Section 6.6 presents the results for internal borders. We offer some conclusions in section 6.7.

6.2 Niger and Its Trade

Niger is a large, sparsely populated, landlocked country in West Africa. The majority of its population consists of rural subsistence farmers who depend upon rain-fed agriculture as their main source of food and income. It is one of the poorest countries in the world. It was ranked last on the United Nations' 2009 Human Development Index.

The primary trading partner of Niger is its southern neighbor, Nigeria, a coastal country that has the largest population in Africa. The 1,500 km border between Niger (a former French colony) and Nigeria (a former British colony) was established by the French and the British in 1906. The border separated the Hausa, Zarma, Fulani, and Kanuri ethnic groups between the two countries. As shown in figure 6.1, the border drawn by the colonial powers also created a Niger that included eight ethnic groups (Hausa, Songhai/

3. The CFA franc was created in 1945, and was devalued in 1948 and 1994 (changing the relative value of the CFA franc to the French franc). The current CFA franc is pegged to the euro.

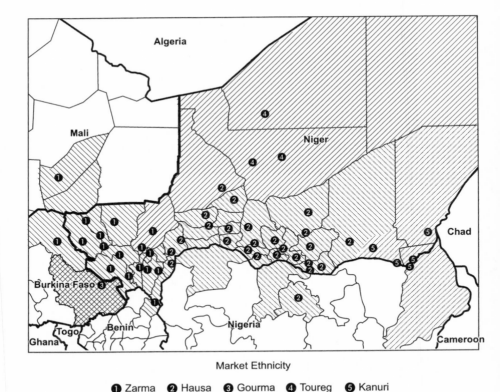

Market Ethnicity

❶ Zarma   ❷ Hausa   ❸ Gourma   ❹ Toureg   ❺ Kanuri

Fig. 6.1   International borders and ethnic groups in Niger and northern Nigeria

Notes: A map of the ethnic and international borders for Benin, Burkina Faso, Mali, Niger, and Nigeria. Created from the authors' household and trader-level data collected between 2005 and 2007, as well as secondary data for markets in Burkina Faso and Mali.

Zarma, Toureg, Fulani, Kanuri, Arab, Toubou, and Gourmantche) which were, for the most part, situated in geographically distinct regions of the country.[4]

The border between Niger and Nigeria was porous and haphazardly patrolled at the time the two countries achieved independence in 1960. Smuggling was a major economic activity.[5] Trade between the two countries was primarily in agropastoral products such as grains, legumes, and livestock (Collins 1976), but "unofficial traders" also brought petroleum and farm-chemical products into Niger (Charlick 1991). There have been

4. A map of Nigeria in 1957–1958 (not shown) also suggests that the geographic location of ethnic groups in Niger and Nigeria seems to be time invariant, as it is similar to the ethnographic maps for 2008.

5. Azam (2007) provides an analytical treatment of the determinants of illegal cross-border trade in the region.

efforts since the early 1970s to harmonize the relationship between the two countries and remove official obstacles to trade. Currently, both countries are members of ECOWAS.

The sample period studied in this chapter is 1999–2007. There were no official trade restrictions or border closings during this time (although there had been border closings in 1983 and 1986, linked to political instability in Nigeria). There are, however, other possible sources of costs of trade between these countries. Nigerien-Nigerian trade could be hampered by costs due to delays, harassment, or banditry. Furthermore, trade between these two countries could be impeded by costs associated with changing currencies between the Communauté Financière Africaine (CFA) franc of Niger and the Nigerian naira. There are also linguistic differences, both between the official languages of Niger and Nigeria (French and English, respectively), and in local languages in different regions of each country.

6.3   Data

The motivation for using prices in different locations to test for the presence of an international border is straightforward; if borders impose costs that undermine trade, then, conditional on distance between markets and other location-specific factors, price differences between markets located in different countries should be larger than those between markets in the same country. Thus our analysis requires both price data and other data used to control for distances between markets and location-specific features in Niger and Nigeria.

The analysis in this chapter uses a data set that draws on both primary and secondary sources in Niger and Nigeria. The price data consist of monthly observations of prices of two grains (millet and sorghum) and a cash crop (cowpeas) over a nine-year period (1999–2007) across forty-eight domestic and cross-border markets.[6] Each of these commodities is produced and consumed in both countries, is heavily traded on an annual basis, and is fairly homogeneous in terms of quality.

Time-series data on gas prices, mobile phone coverage, rainfall, road quality, trade flows, district population levels, mobile phone rollout and coverage, and the official naira-CFA exchange rate were also collected. In addition to these time series, we employ data on the latitude and longitude of each market, the location of the international border, and the road distances between market pairs. These series enable us to calculate the distance to the international and internal border of each market in the data set, as well as the Euclidean distances and actual road distances between market pairs.

6. Grain prices were collected by Niger's agricultural marketing information system, which converted prices in Nigerian markets into CFA using the CFA/naira exchange rate of that day. We do not have access to the original price data in naira, nor to the daily CFA/naira exchange rates used for the price conversion.

Our analysis also uses a unique panel survey of traders, farmers, transporters, and market resource persons collected in Niger by Aker between 2005 and 2007. The survey data draw on interviews with 415 traders and 205 farmers located in thirty-five markets and forty villages across six geographic regions of Niger, as well as in five Nigerian markets. A census of all grain traders was conducted in each market, in which traders and market-resource persons who participated in the survey provided detailed information about their demographic and socioeconomic background and commercial operations. These data allow us to construct measures of the ethnolinguistic fractionalization (ELF) for each market, village, and region, to identify ethnic "borders," and to measure the number of traders operating in these markets over time.

Table 6.1 presents summary statistics for markets located within a 150 km

Table 6.1   **Comparison of observables by country (Niger-Nigeria)**

Observables	Unconditional mean		Difference in means
	Mean (s. d.)	Mean (s. d.)	Difference (s. e.)
A. Market-pair-level data	**Niger-Niger**	**Nigeria-Nigeria**	
Distance between markets (km)	375.29(207)	369(271)	6.29(65)
Road quality between markets	.37(.49)	.6(.52)	–.22(.16)
Mobile phone coverage (2007)	.89(.32)	.6(.52)	.29*(.16)
Transport costs between markets (CFA/kg)	12.35(6.72)	12.19(6.67)	.16(.22)
B. Market-level data	**Niger**	**Nigeria**	
Millet price level (CFA/kg)	124.33(33)	112.96(31)	11.37***(1.83)
Sorghum price level (CFA/kg)	119(36)	104(34.8)	14.35***(2.04)
Cowpea price level (CFA/kg)	173(56)	176 (56)	–3.21(3.36)
Ethnic composition of traders			
Hausa	.58(.51)	.8(.447)	–.21(.21)
Zarma	.29(.464)	0	.29***(.096)
Kanuri	.08(.27)	.2 (.447)	–.12(.19)
Road quality to market	.71(.46)	.75(.5)	.041(.25)
Market size	105.08(90)	176.75(149)	–71.66(69)
Mobile phone coverage (2007)	.95(.020)	.8(.447)	.158(.19)
Drought between 1999 and 2007	.027(.162)	.025(.156)	.002(.007)
Urban center(> = 35,000)	.35(.49)	0.8 (.45)	.45*(.21)

Notes: Data are from secondary sources and the Niger trader survey collected by Aker. In panel A, "Niger" market pairs are pairs where both markets are located in Niger; "border" market pairs are those pairs where both markets are located in a border country (Nigeria, Benin, Burkina Faso). In panel B, "Niger" markets are those that are located within Niger (150 km from the international border), whereas "border" markets are those markets located outside of Niger (but within 150 km of the border). Huber-White robust standard errors clustered by market-pair month (panel A) and by market month (panel B) are in parentheses. Prices are in CFA francs, deflated by the Nigerien Consumer Price Index. The Kolmogorov-Smirnov test tests for the equality of the distribution functions.

***Significant at the 1 percent level.

**Significant at the 5 percent level.

*Significant at the 10 percent level.

radius of the Niger-Nigeria border. In general, prices for staple grains (millet and sorghum) are higher in Niger than in Nigeria, with a statistically significant difference between the two. This is consistent with the direction of trade between the two countries, with Niger importing grains from Nigeria. By contrast, cowpea prices are lower in Niger; while the difference is not statistically significant, the point estimate is as expected since Niger primarily exports to Nigeria. We do not reject the equality of means or distributions for most other observable characteristics, with the exception of mobile phone coverage and the prevalence of the Zarma ethnic group. However, the difference in mobile phone coverage as of 2007 is only statistically significant at the 10 percent level. In addition, the Nigerian markets in our sample are only located in the Hausa region of that country, and none are in Nigeria's Zarma region.[7]

6.4 Analysis of Distributions

Our first analysis of the international border effect for markets in Niger and Nigeria uses the data described above to construct kernel distributions for conditional price differences across countries and within countries. We estimate regressions of the form:

$$(1) \qquad \left| \ln\left(p^i_{jt} / p^i_{kt} \right) \right| = \beta_0 + \beta_1 X_{jkt} + \theta_t + \alpha_{jk} + \varepsilon_{jkt},$$

where p^i_{jt} and p^i_{kt} are the CFA franc prices of good i in markets j and k at time t, deflated by Niger's consumer price index. The regressors in this specification include X_{jkt}, a vector of observable characteristics that affect price dispersion between two markets, including transport costs between markets j and k at time t, a dummy variable that equals 1 if one and only one of the two markets is urban, and another dummy variable that equals 1 if one and only one had a drought at time t. The variable $\theta\alpha_t$ represents time fixed effects. In some specifications market-pair fixed effects, α_{jk}, are also included. Separate regressions are run for market pairs within each country, and also for cross-border pairs. We plot a kernel distribution of the residuals ε_{jkt} from each regression, to examine relative conditional deviations from the Law of One Price.

Figures 6.2A, 6.2B, and 6.2C present the kernel distributions of ε_{jkt} from a regression of equation (1) for millet, sorghum, and cowpeas, respectively, for the entire 1999–2007 period. Each of these three figures includes the kernel distribution for the residuals of a regression using intra-Niger market pairs, a regression using intra-Nigeria market pairs, and a regression using cross-border (Niger-Nigeria) market pairs. Visual inspection of the

7. While members of the Zarma ethnic group live within Nigeria, they represent a small percentage of the population (approximately 88,000 people, or less than .0007 percent) and are geographically focused in the far northwestern region of the country, on the border with Benin and Niger (the Birin n'Kebbi region).

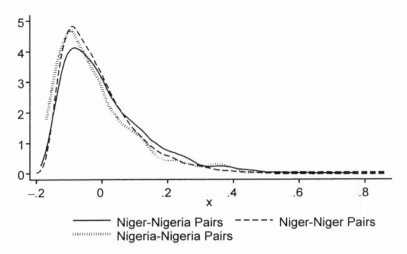

Fig. 6.2A Kernel distributions of millet, sorghum, and cowpeas for Niger and Nigeria (1999–2006), ln price difference for intranational and cross-border pairs: Millet pairs < 300 km: Residuals on ln(transport costs), urban, drought

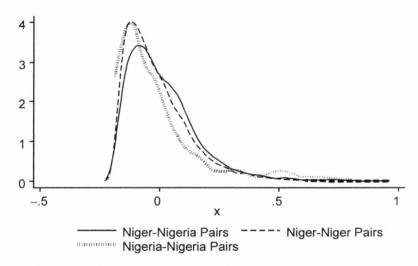

Fig. 6.2B Kernel distributions of millet, sorghum, and cowpeas for Niger and Nigeria (1999–2006), ln price differences for intranational and cross-border market pairs: Sorghum pairs < 300 km: Residuals on ln(transport costs), urban, drought

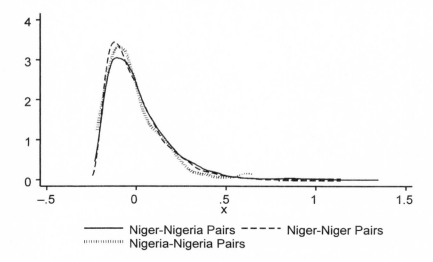

Fig. 6.2C   **Kernel distributions of millet, sorghum, and cowpeas for Niger and Nigeria (1999–2006), ln price differences for intranational and cross-border market pairs: Cowpeas pairs < 300km: Residuals on ln(transport costs), urban, drought**

kernel distributions suggests that the underlying volatilities of market-pair price differentials are similar across countries for grains and cowpeas. The distributions show a modest horizontal displacement across countries, suggesting that even if there is a statistically significant border effect, it may not be economically important.

These cross-sectional results, however, may mask differences across time. In particular, we are interested in investigating whether exchange rate movements between the naira and CFA franc alter relative prices, which would be consistent with a lack of full-market integration across the international border. There was a strong appreciation of the CFA franc relative to the naira between 1999 and 2001 and 2002 and 2004.[8] If cross-border markets were not well integrated, we would expect to see increases in the price of millet, sorghum, and cowpeas in Niger relative to those in Nigeria during these periods.[9]

To investigate conditional price dispersion over time, we estimate equation (1) for cross-border pairs separately for three marketing years (1999/2000, 2000/2001, and 2001/2002) using the observed price differences (rather than absolute values, as above) between Niger and Nigeria for millet, sorghum, and cowpeas, and plot the kernel distributions of the residuals from these

8. There was a 16 percent appreciation of the CFA against the naira between 1999 and 2001.
9. Gopinath et al. (2009) find that relative costs of similar goods in Canada and the United States closely track the exchange rate.

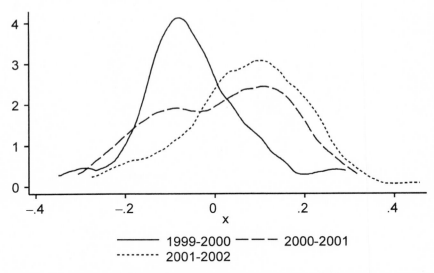

Fig. 6.3A   Kernel distributions for Niger-Nigeria market pairs by year (1999–2001), ln P(Niger) – ln P(Nigeria): Millet residuals on drought, distance < 100 km

regressions in figures 6.3A, 6.3B, and 6.3C. Figures 6.3A and 6.3B show a rightward shift in the distributions of millet and sorghum, respectively, between 1999/2000 and 2000/2001, the period during which there was an appreciation of the CFA/naira exchange rate. This suggests that relative prices follow the CFA franc-naira exchange rate, which could reflect a lack of market integration. A more formal test of market integration is offered by the regression analysis presented in the next section.

6.5   Regression Analysis

In this section we present a more precise analysis of the border effect, following the method of an early and influential contribution to this literature, Engel and Rogers (1996). They compare price dispersion for fourteen categories of goods among 228 market pairs (each pair represents two cities in the United States, two cities in Canada, or one in the United States and the other in Canada) through regressions with the specification:

$$(2) \qquad \sigma_{ij} = \beta_1 \ln\left(d_{ij}\right) + \beta_2 B_{ij} + \sum_{m=1}^{N} \gamma_m D_m + \varepsilon_{ij}$$

where σ_{ij} is a measure of price dispersion between cities i and j, d_{ij} is the distance between these cities, B_{ij} equals 1 if cities i and j are in different countries and 0 otherwise, and D_m is a set of city-specific dummy variables.

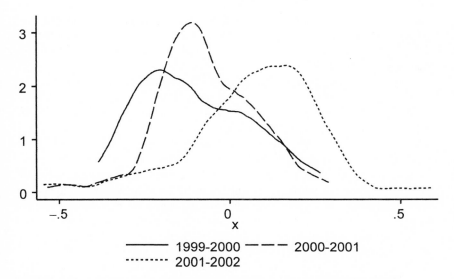

Fig. 6.3B   Kernel distributions for Niger-Nigeria market pairs by year (1999–2001), ln P(Niger) – ln P(Nigeria): Sorghum residuals on drought, distance < 100 km

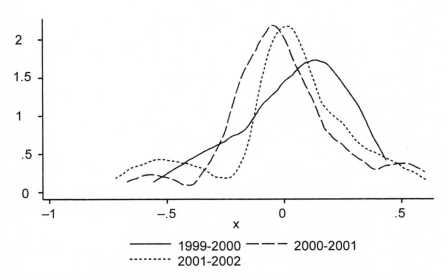

Fig. 6.3C   Kernel distributions for Niger-Nigeria market pairs by year (1999–2001), ln P(Niger) – ln P(Nigeria): Cowpeas residuals on drought, distance < 100 km

The estimated coefficient β_2 represents the conditional change in price dispersion between two cities due to the fact that they are in different countries. The estimated border effect, that is, the distance-equivalent effect of the border, is $exp(\beta_1 / \beta_2)$.

Engel and Rogers find strikingly large effects of the international border on price dispersion; one estimate puts the distance-equivalent effect at over 70,000 km. Other research reports similar magnitudes for border effects between industrial countries. But Gorodnichenko and Tesar (2009) show that differences in underlying price volatility in two countries can result in an upwardly biased estimate of the border effect, since comparing cross-country pairs of prices reflects both differences in underlying price variability in one of the countries as compared to the other as well as the costs associated with crossing the border between the countries. They demonstrate that the inclusion of a dummy variable for pairs of locations within one country can result in very different estimates than those obtained when including a dummy variable for pairs of locations in the other country, if there are wide differences in price volatility across the two countries. For example, with the Engel and Rogers data, the estimated distance-equivalent border effect based on a specification that includes a Canada-Canada fixed effect is 47 km while the one based on a specification that includes a United States-United States fixed effect is 108 million km.

The Gorodnichenko and Tesar effect might be expected to be less of a concern for our analysis than for that of Engel and Rogers since, as shown in figures 6.2A, 6.2B, and 6.2C, the distribution of absolute price differences for Niger-Niger pairs differs very little from the distribution for Nigeria-Nigeria pairs. As will be shown, this conjecture is supported by a comparison of border effects between regressions that include a dummy variable for Niger-Niger pairs and those that use a dummy variable for Nigeria-Nigeria pairs.

To implement the Engel-Rogers approach, we estimate a version of equation (1) with a dummy variable for cross-border market pairs,

$$(3) \qquad \left| \ln(p_{jt}^i / p_{kt}^i) \right| = \beta_1 B_{jk} + \beta_2 X_{jkt} + \sum_{m=1}^{N} \gamma_m D_m + \theta_t + \varepsilon_{jkt}$$

where B_{jk} and D_m are defined as above, X_{jkt} is a vector of variables that might affect price dispersion between two markets, such as drought, road quality, transport costs, and other time-varying factors, and θ_t is a vector of monthly fixed effects. One version of this specification does not include a binary variable for country-specific pairs. In light of the Gorodnochenko-Tesar critique, we estimate two additional versions, one containing an indicator variable that equals 1 if both locations in the pair are in Niger, and the other containing an indicator variable that equals 1 if both locations in the pair are in Nigeria.

Table 6.2 shows the results of the regressions that take the form of equation (3). There is a separate panel for each of the three commodities. Column

Table 6.2 **Estimated international border effects**

Dependent variable: ln(Pit/Pjt)	Millet				Sorghum				Cowpeas			
	(1)	(2)	(3)	(4)	(1)	(2)	(3)	(4)	(1)	(2)	(3)	(4)
Niger-Nigeria border	.026***	.026***	.026***	.020***	.023***	.021***	.024***	.024***	.029***	.029***	.029***	.023***
	(.002)	(.002)	(.002)	(.003)	(.003)	(.003)	(.003)	(.003)	(.003)	(.003)	(.003)	(.003)
Transport costs	.045***	.045***	.045***	.045***	.036***	.036***	.036***	.036***	.063***	.063***	.063***	.063***
	(.002)	(.002)	(.002)	(.002)	(.003)	(.003)	(.003)	(.003)	(.003)	(.003)	(.003)	(.003)
Drought dummy	.004	.004	.004	.004	.046***	.045***	.045***	.046***	-.040***	-.040***	-.040***	-.036***
	(.007)	(.007)	(.007)	(.007)	(.011)	(.011)	(.011)	(.011)	(.009)	(.009)	(.009)	(.009)
Urban status	-.009***	-.009***	-.009***	-.009***	-.008***	-.008***	-.008***	-.008***	-.009***	-.009***	-.009***	-.011***
	(.001)	(.001)	(.001)	(.001)	(.002)	(.002)	(.002)	(.002)	(.002)	(.002)	(.002)	(.002)
Niger market		.002				.001						
		(.008)				(.011)						
Nigeria market			-.002				-.001				-.006	
			(.008)				(.011)				(.010)	
Cell phone coverage				-.005**				-.015***				-.030***
				(.002)				(.003)				(.003)
Border * cell phone coverage				.020***				.008				.004
				(.004)				(.005)				(.007)
Market-pair fixed effects	No	No	No	No	No	No	No	No	No	No	No	No
Monthly time dummy	Yes	Yes	Yes	Yes	Yes	Yes	Yes	Yes	Yes	Yes	Yes	Yes
No. of observations	21,460	21,460	21,460	21,460	15,662	15,662	15,662	15,662	20,421	20,421	20,421	20,421
R-squared	0.0797	0.0797	0.0897	0.0801	0.1081	0.1081	0.1081	0.1091	0.1036	0.1036	0.1036	0.1097
Joint effect of border and interaction				.040**				.032***				.027***
				(.004)				(.005)				(.006)

Notes: Data are from secondary sources and the Niger trader survey collected by Aker. Additional covariates include the presence of drought, mobile phone coverage, and urban status. All regressions are clustered by month to correct for spatial dependence between markets over time.

***Significant at the 1 percent level.

**Significant at the 5 percent level.

*Significant at the 10 percent level.

(1) of each panel shows that the international border is associated with a statistically significant increase in price dispersion for each of the three commodities, contributing a 2.6 percent increase in price dispersion for millet, a 2.3 percent increase for sorghum, and a 2.9 percent increase for cowpeas. The magnitude and statistical significance of the border effect is robust to the inclusion of a binary variable that identifies Niger-Niger market pairs (column [2] in each panel) and another that identifies Nigeria-Nigeria market pairs (column [3] in each panel), suggesting that country-specific differences in price dispersion are not driving our results.[10]

The border effect could arise for a number of reasons. One reason is associated with the difficulty in obtaining timely information on prices across an international border. Aker (2010) has shown that, within Niger, the advent of mobile phone coverage led to a reduction in price dispersion. Does the same effect hold across the Niger-Nigeria border?

Evidence presented in column (4) of each panel shows that the mobile-phone effect does, in fact, hold internationally, as well as within countries. Column (4) augments the basic specification (in column [1]) with two binary variables. The first binary variable is equal to 1 if both markets have mobile phone coverage at time t, and is otherwise 0. The second is an interaction of the mobile phone coverage variable with the border dummy variable. In this specification, the excluded category is internal markets that do not have mobile phone coverage. The coefficient on the border dummy variable therefore represents the border effect for markets that cannot communicate by mobile phone (because at least one of the markets is not covered by mobile phone service), while the coefficient on the mobile phone coverage variable represents the effect of mobile phone coverage on internal market pairs. The border effect for market pairs that can communicate by mobile phone is given by the sum of the coefficients on the border dummy variable and the interaction variable.

The estimates presented in column (4) of each panel of table 6.2 show that mobile phone coverage is associated with a statistically significant decrease in price dispersion across internal markets for all three commodities.[11] Although mobile phones reduce price dispersion for internal market pairs, the border still "matters" for all commodities, even between markets that can communicate by mobile phone, since the joint effect of the border dummy variable and the interaction term remains positive and statistically significant. Not surprisingly, the border effect remains significant for market pairs that cannot communicate by mobile phone, again for all three com-

10. As discussed by Gorodnichenko and Tesar (2009), it is impossible to include the border dummy variable and both market-pair dummy variables because of multicollinearity. The results presented in this table are all robust to the use of dyadic standard errors.

11. Aker (2010) finds the introduction of mobile phones was associated with a negative and statistically significant reduction in price dispersion across millet markets within Niger, and that this effect was the strongest for markets located between 200 and 550 km apart.

modities, as shown by the positive and significant coefficients on the border dummy variable in the column (4) estimates.

6.6   Price Dispersion across Ethnic Regions in Niger

There has been a growing interest recently in economic research investigating the role that ethnic or cultural diversity can play in explaining socioeconomic outcomes. A number of empirical studies have found that ethnic diversity is associated with lower growth rates (Easterly and Levine 1997), more corruption (Mauro 1995), lower contributions to local public goods (Alesina, Baqir, and Easterly 1999), and lower participation in groups and associations (Alesina and La Ferrara 2000). In this section, we contribute to this stream of research by investigating whether ethnic diversity creates "internal borders" to trade, and hence market segmentation.

The process through which borders were established in West Africa resulted in multiple ethnic groups within Niger, as noted above. Also, as mentioned earlier, these ethnic groups generally live in geographically distinct regions of the country. We focus on two of the major ethnic groups in Niger, the Hausa and the Zarma, and consider whether there is a statistically significant and economically meaningful "border" between the regions they inhabit in Niger.

We identify the Hausa and Zarma regions of Niger through the use of both secondary and primary data on the ethnic composition of geographic locations within the country. We use the degree of ethnic diversity across locations to locate the ethnic Hausa/Zarma border as a linear spline running roughly south to north that separates two geographic locations with a low degree of ethnic diversity (i.e., a strong majority of Hausa or Zarma). Markets on the "border" are omitted from the analysis; they have a higher degree of ethnic diversity, that is, a more even mix between Hausa and Zarma, than markets on either side of the border.[12]

Having identified an intra-Niger ethnic border, we now analyze its economic consequences for price dispersion using the two methods employed above to study the effects of the Niger-Nigeria border. We begin with a graphical analysis. Figures 6.4A, 6.4B, and 6.4C show the kernel distributions of the ε_{jkt} of a specification like equation (1) but with a distinction between the Hausa and Zarma regions of Niger rather than the countries of Niger and Nigeria. In this case, the distinction is made between Hausa-Hausa market pairs in Niger, Zarma-Zarma market pairs in Niger, and

---

12. The measure of ethnic diversity used almost universally in the empirical literature is the index of ethnolinguistic fractionalization (ELF), which is a decreasing transformation of the Herfindahl concentration index. In particular, if we consider a society composed of K ≥ 2 different ethnic groups and let p_k indicate the share of group k in the total population, the resulting value of the ELF index is given by $1 - \Sigma(p_k)^2$. Thus, a lower value of the ELF index indicates a higher degree of ethnic homogeneity.

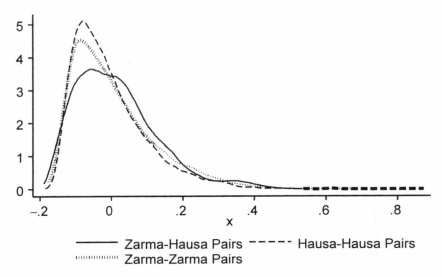

Fig. 6.4A   Kernel distributions for Zarma and Hausa market pairs. Absolute ln price differences: Millet, intra-Niger, < 300km: Residuals on ln(TC), urban, drought

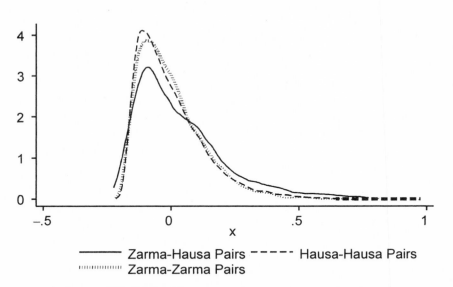

Fig. 6.4B   Kernel distributions for Zarma and Hausa market pairs. Absolute ln price differences: Sorghum, intra-Niger, < 300 km: Residuals on ln(transport costs), urban, drought

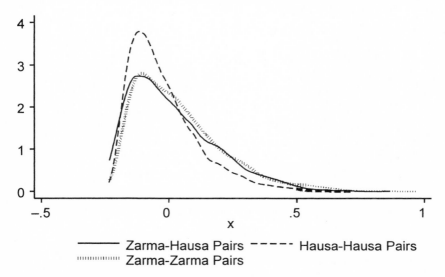

Fig. 6.4C   Kernel distributions for Zarma and Hausa market pairs. Absolute ln price differences: Cowpeas, intra-Niger, < 300 km: Residuals on ln(transport costs), urban, drought

cross-ethnic-border pairs that include one location in the Hausa region of Niger and the other in the Zarma region. These kernel distributions suggest that the underlying price dispersions for millet, sorghum, and cowpeas in each region are similar but, unlike the kernel distributions for Niger-Nigeria market pairs, the distribution of price dispersion between Zarma and Hausa markets seems markedly different than the distributions for intra-Hausa and intra-Zarma market pairs. This suggests that the internal Hausa-Zarma border may have greater consequences for price dispersion within Niger than the Nigerian border does for price dispersion between the two countries.

Regression estimates confirm this impression. The three panels of table 6.3 present the regression estimates of equation (3) for each commodity although, in this case, the sample only includes market-pair data from the Hausa and Zarma regions of Niger and the "border" represents the intra-Niger division between these two regions. These regression results show that this internal border is associated with a positive and statistically significant increase in price dispersion for each commodity. Column (1) of each panel shows that the internal ethnic border between the Hausa and Zarma regions is significant for all three commodities. The magnitude of this intranational ethnic border effect exceeds that of the international border effect in all cases; the estimated ethnic border effect is more than double the international border effect for millet, more than 60 percent larger for cowpeas, and

Table 6.3 Estimated internal border effects

Dependent variable: $|\ln(P_{it}/P_{jt})|$	Millet				Sorghum				Cowpeas			
	(1)	(2)	(3)	(4)	(1)	(2)	(3)	(4)	(1)	(2)	(3)	(4)
Hausa-Zarma border	.056*** (.006)	.061*** (.006)	.043*** (.006)	.052*** (.007)	.026*** (.003)	.024*** (.003)	.037*** (.004)	.026*** (.003)	.047*** (.006)	.060*** (.006)	.018*** (.01)	.037*** (.01)
Transport costs	.041*** (.003)	.040*** (.003)	.040*** (.003)	.040*** (.003)	.053*** (.002)	.052*** (.002)	.052*** (.002)	.052*** (.002)	.060*** (.003)	.060*** (.003)	.060*** (.003)	.060*** (.003)
Drought dummy	.009 (.011)	.011 (.010)	.011 (.010)	.009 (.011)	.022** (.010)	.022** (.010)	.022** (.010)	.022** (.002)	-.024** (.003)	-.023** (.011)	-.023** (.011)	-.024** (.003)
Urban status	-.006*** (.011)	-.006*** (.010)	-.006*** (.010)	-.006*** (.011)	.009*** (.010)	.009*** (.010)	.009*** (.010)	.022** (.010)	-.007** (.011)	-.023** (.011)	-.023** (.011)	-.024** (.011)
Hausa market	-.018*** (.002)	-.018*** (.002)	-.006*** (.002)	-.006*** (.002)	.009*** (.002)	.009*** (.002)	.009*** (.002)	.009*** (.002)	-.007** (.002)	-.007** (.002)	-.007** (.003)	-.006** (.002)
Zarma market		-.018*** (.002)	.018*** (.002)			.012*** (.003)	.012*** (.003)			-.041*** (.003)	.041*** (.003)	-.044*** (.004)
Cell phone coverage				-.012*** (.003)				-.017*** (.003)				.052*** (.014)
Border * cell phone coverage				-.012*** (.003)				.004 (.005)				-.044*** (.004)
Constant				.019 (.016)				.030*** (.004)				.052*** (.014)
Market-pair fixed effects	No	No	No	No	No	No	No	No	No	No	No	No
Monthly time dummy	Yes	Yes	Yes	Yes	Yes	Yes	Yes	Yes	Yes	Yes	Yes	Yes
No. of observations	10,829	10,829	10,829	10,829	26,262	26,262	26,262	26,262	13,195	13,195	13,195	13,195
R^2	0.0873	0.0935	0.0935	0.0844	0.2362	0.2362	0.2362	0.2371	0.1176	0.1329	0.1329	0.1248
Joint effect of border and interaction				.071*** (.014)				.030*** (.004)				.090*** (.012)

Notes: Data are from secondary sources and the Niger trader survey collected by Aker. Cell phone dummy = 1 in period t when both markets have cell phone coverage, 0 otherwise. Drought dummy = 1 in period t when one market in a pair has rainfall less than or equal to two standard deviations below its average rainfall level during the rainy season, or fifteen consecutive days without rainfall during the rainy season, 0 otherwise. Urban status = 1 if one market in a pair is an urban center ($>=$ 35,000 people), 0 if both or neither are urban centers. Regressions include all market pairs no more than 250 km apart. All prices are in CFA francs deflated by the Nigerien Consumer Price Index.

***Significant at the 1 percent level.

**Significant at the 5 percent level.

*Significant at the 10 percent level.

more than 10 percent larger for sorghum. As with the estimates presented in table 6.2, the significance of these results is robust to the inclusion of region-specific fixed effects for intra-Hausa (column [2]) and intra-Zarma (column [3]) market pairs, although the value of the effect is sensitive to the inclusion of these fixed effects in the case of cowpeas. This is consistent with the visual inspection of the kernel distributions in figure 6.4C, which suggested that the underlying price dispersion for cowpeas differed considerably in intra-Hausa and intra-Zarma regions.

Mobile phone coverage diminishes price dispersion within regions. In all three panels in table 6.3, the coefficient on the mobile phone coverage variable is significant and negative, suggesting that mobile phones reduce price dispersion within the Hausa region and within the Zarma region (Aker 2010). The magnitude of this reduction is notable, and equal to 1.2 percent for millet, 1.7 percent for sorghum, and 4.4 percent for cowpeas. But there is less evidence that the reduction in price dispersion occurs across markets on either side of the internal ethnic border: the joint effect of the mobile phone dummy variable and the interaction term is negative and statistically significant for sorghum. While this suggests that mobile phones are less useful across ethnic regions than within them, the result may be confounded to some degree with a nonlinear effect of distance. The cross-border market pairs in these regressions are less than 250 km apart, and Aker (2010) found that mobile phones reduced price dispersion primarily for medium-haul markets, namely, those between 200 and 500 km apart. The joint effect of the border and interaction term, capturing the impact of the internal border on markets connected by mobile phones, remains positive and statistically significant for all specifications.

We might be concerned about potential bias due to correlation between the internal border effect and unobserved covariates. The lower panel of table 6.4 tests for the equality of means of market-level covariates on either side of the internal border. We fail to find evidence of a statistically significant difference for most market-level covariates, including market size, the frequency of drought, road quality, distance between markets, and urban status. The notable exception is mobile phone coverage, with a strong statistically significant difference between the two groups.

6.7   Conclusion

This chapter began by asking whether international market integration is feasible in sub-Saharan Africa. We find evidence of an international border effect between Niger and Nigeria, but the magnitude of this effect is much smaller than that found in industrialized countries. Thus, the border does not pose a deep threat to the success of existing regional economic commissions that have attempted to foster cross-border trade, even when two countries do not share a common currency. These results suggest that the

Table 6.4   Comparison of observables by ethnicity (within Niger)

Observables	Unconditional mean		Difference in means
	Mean (s. d.)	Mean (s. d.)	Unconditional s. e.
A. Market-pair-level data	**Hausa-Hausa**	**Zarma-Zarma**	
Distance between markets (km)	234.08(134)	216.42(161)	17.66(21.54)
Road quality between markets	.43(.49)	.41(.49)	.02(.07)
Cell phone coverage	.81(.39)	.98(.12)	−.17***(.03)
Transport costs between markets (CFA/kg)	8.08(4.34)	7.54(5.06)	.53***(.07)
B. Market-level data	**Hausa**	**Zarma**	
Millet price level (CFA/kg)	123.23(30)	139.01(32)	−15.77***(1.56)
Sorghum price level (CFA/kg)	112.84(32)	134.82(36)	−21.98***(1.90)
Cowpeas price level (CFA/kg)	162.58(48.97)	197.94(55)	−35.37***(2.60)
Road quality to market	.87(.35)	.6(.52)	.28(.21)
Market size	107.63(86)	70.1(50)	37.53(34.43)
Cell phone coverage (2007)	.43(.50)	.35(.48)	.08***(.02)
Drought between 1999–2007	.031(.174)	.031(.174)	−.0000(.008)
Urban center(> = 35,000)	.5(.53)	.4(.52)	.1(.25)

Notes: Data are from secondary sources and the Niger trader survey collected by Aker. In panel A, "Hausa" market pairs are pairs where both markets are located in Hausa regions of Niger, and "Zarma" market pairs are pairs where both markets are located in the Zarma region of Niger. In panel B, "Hausa" markets are markets with a majority of Hausa traders within Niger, and "Zarma" markets are markets with a majority of Zarma traders within Niger. Huber-White robust standard errors are clustered by market-pair month (panel A), and market month (panel B) are in parentheses. All prices are CFA francs deflated by the Nigerien Consumer Price Index. The Kolmogorov-Smirnov test tests for the equality of the distribution functions.
***Significant at the 1 percent level.
**Significant at the 5 percent level.
*Significant at the 10 percent level.

Walrasian auctioneer can be heard across the Niger-Nigeria border. Her voice carries especially well within her ethnic community, or with the aid of a mobile phone.

References

Aker, Jenny C. 2010. "Information from Markets Near and Far: The Impact of Mobile Phones on Agricultural Markets in Niger." *American Economic Journal: Applied Economics* 2 (3): 46–59.

Alesina, Alberto, R. Baqir, and William Easterly. 1999. "Public Goods and Ethnic Divisions." *Quarterly Journal of Economics* 114 (4): 1243–84.

Alesina, Alberto, and Eliana La Ferrara. 2000. "Participation in Heterogeneous Communities." *Quarterly Journal of Economics* 115 (3): 847–904.

Araujo-Bonjean, Catherine, Magali Aubert, and Jonhy Egg. 2008. "Commerce du Mil en Afrique de l'Ouest: Les Frontières Abolies?" Paper prepared for CERDI conference on "Intégration des Marchés et Sécurité Alimentaire dans les Pays en Développement," Université d'Auvergne, Clermont-Fd, France, November 3–4.

Azam, Jean-Paul. 2007. *Trade, Exchange Rate and Growth in Sub-Saharan Africa.* Cambridge: Cambridge University Press.

Charlick, Robert. 1991. *Niger: Personal Rule and Survival in the Sahel.* Boulder, CO: Westview Press.

Collins, D. J. 1976. "The Clandestine Movement of Groundnuts across the Nigeria-Niger Border." *Canadian Journal of African Studies* 10 (2): 259–76.

Crucini, Mario, Mototsugu Shintani, and Takayuki Tsuruga. 2010. "The Law-of-One-Price without the Border: The Role of Geography versus Sticky Prices." *Economic Journal* 120 (544): 462–80.

Crucini, Mario, Chris Telmer, and Marios Zachariadis. 2005. "Price Dispersion: The Role of Borders, Distance and Location." Working Paper, Vanderbilt University.

Daubrée, C. 1995. *Marchés Parallèles et Equilibres Economiques: Expériences Africaines.* Paris: L'Harmattan.

Easterly, William, and Ross Levine. 1997. "Africa's Growth Tragedy: Policies and Ethnic Divisions." *Quarterly Journal of Economics* 112 (4): 1203–50.

Engel, Charles, and John Rogers. 1996. "How Wide is the Border?" *American Economic Review* 86 (5): 1112–25.

Foroutan, Faezeh, and Lant Pritchett. 1993. "Intra-Sub-Saharan African Trade: Is It Too Little?" *Journal of African Economies* 2 (1): 74–105.

Gopinath, Gita, Pierre-Olivier Gourinchas, Chang-Tai Hsieh, and Nicholas Li. 2009. "Estimating the Border Effect: Some New Evidence." Working Paper no. 09-10, Federal Reserve Bank of Boston.

Gorodnichenko, Yuriy, and Linda Tesar. 2009. "Border Effect or Country Effect? Seattle May Not Be So Far from Vancouver After All." *American Economic Journal: Macroeconomics* 1 (1): 219–41.

Longo, Robert, and Khalid Sekkat. 2004. "Economic Obstacles to Expanding Intra-African Trade." *World Development* 32 (8): 1309–21.

Mauro, Paolo. 1995. "Corruption and Growth." *Quarterly Journal of Economics* 110 (3): 681–712.

Oyejide, T. A., I. Elbadawi, and P. Collier, eds. 1997. *Regional Integration and Trade Liberalization in Sub-Saharan Africa, Volume 1: Framework, Issue, and Methodological Perspectives.* London: McMillan.

Oyejide, T. A., E. O. Ogunkola, and A. Bankole. 2005. "Import Prohibition as a Trade Policy Instrument: The Nigerian Experience." In *Managing the Challenges of WTO Participation: 45 Case Studies*, edited by P. Gallagher, P. Low, and A. Stoler. Cambridge: Cambridge University Press.

Parsley, David, and Shang-Jin Wei. 2001. "Explaining the Border Effect: The Role of Exchange Rate Variability, Shipping Costs, and Geography." *Journal of International Economics* 55:87–105.

II

Country Studies

Cape Verde and Mozambique as Development Successes in West and Southern Africa

Jorge Braga de Macedo and Luís Brites Pereira

7.1 Introduction

The global financial crisis turned the risk of excluding African economies from globalization into the certainty that poverty would worsen in most of them. Prior to this crisis, however, Africa accompanied the trend of sustained growth evidenced by emerging economies. Primarily due to the implementation of adequate structural and macroeconomic policies, growth was the strongest in decades (African Economic Outlook [AEO], various issues; World Bank 2009). In sub-Saharan Africa, growth in the gross domestic product (GDP) increased from an average of 3.5 percent in 2000 to 5.7 percent by 2005 and Burkina Faso, Ethiopia, Mali, Mozambique, Tanzania, and Uganda, none of which is a major primary commodity producer, were able to post annual growth rates of over 5 percent in recent years (United Nations 2008).

Jorge Braga de Macedo is professor of economics and director of the Center for Globalization and Governance at Nova School of Business and Economics and a research associate of the National Bureau of Economic Research. Luís Brites Pereira is deputy director of the Center for Globalization and Governance at Nova School of Business and Economics.

We gratefully acknowledge support from the NBER Africa Project, without which our research would not have been possible. This version follows NBER Working Paper no. 16552, November 2010 (except for updating of references), and reflects presentations at the first research conference in Cambridge, Wits Business School, Banco de Moçambique, and Banco de Cabo Verde. We are thankful for comments and suggestions from participants and others, especially Manuel Cabral, Sebastian Edwards, Jeff Frankel, Ernesto Gouveia Gove, Philip Havik, John Luiz, Augusto Nascimento, Léonce Ndikumana, Joaquim Oliveira Martins, Francisco Queiró, Courtenay Sprague, and José Tavares. We also thank João Farinha, José Mário Lopes, Fábio Santos, João Silva, Manuel Melo, and Rita Borges for research assistance at CG&G. The usual disclaimer applies. For acknowledgments, sources of research support, and disclosure of the authors' material financial relationships, if any, please see http://www.nber.org/chapters/c13440.ack.

Indeed, the expansion, diversification, and deepening of trade and financial links between countries over several decades presented an unparalleled opportunity for some to raise their living standards and achieve the millennium development goals (MDG). Notwithstanding Africa's improved economic situation, absolute poverty was still widespread when unprecedented energy and food-price volatility brought worldwide expansion to a halt. Amid dire global economic prospects, growth-enhancing policies needed to be assessed against progress on MDG, including the global partnership on development and prospects for international cooperation.

The evidence suggests that development success under globalization is less a question of relative resource endowments or geographical location than in past waves of globalization. Market perception of the orientation and predictability of national economic policies, and the accompanying institutional arrangements, have proved to be decisive everywhere. The Asian crises of the mid-1990s showed that economic openness must be accompanied by good public- and private-sector governance in order for countries to take full advantage of globalization. Examples of the former include sound macroeconomic policies, unfailing transparency, stable and rational incentive frameworks, and robust financial systems coupled with effective supervisory and regulatory mechanisms.

Severe regulatory failures in developed countries, uncovered by the global crisis, confirmed that there is no universally applicable development model. Adequate governance responses to globalization thus become all the more important as globalization reduces national policy space and increases institutional and economic interdependence at various levels. At the same time, a more integrated global economic context necessarily demands greater policy and institutional coherence, as well the knowledge required to implement the associated reforms and monitor them through effective peer-review mechanisms.

To be sure, even among the highly integrated economies of the Eurozone, neither coherence nor knowledge were able to respond to the challenge posed by the global crisis. Nevertheless, regional economic cooperation remains a valid intermediate step toward the integration of developing countries into the world economy.[1] In addition to benefiting from regional economies of scale, their participation in reform programs within regional organizations also facilitates domestic authorities' work when implementing politically difficult measures. In the wake of the entry into force of the Lisbon treaty, the diverse perspectives of the twenty-seven European Union (EU) member states have at last found an institutional framework. Even though the financial challenges remain daunting for several highly indebted member states,

---

1. The implications of the financial crisis for international governance innovation and for the peer-review mechanism of the IMF for the G20 are contrasted with the Letter to Queen Elizabeth sent by the British Academy in Macedo (2011, 144, note 35; 2015).

especially those inside the Eurozone, alternatives to cooperative responses consistent with regional integration have not been found. Indeed, the success of the EU attests to the advantages among like-minded countries, where a combination of cultural proximity and mutual knowledge facilitated the deepening of the integration process from a free trade area to a single currency and the widening from the original six members through successive enlargements.

With respect to Africa, regional surveillance and peer pressure between the various partners have been set up and implemented over the last eight years: the African Peer Review Mechanism has involved thirty countries of which twelve have been examined.[2] Broader regional surveillance may help reduce the risks of macroeconomic slippage, resulting in a more stable, predictable environment—an essential factor for the private sector to flourish. Among French-speaking countries in West and central Africa (so-called CFA), particularly those pegged to the euro, surveillance has been a driving force of economic policy coordination and integration, even though in the 1980s enforcing the stability of the nominal exchange rate against the French franc led to unstable real effective exchange rates. The monetary allocation mechanism managed by the French Treasury kept the parity between the French franc and the CFA from 1948 until the devaluation of the latter in 1994, which led to a real depreciation in most members of the West African Monetary Union.[3] Their long experience with a monetary policy conducted by a strong institution that must preserve its independence vis-à-vis national governments has accustomed these countries to yielding some of their economic policy matters to a regional organization. In comparison to CFA-common institutions, those in the Economic Community of West African States ([ECOWAS], which includes Benin, Burkina Faso, Cape Verde, Côte d'Ivoire, Gambia, Ghana, Guinea, Guinea-Bissau, Liberia, Mali, Niger, Nigeria, Senegal, Sierra Leone, and Togo), and the Southern African Development Community ([SADC], which includes Angola, Botswana, Democratic Republic of Congo, Lesotho, Madagascar, Malawi, Mauritius, Mozambique, Namibia, Seychelles, South Africa, Swaziland, Tanzania, Zambia, and Zimbabwe) have not yet been effective constituencies for reform. If the ECOWAS and SADC secretariats (in Abuja, Nigeria, and Gabarone, Botswana, respectively) were to cooperate with the Commission

2. Macedo (2010) describes the implications of the crisis for international governance innovation and analyzes the peer-review mechanism of the IMF for the G20 drawing on Niels Thygesen's label on peer pressure by proxy at IMF and by commitment at EU. See also Macedo (2008). Five were examined from July 2002 to 2007, four in 2008, and AEO (2009, 75) expected six, but only three (including Mozambique) were carried out in 2009 (AEO 2010, 72) plus Mauritius in the 13th Forum in Kampala in late July. The effectiveness of mutual control devices reflects the extent to which cooperation overcomes collective action barriers and clears the ground for coherent reforms (Kanbur 2004).

3. Macedo (1986, 358) discusses the paradox of nominal stability and real instability in CFA countries.

for the African Union, or the local offices of global organizations such as the United Nations, the International Monetary Fund, and the World Bank, better interaction between globalization and governance would probably follow. With peer pressure, better information on the fifteen partners in each one of the subregions and beyond would probably be available, facilitating business development and a more active role for civil society.[4]

The idea of producing usable information from within a cooperative framework is what we mean by "mutual knowledge," a term used in a declaration on MDG approved at the 2006 summit of the Community of Portuguese-Speaking Countries (CPLP) held in Bissau.[5] Mutual knowledge is generally more limited and the data harder to compare outside of the Organisation for Economic Co-operation and Development (OECD), so that cooperation at the regional, subregional, and international levels may neither produce knowledge of effective policies or institutions nor create conditions for their implementation. In fact context adjusted, but also widely usable knowledge, only results from identifying an appropriate constituency for each set of related problems and challenges. Reaching the MDG in 2015, for example, presupposed sustained pro-poor economic growth in addition to better governance and more aid, but there were no immediately available recipes on how to bring about a positive interaction between globalization and governance.[6] In other words, alternatives to both the "one size fit all" and "each case is unique" development approaches are urgently needed in a context that cannot draw upon existing experiences of institutional cooperation that foster mutual trust and generate mutual knowledge. Under these circumstances, the quest for African development successes remains a policy as well as a research priority, especially acute in sub-Saharan Africa. In a nutshell, what is at stake for many African countries is how to ensure that current policy and institutional arrangements in the spheres of trade, finance, debt, investment, and technology mutually

4. Some of the group averages below exclude Nigeria and South Africa because their GDP weight is too large. The CPLP and NAFTA both have 1.4 members equivalent. See note 19 below.

5. Aside from five African countries (Angola, Cape Verde, Guinea-Bissau, Mozambique, and São Tomé e Príncipe), Brazil and Portugal are founding members, Timor Leste joined in 2001 and Equatorial Guinea in 2014, while Georgia, Japan, Mauritius, Senegal, and Turkey are associate members of CPLP (Macedo 2015). Macedo (2008) draws on a 2003 report for the OECD secretary general, using labels suggested by Niels Thygesen at an OECD Development Center seminar, such as peer pressure by proxy at IMF and by commitment at EU. Other useful references to work carried out along with the AEO report (produced since 2001) are in OECD (2003) and IICT (2007), the first comparative report on the 2006 Bissau declaration.

6. Bourguignon et al. (2008) underline the heterogeneity of country outcomes and the difficulty in finding patterns, even in fragile states. This heterogeneity is no surprise: to "develop a global partnership for development," the eighth MDG goal, reflects disappointment with the performance of developing countries that seemed to follow the policy recommendations of the "Washington consensus" during the 1990s. As governance improvements were not commensurate with the challenges of globalization, especially in what concerns financial markets, these countries faced recurrent financial crises that interrupted the long-term convergence process.

reinforce each other in support of equitable, rapid, and sustainable growth and development.

Against this background, we assess the extent to which Cape Verde and Mozambique may represent development successes in West and southern Africa. Specifically, we seek to identify lessons for successful governance based on meaningful regional comparisons of Cape Verde and Mozambique's development experience. These lessons will also be drawn from the study of the complementarity of economic policies and accompanying institutional arrangements bearing on trade, finance, and competitiveness. We realize the limitations that lack of data impose on this ambitious agenda but, in our view, identifying such lessons necessarily entails a broader scope of analysis than is usual. Moreover, by analyzing these countries in comparison with their neighbors we may also contribute toward greater mutual knowledge on economic development issues within CPLP and especially among the five Portuguese-Speaking African Countries (PALOP).

The emphasis on identifying the linkages between cultural, institutional, and economic factors that fostered growth and development remains in this chapter, organized as follows: Our interpretative framework, detailed in section 7.2, focuses on the interaction between globalization and governance, which may be positive or negative depending on the policies and accompanying institutional arrangements. Specifically, we hold that economic success under globalization entails, necessarily but not exclusively, positive market perceptions regarding outcomes such as export diversification and narrowing of the income gap with respect to the frontier. Success thus defined must, in turn, be underpinned by good governance and the freedoms that citizens and residents enjoy, which section 7.2 also discusses. Section 7.3, meanwhile, provides a historical and geographical perspective on Africa with comparisons in the subregion as well as PALOP. Section 7.4 estimates the factors that determine export diversification, measured by the number-equivalent Herfindahl index, and income-growth strategies in comparison to subregional averages. Section 7.5 offers a narrative of long-term development in Cape Verde and Mozambique with respect to foreign trade and economic growth and macroeconomic policy and financial reputation. Once again, policy and institutional reforms provide context for good governance indicators and progress toward the MDG in a separate subsection. The concluding section, 7.6, raises the issue of whether cooperative governance and peer-review mechanisms are capable of sustaining African development successes when due account is taken of the diversity of experiences evident from ECOWAS, SADC, and PALOP.

7.2   Interpreting How Globalization and Governance
Interact with Convergence

Policy and institutional responses must necessarily change as the nature of globalization itself changes. Indeed, different waves of globalization

Table 7.1   **Range of variable**

Political rights and civil liberties	Economic freedom
7 = maximum political rights 1 = minimum political rights	10 = maximum economic freedom 0 = minimum economic freedom

(fifteenth, nineteenth, and twentieth centuries, including the past decade) have interacted with different forms of governance responses. The interaction of globalization and governance is always context specific, as defined by space (geography) and time (history). In the wave since the 1990s, the context is captured by convergence, often measured as the gap in per capita income relative to the frontier, and by democracy, often measured in terms of electoral competition and political participation, but best understood by its constituent political and economic elements.[7] To enhance the quality of the democracy measure, we look at the index of political rights and of civil liberties published by Freedom House and at the indexes of economic freedom published by the Fraser Institute and the Heritage Foundation. The Freedom House Index defines democracy as a concept with attributes of political rights and civil liberties. Political rights include the right to vote, fair and free competition for the office, the presence of multiple parties, and decentralized political power. Civil liberties refer to the existence of a free press, open public discussion, and freedom of speech and assembly. The indices are ranked in table 7.1.

Since political rights and civil liberties are highly correlated, we replace them with the average of both (labeled *prcl* in appendix A). This composite indicator performed better in estimation and, in addition, it also had the advantage of being interpretable as an index of political freedom, given that it captures its two main constituent components. We also note that these measures must be used and interpreted with caution due to well-known issues, most of which derive from the process of index construction itself, as pointed out by Oman and Arndt (2006) and Luiz (2009), and that Fedderke, de Kadt, and Luiz (2001) applied an improved method to South Africa. Below we draw on Luiz, Pereira, and Oliveira (2013), which have computed indexes of political and economic governance for Mozambique over the last 100 years.

These caveats should be borne in mind when reading some of our results. Countries are rated according to two seven-point scales, with 1 being the highest score for both scales. The sum of the points obtained in the scales

7. Przeworski et al. (2000) and Garoupa and Tavares (2009) show that higher income increases the survivability of democracy, but they label a country as democratic if its governments are designated through elections in which more than one party competes and the winning party is not always the same. Persson and Tabellini (2006) introduce quality considerations through the concept of democratic capital. The age of democracy is labeled *demage* below.

classifies the country as free (2–5), partly free (6–10), or not free (11–14). The Freedom House Index dates from 1995 and includes data on ten components: business freedom, trade freedom, fiscal freedom, government spending, monetary freedom, investment freedom, financial freedom, property rights, freedom from corruption, and labor freedom. Each component is measured by various indicators and is assigned a grade in a scale of 0 to 100. The ten component scores are then averaged to give an overall economic freedom score for each country. Although the definition of economic freedom is quite vague, and consequently measuring it lacks some precision, the index gains relevance worldwide as several studies reveal that there is an important relationship between economic freedom and positive social and economic values such as per capita income, economic growth rates, human development, democracy, the elimination of poverty, and environmental protection. Political rights are associated with free and fair elections for the executive and legislative branches of power, freedom to constitute political parties, freedom of association, independence from political, religion, and military authorities, real possibilities of the change of power, and other related aspects of the political system. Key elements of civil liberties include freedom of thought, religion, association, free press, and respect for the rights of minorities. The concept of economic freedom is more difficult to define as it may relate only to private ownership, prices being determined by market forces, de jure and de facto entry and exit, efficient rule of law, and official economic regulation guaranteeing competition or also include the financial freedom brought about by currency convertibility, stability of money value, central bank independence, and deep financial markets. Furthermore, the widely used indexes include low taxes, a small share of government spending in GDP, and flexible labor markets, and this appears to some as too extensive a definition of economic freedom. Once again the Luiz, Pereira, and Oliveira (2013) index for Mozambique avoids some of these pitfalls by distinguishing carefully between the rules of the game and their outcomes.

Macedo (2001) reports that trade openness reduces perceived corruption, even after correcting for its endogeneity, and claims that this is the way in which globalization improves governance, given highly significant historical control variables (e.g., Protestant tradition, de facto democracy, and OECD membership). Eichengreen and Leblang (2006) find a two-way interaction between democracy and globalization over the entire 1870–2000 period, distinguishing trade from financial openness but measuring democracy as a dichotomous variable. By introducing the extension of suffrage, for example, a negative interaction between democracy and debt default has been found for the period of the classical gold standard, with a more than proportional effect in capital-poor countries. At the time, parliamentary democracies were seen as sources of financial stability, to the extent that the checks and controls on the sovereign implied a greater ability to tax.[8] This contradicts the widespread view that the repression of democracy facilitated the operation of the pre-1914 international monetary system by making external adjustment easier during the second wave of globalization. Over the period 1970–2004, the different types of freedom interact differently with the trade and financial globalization variables, and the interaction becomes more sensitive to regional context and to stages of national economic and institutional development.[9] Overall, allowing for the quality of democracy lowers the overall effect of globalization on democracy. One reason for this is the hypothesis that globalization's effects on democracy are mediated by slow-moving cultural values, which may, in turn, be associated with weaker constituencies for policy reform. This would imply that such variables might be accounted for by selecting groups of like-minded countries, like the OECD, for which the effect of globalization on freedoms would be stronger, but this would neglect the convergence dimension, more visible on a global scale. Eichengreen and Leblang (2006) also use a measure, "Age of Democracy" (labeled *demage* in appendix A), which counts for each country i at time t the number of uninterrupted years up to time t that country i has been democratic, that is, it measures the length of time a country has been a democracy, which is used in section 7.4. In addition, we employ data from the Political Regime Characteristics and Transitions (POLITY) project, which codes countries' level of democracy as a function of institutional rules.[10] This project is also the source of information on constitutional age. The POLITY project defines constitutional change as occurring either when there is a political transition or when the absolute value of the score changes by at least three points. This allows for constitutional changes in both democracies and dictatorships.

Given these measures, the mutual relationship between globalization, governance, and economic performance can be described along the following lines: a nation's resource endowments and its productivity determine how fast it can grow and the level of its economic well-being in terms of income per capita, both in absolute terms and relative to the income frontier. Feedbacks are possible: a richer country growing fast may invest more resources in scientific research and technology development and thus enjoy higher productivity levels than a poorer, slow-growing economy. Through trade, capital flows, or migration, globalization can influence the level of endowments available in an economy, or even, through international technology transfers, its productivity. Conversely a country's endowments of natural resources, labor, and capital, as well as its geographic location and efficiency of its production structures may determine how much it trades

8. Flandreau and Zummer (2004, 44) report an elasticity of 0.5 for the whole sample and of 1.3 for capital-poor countries.
9. Section 7.4 tests this result (reported in IICT 2007) on ECOWAS and SADC in the form of the diversification-convergence interaction.
10. See http://www.systemicpeace.org/polity/polity4.htm.

with the rest of the world in terms of goods, services, and assets. Similarly, a country with good governance, namely a democratic state with high-quality institutions, effective corruption-free accountable bureaucracies, and a flourishing civil society may likely increase the quality, if not the quantity, of its most important endowment: its own people. Once more, cause and effect can be swapped: well-endowed countries may evolve toward democratic forms of government more easily, or, at least, they may afford investing more resources to build well-functioning institutions.[11]

While these interactions have been at the core of economics, this has not been the case of the issue addressed in this section (how globalization and governance interact with convergence), perhaps because of the interdisciplinary nature of globalization waves and of governance innovation—even when the distance to frontier is not as fundamental as it is for Africa. With respect to the relative strengths of the links between the current wave of globalization, the benchmark measure of freedoms and convergence, the empirical findings of Macedo, Martins, and Pereira (2013) reveal that political rights and civil liberties had a significant impact in the run-up to the third wave of globalization, while feedbacks were somewhat weaker. As mentioned, further work is needed to understand the long-run dynamics and sustainability of this global system, in particular the mechanisms that could enforce or reinforce the expected positive effect of globalization on both convergence and freedoms. The particular interaction that involves democracy reflects historical, geographical, social, cultural, institutional, and economic factors and the method employed focuses on the economic aspect of this relationship. A complementary explanation of the interaction between globalization and governance can be based on the manner in which diversity, be it sociocultural or economic, is addressed by a given society.[12] This is taken up in the next section, with specific reference to the historical roots of CPLP in the first wave of globalization, associated with the Iberian maritime explorations of the fifteenth century.

The available empirical evidence regarding the relationship between economic growth and political regime is weak or inconclusive, as discussed in Kohli (1986), Remmer (1990), and Przeworski and Limongi (1993). In the case of Africa, it is not possible to establish a clear link between political regime and economic growth according to Young (1998), among others. However, the poor economic performance of many of its authoritarian

---

11. Bonaglia, Macedo, and Bussolo (2009). Transport technology also changes costs, sometimes dramatically, making them very different from distance, as documented by Feyrer (2009).

12. Indeed, one of the constants of human organization is the "absolute certainty that man will never be common, he will always de different, he will always give rise to diversity. And society, by managing this diversity, will manage prosperity and the creation of wealth" (Macedo 1996, 194). The same holds true, of course, for the case of political diversity and whether peace or conflict ensues. The distinct processes of colonization of the Americas is chosen to illustrate the importance of diversity and how it is managed as being a crucial determinant of the interaction between economic and political organization in Macedo et al. (2013).

regimes during the 1980s suggests that these failed to promote economic growth. Indeed, Maravall (1995) notes that "a strong case can be made that economic reforms are more likely to succeed in a democratic political context. Political pluralism generates more and better information to use in economic decision making; moreover, democratic institutions may reduce the transaction costs of economic reforms, as well as restrict predation of public resources." Looking at the Economic Freedom Index in sub-Saharan Africa, we see that it is not only the poorest but also the most economically repressed world region: no country belongs in the group of economically free countries, seven are listed in the mostly free group, twenty-eight in the mostly not free, and seven in the repressed group. More worrisomely, in the region, a decline in economic freedom is evident. Factors like corruption, excessive market regulation, or the size of the black market are among the reasons for such a poor result. Using the variables listed in appendix A, results presented in section 7.4 suggest that, in both West and southern Africa, economic convergence increases with political and economic freedom. Even though it warrants further investigation, the focus on the management of diversity as a determinant of positive interactions between globalization and governance pertaining to policy and institutional reform, is especially necessary in connection with Africa. In this case, the knowledge thereabout is certainly less "mutual" than with respect to other regions, even outside of the OECD.

7.3   History and Geography

7.3.1   World Regions

Three "regions" (North America, EU, ASEAN + China, Korea, Japan) each account for one-fourth of world GDP. Africa is in the "rest of the world," which includes over one-half of world population, with other significant actors (Brazil, Russia, India) and salient regions (Middle East). Taking a global view should foster governance innovation, as dominant players have different strengths (Nye 2002). Yet free-rider problems prevent cooperation among abstract regions, especially those where there are no peer-review mechanisms, let alone a culture of cross-cutting intergovernmental cooperation, as seemed to be the case in the rest of the world's significant actors and even in China, certainly before the creation of the Group of 20 (Macedo 2011). In addition, around seventy "fragile states," most of which are located in Africa, are very specific in their fragility (Bourguignon et al. 2008).

Looking at the rest of the world, the share of world GDP accounted for by Africa plus South America combined doubled from 1820 to 1950. The share remained constant at around 10 percent with North America and EU roughly equal to Asia (including Japan, Russia, and Turkey), shares that are comparable to those prevailing in 1820. In 1950, however, North America and the EU accounted for 60 percent and Asia for 30 percent. In terms of

Table 7.2   **Statistics capacity index**

Angola	34
Cape Verde	63
Egypt	83
Ethiopia	78
Guinea Bissau	39
Mauritius	74
Mozambique	62
São Tomé e Príncipe	55
South Africa	78
Tunisia	71

Source: AEO (2010, 47).

population, Africa and South America combined have more than doubled their combined world share from 10 percent in 1820 to 15 percent in 1950 to 22 percent in 2003, while Asia has dropped from three-fourths to one-half and then rose again to two-thirds. In terms of GDP per capita, the relative shares are one-half for Africa and South America combined and over two-thirds for Asia.

As emphasized in AEO (2010, box 2.2), strengthening the capacity of the national statistical systems is required for a results-based management framework, which in turn helps regional integration processes based on peer review.[13] The partnership known as PARIS21, hosted by the OECD, has been in operation since 1999 and on its tenth anniversary produced the Dakar Declaration on the Development of Statistics.[14] Table 7.2 presents a statistical capacity indicator of the five highest-ranking countries and the five PALOP, noting that only three of the former are in sub-Saharan Africa. Indeed, the data drawn from the impressive database of the late Angus Maddison underscores this lack of knowledge. In year 1 there are only estimates of GDP for the five North African countries (Algeria, Egypt, Libya, Morocco, and Tunisia), estimates of GDP for Ghana and South Africa begin in 1820, and for the remaining sub-Saharan African countries in 1950. The share of Africa in world GDP falls from over 4 percent to under 3 percent in 1000, 1 percent in 1500, and around .8 percent until 1820, when it begins to rise to about 1.2 percent in 1913. In 1950, when estimates for thirty-four new countries become available, the Africa share reaches under 4 percent

13. This objective also comprised part of the "capacity building" initiatives in Africa undertaken by the World Bank during the 1990s. These entailed promoting technical expertise and data base construction, for example, population census and socioeconomic surveys.

14. One year before, the *Lisbon Declaration on Science for Global Development* prepared by Jean-Pierre Contzen, adviser to the late Mariano Gago, then minister for science and technology, called for indicators from CGIAR (where IICT represented Portugal) and other organizations in the UN system. Papers presented then include Giovaninni et al. (2008) on statistics and good governance and Macedo (2008) on CPLP, drawing on IICT (2007) and work at OECD in note 5 above.

again, while sub-Saharan Africa remains just under 3 percent. Since then both shares have declined about 1 percentage point of world GDP. As for the share of SSA in Africa, it rose from around 20 percent to 34 percent in 1913 and more than doubled to three-fourths in 1950. Thereafter the sub-Saharan share of Africa GDP declined by more than 10 percentage points, but West (= ECOWAS) and southern (= SADC) shares in sub-Saharan Africa remain at 40 percent and 30 percent, respectively. The increase in population has been such that the relative stability in the share of world GDP implies a decline in GDP per capita of about 20 percentage points, from 42 percent of world GDP per capita in 1950 to 24 percent in 2003. The corresponding figure for sub-Saharan Africa is 18 percent, forecast by the International Monetary Fund (IMF) to rise to 21 percent in 2013.

The views of "development as self-discovery" (Hausman and Rodrik 2003) and the "ladder of competitiveness" (Causa and Cohen 2006) suggest measures of competitiveness that go beyond relative unit labor costs (Branson, Macedo, and Richardson 1987) and other refinements to the country narratives are presented below. The main point, once again, is that diversity must be taken into account. While the impressive database used in Maddison (2007) has been criticized, it allows a "millennial" perspective on world regions and helps to avoid the pitfalls of a purely geographic approach.[15] Regions may be historical rather than geographical, and interaction during the first wave of globalization and even the second did not involve nearly as many players as the current one. The complementarity between globalization and regional integration and the development paradigm based on mutual accountability first contained in the 2002 Monterrey declaration on MDG both suggest that in Africa interaction between globalization and governance has been weak. At the same time, there is evidence that complementary reforms are not a "luxury" for developing countries (Macedo et al. 2014).

7.3.2   Africa and Portuguese-Speaking Countries

The Common Historical Legacy

The combination of Africa and South America is more obvious when the Atlantic side is considered. In effect, Mozambique was ruled from Goa in India during the first wave of globalization and the influence remained after the forced union with the Spanish Crown (1580–1640), but India suffered the competition from Brazil during the 1700s.

Contrary to what is sometimes believed, there was a fair amount of decen-

---

15. Maddison (2001, 71–75) acknowledges the specificity of the Portuguese empire. Amaral (2009) revisits the Portuguese transition to democracy during the second wave of globalization. Macedo and Pereira (2007) were inspired to study the diversity of Portugal's and Portuguese-speaking countries' responses to globalization by drawing on the concept of "diferencialidade" due to Borges de Macedo and discussed in Macedo et al. (2009).

tralization in the Portuguese empire even before the departure of the Crown Regent to Brazil in the wake of the first Napoleonic invasion in 1807 that essentially moved the capital to the New World (Maxwell 2004). The Crown remained in Rio de Janeiro after the congress of Vienna and the liberal revolution of the 1820s. Brazil remained an empire until 1890 and was therefore the sole monarchy in the Americas during most of the nineteenth century. On the other side, the dispute between the two sons of the Regent led to the sole civil war in Portugal's history, which lasted from the independence of Brazil in the early 1820s until the defeat of the absolutist brother Miguel in 1834. In spite of a successful stabilization in the 1850s when it joined the gold standard, Portugal suffered from the 1890 crisis and the currency became inconvertible until 1992 (Macedo, Eichengreen, and Reis 1996). The transition of Brazil from empire to republic coincided with the financial crisis and the first default quickly followed the one of Portugal.

Similarly, the successive revolutions in 1910, 1918, 1926, and 1974 influenced the independence of the former African colonies, together with their own very diverse initial experiences with political and economic freedom. For example, the presumption that political freedom is incompatible with financial freedom instead of complementary damages financial reputations considerably because when political rights decrease the capacity to tax, countries become serial defaulters; but, Reinhart and Rogoff (2009) show that they are also capable of graduating.[16] More recently, the experience of Portugal with IMF adjustment programs may also be relevant to understand how countries like Cape Verde and Mozambique recovered their financial reputations.[17]

Our motivation for studying these countries reflects previous attempts to contribute toward greater mutual knowledge within the CPLP with respect to the MDG (IICT 2007; Macedo 2008). Indeed, the Declaration on MDG in CPLP (approved at the 2006 Bissau summit mentioned in the introduction) sees cooperative governance as capable of producing "mutual knowledge" among the eight member states based on the fact that the standards of appropriateness regarding policy and institutional reform may be less responsive to geography than to historical affinities. In spite of their geographical discontinuity, five Portuguese-speaking African countries formed the PALOP group in 1979, and held ten summits until 1992, when they signed the first Regional Indicative Program with the EU. With Timor-Leste

16. Tables 6.1–2, 4–6, 86–99, record one bankruptcy in Portugal from 1300 until 1812 (against seven in Spain and nine in France), and six are recorded until 1890 (against seven in Spain and zero in France and Brazil). Thus the share of years in default since independence or 1800 is similar in Brazil and Spain (table 10.2, 149), while France stands out for the share in a banking crisis.

17. Bliss and Macedo (1990) and Macedo (2009). Using Reinhart and Rogoff (2009) again, the change from 1979 to 2008 in the credit rating from *Institutional Investor* (table 17.2, 285) is 19 points in Spain and Greece, but 33 in Portugal, reaching 90, 85, and 81, respectively, in 2008 (table 17.2, 285).

joining in 2001, there are now six ACP Portuguese-speaking countries cooperating under the 10th European Development Fund. They signed a Memorandum of Understanding with the European Commission on the eve of the second Europe-Africa summit in late 2007, which extended to CPLP. Future activities, integrated into a multicountry approach, focus on democratic governance as a key determinant for poverty reduction.[18]

Moreover, it is widely recognized within the development community that both countries are actively seeking to overcome adverse developmental conditions, either due to geography (Cape Verde is a small island state devoid of natural resources) or history (Mozambique fought a protracted civil war following independence). Cape Verde, for example, signed a five-year contract in 2005 with the Millennium Challenge Corporation even though it was above the income per capita ceiling that determined eligibility. This was largely seen as an incentive for the country to continue its efforts on the development front. As expected, graduation to middle-income status occurred in late 2007 and, at the suggestion of Luxemburg and Portugal, Cape Verde also signed a special partnership with the EU. Mozambique, meanwhile, was eligible for the Millennium Challenge Corporation since its inception in 2004.

Given Africa's diversity, then, assessing development successes requires comparisons among partners in subregional organizations that include members with different cultural, historical, and strategic affinities. The ECOWAS was established in 1975 and SADC in 1980, and each now includes the fifteen countries listed above. The experience of Cape Verde and Mozambique is systematically compared to the ECOWAS and SADC average, but also to sub-Saharan Africa and PALOP. Table 7.3 summarizes the various sizes relevant to the comparisons in the next section, including comparisons between PALOP and CPLP and the share of both Africa and its sub-Saharan part in the world in terms of GDP, population, and GDP per capita.[19]

Common features in the five PALOP may reflect institutions preceding independence, in spite of very diverse experiences with political and economic freedom since then. Like Portugal during the first half of the nineteenth century and again after the 1890 bankruptcy, financial reputation suffers when political rights decrease the capacity to tax. Like Portugal since 1979, some PALOP have been able to improve their credit rating through appropriate policies. It is therefore useful to preface the estimation of diversification-convergence regimes in West and southern Africa with a reference to the contrasting political culture of Cape Verde and Mozambique.

The comparative evolution of GDP per capita in 1990 international

18. In relation to poverty reduction, see Paul Collier (2007), and especially Collier and Gunning (1999).

19. The weight of Brazil is, of course, overwhelming and the four microstates never rise above 25 basis points of GDP in 1990 international dollars, the number equivalent of NAFTA, as indicated in note 5 above.

dollars from 1950 until 2006 for PALOP and sub-Saharan Africa averages shows a more volatile growth pattern for the former group with more pronounced growth in the 1950s and the last decade (figure 7.1). This reflects civil wars following independence, especially in Angola and Mozambique, the two larger economies. In spite of the common colonial history, the pattern of each one of the five PALOP countries is very specific: figures 7.2A and 7.2B compare GDP per capita in Cape Verde and Mozambique to the

Table 7.3	Relative sizes in 2003		
	GDP (%)	POP (%)	YCAP (%)
CPV/ECOW	0.3	0.2	168
ECOW/SSA	32	31	105
MOZ/SADC	9	11	88
SADC/SSA	41	25	166
SSA/AFR	64	86	74
AFR/WORLD	3	14	24
CPLP/WORLD	3	4	82
PALOP/CPLP	4	14	25

Source: Maddison database (2007). Available at: www.ggdc.net.

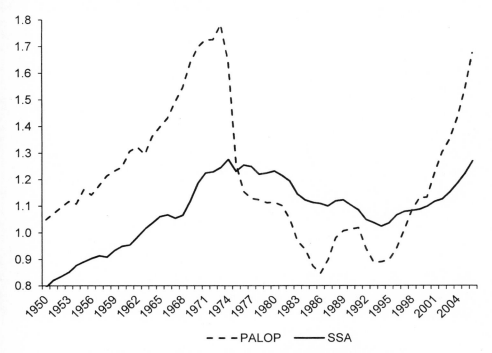

Fig. 7.1   **The PALOP versus SSA (GDP per capita, 1990 international K$)**

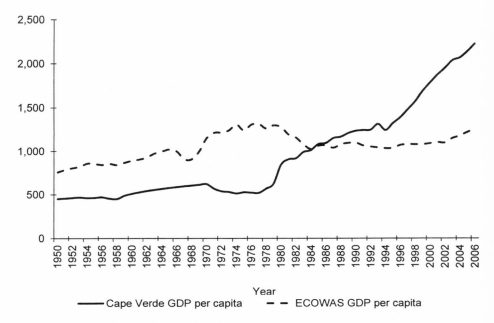

Fig. 7.2A   Cape Verde and ECOWAS (GDP per capita in international $)

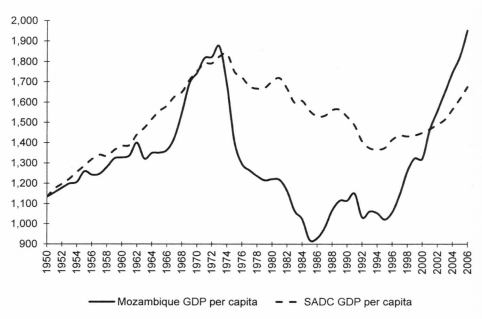

Fig. 7.2A   Cape Verde and ECOWAS (GDP per capita in international $)

Table 7.4   **Diversification index in PALOP**

	1997	1998	1999	2000	2001	2002	2003	2004	2005	2006	2007	2008	AVG
ANG	1	1	1	1	1	1	1	1	1	1	1	1	1
CV	15	10	6	8	9	6	15	14	9	11	15	6	10
GB	2	4	3	2	2	3	2	2	1	2	1	1	2
MZ	7	8	8	9	7	4	3	3	3	3	4	6	5
STP	3	3	5	4	7	3	3	6	4	5	5	2	4

Source: From 2004 AEO (2010); latest from previous issues.

Table 7.5   **Economic freedom index in PALOP**

	2010	2009	2008	2007	2006	2005	2004	2003
CV	62	61	58	57	59	58	58	56
MZ	56	56	57	56	53	56	57	59
A	48	47	47	45	44	—	—	—
GB	44	45	45	45	47	47	42	43

Source: AEO (2010, 75, from Heritage Foundation).

Table 7.6   **Corruption perception index in PALOP**

	Rank 2009	Index 2009	Rank 2008	Index 2008	Rank 2007	Index 2007	Year	Index
CV	46	5.1	47	5.5	53	4.7	—	—
STP	111	2.8	121	2.7	118	2.7	—	—
M	130	2.5	126	2.6	111	2.8	2003	2.7
GB	162	1.9	158	1.9	143	2.3	—	—
A	192	1.9	158	1.9	147	2.2	2002	1.7

Source: AEO from Transparency International (2010, 73, 274–75), previous issues.

respective subregional averages over six decades.[20] According to AEO, Cape Verde, São Tomé e Príncipe, Mozambique, Guinea-Bissau, and Angola is the ranking that applies to export diversification, political and economic freedom, as well as corruption perception in PALOP: Tables 7.4, 7.5, and 7.6 present the latest data available and will be detailed below for the first and third ranked.

In regional terms, current SADC countries showed greater export diversification than those of ECOWAS or the average for sub-Saharan Africa since 1960, as measured by the number-equivalent Herfindahl index. Export

20. The source is the Maddison database, which contains two outliers for GDP of Cape Verde in million GK$. The series is 1990: 430, 1991: 283, 1992: 231, 1993: 434, and the correction was interpolating the two outliers so that GDP per capita growth is smoothed during those years. Frankel (2010) presents governance rankings alongside GDP per capita figures consistent with the ranking in the text.

diversification in Mozambique and Cape Verde also tend to be higher than the sub-Saharan Africa average, but the number equivalent varies a great deal (table 7.7): data for Cape Verde begins in 1976, and in Mozambique recent large-scale investments determined both a strong increase in the exports and an increase in specialization. The decrease in export diversification in Mozambique followed a strong expansion of one single industrial product rather than from a decrease in the exports of other products. In all six governance indicators reported in table 7.8, Cape Verde scores higher than the ECOWAS average and Mozambique performs better than the SADC average in three of them, as detailed in section 7.5.2.

Comparing GDP growth rates of the both countries since 1950 shows a growth differential of almost 2 percent for Cape Verde relative to ECOWAS, whereas Mozambique growth is slightly below that of SADC. The decade averages show the greater volatility of Mozambique's output with two decades of negative growth, whereas in Cape Verde there was a negative differential of 4 percentage points in the 1970s. While this difference has roots in the colonial period, the pattern was reinforced after independence, as described next.

Cape Verde

After achieving independence in 1975, Cape Verde was governed under a one-party system that pursued an inward-looking, activist development program based on central planning and an economically dominant public sector, particularly in banking, transportation, insurance, and energy (IMF 1999). Motivated by the need to overcome the colonial legacy while minimizing the risk of possible political resistance, the new government adopted a protectionist trade regime and controlled the economy directly. As a consequence, there was limited scope for competitive export promotion and foreign direct investment was also discouraged: the resulting loss of competitiveness and the reduction of foreign direct investment became major constraints for sustainable long-run growth (Lourenço and Foy 2003). As of 1988, a wide-ranging program of reforms aimed at trade liberalization and privatization reduced the government's role to essentially that of building badly needed infrastructure, but the country was governed under a one-party system until 1990. Popular dissatisfaction led to free legislative and presidential elections and a constitutional amendment establishing a multiparty system in 1991. Economic reforms gathered further momentum after the country held free elections. The Movement for Democracy (MPD) took power away from the African Party for the Independence of Cape Verde (PAICV) that had led Cape Verde since independence and amended the 1980 constitution to allow for a multiparty democracy. The MPD government continued the economic reforms started by its predecessor, especially those pertaining to financial and foreign exchange markets. Since the adoption of this regime, there have been three legislative elections with results considered to be nonfraudulent and two orderly changes in government.

Table 7.7   Annual change in number-equivalent Herfindahl index (Cape Verde versus ECOWAS, Mozambique versus SADC)

	1961–1965	1966–1970	1971–1975	1976–1980	1981–1985	1986–1990	1991–1995	1996–2000	2001–2005	1976–2005
ECOWAS	0.11	-0.02	-0.02	0.05	0.04	**-0.01**	-0.12	0.21	**-0.03**	0.02
Cape Verde				**0.77**	**0.48**	-0.47	**0.19**	**0.27**	-0.16	**0.18**
SADC	-0.87	-0.32	-0.04	**0.29**	-0.11	**0.04**	**0.02**	-0.05	**-0.01**	-0.1
Mozambique	**0.75**	**0.1**	**0.14**	-0.17	**0.21**	-0.34	-0.62	-0.05	-0.48	**-0.07**

Source: Calculated from Cabral and Veiga (2010, graphs 7–8).

Table 7.8   World Bank Governance Indicators (1996–2007)

	CV	ECOWAS	MOZ	SADC
Rule of law	**0.48**	−0.75	−0.74	−0.44
Voice and accountability	**0.65**	−0.51	**−0.08**	−0.30
Political stability, absence of violence/terrorism	**0.96**	−0.49	**0.05**	−0.24
Government effectiveness	**0.11**	−0.77	**−0.33**	−0.38
Regulatory quality	**−0.25**	−0.65	−0.47	−0.45
Control of corruption	**0.33**	−0.66	−0.65	−0.39

Source: Updated from IICT (2007), same as Lopes and Santos (2010, tables 1a, b); note data are fitted to a normal distribution centered on zero.

Indeed, the fact that democratic governance has taken root is widely recognized by various governance indicators. The 2008 Ibrahim Index of African Governance (Gisselquist and Rotberg 2008) ranks Cape Verde second overall in a sample comprising forty-eight sub-Saharan countries. Cape Verde has good results in terms of safety and security, sustainable economic opportunity, participation, and human rights and human development when compared to its peers, with safety and security obtaining the highest score and sustainable economic opportunity the lowest. Data from the Freedom House Index also confirms the good results of Cape Verde in terms of political stability: Cape Verde is defined as free, obtaining the highest scores (1) for political rights and civil liberties. The presence of "creolisation/métissage" from the first settlers helped promote the view of peace and development. This "peace culture" has been reinforced by the absence of civil strife and by the impressive performance in terms of MDG, reflecting political stability, security, good governance, and functioning democratic institutions. The insular nation, without natural resources, has become an example of best practice: its neutrality in the region lead to its role of mediator—good reputation ("donors' darling"), leadership in United Nations (UN) reform, and using culture as a means of promoting tourism and development.[21]

Mozambique

Three different governance regimes can be identified: the preindependence period (1960–1974); the postindependence period, which was marked by

21. The argument in Santos (2010) is based on a PhD dissertation in peace studies a la Galtung (1996) where she analyzes the thought of Amilcar Cabral (1975, 1999) who led the liberation struggle of Cape Verde and Guinea-Bissau and influenced leaders of several other colonies, especially Angola (Cabral 1995, 1987; Andrade 1978). Surprisingly, she leaves out Cardoso (1986), which is seen as very influential. Another useful reference is the acceptance speech of an honorary doctorate from the Technical University of Lisbon on May 26 by the current head of state (Pires 2010). However, Lourenço and Foy (2003) claim that the resulting loss of competitiveness and the reduction of foreign direct investment became major constraints for sustainable long-run growth during this period.

civil war (1975–1992); and the post-peace-accord period (1993 onward).[22] Following independence, economic growth was stunted by a civil war estimated to have killed up to one million people. It is also affected by the Marxist-socialist ideology espoused by the governments in the immediate postindependence period. Prior to independence, there was significant public investment in infrastructure and also expenditures in health and education during the period 1960–1973, which contributed strongly to Mozambique's growth. In the agricultural sector, it was generally true that large private farms performed better than smaller ones, and therefore accounted for the bulk of agricultural output. However, the postindependence economy was very much government controlled. By 1984, for example, more than half of all registered firms were state owned. Not unexpectedly, the development of a market economy was severely hampered, which impacted negatively on growth. During the 1980s, Mozambique began gradually moving away from a centrally planned economy; for example, price controls on vegetables and fruits were removed. Another example is the enactment of the 1987 Economic Rehabilitation Program, which led to a strong shift toward market-based economic policies and the pursuit of structural reforms. These included the stabilization of the exchange rate, trade liberalization, extensive privatizations, and tariff and financial-sector reforms. However, it was only after the consolidation of peace that any significant improvements had the opportunity to occur. A contributing factor to a quick postconflict development was the UN-led program of exchanging guns for vouchers, which allowed an easier transition from war to peace. While it was soon discontinued because of difficulties in redeeming these vouchers, the program remains a success in confidence building. Following the signing of the 1992 Rome treaty, a new constitution was adopted that allowed for democratic elections and further progress toward a market economy. A prosperous transition after the peace accord allows Mozambique's economic performance to be compared to the best performers in the subregion, namely Mauritius and South Africa. Nevertheless, the rehabilitation and political transition took a few years, before megaprojects such as the MOZAL aluminum smelter plant and the Witbank highway (connecting Mozambique and South Africa) were implemented in 1996–1999, leading to the take off of growth after 2000. According to Tibana (2003), economic activity increased from 1991 until 1995, but slowed down during the preparation and implementation of the megaprojects that came to define the country's export behavior and high rates of economic growth. Over the past decade, Mozambique has again become one of the attractive economies in the subregion, as revealed by Luiz, Pereira, and Oliveira (2013), from where figure 7.3 is reproduced.

22. Tibana (2003) performs a trend and a business cycle analysis in the post-peace accord period, pointing out different growth behaviors within it. Such periods are: an immediate postwar recuperation (1992–1994), a period of slow growth and heavy infrastructure investment (1995–2000), and a strong growth period (2000–2002).

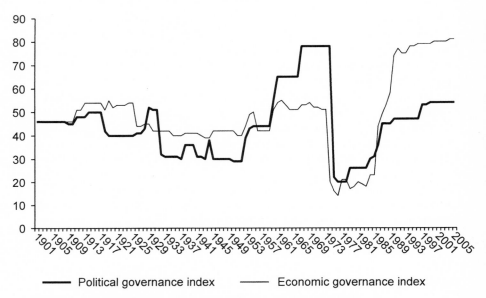

Fig. 7.3   **Political and economic governance index in Mozambique**

7.4   Analyzing the Convergence-Diversification Relationship

In this section, we study the two-way relationship between trade diversification and income convergence motivated by the insights provided by our interpretative framework and the empirical finding that economic development, measured by per capita income, entails more diversification. The general observation is that economies become more diversified as incomes increase before reaching a turning point, which Imbs and Wacziarg (2003) estimate to be around USD 9,000 per capita, beyond which they become less diversified, a stage not yet observed in the sub-Saharan Africa database used by Cabral and Veiga (2010), which includes data disaggregated at five different levels, according to the categories of the Standard International Trade Classification (SITC) trade data (Rev. 2).[23] In other words, development occurs when a country learns how to do new things and focuses on those that it already does well, such as producing new goods, choosing promising export markets, upgrading product quality, and moving into services exports. We note, in passing, that another strand of literature argues that diversification should focus on exporting more sophisticated products, as these entail higher productivity levels conducive to higher growth levels

23. Cabral and Veiga (2010) present mostly results with more disaggregated data, since the results tend to be stronger and more accurate than when the one- and two-digit categories are chosen. They add in note 12, page 15, that the results remain broadly similar, independent of the level of disaggregation used.

(e.g., Hausmann, Hwang, and Rodrik 2007). In this case, a country becomes what it exports, that is, countries converge to the level of income implied by their exports.[24] The common point in both approaches, however, is that product development is undoubtedly an important engine of growth for developing countries.

The study of how economic policy and institutional variables promote or limit the capability of countries to pursue successful export diversification and sophistication strategies serves as background for the identification of the factors that determined the success obtained by Cape Verde and Mozambique. Using regression analysis in a panel of forty-eight countries over forty-five years, Cabral and Veiga (2010) establish that the stage of development and the economy's size are positively correlated with export diversification, and that economies with larger GDPs or populations also have higher export sophistication levels. Moreover, both diversification and sophistication are promoted by trade integration, efforts to reduce transport costs, as well as improvements in institutional, political, and educational factors.

When used to explain export diversification, nineteen out of the twenty-six governance variables presented significant positive signs. The results were particularly robust for the variables reflecting government accountability, respect for the rule of law, political stability, effectiveness, and control of corruption (table 7.8). In export sophistication regressions, fifteen out of twenty-six variables are not statistically significant but "transparency," "accountability," "control of corruption in the public sector," "debt policy and fiscal policy rating, "economic management cluster average," and "policies for social inclusion" have a positive association.

Since 1960, the average of current SADC countries showed greater export diversification, as measured by the number-equivalent Herfindahl index, than ECOWAS or sub-Saharan Africa (Cabral and Veiga 2010, graph 8). It is seen that improving the education standards of the labor force (measured by the share of GDP spent in education or the World Bank index about "building human resources") is associated with export diversification. Moreover, lower levels of education are associated positively with diversification, while higher levels are associated with export sophistication. While equations in which diversification and sophistication were used to explain GDP growth suggested a positive but not robust relationship, higher diversification and sophistication were associated to lower variation in the rate of growth of both GDP and per capita income. The estimated coefficients suggest that a 10 percent increase in diversification leads to a 4.6 percent decrease in the variation of GDP growth and to a 4.4 percent reduction of income per capita variability. Similar results were obtained for sophistication, with country fixed effects models suggesting that increasing sophistication may have a

24. The issue of export sophistication is analyzed in Cabral and Veiga (2010, 16).

stronger marginal effect in decreasing economic instability than diversification in sub-Saharan Africa. In addition, higher diversification and sophistication are associated with lower infant mortality and higher life expectancy. The estimated coefficients are robust and the impact independent of that of diversification and sophistication on income per capita, which is all the more relevant as higher average income does not necessarily translate to better life for the majority of the population.

Export diversification in Mozambique and Cape Verde also tend to be higher than the sub-Saharan Africa average, but the number equivalent varies a great deal (Cabral and Veiga 2010, graph 9): data for Cape Verde begins in 1976, and in Mozambique recent large-scale investments determined both a strong increase in the exports and an increase in specialization. The decrease in export diversification in Mozambique followed a strong expansion of one single industrial product rather than from a decrease in the exports of other products. Figures 7.4 and 7.5, second panel, show the comparative pattern of the number equivalent for ECOWAS and SADC countries, respectively, while figures 7.6 and 7.7, third panel, compares Cape Verde and Mozambique to the group average.

Export diversification and sophistication in Cape Verde and Mozambique relative to the average in sub-Saharan Africa are shown in Cabral and Veiga (2010, graphs 9 and 10). With respect to diversification, Cape Verde ranks higher, whereas Mozambique has improved sophistication. In this regard, Cape Verde is close to 6,000 while ECOWAS is around 5,000, even though in the early nineties it decreases to 3,000 and 2,000, respectively. Mozambique, with a lower sophistication than SADC during the nineties, but its sophistication increased sharply since 2000, overcoming that of SADC. The average annual change in the number equivalent for five-year periods in Cape Verde and ECOWAS shows that, from 1976 to 2005, a new good was being exported by Cape Verde approximately every five and a half years ($1/0.18 = 5.55$). In Mozambique there was significant diversification up to the late seventies, while SADC was actually concentrating. However, from the eighties on, concentration was large, especially in the early nineties and between 2001 and 2005. During the latter period, on average, every two years a product stopped being exported ($1/0.48$).

With this in mind, in this section we seek to identify macrolevel policy and institutional combinations underpinning successful export diversification and economic convergence in ECOWAS and SADC. Just as important, we also expect to establish context-based objective metrics that will subsequently allow us to better assess the relative performance of Cape Verde and Mozambique on both counts in conjunction with evidence of a case-study nature. This indirect approach to study trade-related development success in these two countries is unavoidable as the severe lack of data prevents us from analyzing them empirically. Our study covers the period 1960–2004 and uses annual data obtained from various sources (see appendix A for

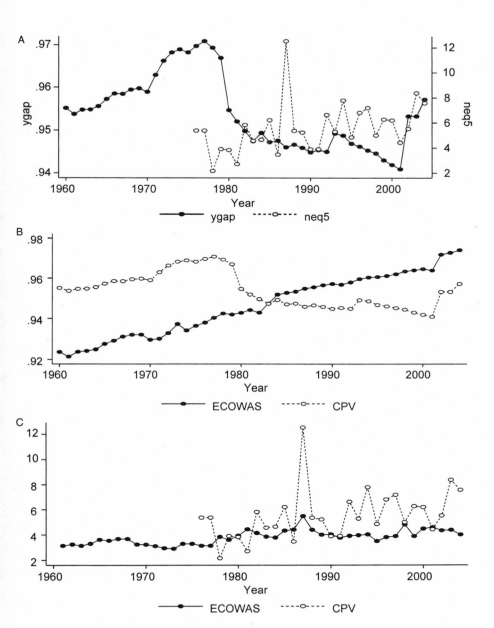

Fig. 7.4　Cape Verde: Relation between income gap and number equivalent

Note: Panel (a): Cape Verde, income gap to frontier and number equivalent; panel (b): Cape Verde versus ECOWAS, income gap to frontier; and panel (c): Cape Verde versus ECOWAS, number equivalent.

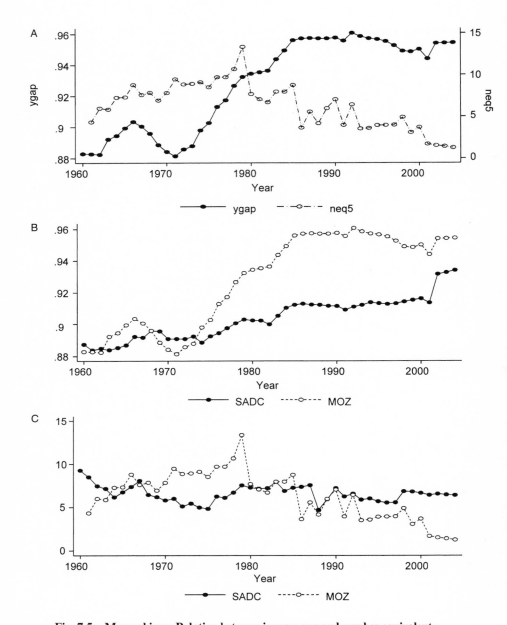

Fig. 7.5   Mozambique: Relation between income gap and number equivalent

Note: Panel (a): Mozambique, income gap to frontier and number equivalent; panel (b): Mozambique versus SADC, income gap; and panel (c): Mozambique versus SADC, number equivalent.

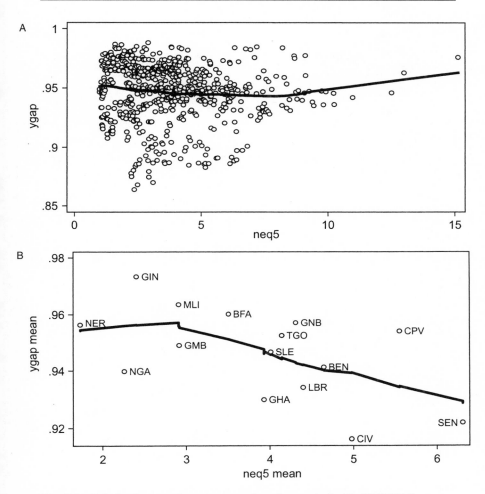

Fig. 7.6   Relation between income gap and number equivalent in ECOWAS

Note: Panel (a): ECOWAS, income gap to frontier versus number equivalent measure, Lowess smoothing, bandwidth = 0.8; and panel (b): ECOWAS, income gap versus number equivalent, country means, Lowess smoothing, bandwidth = 0.8.

full details, including summary statistics, on variables used in our estimations). Before presenting qualitative results from the econometric analysis, a snapshot of eight indicators used in the empirical analysis can be seen in appendix A, figures 7A.1, and 7A.2, for each one of the member countries in ECOWAS and SADC, respectively. Panels (a) through (h) report the following variables: panel (a), convergence: income gap to frontier, country and US GDP per capita, constant 2000 USD; panel (b), diversification: number

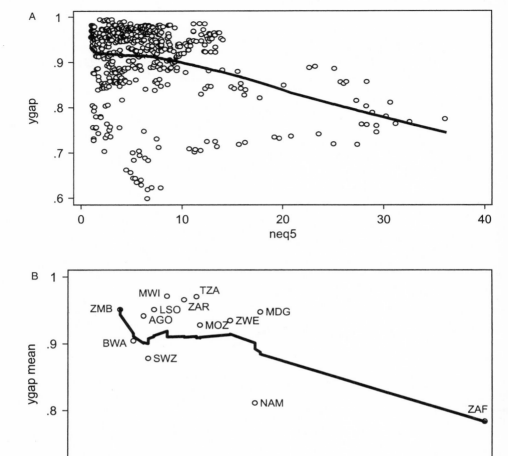

Fig. 7.7 Relation between income gap and number equivalent in SADC

Note: Panel (a): SADC, income gap versus number equivalent, Lowess smoothing, bandwidth = 0.8; panel (b): SADC, income gap versus number equivalent, country means, Lowess smoothing, bandwidth = 0.9; panel (c): SADC (excluding South Africa), income gap versus number equivalent, Lowess smoothing, bandwidth = 0.8; and panel (d): SADC (excluding South Africa), income gap versus number equivalent, country means, Lowess smoothing, bandwidth = 0.9.

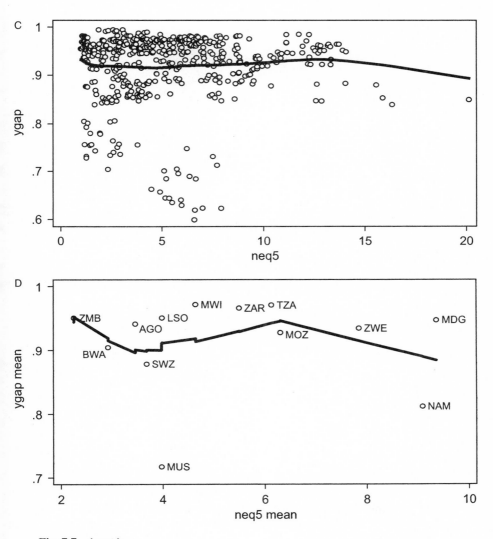

Fig. 7.7   (cont.)

equivalent index of exports at one-, two-, three-, four-, and five-digit SITC; panel (c), monetary stability: inflation in consumer prices; panel (d), fiscal sustainability: government surplus/deficit percent GDP; panel (e), trade openness: exports plus import percent GDP; panel (f), political freedom; panel (g), economic freedom; and panel (h), life expectancy at birth. We also depict the relation between diversification and convergence for Cape Verde and Mozambique over time and also with respect to their respective regional averages. Figures 7.4 and 7.5 compare convergence and diversification indi-

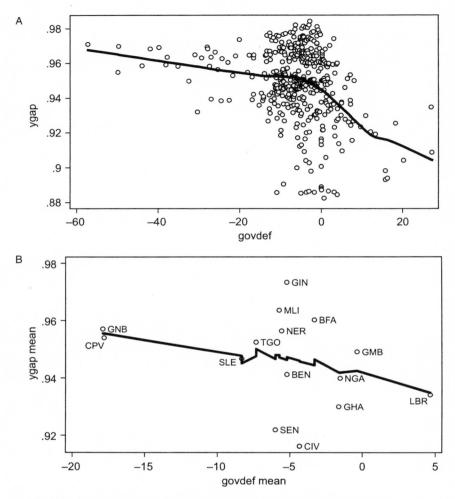

Fig. 7.8   Relation between income gap and government deficit in ECOWAS

Note: Panel (a): ECOWAS, income gap versus government deficit (percent of GDP), Lowess smoothing, bandwidth = 0.8; panel (b): ECOWAS, income gap versus government deficit, country means, Lowess smoothing, bandwidth = 0.8; and panel (c): ECOWAS, income gap versus government deficit, time means, Lowess smoothing, bandwidth = 0.8.

cators in panels (a) through (c) and show the time series of income gap and number equivalent for Cape Verde and ECOWAS, and Mozambique and SADC in panels (b) and (c), respectively. Figures 7.6, and 7.7 show the relation between same variables in terms of the raw data and country means in panels (a) and (b), respectively. The raw data, country means, and time means for the relation between income gap and government deficit is shown in figures 7.8, and 7.9, panels (a) through (c), and the relation between eco-

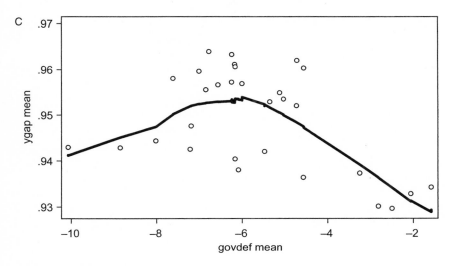

Fig. 7.8   (cont.)

nomic and political freedom in figures 7.10, and 7.11, panels (a) and (b). Account is taken of the different performances by defining "high" and "low" regimes in terms of the variables of interest, and figures 7.10 and 7.11, panel (c), compare the relation between economic and political freedom for the full sample and the two regimes. Figures 7.12 and 7.13, panels (a) through (c), present the indicators in appendix figures 7A.1 and 7A.2, panels (b) through (g), while growth in GDP per capita replaces the distance to frontier in figures 7.12 and 7.13, panel (a). The insights obtained from these graphs, as well those from the Lowess plots (figures 7.6 to 7.11) will help us to better understand and interpret our results, especially with respect to variables identified as being highly significant in our econometric analysis.[25]

The first Lowess plot clearly depicts the expected (negative) relation between diversification and convergence when using the country means, that is, mean ygap and mean neq5 for each country (figures 7.6 and 7.7). When all observations are taken into account, the same is true for SADC, but there is no discernible relation between the two variables for ECOWAS. It is also clear that the strong negative relation exhibited by SADC is largely attributable to South Africa's high level of diversification. Once we exclude

25. Lowess, or locally weighted scatter plot smoothing, is a method that fits simple regression models to localized subsets of the data. The objective is to build up a function that describes, point by point, the deterministic part of the data's variability. For further details, see Cleveland's (1979) seminal contribution and also subsequent developments by Cleveland and Devlin (1988). Note that we only present those Lowess plots in which there is clear and interpretable relationship between the variables under consideration. The others are available from the authors upon request.

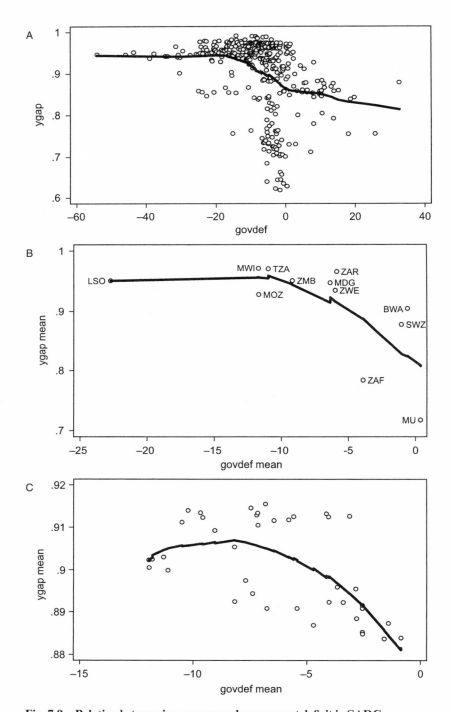

Fig. 7.9   Relation between income gap and government deficit in SADC

Note: Panel (a): SADC, income gap versus government deficit (percent of GDP), Lowess smoothing, bandwidth = 0.8; panel (b): SADC, income gap versus government deficit, country means, Lowess smoothing, bandwidth = 0.8; and panel (c): SADC, income gap versus government deficit, time means, Lowess smoothing, bandwidth = 0.8.

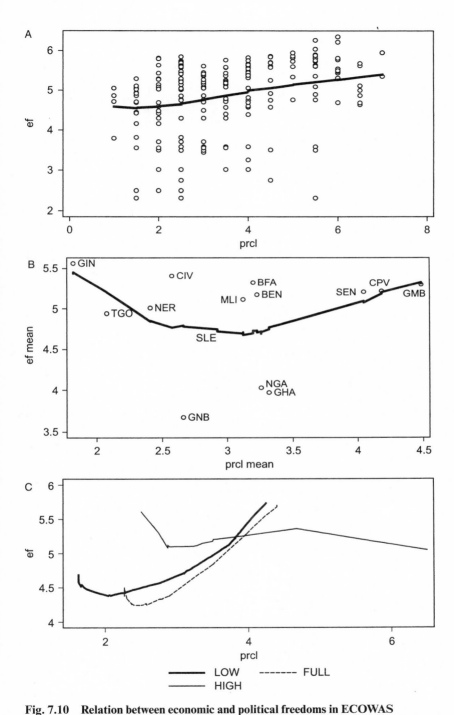

Fig. 7.10 Relation between economic and political freedoms in ECOWAS

Note: Panel (a): ECOWAS, economic freedom versus political freedom, Lowess smoothing, bandwidth = 0.8; panel (b): ECOWAS, economic versus political freedom, country means, Lowess smoothing, bandwidth = 0.8; and panel (c): ECOWAS, economic versus political freedom, Lowess smoothing, bandwidth = 0.8.

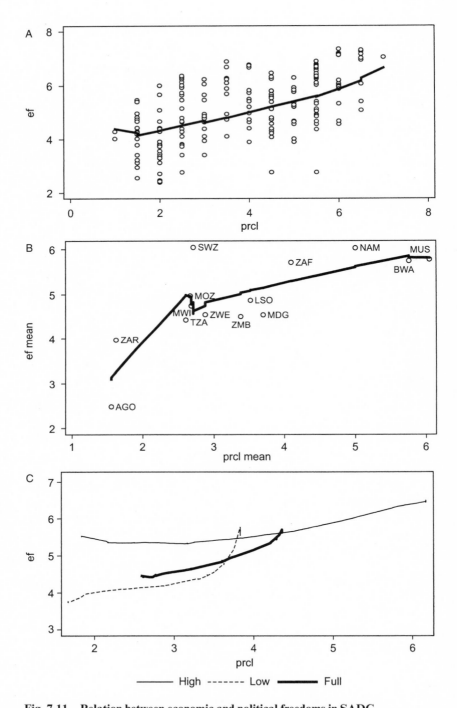

Fig. 7.11   Relation between economic and political freedoms in SADC

Note: Panel (a): SADC, economic freedom versus political freedom, Lowess smoothing, bandwidth = 0.9; panel (b): SADC, economic versus political freedom, country means, Lowess smoothing, bandwidth = 0.8; and panel (c): SADC, economic versus political freedom.

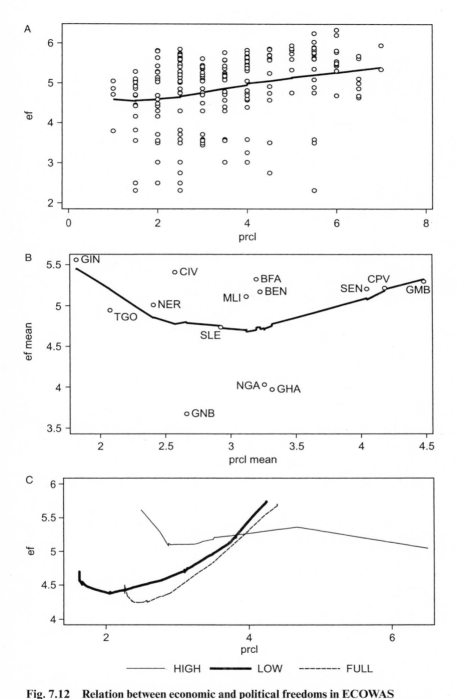

Fig. 7.12   Relation between economic and political freedoms in ECOWAS

Note: Panel (a): ECOWAS, economic freedom versus political freedom, Lowess smoothing, bandwidth = 0.8; panel (b): ECOWAS, economic versus political freedom (country means), Lowess smoothing, bandwidth = 0.8; and panel (c): ECOWAS, economic versus political freedom, Lowess smoothing, bandwidth = 0.8.

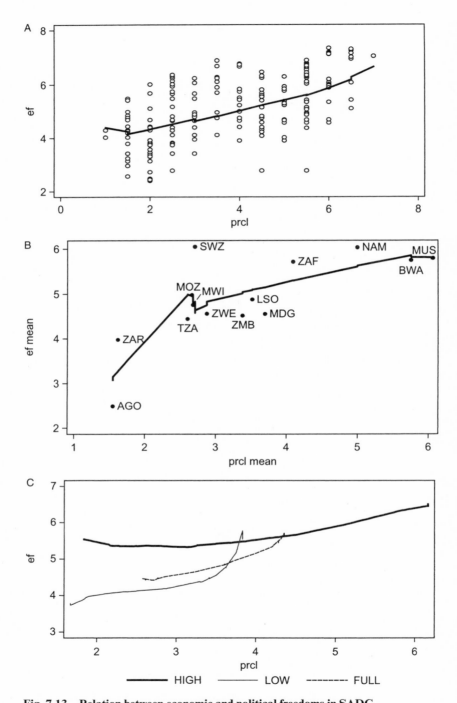

Fig. 7.13   Relation between economic and political freedoms in SADC

Note: Panel (a): SADC, economic freedom versus political freedom, Lowess smoothing, bandwidth = 0.9; panel (b): SADC, economic versus political freedom (country means), Lowess smoothing, bandwidth = 0.8; and panel (c): SADC, economic versus political freedom.

South Africa from the sample, we observe that the relation is now ambiguous and not dissimilar to that of ECOWAS. Regarding government deficits, we observe that lower budget deficits are associated with increased convergence, especially when they are less than 6 percent of GDP for ECOWAS and around 8 percent for SADC (figures 7.8 and 7.9). As for the relation between political and economic freedoms, it is clearly positive in both regions, but more so for SADC based on the visual inspection of the Lowess plot obtained using all observations (figures 7.10 and 7.11). When one uses country averages instead, we see that there is an unequivocal positive relation between freedoms in SADC (figure 7.11, panel [b]), while it is somewhat "U-shaped" in ECOWAS (figure 7.10, panel [b]), which possibly reflects the fact that the region aggregates countries with dissimilar characteristics on this score.

Turning to our empirical analysis, we adopt a system equation approach mainly because we believe that it is better suited to model interdependence between variables. We also seek to address the problem of endogeneity due to simultaneity bias and so make use of the standard three-stage least square method (3SLS). This method incorporates uses all the information provided by the exogenous right-hand-side (RHS) variables to instrument the endogenous (LHS) left-hand-side variables. As such, it avoids the potential pitfall of having to find "good" instruments within a single equation context. Notwithstanding this advantage, we recognize that 3SLS may be more sensitive to the existence of spurious correlations or multi-collinearities among the regressors in one equation, thereby "contaminating" the remaining equations. In our sample, this does not seem to be an issue, however. In order to assess the robustness of our method, we also estimated the diversification-convergence relation using alternative estimation techniques, namely ordinary least squares (OLS) and two-stage least squares (2SLS). Since the results obtained are broadly consistent, tables 7.9A and 7.9B present the 3SLS results while the others are in appendix B.

As for our dependent variables, we measure the distance of a country's GDP per capita (ypc_{it}) compared to that of the United States ($ypc_{USA,t}$) in order to capture economic convergence. Specifically, the income gap is calculated as $ygap_{it} = 1 - (ypc_{it}/ypc_{USA,t})$, which implies that the income gap narrows as ypc_{it} increases. We measure export diversification using the number-equivalent index ($neq5_{it}$), which is calculated as the inverse of the Herfindahl index (five-digits, SITC, Rev. 2). Together with additional control variables, we expect these two variables to be a meaningful characterization of each country's diversification-convergence regime, which will be affected by the interaction between policy and institutional variables. Accordingly, we specify the following two-equation simultaneous system for our analysis:

(1) $ygap_{it} = \alpha_1.neq5_{it} + \delta_1.(Policy_{it}) + \beta_1.(Institutions_{it}) + \gamma_1.Z_{1it} + \varepsilon_{1\cdot it}$

(2) $neq5_{it} = \alpha_2.ygap_{it} + \delta_2.(Policy_{it}) + \beta_2.(Institutions_{it}) + \gamma_2.Z_{2it} + \varepsilon_{2\cdot it}$

Table 7.9A ECOWAS, 3SLS estimation results

Variable type	Variable	Low-regime subsample		Full sample		High-regime subsample	
		lnygap	lnneq5	lnygap	lnneq5	lnygap	lnneq5
Policy	lnygap		−0.569***		−0.398***		−0.751***
			(−3.326)		(−3.812)		(−4.000)
	lnneq5	−0.0972		0.189**		−0.646***	
		(−1.139)		(2.409)		(−3.798)	
	inflation1	−0.0344**	0.0530*	−0.0368***			
		(−2.491)	(1.799)	(−3.400)			
	govdef	0.000174	0.0457***			−0.00618	−0.0153**
		(0.0435)	(4.744)			(−1.407)	(−2.291)
	lnopen1					−0.185**	−0.229**
						(−2.112)	(−2.156)
Institutional	lnprcl	−0.0147	−0.157	−0.172***	0.0620	−0.0477	0.299**
		(−0.339)	(−1.646)	(−2.723)	(0.579)	(−0.395)	(2.157)
	lnef	0.114	0.399*	−0.497***	0.840***	0.201	1.610***
		(1.487)	(1.888)	(−2.606)	(2.710)	(0.456)	(2.923)
	demage	−0.0319***		−0.0312***	−0.0444*		
		(−3.498)		(−2.963)	(−1.879)		
	demtot			0.00804***			
				(11.12)			
	dictrans		−0.179**				
			(−2.459)				

Control						
lnk	-0.107***		-0.0879***			
	(-4.441)		(-3.290)			
lnltotal						
lnpopdens		0.666***		0.191***	0.961***	
		(5.132)		(3.293)	(4.396)	
Dummies						
capcont				0.552***		
				(3.193)		
landlock	0.345***		0.322***	0.322***		
	(7.128)		(4.163)	(4.163)		
oil			-0.427***	-0.427***	-3.601***	
			(-7.158)	(-7.158)	(-4.657)	
cpv			-0.299***	0.438**		
			(-3.267)	(2.346)		
sen			-0.370***	0.504***	-2.827***	0.473***
			(-6.040)	(4.982)	(-3.871)	(6.759)
legaleng			-0.108**		-2.418***	
			(-2.347)		(-4.918)	
Constant	6.254***	2.790***	5.469***	0.904	-5.875**	2.334*
	(14.00)	(3.268)	(11.34)	(1.426)	(-2.359)	(1.828)
Model diagnostics						
Observations	40	40	99	99	32	32
R-squared	0.860	0.703	0.876	0.604	0.866	0.688
F-test	30.87	13.95	62.61	18.63	44.60	14.27
Prob > F	0	0	0	0	0	0

Note: The *t*-statistics are in parentheses.

***Significant at the 1 percent level.

**Significant at the 5 percent level.

*Significant at the 10 percent level.

Table 7.9B   SADC, 3SLS estimation results

Variable type	Variable	Low-regime subsample		Full sample		High-regime subsample	
		lnygap	lnneq5	lnygap	lnneq5	lnygap	lnneq5
	lnygap		1.340*** (6.654)		−0.782*** (−9.407)		−1.067*** (−6.012)
	lnneq5	0.617*** (6.624)		−0.276** (−2.571)		−0.659*** (−5.961)	
Policy	inflation1	0.0533*** (2.662)	−0.0765** (−2.532)				
	govdef			−0.0399*** (−6.492)	−0.0517*** (−4.202)	0.0259 (1.322)	0.0649*** (2.836)
	lnopen1	0.779*** (6.829)	−1.160*** (−7.293)	−0.276 (−1.622)	−0.691*** (−2.813)		
Institutional	lnprcl	−0.812*** (−10.64)	1.070*** (5.112)	−0.147** (−2.458)	−0.182** (−1.969)	−0.396*** (−4.609)	−0.323** (−2.028)
	lnef	−1.171*** (−6.261)	1.751*** (6.795)	0.766*** (4.175)	1.526*** (6.154)	−2.386*** (−6.059)	−2.306*** (−2.991)
	constage				0.00610** (2.537)		
	demage	0.121*** (5.235)	−0.169*** (−4.294)		−0.0179* (−1.686)		
	demtot	0.0127*** (8.015)	−0.0160*** (−3.998)				

Control		(1)	(2)	(3)	(4)	(5)	(6)
Control	lnk	-0.412*** (-9.979)					
	lnltotal	0.379*** (6.551)	0.419*** (4.502)				
Dummies	landlock	0.152* (1.806)	0.859*** (4.352)				
	mus	-0.833*** (-5.429)		-0.972*** (-4.263)	-1.578*** (-9.644)		
	moz	-0.728*** (-4.403)	-1.313*** (-4.507)				
	legaleng		-0.750** (-3.485)				
	Constant	6.939*** (5.027)	-1.130 (-0.488)	9.409*** (12.76)	10.55*** (5.822)	1.856*** (3.672)	-2.137** (-2.285)
Model diagnostics	Observations	156	156	51	51	39	39
	R-squared	0.893	0.530	0.847	0.745	0.850	0.645
	F-test	150.1	30.28	76.55	38.08	48.47	19.68
	Prob. > F	0	0	0	0	0	0

Note: The *t*-statistics are in parentheses.

***Significant at the 1 percent level.

**Significant at the 5 percent level.

*Significant at the 10 percent level.

where $i = 1, \ldots, N$ countries and $t = 1960–2004$. For each country, Policy$_{it}$ and Institutions$_{it}$, respectively, represent economic policy variables (inflation, government deficit, and degree of openness) and institutional ones (political and economic freedom, age of constitution, age of democracy, and number of prior transitions to dictatorship, among others). The $\{Z_i\}$ denotes a set of control variables (see appendix A) where the economic variables (such as capital and labor endowments) are used together with geographic variables (such as distance or landlockedness). Our initial estimation process revealed that the inclusion of certain key variables of interest, such as the real effective exchange rate and measures of exchange market pressure (EMP), dramatically reduced the number of observations that were available to be used in our models. We subsequently dropped these variables from our analysis, but evidence on conditional EMP is presented in the next section.

Regarding our estimation strategy, we first estimate the log-log equivalent of equations (1) and (2) for each region in order to identify the determinants of diversification and convergence at the regional level. Then, we reestimate these two equations for regional subsamples that capture two different diversification-convergence scenarios. The first subsample, denoted as the high regime, comprises countries that simultaneously exhibit high diversification and high convergence while the second, the low regime, comprises those that exhibit the opposite combination. We expect that this strategy will allow us to highlight differences and commonalities in performance across regimes and regions.

We identify the criteria used to divide the sample from the visual inspection of the partial relation between income gap and number-equivalent index averages (see figures 7.8 and 7.9, panel [b]). We define high regime as those observations satisfying the condition $\{ygap < 0.945 \ \& \ neq5 > 4.5\}$ and low regime as those where $\{ygap > = 0.945 \ \& \ neq5 < = 4.5\}$ in the case of ECOWAS. In effect, we are isolating the upper-left and bottom-right quadrants for further analysis. Moreover, we identify Senegal as a potential regional benchmark with which to compare Cape Verde, given its high intraregional diversification-convergence combination. We adopt the same conditions for SADC to facilitate interregional comparisons and identify Mauritius and South Africa as potential benchmarks. Estimation results are given in tables 7.9A and 7.9B, which includes both the full sample and two subsamples for ease of comparison.

With respect to ECOWAS, we find a two-way relationship between convergence and diversification, but only under the high regime. Moreover, the estimated coefficient of the impact of diversification on convergence is relatively and highly significant (–0.646 at 1 percent level). Under the low regime, the relation is only 1-way, as more convergence always increases diversification, but not the other way around. For the region as whole diversification increases with more convergence, but more diversification actually leads to *less* convergence. This result is unexpected but plausible given the ambiguous relationship between these two variables in ECOWAS, as depicted in figure 7.8 (panel [a]), and nonlinearities that characterize many of the partial relations between variables. The impact of convergence on diversification is also weaker when compared to the high regime, as the estimated coefficient is about half as large (−0.398 vs. −0.751). Together, these results appear to indicate that a critical level of diversification is needed before one observes a two-way relationship, ceteris paribus.

For SADC, the two-way relationship between convergence and diversification occurs under the high regime and, significantly, also for the full sample. These findings contrast with the one obtained for ECOWAS, where only the high regime exhibited such behavior. It is probably due to the influence that highly diversified countries such as South Africa and, perhaps to a lesser extent, Mauritius, exert on the region.[26] It may also be due to the fact that SADC is almost 70 percent more diversified than ECOWAS (6.47 vs. 3.83 mean neq5 as reported in table 7A.2). In contrast, the two-way relation is *positive* under the low regime: more diversification leads to *less* convergence and less convergence leads to more diversification. This result implies that SADC countries experiencing low levels of diversification may well need to specialize in order to ensure more convergence. This could be the rationale for Mozambique's move toward lower diversification, albeit accompanied by higher GDP per capita growth rates, as discussed below.

In order to better interpret our empirical findings, as well as to highlight possible differences and commonalities in performance, we also look at how key model variables differ across high and low regimes for each country (see figures 7B.1 and 7B.2). Note that we use each country's GDP per capita growth rate in lieu of its rate of convergence to the income frontier, as the latter measure would also reflect changes in the United States' GDP per capita. Interestingly, almost all of the highly diversified countries in ECOWAS register *negative* GDP per capita growth rates, with the exception of Cape Verde. Indeed, it is striking that Cape Verde exhibits not only the highest GDP per capita growth rate in ECOWAS, but also one that is fairly consistent across both regimes. This finding accords with our findings in section 7.3 and is also reflected in our estimates, as the Cape Verde dummy contributes toward more convergence under the full sample. Moreover, its effect for the Cape Verde dummy is almost on par as that of the benchmark. Note also that while Cape Verde is not as diversified as Senegal, it has increased its number equivalent appreciably between regimes as a result of its positive diversification trend over time.

For SADC, GDP per capita growth rates are positive under the high regime with the exception of Madagascar, Mozambique, and Zimbabwe.

---

26. Indeed, our initial OLS and 2SLS scoping estimations indicated that the determinants of diversification and convergence are broadly similar for ECOWAS and SADC when South Africa is excluded from the latter sample. These results are available from the authors upon request.

In the case of Mozambique, however, the move toward less diversification is accompanied by positive GDP per capita growth, which appears to be a notable reversal of fortune. Indeed, Mozambique's growth under the low regime compares very favorably with that of Mauritius, which is highly diversified and so has no observations falling in the low-regime subsample (see figure 7.13).

Turning to the other policy variables, we find that more inflation leads to more convergence under the full sample and low regime. In the case of the latter more inflation also leads to diversification, as does a higher budget deficit. This result could mean that increased diversification is associated with less macroeconomic stability, but this intuition needs to be confirmed. For the high regime we find no relation between inflation and diversification, while increased budget deficits lead to *less* diversification and have no effect on convergence. A greater degree of openness leads to less diversification and more convergence under this regime and has no impact whatsoever on the others. Our reading of figure 7.12 reinforces these findings: inflation is generally lower under the high regime for countries experiencing both regimes (with the exception of Ivory Coast), while government deficits are higher, but only moderately so in most cases, and always less than 10 percent of GDP. For Cape Verde, the result of government deficit consolidation as diversification increased is very clear, as is the dramatic lowering of its inflation rate. Diversification coupled with convergence also appears to go hand in hand with an average degree of openness in the range of 60–80 percent of GDP based on Ivory Coast, Cape Verde, and Senegal's performance on this score.

The results obtained for policy variables in SADC differ from those in ECOWAS when compared on a sample-by-sample basis. We find that more inflation leads to *less* convergence and *less* diversification under the low regime, as does greater openness. Greater openness is also associated with *less* diversification in the full sample. Increased government deficits lead to more convergence and *less* diversification for the same sample, but increase diversification under the high regime. Our reading of figure 7.13 is that more inflation, larger budget deficits, and being less open are a greater concern for countries under the low regime. Regarding Mozambique the shift toward less diversification is accompanied by lower inflation, but also higher deficits, and it appears that there is scope for it to increase its degree of openness. With the exception of the sole effect mentioned above, we note that the effect of policy variables is not as pronounced under the high regime as in the others, which we take to be a sign of policy credibility.

As for the institutional variables, convergence increases as political and economic freedom increases in ECOWAS. Also, there is more convergence as the age of democracy increases, and this holds true for the low regime. However, an increase in the number of democracies in the system unexpectedly reduces convergence. Under the high regime, diversification increases with more political and more economic freedom. In the other two cases, diversification is associated with more economic freedom only. Indeed, we observe that the effect of economic freedom is pervasive across all samples and its effect is largest precisely under the high regime. In the full sample, being an older democracy also leads to less diversification, as do a larger number of prior transitions to dictatorship in the low regime. There is also more convergence under an English legal tradition. While these results are interesting, they clearly need to be further explored.[27]

For now, we take away the insight that a positive relation must exist between economic and political freedoms, which may have to exceed some critical threshold in order for there to be an environment conducive to convergence (full sample). In addition, economic freedom may be a necessary, but not sufficient, condition to underpin successful diversification in ECOWAS. The insight applies to SADC: an increase in both political *and* economic freedoms increases convergence in both the low and high regimes. This does not happen in the full sample, possibly because of a composition effect (we have the combined effect of two opposing effects associated with more economic freedom, which leads to more diversification under the low sample and less under the high). Moreover, an increase in both freedoms increases diversification under the low regime but has the opposite effect under the high. Here again, the full sample exhibits mixed results. Even though this is not the main focus of analysis in this section, most control variables display the expected signs.[28] Additional insights against which to interpret both countries' performance with respect to political and economic governance and the convergence-diversification relationship relative to their subregional partners is provided in the next section.

7.5   Comparative Description of Cape Verde and Mozambique

We seek to embed the insights from the estimation of diversification-convergence regimes to successful development experiences in Cape Verde and Mozambique into a comparative description of the broad dimensions of economic growth and foreign trade on the one hand and macroeconomic policy and financial reputation on the other. Going back to the interaction between globalization and governance in Africa, section 7.5.3 presents progress on the MDG and other governance indicators.

---

27. This task requires a better understanding of how freedoms interact with one another and how they relate to alternative legal, political, and constitutional arrangements, as discussed in Macedo et al. (2013).

28. For example, more capital and more oil both lead to more convergence, while landlockedness has the opposite effect in ECOWAS. On the other hand, total labor force and population density have unexpected signs.

7.5.1   Economic Growth and Foreign Trade

Cape Verde

During the 1970s, the growth rate of GDP was positive (0.18 percent) but below the ECOWAS average (1.18 percent). In contrast it averaged 6.85 percent during the 1980s, while ECOWAS reported a decline of –0.64 percent. The reversal of fortunes continued during the 1990s, with a growth rate above the ECOWAS average (3.89 percent vs. –0.20 percent) and over the 2000–2006 period (1.04 percent vs. 0.86 percent). Although the causal study of growth is beyond the scope of our research, Cape Verde's improved growth performance follows the policy and institutional reforms described above. Describing their impact on exports, these were derived mainly from a relatively limited natural resource base. During 1988–1997, exports consisted mainly of primary-sector products, namely fish and crustacean, and so were neither diversified nor high value added. The 1976 decision to join ECOWAS was possibly one of the few exceptions to the otherwise protectionist trade policy. In practice, ECOWAS trade is of reduced importance, as ECOWAS members produce similar manufactured products. Clearly of greater importance was the decision to diversify production during 1992–1996, which went hand in hand with greater trade openness and a market-orientated policy stance. As a result, exports grew substantially. After a dramatic decline of over 40 percent in 1993, exports surged to almost 4 percent in 1997 (IMF 1998). The destination of exports also changed, as these were now directed mainly toward the European Union, particularly Portugal and Spain. Most of the export growth, however, has been in tourism, notwithstanding the cyclical efforts to diversify the fishing and industrial sectors since the 1990s.

When the government shifted away from a policy of state control to a free market one in 1988, tourism also began to develop substantially. In line with this policy change, Werlin (1996) observes that this sector's development entailed the synchronization of public and private investment in infrastructure. Legislation was also passed to encourage tourism, which included streamlining approval of qualified projects, allowing for a gaming industry, and setting up a regulatory and enforcement framework. Furthermore, a standard service fee was levied on the users, as opposed to service providers, which helped finance tourism. Direct public investment in infrastructure construction, such as hotels and transportations, was also pursued. Tourism's contribution to GDP increased from approximately 2 percent in 1995 to 5 percent in 2000 and 10 percent in 2005 (Mitchell 2008). As noted in IMF (2008a), the balance of payments changed from being very dependent on international aid and emigrants' remittances to being based on tourism and tourism-related foreign direct investment. In 2001, services exports and foreign direct investment surpassed transfers for the first time as a percentage of GDP. Indeed, Cape Verde became the fastest-growing market within the group of tourism-based economies whose travel exports have exceeded 10 percent of GDP for at least one year during 1998–2007, reporting an average annual growth rate of tourism services around 30 percent during 2000–2006. During the same period Croatia registered an average annual growth rate of 20 percent, the second highest. Tourism is highly procyclical, however, so an excessive reliance on it increases output volatility unless exports of goods and services are sufficiently diversified. Unfortunately, tourism is absent from the OECD database used in our empirical work.

When it returned to power in 2001, PAICV pursued growth-orientated policies while rationalizing and reducing import taxes and seeking to rein in the budget deficit. It also promoted trade integration through increased access to preferential markets, such as the United States (African Growth and Opportunity Act [AGOA]), and European Union (Cotonou agreement). Joining the World Trade Organization in 2008 required a transparent and predictable trade and foreign investment environment, which accelerated Cape Verde's global integration. Although recently graduated to middle-income status, it still benefits from preferential market access for least developed countries. Recent governments have continued the reform process, including those of relevance to financial and exchange markets. Growth has been sustained by the service sector, namely transports, hotel, and restaurants and communications, and also due to increased spending on education and improved governance. Indeed, the importance of the service sector, largely in tourism, was evident as early as 1980. Its continued success depends on further improving required infrastructure, namely good communications and a liberalized air transport market (Lourenço and Foy 2003). Cape Verde's business cycles have thus become more synchronized with developed economies following increasing trade and financial integration into the world economy: Ribeiro, Loureiro, and Martins (2008) make this an argument for "euroization" and the stability of a real effective exchange rate where the euro and dollar shares are equal to one-half (table 7.10) and could be used in supporting such policy recommendation. On the other side, the labor market is relatively rigid and administered prices still exist, for example, in the energy sector. Thus structural problems persist and they make adjustment to external shocks more difficult.

Regarding foreign financing sources, emigrant's remittances accounted for 12 percent of GDP in 2006, and their low volatility has allowed for consumption smoothing in response to external shocks. However, remittances have become more procyclical in recent years; for example, the correlation between (detrended) GDP and remittances was around 65 percent for the period 1980–2006. This fact may be associated with investment-driven flows rather than traditional consumption-smoothing behavior. Since financial flows are far more volatile and less prone to act as a buffer in times of crisis, this is another challenge to Cape Verde: reforms are a necessary but not sufficient condition for success. Adequate implementation and control is also

Table 7.10   Nominal and real effective exchange rates based on consumer prices

	CVP NEX	CVP R CPI	MOZ NEX	MOZ R CPI
1990	85	100	8	70
1991	86	95	13	84
1992	83	93	23	107
1993	94	103	33	114
1994	96	104	52	113
1995	95	98	81	117
1996	100	100	100	100
1997	107	100	97	92
1998	112	102	99	94
1999	115	102	104	97
2000	124	116	115	99
2001	125	117	154	124
2002	122	114	181	127
2003	112	105	199	126
2004	106	104	198	114
2005	106	107	202	112
2006	106	104	224	112
2007	101	97	238	113
2008	98	91	232	103
2009	100	91	244	105
2010	91	81	243	96
2011	91	80	243	94

required to ensure that increased foreign direct investment translates into higher growth and employment.

Industrial policy in the 1980s was characterized by less state intervention and more privatization, which led to the creation of a vibrant private sector that contributed positively to growth. On this score, the literature shows a clear link between private ownership and economic growth. According to Plane (1997), privatizations are a means to reduce government loans, equity, subsidies, and explicit or implicit government guarantees for borrowing, which contributes toward competitiveness and a more efficient market economy.

In terms of competitiveness, the relative stability of Cape Verde's real effective exchange rate since 1992 has already been mentioned. This is largely attributable to the Cape Verde escudo's peg, first to a basket of currencies during 1977–1998 and to the euro thereafter (table 7.10). Thus, exchange rate changes have not played a major role in engineering gains in competitiveness. Moreover, the low volatility reflects the control of inflation over the 1990s.

Mozambique

The GDP data show a similar, though slightly worse, comparative performance in the preindependence period, where the country grows at an average rate of 4.6 percent, while the SADC average was close to 5 percent, then the period of social and political unrest, where we watch a general regional slowdown and a severe recession in Mozambique (an average rate of –1.6 percent while SADC average growth rate equals 1.7 percent), and finally, in the postwar period, Mozambique grows at a fast rate (averaging about 8.5 percent per annum [p. a.]), while the region grows at a considerably slower rate of 3.4 percent, less than half of Mozambique's. The civil war is characterized by both a regional slowdown and a significant decrease in Mozambique's GDP per capita. While SADC still manages to grow at a rate of less than 1 percent per year, Mozambique's GDP per capita falls, on average, 3 percent per year. After the severe recession of the late 1970s and 1980s, when Mozambique fell back in comparison to its neighbors, Mozambique more than doubles its GDP per capita and starts to close the gap relative to the SADC average.

Export specialization has gone hand in hand with GDP growth, possibly due to the megaproject-related exports, which increased appreciably since 2000. Products such as aluminum and electrical energy now dominate exports, while prawns and cashews lost significance. The average trade share of world exports more than doubled in the 2001–2006 period relative to 1991–2000, but remains lower than in comparator groups in Africa and Asia.[29] While most Mozambican exports are directed to OECD countries, SADC is also a preferred destination, making up over 20 percent of the 2007 total, of which sixteen is accounted for by South Africa. This increase is due almost exclusively to megaproject-related exports, rather than a diversified performance associated with extensive competitiveness gain. Mozambique's revealed comparative advantages are in the production of aluminum, gas, electrical energy, and wood articles, reflected in terms of trade that improved significantly more than in comparator groups in Africa and Asia. As aluminum prices rose, the terms of trade improved by 7 percent in 2001–2006 as opposed to 0.5 percent during 1991–2000. These industrial exports are directed mainly to developed countries, whose share in the share in total exports toward those countries are from 40.1 percent in 1991–2001 to 63.9 percent in 2002–2005 (Lledó, Peiris, and Kvintradze 2007, 61). Considering traditional exports, Mozambique's main agricultural exports are cashew nuts, sugar cane, cotton fiber, and timber. Other products include sisal, tobacco, and fruits such as bananas, citrus, and mango. The main fisheries product, prawns (shrimp), continues to be among the country's top exports (and the largest agricultural export in 2007). Unlike the typical cases of export specialization, in Mozambique these grew by an annual

29. Lledó, Peiris, and Kvintradze (2007) compare Mozambique with sub-Saharan Africa (SSA) and Indonesia, Malaysia, the Philippines, and Thailand (ASEAN4) instead of SADC average. It rose from 0.01 to 0.02, whereas SSA rose from 1.5 to 1.6 and ASEAN4 remained constant. Since the early 1990s, exports have expanded at an average rate of 10 percent per year. According to the 2007 WTO Trade Policy Review, exports reached over $2.4 billion.

average rate of 4 percent, whereas the growth of megaproject-related exports was over 10 percent yearly, on average (additional evidence in Easterly and Resheff 2010).

In terms of competitiveness, Mozambique's real effective exchange rate (shown in table 7.10, with euro and dollar shares equal to one-half) has tracked the SADC average since the mid-1990s, whereas before it was clearly less competitive than the subregion. Nevertheless, both Mozambique and SADC are less competitive than South Africa, especially in recent years. Based on our reading of the 2006 and 2007 World Bank Enterprises surveys in section 7.5.3, trade liberalization has yet to yield substantial improvements in firm-level competitiveness. While Mozambique has better infrastructures (particularly on water, electricity, and Internet), less corruption, and a generally better regulatory environment than SADC, PALOP, and sub-Saharan Africa, it has less developed financial markets, a state where rule of law grounded less export-oriented firms, and less technology licensed to foreigners than the benchmarks (additional evidence in La Porta and Schleifer [2010]).

Notwithstanding the progress achieved thus far, Mozambique also faces a number of challenges. As it depends on foreign aid, revenue and administration reform, as well as a stronger fiscal regime toward mineral and oil resources, will be required for the government to enforce an "exit strategy" that enables it to raise revenue for its own, to finance at least current expenditure as soon as the MDGs are achieved (Lledó, Peiris, and Kvintradze 2007). While it is true that Mozambique has a strong export record when one considers its share of world exports over the last few years, this achievement has been primarily due to specific megaprojects, most noticeably in the aluminum sector. Moreover, its trade pattern is sometimes the result of protectionist policies, such as tax exemptions and qualification as export-processing zones that allow companies to import goods duty free and benefit from tax incentives. Two examples are the sugar and cashew industries. In the late 1990s, an import tax on sugar led to increased domestic sugar production, and an export tax on raw cashew nuts penalized small exporters while encouraging small- and medium-sized cashew processing. In this case, the pattern of specialization is clearly linked not only to comparative advantage, but also to trade policy.

That said, Mozambique's trade regime is not too restrictive. In 2006, the average tariff was in line with the rest of SADC, there were no significant nontariff barriers according to the IMF, and the process of tariff disarmament will likely continue. As a result, the maximum tariff has declined from 35 percent in 1999 to 20 percent in 2006. Mozambique's business environment is still relatively weak. The *Ease of Doing Business* indicators for 2006 suggest that custom procedures, business registration, and contract enforcement still perform poorly against other SADC members. Mozambique was one of the countries that benefited most from the Heavily Indebted Poor

Countries and Multilateral Debt Relief Initiatives (IMF 2008b). Coupled with a cautious macroeconomic stance, debt relief has allowed for increased spending, especially in the health and education sectors. However, long-term fiscal sustainability hinges crucially on the widening of the tax base and on economic growth underpinned by high-quality structural investments.

7.5.2   Macroeconomic Policy and Financial Reputation

Exchange Market Pressure

The empirical results in section 7.4 did not use EMP and real effective exchange rate indices due to database incompatibilities, but they did establish that lower budget deficits (less than 7 percent of GDP) are associated with convergence for both ECOWAS and SADC. Not unrelated, Cape Verde and Mozambique also compare favorably to respective subregional averages in financial reputation. As discussed in Macedo, Pereira, and Reis (2009), this can be proxied by EMP, a weighted sum of the nominal depreciation rate, changes in foreign reserves (excluding gold), and changes in the interest-rate differential,[30] that is,

$$EMP_t = \Delta e_t + \eta_r \Delta r_t + \eta_i \Delta (i_t - i_t^*).$$

The weights for reserves and for the interest rate differential are given by the standard deviation of depreciation relative to the respective variable, to avoid that the most volatile components of EMP dominates the others. As mentioned, according to the governance indicators reported in table 7.8, Cape Verde compares well to the ECOWAS average. Lopes and Santos (2010) note, however, that this institutional portrait misses the "financial credibility factor" that they analyze through EMP using monthly data from 1990 to 2005, both in a descriptive sense and in a model-dependent framework. Mozambique's mixed record compared to the SADC average is shown in table 7.8. Yet, it behaves well in terms of political stability and voice and accountability.[31]

Lopes and Santos (2010) distinguish between fixers and floaters as follows: The seven franc CFA countries (Benin, Burkina Faso, Côte d'Ivoire, Mali, Niger, Senegal, and Togo) and Guinea-Bissau peg to the euro in ECOWAS, while Seychelles and Zimbabwe peg to the dollar in SADC.[32] Ghana, Nigeria, Sierra Leone, and Gambia are floaters in ECOWAS and Zambia, Tanzania, Mauritius, Malawi, Madagascar, and South Africa are floaters in

30. From *International Financial Statistics* and central banks' websites.
31. Figure 1 in Lopes and Santos (2010) shows the tremendous improvements in Mozambique as soon as the war is over, compared to SADC and Great Britain. Again it misses the "financial credibility" factor.
32. Botswana, Lesotho, Namibia, and Swaziland peg to the rand, so they float relative to the dollar. Lopes and Santos (2010) acknowledge that this makes them effectively neither fixers nor floaters, but a third category.

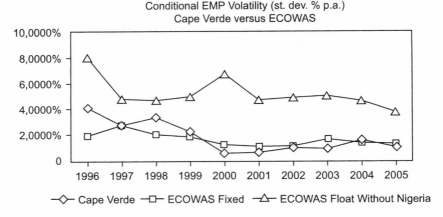

Fig. 7.14A   Conditional volatility of EMP Cape Verde versus ECOWAS
Source: Lopes and Santos (2010).

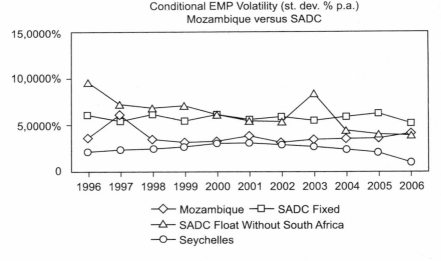

Fig. 7.14B   Conditional volatility of EMP Mozambique versus SADC
Source: Lopes and Santos (2010).

SADC. They also find that real exchange rate depreciation improves financial reputation in Cape Verde while doing the opposite in Benin, where it increases EMP mean and volatility.

If financial reputation is defined as low EMP with low volatility, then fixers behave better than floaters both in ECOWAS and SADC. Conditional volatility and mean EMP, reported in figures 7.14A, 7.14B, 7.15A and 7.15B for ECOWAS (without Nigeria) and SADC (without South Africa), strengthen

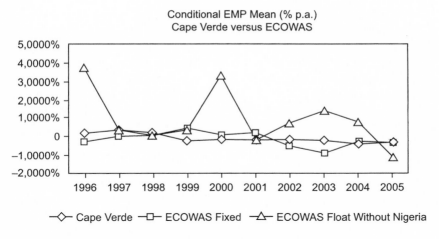

Fig. 7.15A   Conditional mean of EMP Cape Verde versus ECOWAS
Source: Lopes and Santos (2010).

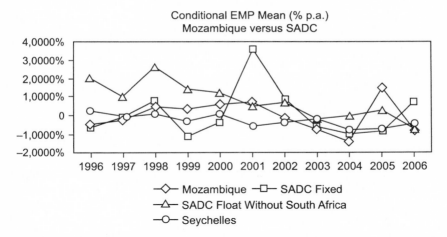

Fig. 7.15B   Conditional mean of EMP Mozambique versus SADC
Source: Lopes and Santos (2010).

conclusions from the unconditional volatility and mean EMP. Comparing Mozambique's EMP performance to SADC, except South Africa (which dominates the weighted average), Botswana, Lesotho, Namibia, and Swaziland because they are pegged to the rand, and Zimbabwe because of the huge devaluations in 1998 and 2000, the standard deviation of Mozambique's EMP has converged to that of Seychelles. The fixers, taken as a whole, behave very similarly to South Africa, given that Lesotho and Namibia are pegged to the rand and Botswana is pegged to a basket of currencies where the South African rand has an overwhelming weight. From 1994 to 2008, Mozambique's EMP mean has behaved similarly to the one of South Africa but, from 1999 on, its volatility has converged more sharply toward the one of Seychelles. Mozambique also has a few EMP "crises" (taken to be extreme values of EMP), none of which are severe, behaving better on this account than several economies in the region, such as Tanzania, Mauritius, and Malawi. In SADC, the gap between fixers and floaters is not as wide as in ECOWAS.

For the impact of domestic credit in EMP variance, Mozambique appears with a positive relationship that indicates the opposite of Cape Verde. It seems that these countries did not avoid the volatility and uncertainty on EMP with monetary expansions through domestic credit. But if we complement this result with the one obtained for the coefficient of domestic credit variation in the mean equation for Mozambique, then volatility is not as harmful given that Mozambique was able to reduce its mean EMP when credit was expanded, although they did not behave so well in controlling the volatility. In Mozambique, moreover, the initial real depreciation is followed by nominal depreciations, which increase EMP and incite speculation.

In the SADC floaters group, Mauritius and South Africa display the most credible results on our key indicators, as well as other coefficients. However, Mozambique also has some positive conclusions, as the risk-return relationship or the domestic credit effect on the EMP mean. Cape Verde has had a remarkable degree of credibility and sophistication of its exchange markets, undoubtedly due to the quality of the institutional framework. Due to its natural focus on political freedom and accountability, the governance indicators presented in table 7.8 and below overlook the effect of financial expectations. Mozambique, too, despite lagging behind Cape Verde, also has some good results, very much in line with other floaters in the region, and better in some accounts (namely, the absence of any severe crises, a conditional volatility close to a fixer's, and a risk-return effect pointing the right way, unlike many other countries in the region). While Mozambique's financial reputation is weaker than Cape Verde's, it seems to be heading the right way. We now described the foreign exchange market in greater detail for each of the two countries.

Cape Verde

On this score, Cape Verde's track record improved substantially given that, following independence, high budget deficits were the order of the day. The reason for expansionary fiscal policy was the relatively large expenditures required to improve living conditions, run the state-controlled industrial sector, and pay for the high level of imports. The deficit was also high due to interest payments on domestic and foreign debt, leading to a loss of foreign exchange reserves and financial reputation. It was only in the late 1990s that the deficit was reduced. This change was accompanied by measures to control inflation and strengthen the financial sector. In 1997, a program was adopted that did away with domestic bank financing to be substituted by that obtained from foreign sources. As a result, the 1998 budget deficit was financed entirely by foreign creditors, whereas domestic creditors had accounted for 10 percent of GDP and foreign ones almost 1 percent in 1997. The peg to the euro, which allowed for low inflation rates and increased financial reputation, was crucial in obtaining the needed international finance. The government also speeded up the privatization process, improved tax collection, and increased the recovery of debt obligations from public enterprises. Current primary expenditure was curtailed to offset higher interest revenue and the government abstained from prefinancing, donor-supported investment projects. The composition of the expenditures was also modified while maintaining their level. With these measures, the budgetary position changed from a deficit 15.1 percent of GDP in 1997 to a surplus of 0.5 percent in 2000.

The 2001 elections brought about some fiscal slippage, but the newly elected PAICV government then sought to reduce the deficit, as well as domestic and external public debt, without overly increasing the tax burden. More recent reforms have streamlined and rationalized taxes on imports, accompanied by a general reduction of customs duties and excises. At the same time, public spending was redirected toward education, health, and other priority areas, in accordance with the government's poverty-reduction strategy. Transfers and subsidies were also reduced substantially, notably subsidies to large public enterprises. As a consequence, current revenues increased from approximately 21 percent of GDP in 2001 to 23 percent of GDP in 2004, while current public expenditures were kept constant at around 21–22 percent of GDP during the same period. The adoption of an IMF mid-term program in 2006, supported by a new nonfinancial instrument—Policy Support Instrument (PSI)—confirmed Cape Verde's commitment to maintain the pace of reforms and close dialogue on macroeconomic policy. The program, which will be completed in 2010, will assist Cape Verde in reducing fiscal risks and minimize the impact of external shocks on its economy by promoting the necessary structural reforms under IMF advice and supervision. While AEO (2010) maintains a positive assessment on financing, the threats to the EU financial system are bound to have a negative effect going forward.

In 1976, Banco de Cabo Verde started operations, succeeding Banco Nacional Ultramarino (the former issuing bank) and Banco de Fomento Nacional (a state-owned development bank). The currency was pegged to the escudo but in 1977, following Portugal's devaluation, the peg shifted to a basket of currencies. During the eighties, several reforms were put in place, namely through the use of information and communication technologies in the central administration and a network of bank offices spreading through the archipelago: A newly created investment department managed programs supporting productive activities. From 1988 on, a vast program of reforms began promoting trade liberalization and privatizations while the government remained responsible for infrastructures. Successive governments continued these reforms, accompanied by an increasing concern with the role of education and good governance. High growth in transports, hotels, restaurants, and communications was associated with these reforms, making Cape Verde largely dependent on services by 1980.

In 1990 monetary and exchange rate policies, as well as the supervisory and lender of last resort roles of the central bank, were reinforced by new by-rules but commercial and development activities continued until September 1993. Starting April 1, 1998, the Cape Verde escudo was pegged to the euro in the framework of an agreement with Portugal. Ribeiro, Loureiro, and Martins (2008) describe the agreement, while Macedo and Pereira (2006) associate it with a substantial reduction in EMP and lower inflation, as described above. In 2002, deficit financing by the central bank was also formally prohibited. In practice, the government has not needed to rely on this type of financing due to the receipt of donor aid and the sale of treasury bonds with medium-term maturities. Fiscal policy has also been prudent with a medium-term fiscal strategy for 2008–2010 approved by the IMF. Fiscal reforms were accompanied by an increase in tax effort, particularly of income tax, as corporate tax rates are still relatively low. Together, this environment of fiscal responsibility has allowed debt sustainability analysis to classify Cape Verde's debt risk as low. The external position continues to depend on transfers, mostly migrants' remittances. The decreasing role of transfers and the increasing role of portfolio and direct investment from abroad erodes remittances' role as a buffer for households. It is likely that second and third generation emigrants will be less inclined to send remittances and will only invest in Cape Verde when it is profitable to do so. The government will have to take cognizance of this fact when designing and implementing its medium-term development strategy.

Mozambique

Mozambique's economic recovery in recent years has clearly entailed a more effective and prudent fiscal policy. After the 1992 peace accord, there was a significant reduction of current expenditures (from 20 percent in 1992 to 10 percent three years later). In fact, except during 2000–2002, revenues have exceeded current expenditure since 1995, while investment expenditure (mainly on megaproject-related investments) has been paid with grants. Such a strategy, in combination with a sound monetary policy (particularly since 1996–1997) and significant trade liberalization (as discussed above), has allowed for higher growth rates, private investment, and lower inflation. We also observe a shift in the utilization of public resources, with new emphasis being given to sectors such as health, education, and agriculture, along a poverty-reduction strategy undertaken principally since 1998.[33] At present, it seems that budget equilibrium is not a goal for the Mozambican policymakers. Moreover, the tax effort is still very low, although it has increased recently. As such, it is important for government to increase taxes on big projects and to create procedures that increase compliance in order to widen the future tax base.

Mozambique's currency, the metical, was created on June 16, 1980, by Law 2/80 and the colonial administration's banknotes ceased to circulate. The first credit conceded by the International Development Association, though, was only granted in 1985; the second was in 1987 and successive agreements were signed in the following years. Mozambique has benefited widely from the support of the IDA, either financially or through its technical expertise. The main accomplishments, as reported in IDA (2007), involve the liberalization of trade, financial sector reform (with a separation between the commercial and central banking, with competition in commercial banking), improved health conditions, good investment climate, and privatizations in several sectors. On January, 31, 1987, the metical was pegged to the US dollar instead of being pegged to a basket of six currencies reflecting shares in goods and services transactions, but authorities reverted to a basket of ten currencies in April 1988.

In the late eighties/early nineties, policymakers started aiming at transforming Mozambique into a market economy. Throughout 1989, several capital account liberalization measures were pursued: agencies of the bank were allowed to conduct foreign operations (April) and private financial firms were given more freedom to conduct foreign exchange operations (July). On November 30, finally, the new Constitution declared that Mozambique would aim at being a market economy.

In May 1993, interest rates were semiliberalized and left to the free market, with the central bank determining maximum and minimum bounds. In June, exchange rates from the Secondary and Official Exchange Markets were unified. By 1994, the interest rates were completely liberalized. Through the following years, several liberalizing measures were undertaken and the legal foundations of the exchange market were perfected.

In June 1999, in a move that was very important for Mozambique's development, external debt in the amount of $3.7 billion is erased by the Heavily Indebted Poor Countries Initiative of the IMF. In 2000, a reinforced initiative was put in place to the favor of Mozambique. In 2003, further measures were taken to ease capital operations by nonresidents in the stock exchange. In fact, AEO (2008) claims that debt relief early in the twenty-first century was a condition for most of the development Mozambique is experiencing today. In 2005, Banco de Moçambique started intervening in the Interbank

33. For instance, according to official budget figures from 1998 to 2000, health and education accounted for 26–28 percent of central governmental spending.

Foreign Exchange Market through weekly auctions of foreign exchange and a Multilateral Debt Relief Initiative was launched.

Mozambique's inflation rate has been under control for some time now and it now ranks among the lowest in the SADC. Indeed, the control of inflation has been the main objective of monetary policy since 1987, upon the approval of an economic recuperation plan, and even more so since the early 1990s. The data show that Mozambique managed to control inflation since 1991, averaging consistently below its SADC counterparts, particularly Angola. The inflation rate has been about half of the average in SADC since the nineties. This accomplishment is significant if we consider that in this period Mozambique experienced a transition from a central-planned, public-owned economy to a free-market economy, which is known to create an upward pressure on inflation.[34] More recently, Banco de Moçambique has also adopted several important measures, namely, daily liquidity forecasting and sterilization of changes in the monetary base, which improved the conduct of monetary policy.

This relative stability in inflation has been accompanied from the 1990s onward by a steady depreciation of the Mozambican metical's exchange rate against the US dollar, which is in line with other depreciation rates of SADC currencies. Regarding its external position, Mozambique has experienced trade deficits and negative factor incomes balances, which have been partially compensated by transfers (with the exception of 2006, where transfers were in excess of the shortfalls). The trade balance improved up till 2006 due to high aluminum prices and export growth of cashew nuts, sugar, prawns, and tobacco. However, the increase in the oil price and a decrease in traditional exports in 2007 deteriorated the trade balance. Indeed, financing a current account deficit, which reached 22 percent of GDP in 1999, required debt relief.

7.5.3 Millennium Development Goals and Governance Indicators

The information on MDG is drawn from a report prepared at the request of the Guinean presidency of CPLP (IICT 2007) and from AEO: the percentage of satisfactory outcomes in PALOP is 31 percent according to the first source, but 26 percent according to the second, as shown in table 7.11. The corresponding percentage for the whole AEO sample of fifty-three countries is 31 percent in 2007 and 41 percent in 2009 and 2010. Fewer entries with missing data appear in AEO (2009, 2010) than in previous issues, at least for PALOP, and the criteria used seem to have stabilized together with the percentage. The ranking found in the first source remains that found in tables 7.4 through 7.6, Cape Verde followed closely by Sao Tome, and Mozambique only marginally above Guinea Bissau and Angola, whereas the Sao Tome and Mozambique have the same average AEO score. Table

---

34. See Andersson and Sjöö (2002) for the structural adjustment's impact on inflation.

Table 7.11   **The MDGs in PALOP before and after crisis**

No. Indic.	1 pov.	2 schl.	3 rat.	4 < 5 m	5 mm	6 dis.	7 wat.	No. sat.
A	S	R	S	R	R	R	C	1
CV	A	R	A	A	A		A	5
GB	R	S	S	R	R	R	A	1
M	S	C	S	S	S	R	S	1
STP	R	A	A	S	R		A	3
No. percent sat.	1	2	2	1	1	0	4	31
2007								
A	C							1
CV		C	C	C				3
GB								0
M	C							1
STP	C	C		C		C		4
No. percent sat.	3	2	1	2	0	1	0	26
2009								
A	R	S	S	S	S	R	S	0
CV	R	A	A	S	A		C	4
GB	S	A	A	S	S	S	A	3
M	S	C	C	S	S		S	2
STP	R	R	S	S	R	S		0
No. percent sat.	0	3	3	0	1	0	2	26
2010								
A	S	S	R	S	R	S	S	0
CV	A	R	S	A	S	S	A	3
GB	R	S	S	S	R	S	S	0
M	S	C	S	C	A	R	S	3
STP	R	A	A	S	R		C	3
No. percent sat.	1	2	1	2	1	0	2	26

Source: First panel, Macedo, Martins, and Pereira (2007); others AEO of year indicated.
Note: A = achieved/early achiever; C = on course/on track; S = slow progress/off track; and R = regress satisfactory (A + C).

7.12 provides more detail on the quantified MDG presented in table 7.11 and compares Cape Verde and Mozambique to the ECOWAS and SADC average as before.

On the eradication of poverty, Cape Verde has one of the lowest shares of the poorest quintile in national consumption. Using the data available, we see that it is slightly worse than the average ECOWAS member. Angel-Urdinola and Wodon (2007) argue that relative poverty increased between the 1988/89 and 2001 surveys, based on the increase in the Gini coefficient from 50.2 percent to 53.83 percent), while absolute poverty measures decreased dramatically. Mozambique, meanwhile, has a slightly larger share (5.4 percent) of consumption of poor people when compared to the SADC average. Although the United States has a comparable figure, its definition of poverty is a relative and not absolute one. In view of Mozambique's recent

Table 7.12 **Millennium development goals**

1. Share of poorest quintile in national consumption (%)

Cape Verde	4.4	1990–2003
ECOWAS	5.3	
Mozambique	5.5	1991–2004
SADC	5.0	

2. Net enrollment ratio in primary education

	1991–2006	1991–1999	2000–2006	90s–00s (%)
Cape Verde	942	953	938	−1.5
ECOWAS[a]	575	508	602	9.5
Mozambique	614	470	663	19.3
SADC[b]	808	720	835	11.5

3. Ratio of girls to boys in primary education

Cape Verde	95	95	96	0.6
ECOWAS	80	75	81	7.8
Mozambique	79	74	81	9.0
SADC	91	92	91	−1.4

4. Children under five mortality rate per 1,000 live births

	1990	1995	2000	2005	2006
Cape Verde	60	50	42	35	34
ECOWAS	213	207	190	181	179
		90s	00s	90s–00s (%)	
Mozambique		224	154	−7.0	
SADC		155	143	−1.2	

5. Maternal mortality ratio per 100,000 live births 2005

Cape Verde	210
ECOWAS	1,027
Mozambique	520
SADC	819

6. Tuberculosis incidence rate per year per 100,000 population

	90s	00s	90s–00s (%)
Cape Verde	1,642	1,672	0.0
ECOWAS	2,076	2,817	0.7
Mozambique	2,854	4,330	1.5
SADC	3,066	4,708	1.6

7. Proportion of population using an improved drinking water source

Cape Verde	79	80	1.0
ECOWAS	52	57	4.2
	1995	2000	2006
Mozambique	39	41	42
SADC	57	60	63

8. Debt service as a percentage of exports of goods and services

	1990–1994	1995–1999	2000–2006
Cape Verde	136	118	82
ECOWAS	171	179	102
Mozambique	238	252	33
SADC[c]	132	121	71

Source: Same as table 7.8.

[a]Except Sierra Leone.

[b]Excluding Angola and DR Congo due to insufficient data.

[c]Except Zimbabwe, Zambia, and DR Congo.

evolution, the IMF considered it likely that this goal will be attained by 2015, and the 2009 and 2010 AEO percentages of satisfactory performance are uniformly better than in 2007. In fact, they are higher in 2010 than in 2009, so that they do not yet show any effect of the crisis—except for objectives 5 and 7, maternal mortality, and access to water, which fall to one-half of the previous value.

On MDG 2, net enrollment in primary education, Cape Verde has actually decreased slightly. However, the enrolment level is very high, even by the developed world's standards. Notably, Cape Verde is well ahead of its ECOWAS partners, which reflects its focus on education and the quality thereof. For Mozambique, the net enrollment in primary education has increased significantly since the 1990s, especially during 2000–2006. Indeed, Mozambique has improved remarkably when compared to most SADC countries, but stills lags behind them. The same can be said for its level of literacy. On MDG 3, gender parity, Cape Verde is better placed than its ECOWAS partners, but some of them are now catching up fast. Gender parity in Mozambique is one of the poorest in SADC but, at the same time, it registers a sustained and strong improvement. With respect to child mortality, MDG 4, Cape Verde's is by far the lowest in ECOWAS, but still far short of the level in developed countries. Even so, it has decreased significantly. On this score, Mozambique is improving rapidly, as its child mortality rate has decreased to 153.67 per thousand, which is much better than the SADC average. The IMF foresees that this MDG will probably be reached by 2015. For maternal health, MDG 5 (for which there is only one observation, and a higher percentage of satisfactory performance was reached in 2009 than in 2010), Cape Verde is the best in ECOWAS. Mozambique's maternal mortality rate was below the SADC average in 2005, which is in line with the improvement in child mortality and in public health as a whole. The MDG 6, the incidence, prevalence, and death rates associated with tuberculosis, show much lower figures in Cape Verde than for ECOWAS. There is no data on HIV prevalence in Cape Verde as far as we are aware. The prevalence and death rate of tuberculosis grew more in Mozambique than in SADC members, while HIV/AIDS statistics show a worrying increase in infection rates among young people.

The goal of sustainable development is often proxied by the proportion of the population having access to safe drinking water sources. It is much higher in Cape Verde than in ECOWAS. Similarly, the proportion of the urban population is also higher in Cape Verde, but a significant catching up is noticeable in ECOWAS member states. In Mozambique, the proportion of population having access to improved sanitation facilities has increased from 22 percent to 31 percent between 1995 and 2006: it lags behind other SADC partners but is quickly narrowing the gap. The same can be said of the proportion of the population living in slums, which has fallen drastically since 2001 (whereas in the SADC partners the reduction has been modest).

The weak spot of this MDG lies in the water quality since the improvement in the proportion of population having access to an improved drinking water source has been negligible, while the proportion of the urban population has actually decreased from 83 percent to 71 percent when comparing 1995 to 2006. This is again a case where the percentage of satisfactory performance reached in 2009 was about double that reported in 2010, under 30 percent as opposed to slightly over 60 percent.

The global partnership for development is often illustrated by debt service as a percentage of exports of goods and services, as done in table 7.12. This has been historically lower in Cape Verde when compared to ECOWAS and has decreased over time, but ECOWAS decreased more markedly when looking at the year-by-year numbers. Mozambique's debt service has fallen markedly and the period of high growth coincides with that of the donor community's relief of debt, as discussed in the previous subsection.

Coming back to the comparison of governance and freedom indicators appearing in tables 7.5, 7.6, and 7.8, Cape Verde's Economic Freedom Index has improved since 1996, when it obtained 49.7 points. However, trade freedom (45), government spending (30.9), financial freedom (10), and freedom from corruption (30) were below average. The lack of financial freedom was due to commercial banks' weak independence, and excessive government spending was due to weak industrial policies in the transition to independences. Financial freedom only ranked higher in 2002 (50 points), when a law that gave more independence to the central bank was approved. As for government spending, this category reached similar values to current ones in 2004 (around 70 points) because political measures aimed at controlling the budget deficit started to be effective. In the years following 1996, the country's score has been improving when compared on a year-to-year basis, except during 1997, 2003, 2005, and 2007. In 2010, Cape Verde reached its maximum score (61.8) and is classified as the 78th freest economy in the world. Above average items include business freedom (63.3), trade freedom (65.5), fiscal freedom (65.6), government spending (65.3), monetary freedom (74.5), and property rights (65). Freedoms in need of improvement were investment freedom (69), financial freedom (60), freedom from corruption (51), and labor freedom (48.1). In comparative terms, Cape Verde ranked seventh out of forty-six countries in sub-Saharan Africa, with a regional score much higher than the average.[35] Luiz, Pereira, and Oliveira (2013) present a set of institutional indicators for Mozambique for the period 1900 through to 2005, reproduced in figure 7.3. The first tracks political freedoms

35. This happens not only due to relatively good performances in the above-mentioned categories, but also due to the fact that its regional partners perform even worse in those categories where Cape Verde performs poorly. For example, Cape Verde ranks 47th out of 179 countries in Transparency International's 2008 Corruption Perceptions Index regarding the "freedom from corruption" indicator. However, Cape Verde ranks third when looking at only African countries, coming in after South Africa (first) and Botswana.

and is unique in its duration and complexity, even though it correlates highly with the Freedom House combined index of political and civil liberties. The second index constructs a property rights measure, which has not existed previously, but also reveals a fairly strong correlation with the other index. They explain this as follows: "The Portuguese government during several phases of its colonial administration went to great lengths to develop a more formal system of property rights even whilst politically suppressing the participation of the vast majority of its population and this drives down the correlation between these two indices to 0.46 under colonialism. If we focus on the post 1975 period the correlation shoots up to 0.93 which indicates that a deterioration in political freedom from independence onwards is associated with a lack of economic freedom and security, whilst an improvement sees a rise in economic freedoms as well."

The IICT (2007) includes the following six governance indicators from the World Bank Institute: freedom and accountability (FREE), stability and absence of violence (STAB), government efficiency (EF GV), quality of regulation (Q REG), quality of justice (JUST), and control of corruption (CORR), which were reported in table 7.8. Good governance has been one of the main features of Cape Verde's development. Rule of law and accountability stem from the fact that democracy is well established and that free elections take place regularly with the results not being disputed. The only aspect that fares worse is regulatory quality, but this indicator still fares better than most ECOWAS member states. Education is a major concern for Cape Verde governments: between 1970 and 1990, the number of children leaving school with secondary education increased dramatically. In 1990, half of the children in rural areas attended secondary school and 60 percent of girls received secondary education in urban areas (see Goujon and Wils 1996). The literacy rate in the people between fifteen and twenty-four years old is the highest in all ECOWAS. With respect to Mozambique, no significant evolution is noticeable between 1996 and 2006 for most indicators, and then it improves gradually. The exception is the indicator of political stability and the absence of violence/terrorism, which has improved markedly.

The twenty-eight indicators in the 2006 and 2007 World Bank Enterprise Surveys, for which both Cape Verde and Mozambique report at least ten answers, are in table 7.13, panels (a) through (e). The indicators for regional groupings and sub-Saharan Africa are simple averages of the countries, some of which are missing (two out of fifteen from ECOWAS and SADC, twelve in sub-Saharan Africa). Relative to the average of their comparator countries (in parentheses), then Cape Verde has more developed financial markets, greater macroeconomic stability, less corruption, and a state where rule of law is more grounded than ECOWAS, PALOP, and sub-Saharan Africa, but less export-oriented firms, less technology licensed to foreigners, higher taxes, and a heavier regulatory framework than the benchmarks. Mozambique has better infrastructures (water, electricity, and Internet)

Table 7.13   **World Bank Enterprise Survey**

A. International trade (= 5, <u>best</u>/**worst**)

Country/comparator	CV	MZ	SSA	SAD	ECW	LOP	Code
Exporting firms	**4**	6	13	<u>16</u>	11	5	%
Time imports	11	11	11	<u>10</u>	<u>10</u>	**17**	Day
Import license days	<u>06</u>	13	18	**21**	16	15	Day
Foreign technology	**2**	<u>33</u>	11	16	8	12	%
Foreign shareholder	**10**	20	19	<u>25</u>	12	14	%

B. Infrastructure (= 5, <u>best</u>/**worst**)

Country/comparator	CV	MZ	SSA	SAD	ECW	LOP	Code
No. electricity outages	**21**	<u>3</u>	14	12	16	10	No./mo.
No. Internet outages	4	<u>3</u>	46	32	**86**	<u>3</u>	No./mo.
No. water outages	13	<u>4</u>	8	6	9	7	No./mo.
Transportation	36	37	44	<u>35</u>	**49**	40	Percent bad
Access to land	<u>19</u>	26	34	31	**36**	28	Percent bad

C. Finance, competition, and education (<u>best</u>/**worst**)

Country/comparator	CV	MZ	SSA	SAD	ECW	LOP	Code
Credit line	<u>47</u>	**13**	24	24	20	17	Percent good
Investment own funds	<u>51</u>	<u>88</u>	77	74	80	78	Percent good
Access to finance	<u>48</u>	62	60	51	**68**	64	Percent bad
Number competitors	4	<u>3</u>	4	4	4	4	No.
Education workers	**43**	<u>33</u>	34	37	<u>28</u>	32	Percent bad

D. Institutions: stability, corruption, and rule of law (<u>best</u>/**worst**)

Country/comparator	CV	MZ	SSA	SAD	ECW	LOP	Code (%)
STAB crime theft and disorder	47	**50**	41	49	<u>35</u>	45	Bad
CORR corruption	<u>25</u>	37	46	43	**48**	42	Bad
CORR informal payments	<u>0</u>	2	**5**	3	5	2	Bad
JUST sales on credit	30	<u>19</u>	29	**36**	25	<u>19</u>	Bad
JUST government predictability	**59**	<u>21</u>	49	50	47	29	Good
JUST court impartiality	**62**	<u>15</u>	44	46	44	30	Good
JUST legal conflict resolution	**29**	<u>14</u>	23	21	25	27	Bad

E. Quality of regulation (<u>best</u>/**worst**)

Country/comparator	CV	MZ	SSA	SAD	ECW	LOP	Code (%)
Time senior mgt. regulations	**14**	<u>4</u>	7	8	8	7	Bad
Tax administration	41	<u>31</u>	46	36	**48**	36	Bad
Tax rates	**74**	<u>53</u>	59	51	61	57	Bad
Licensing permits	<u>29</u>	30	33	29	33	**37**	Bad
Labor regulations	**28**	17	20	21	<u>16</u>	18	Bad
Customs & trade regulations	**38**	<u>26</u>	33	28	30	33	Bad

Source: World Bank Enterprise Survey, courtesy of Francisco Queiró.

and less corruption than SADC, PALOP, and sub-Saharan Africa, but less developed financial markets, a state where rule of law is less grounded, less export-oriented firms, and less technology licensed to foreigners than the benchmarks.

7.6 Conclusions

The expansion, diversification, and deepening of trade and financial links between countries over several decades presented an unparalleled opportunity to raise living standards and achieve the MDG. Development success under globalization, meanwhile, is less a question of relative resource endowments or geographical location than in past waves of globalization. Moreover, adequate development responses to globalization become all the more important as globalization increasingly affects political and economic governance, mainly by reducing national policy space and increasing institutional and economic interdependence at various levels. Under these conditions, interactions between globalization and governance can be either positive or negative, depending on the orientation and predictability of economic policies and the accompanying institutional arrangements, but also on linkages between cultural, institutional, and economic factors.

Against this background, we want to determine whether the interaction between globalization and governance is positive or not in Cape Verde and Mozambique so as to assess the extent to which they represent development successes in West and southern Africa. Specifically, we attempt to identify lessons for successful governance based on meaningful national and regional comparisons of Cape Verde and Mozambique's development experience. Economic success under globalization for these countries entails necessarily, but not exclusively, positive market perceptions regarding outcomes such as trade diversification and narrowing of the income gap relative to the frontier. This aspect of success has to be, in turn, sustained by good governance and a level of political and economic freedom that their citizens and residents enjoy. As such, policy and institutional reforms provide the context against which to interpret governance indicators and progress toward the MDG.

To identify macrolevel policy and institutional combinations underpinning successful export diversification and economic convergence in ECOWAS and SADC, the empirical analysis establishes context-based objective metrics that assess the relative performance of Cape Verde and Mozambique in conjunction with evidence of a case-study nature. Given the severe lack of data over the period 1960–2004, this indirect approach to study trade-related development success in these two countries is unavoidable. We apply three-stage least squares and other estimation techniques, with broadly consistent results, to two main variables: the distance of a country's GDP per capita compared to that of the United States in order to capture economic convergence (ygap), and the inverse of the Herfindahl index (neq5) as a measure of export diversification. Together with additional control variables, these two variables are a meaningful characterization of each country's diversification convergence, which will be affected by the interaction between policy and institutional variables.

We first identify the determinants of diversification and convergence at the regional level. Then, we reestimate the model for subsamples that capture two different diversification-convergence scenarios in each subregion. The first subsample, denoted as the high regime, comprises countries that simultaneously exhibit high diversification and high convergence {ygap < 0.945 & neq5 > 4.5} while the second, the low regime, comprises those that exhibit the opposite combination{ygap > = 0.945 & neq5 < = 4.5}. This strategy allows us to highlight differences and commonalities in performance across regimes and regions including regional benchmarks, namely, Senegal for ECOWAS and Mauritius and South Africa for SADC.

The principal differences are that ECOWAS high-regime countries are becoming more diversified, while those of SADC are becoming less diversified. Opening up to trade is also an important driver of both convergence and diversification for the former, especially in the range of 45–75 percent of GDP, but not for the latter. In SADC high-regime countries, economic and political freedom drive convergence, suggesting effective institutional arrangements. As for the commonalities or lessons present in the high regimes, we find that: (a) the expected two-way relationship always exists; (b) convergence always entails macroeconomic stability (inflation < 9 percent, budget deficits < 7 percent of GDP); (c) political and economic freedoms are always greater, on average, when compared to the other cases; and (d) freedoms always affect diversification policy as do government deficits, albeit in different directions across both subregions. However, increasing deficits always counteract prevailing diversification stance in both subregions, which we take to be a sign of regime credibility. The comparison across subregions, meanwhile, serves to highlight the importance of institutions irrespective of the sample chosen: economic freedom always affects diversification in ECOWAS, while both freedoms affect it in SADC, where they affect convergence too. Efforts at monitoring the MDGs complement the context for export diversification across sub-Saharan Africa (Cabral and Veiga 2010) and for financial reputation in PALOP, ECOWAS, and SADC (Lopes and Santos 2010).

The estimated impact that Cape Verde and Mozambique have on their respective subregions, which accords with the intuition and implications of the posited two-way relationship, confirms the narrative of their long-term development. Based on our reading of this narrative, we identify the following common drivers of macrolevel policy and institutional combinations as being associated with the (different) two-way relationship of both countries: moving toward a market economy; opening up to regional and global trade; increasing economic and political freedom; pursing macroeconomic stability and financial reputation; ensuring policy continuity (especially in trade and industrial sectors), and focusing on human development (especially poverty reduction and education). These two case studies of positive G&G interaction reflect on the potential for cooperative governance and peer-review mechanisms outside of its usual domain among OECD and EU member countries. For Cape Verde, in particular, the effects of the "culture of peace" should be stressed again, as it helped sustain the move toward a market economy, through greater trade integration, especially with the European Union and the United States, culminating in membership in the World Trade Organization. Multiparty democracy and greater political freedom and civil liberties allowed policy continuity across the political divide and improved human development. This is not to say that human development is sustainable in the face of the current global crisis. In effect, macroeconomic stability was threatened from outside, but also through an insufficient attention to public and external deficits. If not appropriately monitored, this could threaten the positive interaction attained between globalization and governance.

Appendix A

The acronyms of the different variables used in the regressions are given above. The data are annual and cover the period 1960–2004, but some variables have shorter spans (e.g., data on political and civil liberties, economic freedom) as these only became available later. Capital controls are measured in the manner of the Annual Report on Exchange Arrangements and Exchange Restrictions of IMF, which seeks to capture whether there are explicit legal restrictions on capital transitions (supplemented with historical sources introduced by Eichengreen and Leblang [2006]). For data on the real effective exchange rate, the International Financial Statistics gives an index based on 2005 = 100, where an increase reflects an appreciation. A real effective exchange rate index represents a nominal effective exchange rate index adjusted for relative movements in national price or cost indicators of the home country and selected countries. A nominal effective exchange rate index, meanwhile, represents the ratio (expressed on the base 2005 = 100) of an index of a currency's period-average exchange rate to a weighted geometric average of exchange rates for the currencies of selected countries.

Table 7A.2 reports summary statistics for the ECOWAS and SADC averages of all the variables and table 7A.3 reports correlations for both samples of the final model variables.

Table 7A.1   **Data description**

Variable type	Variable	Description	Source
Policy	ygap	Income gap to frontier (country and US GDP per capita, constant 2000 USD)—see text for definition	World Bank & own calculations
	ypc	GDP per capita (constant 2000 USD)	World Bank
	neq 1, 2, 3, 4, 5	Number equivalent index (1-, 2-, 3-, 4-, 5-digit SITC rev. 2)	OECD
	inflation1	Inflation, consumer prices (annual %)	World Bank
	govdef	Government surplus/deficit (% GDP)	World Bank
	open1	Exports plus import (% of GDP)	World Bank
	reer	Real effective exchange rate (% change)	IMF-IFS
	emp	Exchange market pressure (% change)	Own calculations
Institutions	pr	Index of political rights	Freedom House
	cl	Index of civil liberties	Freedom House
	ef	Index of economic freedom	Fraser Institute
	constage	Constitutional age	Polity
	demage	Age of democracy	Eichengreen and Leblang (2006)
	demtot	Number of other democracies in system	Polity
	dictrans	Number of prior transitions to dictatorship	Polity
Controls	k	Gross capital formation (constant 2000 USD)	World Bank
Economic	ltotal	Labor force, total	World Bank
Geographic	land	Land (sq. km)	World Bank
	landagri	Agricultural land (% of land area)	World Bank
	landarbl	Arable land (% of land area)	World Bank
	disteur	Minimum distance to the European Union	CEPII
Demographic	poptotal	Population, total	World Bank
	popdens	Population density (people per	World Bank
	popurban	Urban dwellers (% population)	World Bank
	life	Life expectancy at birth, total (years)	World Bank
Dummies	landlock	Landlocked countries	United Nations
Economic	oil	Net oil exporter	United Nations
	capcont	Capital controls	IMF-EAER
	legaleng	British legal origin	Polity
	cpv	Cape Verde	IFS country codes
	gha	Ghana	IFS country codes
	mus	Mauritius	IFS country codes
	moz	Mozambique	IFS country codes
	sen	Senegal	IFS country codes
	zaf	South Africa	IFS country codes

Table 7A.2 **Summary statistics (all variables)**

Variable	Obs.	Mean	Median	Std. dev.	Minimum	Maximum
			ECOWAS			
ygap	675	0.95	0.95	0.02	0.86	0.99
ypc	612	356.70	284.39	217.94	56.47	1,266.81
ypcgrowth	597	0.23	0.66	7.32	−50.49	90.47
neq5	637	3.83	3.46	2.09	1.00	15.12
inflation1	574	12.83	6.89	20.09	−34.40	178.70
govdef	450	−5.70	−4.65	9.19	−57.26	27.17
open1	592	59.01	54.58	26.57	6.32	140.86
reer	144	−0.04	−0.01	0.26	−1.88	0.79
averageempusd	106	0	0	0.04	−0.13	0.21
pr	490	2.87	2.00	1.78	1.00	7.00
cl	490	3.23	3.00	1.34	1.00	7.00
prcl	490	3.05	2.50	1.50	1.00	7.00
ef	295	4.81	5.05	0.90	2.31	6.34
constage	596	13.11	7.00	19.98	0.00	105.00
demage	660	0.72	0.00	2.16	0.00	14.00
demtot	660	64.72	54.50	26.48	36.00	110.00
dictrans	626	0.39	0.00	0.73	0.00	3.00
k	415	4.35e + 08	3.00e + 08	5.04e + 08	4.90e + 06	3.60e + 09
ltotal	375	4.97e + 06	2.66e + 06	8.95e + 06	88,445.88	5.00e + 07
disteur	675	4,889.93	5,020.85	302.59	4,244.89	5,283.33
landagri	660	42.49	41.81	17.32	13.04	81.40
land	660	335,343.33	192,530.00	415,989.64	4,030.00	1.27e + 06
landarbl	660	12.39	9.43	9.89	1.34	46.15
poptotal	675	1.01e + 07	4.49e + 06	2.06e + 07	196,351.00	1.38e + 08
popdens	660	42.83	35.96	31.32	2.49	157.07
popurban	576	0.11	0.10	0.08	0.00	0.39
life	240	47.50	46.90	7.75	32.28	69.84
			SADC			
ygap	630	0.9	0.94	0.08	0.6	0.99
ypc	507	945.54	459.1	1,040.85	81.01	4,264.32
ypcgrowth	493	1.13	1.07	5.69	−27.14	23.75
neq5	554	6.47	4.96	5.75	1	36.09
inflation1	495	109.59	12.14	1,114.9	−9.62	23,773.13
govdef	370	−7.37	−6.15	10.29	−54.09	32.68
open1	502	80.63	68.23	40.54	14.33	198.91
reer	129	−0.02	−0.02	0.2	−0.91	1
averageempusd	106	0.01	0.00	0.04	−0.08	0.18
pr	441	3.38	3	1.85	1	7
cl	441	3.41	3	1.56	1	7
prcl	441	3.4	3	1.65	1	7
ef	316	4.91	4.84	1.10	2.39	7.35
constage	509	13.06	8	16.35	0	81
demage	600	1.76	0	5.53	0	37
demtot	600	65.02	55.5	26.72	35	110
dictrans	572	0.15	0	0.36	0	1
k	466	2.03E + 09	4.35E + 08	4.85E + 09	2.26E + 06	2.79E + 10
ltotal	350	5.60E + 06	4.28E + 06	5.69E + 06	170,025.2	2.28E + 07
disteur	630	8,253.78	8,491.14	978.51	6,257.08	9,571.16
landagri	616	50.26	46.94	20.09	9.68	87.97
land	616	688,990	662,465	596,625.63	2,030	2.27E + 06
landarbl	616	9.62	6.77	11.76	0.61	49.26
poptotal	630	1.02E + 07	6.74E + 06	1.14E + 07	326,000	5.69E + 07
popdens	616	55.93	18.2	121.74	0.75	607.58
popurban	497	0.14	0.13	0.13	0	0.78
life	237	50.9	49.25	8.69	33.19	71.97

Table 7A.3 Correlations (final model variables only)

	lnygap	lnneq5	inflation1	govdef	lnopen1	lnprc1	lnef	constage	demage	demtot	dictrans	lnk	lnpopdens
lnygap	1												
lnneq5	−0.126	1											
inflation1	0.08	−0.012	1										
govdef	−0.128	−0.043	−0.011	1									
lnopen1	−0.396	−0.027	−0.016	−0.017	1								
lnprc1	−0.242	0.18	−0.042	0.035	0.212	1							
lnef	−0.264	0.296	−0.09	0.069	0.321	0.362	1						
constage	−0.225	0.176	−0.038	0.102	0.246	0.022	0.148	1					
demage	−0.189	0.073	−0.013	0.009	0.143	0.376	0.282	0.008	1				
demtot	0.244	0.064	0.044	−0.148	0.162	0.26	0.282	−0.01	0.24	1			
dictrans	0.042	0.003	−0.018	−0.04	−0.183	0.202	−0.046	−0.121	0.266	0.241	1		
lnk	−0.392	0.335	−0.035	0.15	−0.084	0.096	0.221	0.427	0.031	0.123	0.243	1	
lnpopdens	0.107	0.144	−0.013	−0.129	−0.104	0.24	0.074	−0.046	0.283	0.246	0.19	−0.029	1

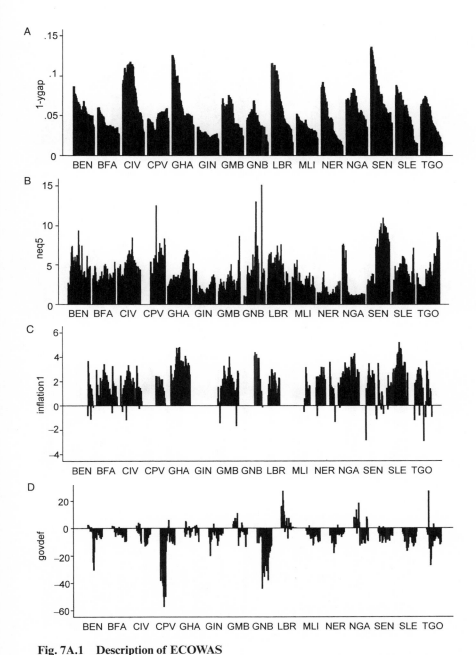

Fig. 7A.1 Description of ECOWAS

Note: Panel (a): ECOWAS, income gap (reverse scale) 1960–2004, read from left to right; panel (b): ECOWAS, number equivalent, 1960–2004, read from left to right; panel (c): ECOWAS, inflation (consumer prices, annual percentage, log), 1960–2004, read from left to right; panel (d): ECOWAS, government deficit (percentage of GDP) 1960–2004, read from left to right.

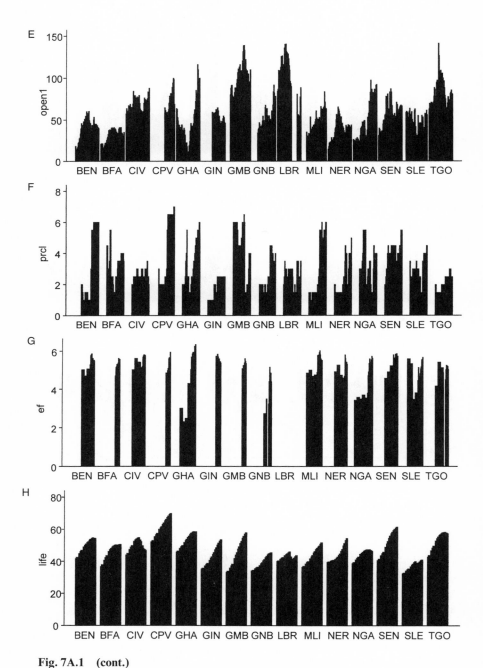

Fig. 7A.1 (cont.)

Note: Panel (e): ECOWAS, openness (X + M/GDP), 1960–2004, read from left to right; panel (f): ECOWAS, composite index of political and civil freedoms, 1960–2004, read from left to right; panel (g): ECOWAS, index of economic freedom, 1960–2004, read from left to right; and panel (h): ECOWAS, life expectancy at birth, 1960–2004, read from left to right.

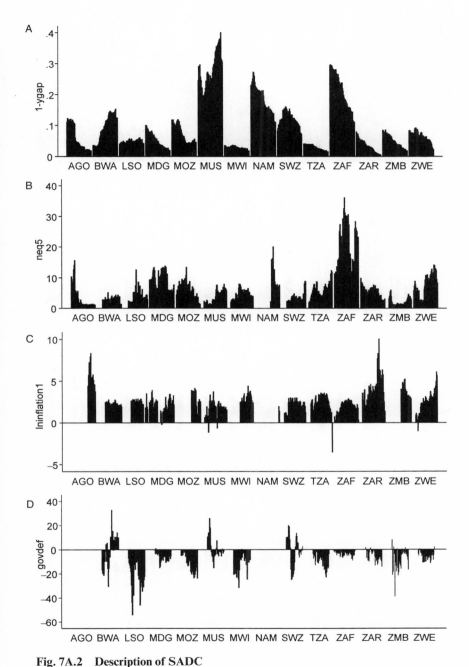

Fig. 7A.2   Description of SADC

Note: Panel (a): SADC, income gap (reverse scale), 1960–2004, read from left to right; panel (b): SADC, number equivalent, 1960–2004, read from left to right; panel (c): SADC, inflation (consumer prices, annual percentage, log), 1960–2004, read from left to right; panel (d): SADC, government deficit (percentage of GDP), 1960–2004, read from left to right.

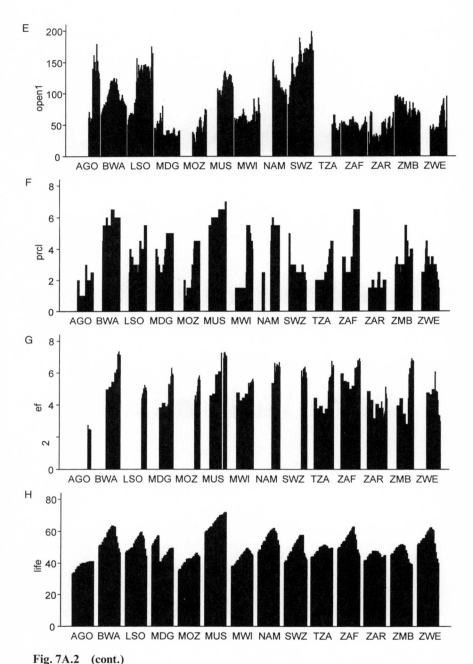

Fig. 7A.2   (cont.)

Note: Panel (e): SADC, degree of openness (X + M/GDP), 1960–2004, read from left to right; panel (f): SADC, political freedom index, 1960–2004, read from left to right; panel (g): SADC, economic freedom index, 1960–2004, read from left to right; and panel (h): SADC, life expectancy at birth, 1960–2004, read from left to right.

Appendix B

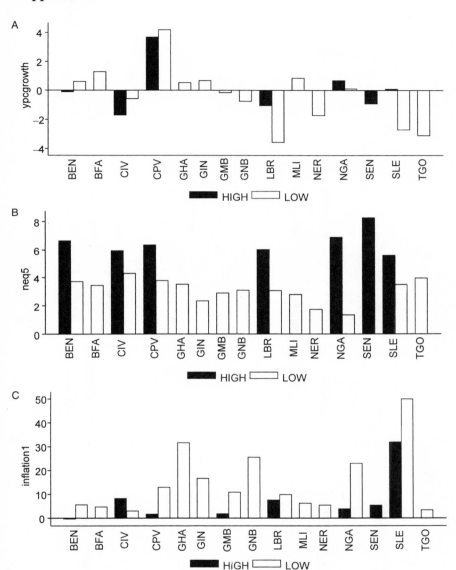

Fig. 7B.1   Comparison of high and low regimes in ECOWAS

Note: Panel (a): ECOWAS, GDP per capita growth, low versus high regime; panel (b): ECOWAS, number equivalent, low versus high regime; panel (c): ECOWAS, inflation, low versus high regime.

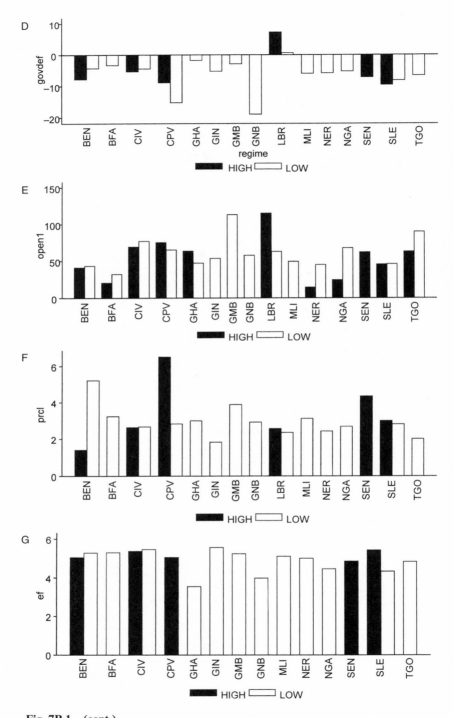

Fig. 7B.1   (cont.)

Note: Panel (d): ECOWAS, government deficit, low versus high regime; panel (e): ECOWAS, openness, low versus high regime; panel (f): ECOWAS, political freedom, low versus high regime; and panel (g): ECOWAS, economic freedom, low versus high regime.

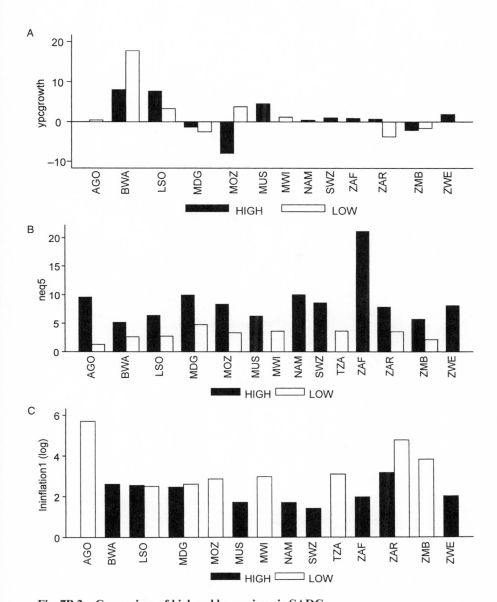

Fig. 7B.2   Comparison of high and low regimes in SADC

Note: Panel (a): SADC, GDP per capita growth, high versus low regime; panel (b): SADC, number equivalent, high versus low regime; panel (c): SADC, inflation, high versus low regime.

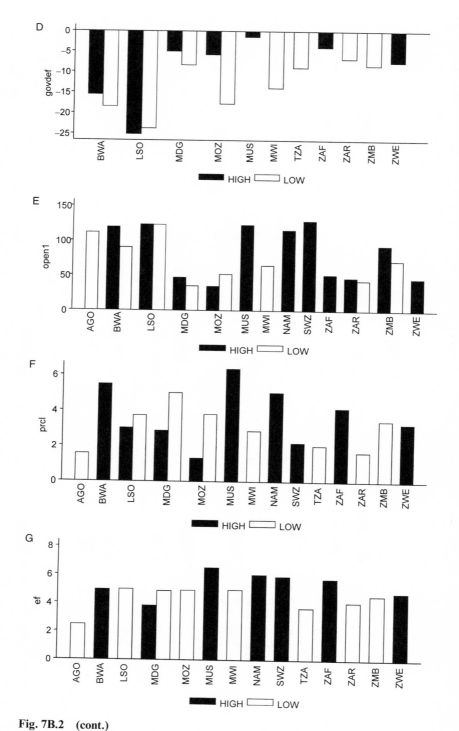

Fig. 7B.2 (cont.)

Note: Panel (d): SADC, government deficit, high versus low regime; panel (e): SADC, openness, high versus low regime; panel (f): SADC, political freedom, high versus low regime; and panel (g): SADC, economic freedom, high versus low regime.

OLS and 2SLS Estimation Results

Table 7B.1   Determinants of diversification in ECOWAS (OLS)

			lnneq5		
Variable type	Variables	OLS pooled	OLS random effects	OLS between effects	OLS fixed effects
Policy	lnygap	−0.263***	−0.241***	−0.793***	−0.214**
		(−3.550)	(−2.812)	(−3.626)	(−2.711)
	govdef	−0.0109***	−0.0106***		
		(−2.971)	(−2.677)		
Institutions	lnprcl	0.0484	0.0651		0.0875
		(0.908)	(1.203)		(1.069)
	lnef	0.264**	0.380***		0.516**
		(2.217)	(3.418)		(2.282)
	demage	−0.0353*	−0.0482**		−0.0483***
		(−1.945)	(−2.367)		(−3.787)
	demtot				−0.00773*
					(−2.029)
Control	lnpopdens	0.208***	0.176***		
		(4.100)	(2.678)		
	lnltotal				1.164**
					(2.333)
	lndisteur	7.313***	7.262***		
		(6.185)	(3.515)		
Dummies	landlock	0.811***	0.766**		
		(3.717)	(2.115)		
	cpv	0.609***	0.760***		
		(4.280)	(4.196)		
	gha	−1.200***	−1.225***	−0.861***	
		(−20.55)	(−13.54)	(−3.362)	
	sen	1.267***	1.292***		
		(8.722)	(5.502)		
	legaleng	−0.123**			
		(−1.984)			
	Constant	−61.19***	−60.95***	4.423***	−15.48**
		(−5.967)	(−3.426)	(5.035)	(−2.168)
Model diagnostics	Observations	223	223	592	228
	R-squared	0.853		0.635	0.171
	Adjusted R-squared	0.844		0.574	0.149
	F-test	318.2		10.44	30.54
	Prob. > F	0		0.00236	9.52e − 07
	Number of countries		14	15	14
	R-squared within model		0.151		
	R-squared between model		0.954		
	R-squared overall model		0.848		
	Wald Chi^2		973.2		
	Prob. > W		0		

Note: Robust *t*-statistics are in parentheses (except for the case of between effects).

***Significant at the 1 percent level.

**Significant at the 5 percent level.

*Significant at the 10 percent level.

Table 7B.2   **Determinants of diversification in ECOWAS (2SLS)**

		lnneq5		
Variable type	Variables	2SLS random effects	2SLS between effects	2SLS fixed effects
Policy	lnygap	−0.138	−0.945***	−0.358**
		(−1.599)	(−3.910)	(−2.501)
Institutions	lnprcl	0.149**		0.130**
		(2.473)		(2.216)
	lnef	0.374***		0.351***
		(3.226)		(2.852)
	demage	−0.0342**		−0.0334*
		(−1.991)		(−1.816)
	demtot			−0.00852***
				(−2.929)
Control	lnpopdens	0.210**		
		(2.409)		
	lnltotal			1.463***
				(4.074)
	lndisteur	7.244***		
		(4.097)		
Dummies	landlock	0.750**		
		(2.345)		
	cpv	0.599**		
		(2.536)		
	gha	−1.290***	−1.409***	
		(−7.445)	(−5.242)	
	sen	1.275***		
		(5.474)		
	Constant	−61.34***	5.183***	
		(−4.051)	(5.256)	
Model diagnostics	Observations	200	315	183
	R-squared			0.227
	Adjusted R-squared		0.721	0.138
	Number of countries	13	14	13
	R-squared within model	0.153	0.0278	
	R-squared between model	0.966	0.764	
	R-squared overall model	0.860	0.328	
	F-test	0	0.000370	0
	Prob. > F		0.721	0.138

Note: The *t*-statistics are in parentheses (robust in the case of fixed effects).

***Significant at the 1 percent level.

**Significant at the 5 percent level.

*Significant at the 10 percent level.

Table 7B.3   **Determinants of diversification in SADC (OLS)**

Variable type	Variables	lnneq5 OLS pooled	lnneq5 OLS random effects	lnneq5 OLS between effects	lnneq5 OLS fixed effects
Policy	lnygap	−0.132***		−0.315	
		(−2.839)		(−1.626)	
	lnopen1	−0.468***			
		(−7.422)			
Institutions	lnef	0.803***	0.886***	2.278***	0.619***
		(5.081)	(4.988)	(3.327)	(4.274)
	dictrans		−0.328***		
			(−3.793)		
Physical	lnk				0.148*
					(1.839)
	lnpopdens				−4.949***
					(−3.108)
	lnltotal			0.471***	4.155**
				(4.570)	(2.635)
	landlock				
	mdg	0.633***	0.972*		
		(5.062)	(1.847)		
	moz	−0.275**		−0.805*	
		(−1.997)		(−1.912)	
	tza	0.584***			
		(7.243)			
	zaf	1.197***	1.557**		
		(9.883)	(2.364)		
	zwe	0.854***	0.963***		
		(9.927)	(2.668)		
	Constant	2.619***	0.0189	−7.705***	−48.18**
		(4.926)	(0.0657)	(−3.539)	(−2.538)
Model diagnostics	Observations	254	290	217	237
	Number of countries		14	14	13
	R-squared	0.641		0.789	0.142
	Adjusted R-squared	0.630		0.696	0.127
	R-squared within model		0.0964		
	R-squared between model		0.672		
	R-squared overall model		0.555		
	F-test	67.08		8.439	10.31
	Prob. > F	0		0.00410	0.00122
	Wald Chi^2		49.57		
	Prob. > W		1.70e–09		

Note: Robust t-statistics are in parentheses (except for the case of between effects).

***Significant at the 1 percent level.

**Significant at the 5 percent level.

*Significant at the 10 percent level.

Table 7B.4　　　　**Determinants of diversification in SADC (2SLS)**

Variable type	Variables	lnneq5		
		2SLS random effects	2SLS between effects	2SLS fixed effects
Policy	lnygap	−0.380***	−0.242*	−0.310**
		(−3.976)	(−2.164)	(−2.091)
Institutions	lnef	0.936***	2.505***	1.196***
		(5.791)	(3.831)	(6.992)
	constage	0.00611***		0.00602**
		(3.427)		(2.006)
Physical	lnpopdens			−4.974***
				(−3.415)
	lnltotal	0.401***	0.512***	4.415***
		(5.909)	(9.075)	(3.587)
	moz		−0.508*	
			(−2.273)	
	zwe	0.753**	0.628**	
		(2.603)	(2.897)	
	Constant	−4.563***	−9.092***	
		(−5.020)	(−5.444)	
Model diagnostics	Observations	156	156	156
	Number of countries	12	12	12
	R-squared			0.350
	Adjusted R-squared		0.899	0.270
	R-squared within model	0.258	0.148	
	R-squared between model	0.850	0.945	
	R-squared overall model	0.734	0.663	
	F-test	19.62	20.63	35.51
	Prob. > F	0	0.00102	0

Note: The *t*-statistics are in parentheses (robust in the case of fixed effects).
***Significant at the 1 percent level.
**Significant at the 5 percent level.
*Significant at the 10 percent level.

Table 7B.5 **Determinants of convergence in ECOWAS (OLS)**

Variable type	Variables		lnygap		
		OLS pooled	OLS random effects	OLS between effects	OLS fixed effects
Policy	lnneq5	−0.157***		−0.340***	
		(−5.848)		(−3.680)	
	inflation1		−0.0435***		
			(−3.658)		
	govdef				−0.00222*
					(−1.932)
	lnopen1				−0.0498***
					−0.00222*
Institutions	lnprcl	−0.0764***	−0.0833**	−0.414**	
		(−2.827)	(−2.166)	(−2.475)	
	lnef		−0.309***		−0.166**
			(−5.831)		(−2.460)
	demage	−0.0696***	−0.0504***		−0.0216**
		(−10.44)	(−6.215)		(−3.153)
	demtot	0.00897***	0.192***		−0.00162**
		(22.17)	(6.243)		(−2.610)
	dictrans	0.148***	0.00828***		
		(5.416)	(15.00)		
Control	lnk				−0.0830***
					(−3.922)
	lnpopdens				−3.145**
					(−2.720)
	lnltotal				4.296***
					(3.737)
	landlock	0.0997***	0.209***		
		(2.932)	(3.945)		
Dummies	oil	−0.610***	−0.497***	−0.564***	
		(−18.17)	(−7.637)	(−4.766)	
	cpv		−0.219***		
			(−4.714)		
	gha	−0.351***	−0.452***		
		(−6.363)	(−9.250)		
	sen	−0.379***	−0.359***		
		(−10.07)	(−7.010)		
	legaleng	−0.212***	−0.133***		
		(−6.335)	(−3.417)		
	Constant	3.880***	4.177***	4.975***	−45.71***
		(65.32)	(44.93)	(30.59)	(−3.491)
Model diagnostics	Observations	441	181	444	140
	R-squared	0.732		0.811	0.917
	Adjusted R-squared	0.725		0.759	0.912
	F-test	154.7		15.73	64.62
	Prob. > F	0		0.000271	9.04e − 06
	Number of countries		13	15	11
	R-squared within model		0.739		
	R-squared between model		0.920		
	R-squared overall model		0.849		
	Wald Chi^2		785.3		
	Prob. > W		0		

Note: Robust t-statistics are in parentheses (except for the case of between effects).

***Significant at the 1 percent level.

**Significant at the 5 percent level.

*Significant at the 10 percent level.

Table 7B.6   **Determinants of convergence in ECOWAS (2SLS)**

		lnygap		
Variable type	Variables	2SLS random effects	2SLS between effects	2SLS fixed effects
Policy	lnneq5	0.790*** (5.400)	−0.326*** (−3.613)	
	lnopen1			−0.0728*** (−4.100)
Institutions	lnprcl	−0.234*** (−4.391)		
	lnef			−0.178*** (−4.876)
	demage		−0.0868** (−2.702)	
	demtot	0.00622*** (6.262)	0.0150*** (3.338)	−0.00242*** (−4.113)
Control	lnk	−0.197*** (−6.001)		−0.0901*** (−5.150)
	lnpopdens			−3.222*** (−5.026)
	lnltotal			4.506*** (7.162)
Dummies	landlock	0.606*** (6.985)		
	oil	−0.401*** (−3.704)	−0.530*** (−4.506)	
	cpv	−0.537*** (−4.387)		
	sen	−0.494*** (−4.256)		
	Constant	6.577*** (11.71)	3.507*** (9.792)	
Model diagnostics	Observations	208	313	118
	R-squared			0.939
	Adjusted R-squared		0.762	0.930
	Number of countries	10	14	10
	R-squared within model	0.371	0.566	
	R-squared between model	0.913	0.835	
	R-squared overall model	0.613	0.654	
	F-test	28.90	11.42	215.7
	Prob. > F	0	0	0

Note: The *t*-statistics are in parentheses (robust in the case of fixed effects).
***Significant at the 1 percent level.
**Significant at the 5 percent level.
*Significant at the 10 percent level.

Table 7B.7   **Determinants of convergence in SADC (OLS)**

Variable type	Variables	lnygap			
		OLS pooled	OLS random effects	OLS between effects	OLS fixed effects
Policy	lnneq5	−0.222***	−0.0351		
		(−6.120)	(−1.193)		
	open1			−0.532**	
				(−2.327)	
	lninflation1				0.0327**
					(2.304)
Institutions	lnprcl		−0.0549*		−0.166**
			(−1.704)		(−2.545)
	lnef			−1.940***	
				(−3.707)	
	demage	−0.00638*		−0.0553**	
		(−1.678)		(−2.479)	
	demtot				0.00759***
					(5.016)
	dictrans	0.262***	0.184***		
		(5.978)	(3.649)		
Physical	lnk	−0.138***	−0.286***		−0.349***
		(−3.798)	(−9.104)		(−5.390)
	lnpopdens	0.165***			
		(9.680)			
	lnltotal	0.401***	0.510***		
		(18.00)	(7.454)		
	oil	0.239**			
		(2.392)			
	moz	−0.302***			
		(−4.752)			
	mus	−1.707***	−1.014***		
		(−15.81)	(−6.400)		
	zaf	−1.247***	−1.098***	−1.235**	
		(−11.66)	(−4.958)	(−2.740)	
	Constant	0.642	2.281**	9.321***	10.31***
		(0.949)	(2.221)	(7.609)	(8.000)
Model diagnostics	Observations	265	253	254	278
	Number of countries		13	14	12
	R-squared	0.898		0.845	0.657
	Adjusted *R*-squared	0.894		0.776	0.652
	R-squared within model		0.471		
	R-squared between model		0.917		
	R-squared overall model		0.891		
	F-test	640.6		12.26	13.21
	Prob. > F	0		0.00109	0.000576
	Wald Chi²		362.8		
	Prob. > W		0		

Note: Robust *t*-statistics are in parentheses (except for the case of between effects).

***Significant at the 1 percent level.

**Significant at the 5 percent level.

*Significant at the 10 percent level.

Table 7B.8 **Determinants of convergence in SADC (2SLS)**

		lnygap		
Variable type	Variables	2SLS random effects	2SLS between effects	2SLS fixed effects
Policy	inflation1	−0.356***	−0.600	−0.101
		(−3.216)	(−1.633)	(−1.098)
Institutions	lnprcl		−5.893***	
			(−3.645)	
	lnef		−1.389*	−0.120***
			(−2.280)	(−3.065)
	demage	−0.591***		−0.372***
		(−6.474)		(−4.585)
	demtot	−0.591***		−0.372***
		(−6.474)		(−4.585)
Physical	lnk	−0.591***		−0.372***
		(−6.474)		(−4.585)
	lnltotal	0.561***		0.730***
		(6.187)		(5.226)
	Constant	8.115***	16.42***	
		(4.910)	(4.400)	
Model diagnostics	Observations	190	178	190
	Number of countries	12	12	12
	R-squared			0.358
	Adjusted R-squared		0.690	0.299
	R-squared within model	0.191	0.0726	
	R-squared between model	0.919	0.775	
	R-squared overall model	0.809	0.235	
	F-test	24.09	10.11	22.96
	Prob. > F	0	0.00426	0

Note: The *t*-statistics are in parentheses (robust in the case of fixed effects).

***Significant at the 1 percent level.

**Significant at the 5 percent level.

*Significant at the 10 percent level.

References

African Economic Outlook (AEO). Various years. Paris: African Development Bank and OECD Development Centre.

Amaral, Luciano. 2009. "Old but New Questions Back to the Passage from Ancient Régime to Liberalism." In *Nove Ensaios na Tradição de Jorge Borges de Macedo*, edited by Jorge Braga de Macedo, Luciano Amaral, Álvaro Ferreira da Silva, and António Castro Henriques. Lisboa: Tribuna da História em Colaboração do CG&G e IICT.

Andersson and Sjöö. 2002. "O Sucesso Moçambicano no Controle da Inflação Durante a Transição para uma Economia de Mercado (1991–1996)." Gabinete de Estudos do Ministério do Plano e das Finanças Moçambique.

Andrade, Mário D., ed. 1978. *Obras Escolhidas de Amílcar Cabral, a Arma da Teoria, Unidade e Luta I*. Lisboa: Seara Nova.

Angel-Urdinola, Diego, and Quentin Wodon. 2007. "Assessing Absolute and Relative Poverty Trends with Limited Data in Cape Verde." *Growth and Poverty Reduction: Case Studies from West Africa*, edited by Quentin Wodon, 95–197, World Bank Working Paper Series no. 79. Washington, DC: World Bank.

Bliss, Christopher, and Jorge Braga de Macedo, eds. 1990. *Unity with Diversity in the European Economy: The Community's Southern Frontier*. Cambridge: Cambridge University Press.

Bonaglia, Federico, Jorge Braga de Macedo, and Maurizio Bussolo. 2009. "How Globalisation Improves Governance." In *The Law and Economics of Globalisation*, edited by Linda Yueh, 193–224. Cheltonham, UK: Edward Elgar.

Bourguignon, François, Agnès Bénassy-Quéré, Stefan Dercon, Antonio Estache, Jan Willem Gunning, Ravi Kanbur, Stephan Klasen et al. 2008. "Millennium Development Goals at Midpoint: Where Do We Stand and Where Do We Need to Go?". European Report on Development, Department of International Development, London, September. http://www.kanbur.aem.cornell.edu/papers/MDGsAtMidpoint.pdf.

Branson, William, Jorge Braga de Macedo, and David Richardson. 1987. "Ford Foundation Proposal: Measurement and Estimation of Changes in International Competitiveness." Unpublished Manuscript, NBER, May.

Cabral, Amilcar. 1975. *Análise de Alguns Tipos de Resistência*. Lisboa: Seara Nova.

———., ed. 1987. *Pour Cabral*. Paris: Présence Africaine.

———. 1999. *Nacionalismo e Cultura*. Santiago de Compostela: Edicións Laiovento.

Cabral, Ana Maria. 1995. "Programa da Comemoração do XX Aniversário da Independência de Cabo Verde." Washington, DC, Festival of American Folklore, Smithsonian Institution. http://solidariedadesemfronteiras.blogspot.com/2008/06/programa-da-comemoracao-do-33-aniversrio.html.

Cabral, Manuel Herédia Caldeira, and Paula Veiga. 2010. "Determinants of Export Diversification and Sophistication in Sub-Saharan Africa." FEUNL Working Paper no. 550, July, Faculdade de Economia da Universidade Nova de Lisboa.

Cardoso, Renato. 1986. *Cabo Verde: Opção para uma Política de Paz*. Praia: Instituto Cabo-Verdiano do Livro.

Causa, Orsetta, and Daniel Cohen. 2006. *The Ladder of Competitiveness and How to Climb It*. Paris: OECD Development Centre.

Cleveland, W. S. 1979. "Robust Locally Weighted Regression and Smoothing Scatterplots." *Journal of the American Statistical Association* 74 (368): 829–36.

Cleveland, W. S., and S. J. Devlin. 1988. "Locally-Weighted Regression: An Approach to Regression Analysis by Local Fitting." *Journal of the American Statistical Association* 83 (403): 596–610.

Collier, P. 2007. *The Bottom Billion: Why the Poorest Countries are Failing and What Can Be Done about It*. Oxford: Oxford University Press.

Collier, P., and J. W. Gunning. 1999. "'The IMF' Role in Structural Adjustment." *Economic Journal* 109 (459): F634–51.

Easterly, William, and Ariell Reshef. 2010. "African Export Successes: Surprises, Stylized Facts and Explanations." Paper presented at the NBER research conference 2, Accra, Ghana, July.

Eichengreen, Barry, and David Leblang. 2006. "Democracy and Globalization." NBER Working Paper no. 12450, Cambridge, MA.

———. 2008. "Democracy and Globalization." *Economics & Politics* 20 (3): 289–334.

Fedderke, J. W., R. H. J. de Kadt, and J. M. Luiz. 2001. "Indicators of Political Liberty, Property Rights and Political Instability in South Africa: 1935–97." *International Review of Law and Economics* 21 (1): 103–34.

Feyrer, James. 2009. "Trade and Income: Exploiting Time Series in Geography." Working Paper, Department of Economics, Dartmouth College.

Flandreau, Marc, and Frédéric Zummer. 2004. *The Making of Global Finance 1880–1913*. Paris: OECD Development Centre Studies.

Frankel, Jeffrey. 2010. "Mauritius: African Success Story." Paper presented at the NBER research conference 2, Accra, Ghana, July.

Galtung, J. 1996. *Peace by Peaceful Means, Peace and Conflict, Development and Civilization*. New Delhi: Sage.

Garoupa, Nuno, and Jose Tavares. 2009. "Institutions and Portuguese Economic History: Implications and (Brief) Applications." In *Nove Ensaios na Tradição de Jorge Borges de Macedo*. Lisboa: Tribuna da História em Colaboração do CG&G e IICT.

Giovannini, Enrico, Joaquim Oliveira Martins, and Michaela Gamba. 2008. "Statistics, Knowledge and Governance." Presented at Committing Science to Global Development Workshop, IICT, September 26. http://www.iict.pt/workshop/Papers/2008092903.pdf.

Gisselquist, Rachel, and Robert Rotberg. 2008. "Strengthening African Governance: Ibrahim Index of African Governance, Results and Rankings." Harvard University. http://belfercenter.ksg.harvard.edu/project/52/intrastate_conflict_program.html?page_id=224.

Goujon, Anne, and Annababette Wils. 1996. "The Importance of Education in Future Population. Global Trends and Case Studies on Cape Verde, Sudan, and Tunisia." IIASA Working Paper no. 96-138, November, International Institute for Applied Systems Analysis. http://www.iiasa.ac.at/publication/more_WP-96-138.php.

Hausmann, R., J. Hwang, and D. Rodrik. 2007. "What You Export Matters." *Journal of Economic Growth* 12 (1): 1–25.

Hausmann, R., and D. Rodrik. 2003. "Economic Development as Self-Discovery." *Journal of Development Economics* 72:603–33.

Instituto de Investigação Científica Tropical (IICT). 2007. "Relatório Sobre CPLP e Objectivos de Desenvolvimento do Milénio." A report for the executive secretary of CPLP by Jorge Braga de Macedo, Luís Brites Pereira, Joaquim Pina, and João Jalles. Lisbon: Tropical Research Institute (IICT), October.

International Development Association (IDA). 2007. "L'IDA en Action—Le Mozambique: Du Reddressement d'Après-Guerre à la Relance de la Croissance." April.

International Monetary Fund (IMF). 1998. "Cape Verde: Statistical Tables." Country Report no. 98/31, Washington, DC, IMF.

————. 1999. "Cape Verde: Recent Economic Developments." Staff Country Report no. 99/58, Washington, DC, IMF.

————. 2008a. "Cape Verde Growth and Poverty Reduction Strategy Paper II (2008–11)." Staff Country Report no. 08-244, Washington, DC, IMF.

————. 2008b. "Heavily Indebted Poor Countries (HIPC) Initiative and Multilateral Debt Relief Initiative (MDRI)—Status of Implementation." September. http://www.imf.org/external/np/pp/eng/2008/091208.pdf.

Imbs, J., and R. Wacziarg. 2003. "Stages of Diversification." *American Economic Review* 93 (1): 63–86.

Kanbur, Ravi. 2004. "The African Peer Review Mechanism (APRM): An Assessment of Concept and Design." *Politikon* 31 (2): 157–66.

Kohli, A. 1986."Democracy and Development." In *Development Strategies Reconsidered*, edited by J. P. Lewis and V. Kallab. New Brunswick: Transaction Books.

La Porta, Rafael, and Andrei Schleifer. 2010. "The Unofficial Economy in Africa." Paper presented at the NBER research conference 2, Accra, Ghana, July.

Lledó, V., S. Peiris, and E. Kvintradze. 2007. "Republic of Mozambique: Selected Issues." IMF Country Report no. 07/258, July, International Monetary Fund.

Lopes, Jose Mario, and Fabio Santos. 2010. "Comparing Exchange Market Pressure in West and Southern African Countries." FEUNL Working Paper no. 549, July, Faculdade de Economia da Universidade Nova de Lisboa.

Lourenço, Jaime, and Colm Foy. 2003. "Cap Vert: Gouvernance et Développement." Centre de Développement de l'OCDE, Document de travail No. 225, Novembre.

Luiz, John. 2009. "Institutions and Economic Performance Implications for African Development." *Journal of International Development* 21:58–75.

Luiz, John, Luis Brites Pereira, and Guilherme Oliveira. 2013. "Indicators of Political and Property Rights in Mozambique, 1900–2005." *Governance* 26 (4): 688–92.

Macedo, Jorge Borges de. 1996. "Mares Abertos e Mares Fechados. Da Dialéctica do Confronto aos Problemas da Cooperação." *Actas dos 2.º Cursos Internacionais de Verão de Cascais*, vol. 1, 185–94. Cascais: Câmara Municipal de Cascais.

Macedo, Jorge Braga de. 1986. "Collective Pegging to a Single Currency: The West African Monetary Union." In *The Real Exchange Rate and Adjustment in Developing Countries*, edited by Sebastian Edwards and Liaquat Ahamed, 333–62.Chicago: University of Chicago Press.

————. 2001. "Globalization and Institutional Change: A Development Perspective." In *Globalization Ethical and Institutional Concerns*, edited by Louis Sabourin and Edmond Malinvaud, 223–67. Vatican City: The Pontifical Academy of Social Sciences, Acta 7.

————. 2008. "Regional Integration and Mutual Knowledge: The Case of the CPLP." Presented at Committing Science to Global Development Workshop, IICT, September 26. http://www.iict.pt/workshop/Papers/2008091401.pdf.

————. 2009. "Economic Advice and Regime Change in Portugal." In *Challenges Ahead for the Portuguese Economy*, edited by Francesco Franco, 201–29. Lisbon: ICS.

————. 2011. "Global Crisis and National Policy Responses: Together Alone?" In *Ética, Crise e Sociedade*, edited by Michel Renaud and Gonçalo Marcelo, 91–159. Vila Nova de Famalicão, Portugal: Húmus.

————. 2015. Energy@CPLP Drives Portugal's Strategy for Open Economy." In *Writing to Queens While Crises Proceed,* 2nd ed. (in memory of Manuel Jacinto Nunes), edited by Jorge Braga de Macedo, 113–33. CG&G and IICT.

Macedo, Jorge Braga de, Luciano Amaral, Álvaro Ferreira da Silva, and António

Castro Henriques, eds. 2009. *Nove Ensaios na Tradição de Jorge Borges de Macedo*. Lisboa: Tribuna da História em colaboração do CG&G e IICT.

Macedo, Jorge Braga de, and Luís Brites Pereira. 2006. "The Credibility of Cabo Verde's Currency Peg." FEUNL Working Paper no. 494, September, Faculdade de Economia da Universidade Nova de Lisboa.

———. 2007. "Diferencialidade Portuguesa na Globalização." *Negócios Estrangeiros* 11 (2): 223–36.

Macedo, Jorge Braga de, Barry Eichengreen, and Jaime Reis, eds. 1996. *Currency Convertibility: The Gold Standard and Beyond*. London: Routledge.

Macedo, Jorge Braga de, Joaquim Oliveira Martins, and Luís Brites Pereira. 2007. "How Freedoms Interact with Globalization." Presented at Conference on Globalization and Democracy, Princeton University, September 27–28, revision in progress.

Macedo, Jorge Braga de, Luís Brites Pereira, and Afonso Mendonça Reis. 2009. "Comparing Exchange Market Pressure across Five African Countries." *Open Economies Review* 20 (5): 645.

Macedo, Jorge Braga de, Joaquim Oliveira Martins, and Bruno Rocha. 2014. "Are Complementary Reforms a 'Luxury' in Developing Countries?" *Journal of Comparative Economics* 42 (2): 417–35.

Maddison, Angus. 2001. *The World Economy: A Millennial Perspective*. Paris: OECD.

———. 2007. *Contours of the World Economy 0–2030 AD*. Oxford: Oxford University Press.

Maravall, J. M. 1995. "The Myth of the Authoritarian Advantage." In *Economic Reform and Democracy*, edited by L. Diamond and M. F. Plattner. Baltimore: Johns Hopkins University Press.

Maxwell, Kenneth. (1973) 2004. *Conflicts and Conspiracies: Brazil and Portugal, 1750–1808*. New York: Routledge.

Mitchell, J. 2008. "Tourism Development in Cape Verde: The Policy Challenge of Coping with Success." Overseas Development Institute. http://www.odi.org /projects/900-tourist-development-cape-verde-policy-challenge-coping-success .http://www.odi.org/projects/900-tourist-development-cape-verde-policy -challenge-coping-success

Nye, Joseph. 2002. "A Whole New Ball Game." *Financial Times*, December 28.

Oman, Charles, and Christiane Arndt. 2006. *Uses and Abuses of Governance Indicators*, Paris: OECD Development Centre.

Organisation for Economic Co-operation and Development (OECD). 2003. *Globalisation and Governance: Main Results of the OECD Development Centre Programme of Work 2001/2002*. Paris: OECD.

Persson, Torsten, and Guido Tabellini. 2006. "Democratic Capital: The Nexus of Political and Economic Change." NBER Working Paper no. 12175, Cambridge, MA.

Pires, Pedro. 2010. "Discurso proferido por Sua Excelencia o Senhor Presidente da Republica de Cabo Verde na Cerimonia de Atribuicao do Grau de Doutor Honoris Causa pela Universidade Tecnica de Lisboa." Unpublished Manuscript, June.

Plane, P. 1997. "Privatization and Economic Growth: Reflections and Observations." In *Privatization at the End of the Century*, edited by H. Giersch. Heidelberg, Germany: Springer.

Przeworski, Adam, M. Alvarez, J. A. Cheibub, and F. Limongi. 2000. *Democracy and Development: Political Institutions and Well-Being in the World, 1950–1990*. Cambridge: Cambridge University Press.

Przeworski, Adam, and Fernando Limongi. 1993. "Political Regimes and Economic Growth." *Journal of Economic Perspectives* 7:51–69.

Reinhart, Carmen, and Kenneth Rogoff. 2009. *This Time is Different: Eight Centuries of Financial Folly*. Princeton, NJ: Princeton University Press.

Remmer, K. L. 1990. "Democracy and Economic Crisis: The Latin American Experience." *World Politics* 42:315–35.

Ribeiro, Ana Paula, João Loureiro, and Manuel M. F. Martins. 2008. *Assessment of the Exchange Rate Cooperation Agreement Cape Verde-Portugal*. Ministry of Finance, October.

Santos, Vanda. 2010. *Post-colonial Cape Verdean Culture as a Contributor to a Culture of Peace*. Presentation to African Development Successes course module, FEUNL based on PhD dissertation presented to Universitat Jaume I, "La Cultura Postcolonial en Cabo Verde Como Sporte a Una Cultura de Paz."

Tibana, Roberto J. 2003. "The Composite Indicator of Economic Activity in Mozambique (ICAE): Filling in the Knowledge Gaps to Enhance Public-Private Partnership (PPP)." OECD Development Centre Working Paper no.227, November, Organisation for Economic Development and Co-operation.

United Nations Department of Economic and Social Affairs. 2008. *Trends in Sustainable Development: Africa Report*. New York: United Nations.

Werlin, L. 1996. "Cape Verde: Emerging Tourist Destination." A paper presented to the Department of Tourism, George Washington University, Washington, DC, January. http://www1.umassd.edu/SpecialPrograms/caboverde/werlin.html.

World Bank. 2009. *World Development Indicators*. Washington, DC: World Bank.

Young, C. 1998. "Africa: An Interim Balance Sheet." In *Africa: Dilemmas of Development and Change*, edited by P. Lewis. Boulder, CO: Westview Press.

8

Mauritius
African Success Story

Jeffrey Frankel

Some might be tempted to put a question mark after a title like "Mauritius: African Success Story." But this would only be because some ask if the country off the eastern coast of Madagascar is truly African, in light of its unusual ethnic composition.[1]

There cannot be much doubt about the word "story." The country's story is a fascinating one.

Nor can there be much doubt that it is a "success": of all countries identified as being in the geographical region of Africa, Mauritius appears at the top of the governance rankings, as table 8.1 shows. The Rule of Law

Jeffrey Frankel is the James W. Harpel Professor of Capital Formation and Growth at the Harvard Kennedy School and a research associate and director of the International Finance and Macroeconomics Program at the National Bureau of Economic Research.

This chapter was presented at the NBER Conference on African Successes, Accra, Ghana, July 18–20, 2010. The author would like to thank for research assistance Oyebola Olabisi, Jesse Schreger, Diva Singh, and Cristobal Marshall. He benefited from numerous discussions with the people of Mauritius, but is especially indebted to Ali Mansoor. Among many others from whom he absorbed ideas are Vinaye dey Ancharaz, Abhijit Banerjee, and Arvind Subramanian in academia; Central Bank Governor Rundheersing Bheenik, Prime Minister Navin Ramgoolam, and Finance Minister Ramakrishna Sithanen in the government; and others in Mauritius including Nando Bodha and Anubhava Katiyar. The author also thanks for comments on an earlier draft Jorge de Macedo, other participants at the Accra conference, and Avnish Gungadurdoss. This study was part of an NBER project on African Successes, organized by Sebastian Edwards, Simon Johnson, and David Weil. For acknowledgments, sources of research support, and disclosure of the author's material financial relationships, if any, please see http://www.nber.org/chapters/c13441.ack.

1. Today, 68 percent of the population has Indian forbears. Even inside this share are ethnic cleavages between Hindu and Muslim, and between those whose ancestors immigrated from the Ganges plain and those who emigrated from elsewhere (especially Tamils). Major remaining shares include Creoles, Franco-Mauritians, and Sino-Mauritians. (An ethnic composition that features a small number of large ethnic groups is usually considered a negative factor for development.)

Table 8.1   **Sub-Saharan countries ranked by governance, with other indicators**

Index of African Governance ranking (2007)	Country	GDP per capita, PPP in constant 2005interntl. $ (2008)	UN Human Development Ranking (2007)	Worldwide Governance Indicators, Rule of Law index ranking (2008)
1	Mauritius	11,412	2	1
2	Seychelles	19,758	1	5
3	Cape Verde	2,957	5	3
4	Botswana	12,537	6	2
5	Ghana	1,351	18	7
6	Namibia	5,909	7	4
7	South Africa	9,343	8	6
8	São Tomé & Príncipe	1,615	9	18
9	Gabon	13,461[b]	3	24
10	Benin	1,361	27	22
11	Malawi	744	26	10
12	Gambia	1,259	33	8
13	Senegal	1,656	31	12
14	Madagascar	974	14	15
15	Burkina Faso	1,072	41	14
16	Tanzania	1,201	17	9
17	Mauritania	1,810[a]	20	30
18	Lesotho	1,444	23	11
19	Zambia	1,253	29	16
20	Comoros	1,081	11	31
21	Rwanda	949[b]	32	17
22	Kenya	1,432	15	28
23	Uganda	1,077	22	19
24	Niger	631	46	27
25	Mali	1,043	43	13
26	Mozambique	774	37	25
27	Djibouti	1,975	21	21
28	Cameroon	2,027	19	29
29	Togo	767	25	26
30	Sierra Leone	723	45	32
31	Guinea-Bissau	496	38	40
32	Ethiopia	802	36	23
33	Nigeria	1,939	24	34
34	Burundi	354	39	33
35	Liberia	358	34	36
36	Equatorial Guinea	31,309	4	39
37	Swaziland	4,551	12	20
38	Congo (Brazzaville)	3,647	10	35
39	Guinea	975	35	45
40	Zimbabwe	185[b]	n/a	47
41	Angola	5,375	13	38
42	Eritrea	592	30	37
43	C. A. R.	685	44	41
44	Cote d'Ivoire	1,526	28	43
45	Congo (DR)	290	42	46
46	Chad	1,234	40	44
47	Sudan	1,990	16	42
48	Somalia	—	n/a	48

Notes: Ranking is among African countries excluding North Africa.

[a] Data from 2007.

[b] Data from 2005.

index from the Worldwide Governance Indicators puts Mauritius first in sub-Saharan Africa, followed by Botswana and Cape Verde. The Index of African Governance compiled by Rotberg and Gisselquist (2009), which attempts to rely less on subjective measures, again puts Mauritius in the number one spot, followed by Seychelles, Cape Verde, and Botswana.[2] Mauritian growth in gross domestic product (GDP) per capita rate averaged 5.4 percent over the period 1970–2010, during which the growth rate in the rest of Africa was only about 1 percent. By 2010 Mauritius had achieved a per capita income of about $7,000 at current exchange rates. (The number is higher, of course, in purchasing power parity [PPP] terms: $11,000.) An oil-rich country such as Equatorial Guinea has higher income, but as a result of poor governance, few people outside the elite enjoy improved quality of life. The Human Development Index from the United Nations Development Program, a more comprehensive measure, classifies Mauritius in the "High Human Development" quartile globally: it ranks number 81 out of 182 countries, well ahead of other African countries.[3] Life expectancy is 72.8 years, for example.[4] Table 8.2 reports additional statistics for all African countries, standardized for the common year 2006.

Others may wonder if the country is too small to hold important lessons for typical-sized countries. The land area is only 1,865 square kilometers, or 720 square miles. But given the population of 1.25 million and the current relatively high level of income per capita, GDP puts the country at the median among African countries in economic size, ahead of Namibia.[5]

Still, others may wonder if the uniqueness of the story of Mauritius prevents generalizing to lessons that can be useful elsewhere. Of course, every country is unique. If econometricians have run "two million cross section regressions" looking for the determinants of countries' economic performance,[6] it sometimes seems that others have complained two million times that the institutional, cultural, and historical particularities of individual countries can never be captured by the data fed into a computer. This chapter uses cross-country regressions as one input into the analysis— but only one. Two other kinds of inputs enter as well. One is the relevant

2. The next countries in the governance rankings are South Africa, Namibia, and Ghana, with the sequence depending on the precise measure and year.

3. Tiny Seychelles is ahead, at 57. The next nearest competitors in sub-Saharan Africa are: Gabon at 103, Equatorial Guinea at 118, Cape Verde at 121, Botswana at 125, South Africa at 129, and Sao Tome and Principe at 131. Most fill out the bottom ranks. (Human Development Report 2009, United Nations Development Programme; at http://hdr.undp.org/en/statistics/.)

4. World Development Indicators (2009) and Rotberg and Gisselquist (2009) show the Seychelles as just surpassing Mauritius in lifespan in 2007, followed by Cape Verde, Western Sahara, Sao Tome and Principe, Comoros, Mauritania, Senegal, and Ghana. (Source: United Nations, for 2005–2010.) Table 2 reports additional statistics for all African countries, standardized for the common year 2006.

5. Namibia has twice the population and 400 times the land area. Total GDP in Mauritius also surpassed Mali, Madagascar, and the Congo in 2009.

6. Sala-i-Martin (1997).

Table 8.2   Performance of sub-Saharan African countries (2006 unless otherwise noted)

Country	GDP per capita, PPP (constant 2005 international $)	Population, millions	Average annual GDP growth rate (constant 2000 $)		Worldwide Governance Indicators, Rule of Law index ranking	Index of African Governance ranking	UN Human Development ranking
			1968–1976 (%)	1977–2006 (%)			
Angola	4,163.76	16.56		3.81	39	44	13
Benin	1,319.02	8.76	1.55		18	13	26
Botswana	12,252.27	1.86	15.28	7.85	2	4	6
Burkina Faso	1,060.48	14.36	3.17	4.49	14	20	41
Burundi	347.02	8.17	3.53	1.42	34	35	40
Cameroon	1,972.82	18.17	4.29	3.15	32	25	19
Cape Verde	2,796.55	0.52			3	3	5
C. A. R.	670.82	4.26	3.00	0.68	45	43	43
Chad	1,304.66	10.47	1.88	4.16	42	46	38
Comoros	1,116.86	0.61			29	14	11
Congo (Brazz.)	3,640.58	3.69	6.63	4.10	38	28	10
Congo (DR)	271.55	60.64	1.87	-0.94	47	47	42
Cote d'Ivoire	1,536.51	18.91	7.78	1.09	44	42	28
Djibouti	1,889.75	0.82			22	26	21
Eq. Guinea	24,416.68	0.50			37	36	4
Eritrea	609.91	4.69			31	41	30
Ethiopia	683.38	77.15			19	31	36
Gabon	12,933.20	1.31	15.95	0.68	25	8	3
Gambia	1,181.91	1.66	5.24	3.65	9	27	33
Ghana	1,242.08	23.01	1.29	3.46	7	7	20
Guinea	955.95	9.18			43	40	35
Guinea-Bissau	489.09	1.65		2.02	40	30	39
Kenya	1,386.43	36.55	6.43	3.51	28	17	15

Lesotho	1,345.99	1.99	4.79	3.82	8	12	22
Liberia	334.31	3.58	3.29	-3.55	30	38	34
Madagascar	901.25	19.16	1.10	1.59	12	16	14
Malawi	660.13	13.57	5.91	2.83	15	11	27
Mali	1,012.80	11.97	4.40	2.95	11	23	44
Mauritania	1,820.52	3.04	2.92	2.86	20	32	18
Mauritius	10,476.46	1.25	8.00[a]	4.34	1	1	2
Mozambique	707.77	20.97			26	22	37
Namibia	5,659.85	2.05			6	6	8
Niger	602.68	13.74	-1.86	2.07	27	24	46
Nigeria	1,800.82	144.70	9.97	2.71	35	39	23
Rwanda	833.97	9.46	4.77	3.11	23	18	32
Sao Tome & P.	1,486.65	0.16			17	9	9
Senegal	1,611.75	12.07	2.71	2.78	10	10	31
Seychelles	18,414.93	0.08	7.19	3.76	5	2	1
Sierra Leone	678.64	5.74	3.45	1.54	36	37	45
Somalia		8.45			48	48	n/a
South Africa	8,861.93	47.39	3.73	2.42	4	5	7
Sudan	1,743.57	37.71	5.70	3.82	41	45	16
Swaziland	4,410.90	1.14		5.02	24	34	12
Tanzania	1,104.95	39.46			13	15	17
Togo	782.19	6.41	3.62	2.25	33	29	25
Uganda	966.31	29.90			16	19	24
Zambia	1,168.84	11.70	2.75	1.62	21	21	29
Zimbabwe		13.23	7.01		46	33	n/a

[a]Estimated.

economic, political, and historical literature. Another kind of input is what the author—with no previous background in Mauritius—learned from exploring the country.

The many global econometric cross-country studies have produced a variety of important conclusions, notwithstanding their limitations and ambiguities. Some of the more robust findings include that remoteness, landlockedness, tropical location, and small population size[7] are bad for economic performance, other things equal. These variables help explain why incomes are lower in Africa than in other parts of the world. Access to the sea, education, and national saving tend to be good for economic performance. High population density is often bad. Two of the most consequential findings are that openness to trade and the quality of institutions are major determinants of economic performance, but there are valid questions regarding the measurement of those two variables, and about the exogeneity of the relationships. Clearly a major reason that remoteness and landlockedness hurt economies is that they impede international trade.

A common finding is a negative dummy variable for Africa. It often can be attributed to some of the other variables, however, especially tropical location,[8] as becomes evident when the econometrician controls for them and the apparent Africa effect disappears.

While some of these variables may help explain the negative dummy for Africa, they do not necessarily help explain variation within Africa. Indeed, when using regression analysis to learn about differences in growth performance among African countries, one major finding is that many of the variables that are most significant on global data sets do nothing for us within this continent.

The reader who has looked at table 8.1 may have noticed a striking fact: not only is the highest performer in Africa reported to be a small island country (Mauritius), but so are numbers two and three (Seychelles and Cape Verde, respectively). Not until we get to fourth place do we see a country on the mainland (Botswana), and not until fifth place do we see a country of substantial size (Ghana, in 2008). Is it just a coincidence that the top performers are island countries? There exists at least one small African island country with poor performance: the Comoros. What explains the difference?[9]

Island countries provide an intriguing subset of self-contained data points. There is less likely to be an issue of endogenous borders, for example.

7. Frankel and Romer (1999, table 3), to take just one example.

8. Probably the best interpretation of why tropical location seems to be bad for economic growth is the presence of malaria and other tropical diseases. Sachs (2003) shows that specific determinants of malaria are correlated with slow growth across countries.

9. Madagascar is an island, but we are not counting it as small. As noted, Equatorial Guinea shows high income per capita, but consistent with natural resource curse the benefits from its oil discoveries have gone to the elite rather than the general population. In any case, only part of it is an island.

The econometric analysis of the determinants of economic performance in this chapter includes a cross section of island countries, before we turn to a within-Africa data set.

We begin with a short history of Mauritius, however. Next comes an overview of the competing hypotheses that others have put forward to explain Mauritian success. Then the econometrics, followed by an attempt to put everything together. When we are done, we will not be able to claim a definitive answer as to the single reason for the island's success, nor will we ever attempt to answer whether it is African. But the story will be of interest, or so the author hopes. Most importantly, notwithstanding the uniqueness of the country, there are potentially valuable lessons for others seeking to achieve economic development in Africa.

8.1   A Brief History of the Island

Our account will just briefly hit the highlights, but will slow down a bit when we get to the postindependence history.

8.1.1 ˙ Globalization at Its Worst

The first two centuries of Mauritius' history could be described as globalization at its worst.[10] The Dutch arrived in 1598 and the Dutch East India Company left a settlement in 1638. They immediately stripped the island of its ebony trees, using slaves imported from Madagascar for the work, and famously killed off the dodo birds. Today, less than 1 percent of the indigenous forests are left. When the Dutch decamped for the Cape Colony in 1710, they left the island nothing useful but its name.

In 1721 the French landed. A competent governor Bertrand Mahe de Labourdonnais built a port/capital at Port Louis on the western coast and made many improvements in the land that the colonizers called Ile de France. They began to grow sugar for export—the first factory was built in 1744—and other crops. But the expanding sugar economy depended on slavery, the ultimate evil of the age. As if to complete a list of evils of globalization, passing ships occasionally brought either pirates or cholera, wreaking havoc on the population.

The island officially passed from France to Britain with the defeat of Napoleon in 1814.[11] The British valued their new possession, but as a coveted way station on the route to India and the Far East. They had no particular desire to settle the island, and were happy to leave the Franco-Mauriciens

10. I am counting from 1638. The island was visited by Arabs one or more times in the seventh to ninth centuries, but they did not stay. The same with the Portuguese in the early sixteenth century. This section of the chapter draws in part on Lutz and Wils (1990) and Selvon (2005).

11. Ironically, the French navy in 1810 scored the strongest of its very few victories of the Napoleonic Wars in the Battle of Grand-Port, on the eastern edge of Mauritius. But de facto possession of the island passed to the British later that year; 2010 is the 200th anniversary.

in place as the land-owning elite. The French Napoleonic code was retained, and still constitutes an important component of the legal system.

Slavery had already been abolished in the British Empire in 1807. The French landowners were reluctant to comply, however, and it wasn't until 1835 that slavery was finally ended on the island. The abolition of slavery marks the end of what I am calling the period of globalization at its worst.[12]

8.1.2 Globalization at Its Best

The next phase of Mauritian history began with a problem for the sugar-based economy. The abolition of slavery had left a shortage of labor. The freed slaves were understandably reluctant to go to work for their former masters. Who would work the plantations? The solution was a "Great Experiment": indentured workers were brought from India. From 1849 to 1923, a half million indentured Indian laborers passed through the immigration depot at the dock called Aaprivasi Ghat, the Ellis Island of Mauritius. Although their lot was hard, most of them chose it voluntarily because the conditions were better than what they were leaving behind.[13] Production and exports from the plantations grew rapidly. The experiment was sufficiently successful that it was copied in other sugar-growing parts of the world such as Fiji and the Caribbean.

Eventually locals and even nonwhites gained some political rights. Under the 1886 Constitution, which lasted sixty years, the British governor allowed a Creole elite to join the Franco-Mauritians among the national representatives. When a new constitution extended the franchise to all adults who could write in 1948, the Indian-dominated Labour Party suddenly won a majority in the Legislative Council seats. Its members were mainly rural workers and its platform was mainly socialist. It was opposed by the Franco-Mauriciens, who accurately described themselves as "oligarchs," and who feared "Hindu hegemony." This phrase referred to what the majority ethnic group were expected to do if and when the country became independent, which the Franco-Mauriciens opposed.

The Labour Party became more moderate under the leadership of Seewoosagur Ramgoolam. By 1960 it had renounced its previous position that the sugar plantations should be nationalized.[14] This decision was to prove a key turning point in several respects. First, it helped establish the important precedent of safeguarding property rights. Second, it contrasted with other African countries that have either expropriated natural resources, taxed

---

12. Many slaves had escaped to the wild over the years. Reportedly, when British soldiers came to bring news of their liberation, some of the escapees thought they were to be arrested, and so instead jumped to their deaths over the vertical sides of the mountain that was thenceforth called Le Morne.

13. In his novel *Sea of Poppies*, Amitav Ghosh describes a variety of circumstances that would inspire residents of the Ganges Plain to seek a better life in far-off Mauritius.

14. Selvon (2005, 404).

them away, or discouraged production through other devices, such as marketing boards.[15] Third, it eventually helped reconcile the Franco-Mauritians to independence.

8.1.3   Independence

In the early 1960s the British prepared for independence,[16] but communal or sectarian tensions were strong. Creoles, the descendants of the original slaves, many of whom had acquired positions in the civil service and in the growing private sector, aligned with Franco-Mauritians in their fears regarding independence, adding to the voting strength of the latter. Chinese, Muslim, and Tamil minorities were also afraid that those Hindus descended of immigrants from the Ganges Plain would dominate an independent country. The Mauritian Social Democratic Party (PMSD), composed of Franco-Mauritians and Creoles, lost elections to the Hindu-dominated Labour Party in 1967. This election confirmed the narrowly drawn fault lines regarding the independence issue: only 55 percent voted for the independence platform. Riots along ethnic lines took place periodically in the 1960s, especially as the date of independence drew near. The Labour Party government had to call in British troops to restore order in January 1968.

Mauritius became an independent country in March 1968, with Ramgoolam as prime minister. He had won respect by avoiding divisive appeals and cooperating with all factions. He was to serve in that post for fourteen years.

The PMSD boycotted the independence ceremony. It soon became reconciled to independence and the need for nation building, however, to some extent reassured by minority rights, and especially pushed by two powerful constituencies who favored stability: business leaders, including plantation owners (who were financial backers of the party), together with the foreign diplomatic community. The PMSD joined in a series of changing coalition governments. All governments have been coalitions, and each has included either Labour, the PMSD, or often both. The precedent that the parties must enter coalitions was set by the British governor, before independence.

The leftist niche was staked out by a new party, the Mouvement Militant Mauricien (MMM). The government responded in a heavy-handed way in 1971, first by postponing elections scheduled for the following year and then, when the MMM called strikes, by imprisoning its leader, a Franco-Mauricien named Paul Bérenger. The strategy seemed to work, at any rate. Bérenger subsequently moved to the right, perhaps as the policies of the ruling party were seen to be successful. (Economic growth averaged over 8 percent during the years 1970–75.) Eventually Bérenger entered a coali-

---

15. One example of Ghana's past treatment of its cocoa farmers (Frankel 1974).

16. This section draws on Bowman (1991, 33–42), Brautigam (1999), Bunwaree and Kadenally (2006), Selvon (2005), and Simmons (1982), among others.

tion government with Anerood Jugnauth, when he was elected the second prime minister in 1982. Jugnauth served through 1995, in six coalition governments.

There are many parties, but two broad alliances usually dominate: one built around Labour, the MLP, and the other built around the MMM. The son of the founding premier, Navin Ramgoolam, at the head of Labour, became the third prime minister from 1995 to 2000 and was returned to office in 2005, which he held for ten years.

8.1.4 Which Colonial Heritage?

Some economists and historians have sought to discern if one national brand of colonialism in Africa and elsewhere left behind better institutions than another.[17] This test would be impossible to perform in the case of Mauritius, because of the impossibility of saying who left the colonial heritage. The Dutch? They first colonized the island, and named it. The French? They left the landowning elite and gave the island its dominant language. The British? Cars drive on the left and, remarkably, the country's Supreme Court is Britain's Privy Council, even though it became a Republic—Queen Elizabeth ceased to be the head of state—in 1992. Or perhaps it could be described as India's colony. Three languages appear on the money: English, Hindi, and Tamil.

8.1.5 Stages of Development

The traditional three stages of development worldwide feature gradual shifts in the composition of a country's economy, from the primary sector to manufactures, and then on to the service economy. This stylized model happens to fit Mauritius in a literal way. The commodities at the primary stage were agricultural, particularly sugar, as we have seen. Industrialization began in the 1970s, consisting largely of textiles and apparel. More recently, the desired and actual share of services has risen, especially tourism but also financial services, information and computer technology (ICT), and others. When economists ponder the island's success, they are usually talking about the solid achievement of that critical first stage of development: labor-intensive manufacturing, especially clothing exports.[18] But we need equally to consider the subsequent phase of adaptation to trade shocks, especially the decline of clothing export markets.

8.1.6 Adapting to External Shocks

While globalization carries gains from trade and other benefits, it also can also increase exposure to external fluctuations. Mauritius has experienced

---

17. For example, Feyrer and Sacerdote (2009).

18. Basic manufactures at the beginning also included wigs, toothpaste, and simple electronics, among other things.

many external shocks in its history, inevitably suggesting the metaphor of a small ship on stormy seas. Whether through luck or skill, however, the country has usually been able to adapt to changed circumstances over the years. Consider four.

Labor Shortage

We have already discussed the big adaptation to the labor shortage on the sugar plantations that followed the abolition of slavery in 1835: the import of indentured workers from India.

Independence

The second big shock was independence in 1968, under inauspicious conditions that will be elaborated in the next section of the chapter. The country soon achieved trade-led growth in the 1970s, despite protectionist import policies.

The 1974–1980 Increases in World Oil Price

Like most other oil-importing developing countries, Mauritius initially responded to its higher import bill by borrowing, running large current account deficits in the late 1970s. But it undertook successful adjustment ahead of most of the others.[19] The adjustment took place in macroeconomic policy, when it devalued twice in compliance with International Monetary Fund (IMF) programs,[20] as well as in microeconomic policy, featuring an important trade reform in 1984[21] consistent with a World Bank Structural Adjustment Facility. The reforms were implemented over three successive governments; a number of observers have highlighted what this says about the stability of the political system and its ability to do what is best for the country, even while simultaneously squabbling furiously over personal and factional politics.[22] There followed a period of strong economic performance that can be said to have carried the country into tiger status by the end of the 1990s.

Further Trade Shocks over the Years 2004–2009

The worst of the latter-day trade shocks was the end of favored treatment abroad of its most important exports: the loss of sugar preferences in 2004 and the loss of MFA clothing preferences around the same time, as the Multi-Fiber Agreement (MFA) system was dismantled, the world market became free and open, and low-wage manufacturers in China displaced

19. Gulhati and Nallari (1990); Selvon (2005).
20. Twenty-three to thirty percent (depending on the measure) in 1979 and almost as much again in 1981; Ancharaz (2004, 6), Brautigam (1999, 156–57), Gulhati and Nallari (1990), and Imam and Manoiu (2008).
21. Ancharaz (2004).
22. Brautigam (1999, 156–57) and Subramanian (2001).

textiles and apparel in many developing countries.[23] In Mauritius the sector suffered a 30 percent fall in output and 25 percent drop in employment. The balance of payments deficit, budget deficit, and unemployment all deteriorated. The adverse trend in the terms of trade continued with the rise in world prices of oil and food over the period 2003–2008. Finally the great global recession hit all export-oriented countries in 2008–2009.

The incoming Labour government that was returned to power in 2005 responded to the loss of trade preferences and current account deficit in several ways.[24] A multifaceted reform program in 2006 included a Business Facilitation Act to eliminate obstacles to investment and hiring, steps to make it easier for desired immigrants to become citizens,[25] and a simplified tax system with a flat 15 percent tax rate for individuals and companies. Soon the government was able to claim tangible results: (a) the country climbed even higher in international rankings of climate for business,[26] and (b) the budget deficit fell, so that by 2007 the primary deficit was almost down to zero.[27]

The government had achieved enough reduction in the budget deficit, and had enough foresight when the US subprime mortgage crisis lingered a year after its origins in mid-2007, to ease a bit fiscally as early as mid-2008, just in time for the global recession.[28] This sort of example of countercyclical fiscal policy—allowing deficits to fall in booms and rise in downturns—had been rare among developing countries in the past, but was newly achieved by some in 2008–2009.

With the loss of MFN preferences for clothing exports, and the new competition from China in all manufactures, Mauritians described the way forward as "the third sector," that is, services. Tourism was already the leading service export (Durbarry 2004), and was now joined by banking and ICT, looking to Singapore as a model. (Join the club!)

Is the move to banking a wishful-thinking pursuit of a mirage in the desert? Not quite. But neither should the island see itself as the next Singapore. Subramanian (2009, 20–21) explains: "the offshore financial sector has grown because of the Indian diaspora which led to the signing of a double taxation treaty between Mauritius and India. As a result, Mauritian

23. Ancharaz (2009) and Imam and Manoiu (2008).

24. Rama Sithanen, finance minister (Labor Party), said: "When we came to power in 2005, the situation was awful" (Hawkins 2008).

25. Needless to say, most countries are less welcoming to immigrants. Think of South African attacks on recent Mozambiquan and Zimbabwean immigrants in 2008, Ivoirian attacks on its immigrants in 2002, or Uganda booting out its entire Indian population in 1972.

26. The Business Facilitation Act evidently succeeded in boosting the climate for business in Mauritius as judged by the *Doing Business Report* of the World Bank and the *Global Competitiveness* measure from the World Economic Forum (especially low barriers to trading across borders, such as days required for importing and exporting).

27. Down from 1.5 percent of GDP in 2005/06. For example, subsidies on rice and flour were removed. African Economic Outlook (2008, 434).

28. Ministry of Finance (2008).

offshore centres have mediated large financial flows to India and Mauritius has become the largest investor in India." If the financial center is built on Indians using a bilateral investment treaty for round-tripping, it is unlikely to be durable.

More recent plans call for expansion in a variety of other sectors: a seafood hub, an "integrated resorts" scheme, and more. They are characterized as "pillars" of the new economy.[29]

Even within the textiles and apparel sector, when a country loses low-end exports to low-wage competition, a reduced subset of the industry can be reborn through innovation. This describes northern Italy, for example, and it also describes Mauritius.

One can see tangible evidence of precisely such adaptation if one visits the successful Compagnie Mauricienne de Textiles. Rather than closing its clothing factory when the MFA ended, the company brought in an experienced new manager from India, opened a textile factory just across the parking lot, adopted current Asian technology, and is now fully integrated.[30] On one side of the parking lot, the textile plant is so highly automated that it requires only a few young workers, who get around the large building on roller skates to tend the machines. Meanwhile, the apparel plant next door is still a beehive of low-skilled workers. The textile factory takes raw cotton and turns it into yarn and fabric. The apparel factory takes the fabric and turns it into finished garments. Although the integrated process can be run continuously from beginning to end, CMT also keeps inventories of many kinds of cloth, so as to be able to respond even more rapidly to the sort of sudden new requests that are standard in the world of fashion.

One plausible way forward for Mauritius is as a platform for firms from India and China wishing to do business in Africa. Everyone's favorite entrepôt, Singapore, is an obvious model. (Mauritius has the second big-

---

29. When one hears of the sectors that have been designated as promising priorities for the future, it is difficult to discern the balance of government versus private participation in these plans. The government intervenes in many markets. (Lange [2009] declares Mauritius a "developmental state"—for which he credits direct British colonial rule!) The strategic documents describing "pillars" are from the government, but officials deny that they are directing investment in the manner of socialist five-year plans. Perhaps the "administrative guidance" of some East Asian countries is a parallel. Perhaps, in a sufficiently small country, a meeting to plan an integrated resort (a luxury hotel and villa development intended to attract foreign investors), even though it is called by government officials, need not operate fundamentally differently from the sort of meeting among private developers that would take place in a larger, more purely capitalist, country.

30. The primary motivation for integrated production was the African Growth and Opportunity Act (AGOA), under which the United States decided in 2000 to grant duty-free access to African apparel exports provided that the fabric or yarn not be imported from Europe, but rather be either homemade or imported from the United States. Mauritius was one of the first two countries (with Kenya) to be approved for AGOA, which has proven successful (Frazer and Van Biesebroeck 2010, 130) to a surprising extent. The AGOA benefits are no longer relevant, but once established, CMT's integrated production is profitable regardless. (The manager told us that he knew this ahead of time, but that the owners who hired him did not.)

gest container cargo in sub-Saharan Africa.) But another possible model is Hong Kong, which long had a favored position as the window or platform for investing into China. Another possible analogy more recent in origin is Dubai, which can be viewed as the platform for investing into the volatile Middle East. These city-states share the traits of being open, stable, well functioning, cosmopolitan, and adaptable.[31]

8.2   Economists' Hypotheses Regarding Mauritian Economic Performance

We review six explanations that have been put forward for the success of Mauritius. (This section owes much to the cataloging of theories in Subramanian [2009].[32]) Each of these explanations will be rejected at least in part, suggesting that the field is still open.

8.2.1   Initial Conditions

After the fact, success often looks preordained. So any recounting of the performance of the pearl of the Indian Ocean must start by relating how two Nobel Prize winners, around the time of independence, independently forecast doom instead of success. The first, James Meade (1961a), was later to win the Nobel Prize in Economics: "Heavy population pressure must inevitably reduce real income per head. . . . That surely is bad enough in a community that is full of political conflict . . . the outlook for peaceful development is poor." The second, V. S. Naipaul (1972), had a more literary vantage point, but came to the same conclusion: "The disaster has occurred . . . now given a thing called independence and set adrift, an abandoned imperial barracoon, incapable of economic or cultural autonomy."

There were excellent reasons for such fears. Three were perhaps uppermost in the minds of observers at the time; three more would have been particularly worrisome given empirical regularities that we know about today.

- Geography. A country that is small lacks internal economies of scale and a complete array of endowments. Many small countries make up for these limitations through international trade. But a country that is located remotely from the centers of population and economic activity is at a disadvantage for trade. Mauritius ranks as more disadvantaged than Madagascar, and alongside eleven South Pacific countries, as the most remote in the world.[33]
- Ethnic tensions. Mauritius had, and has, a split of several major ethnic groups that would normally not be considered conducive to growth.

31. China has already begun to use Mauritius as a platform for investment into Africa (Ancharaz 2009, 6, 19).

32. Also Brautigam (1997, 1999), Russell (2008), and others.

33. Remoteness is measured as a weighted average of log distance from other countries, with shares of either GDP or population used as weights.

Social scientists generally consider a low degree of ethnic fragmentation to be the best for growth (Sweden, Japan, Botswana).[34] A widely used measure of ethnic, linguistic, and religious fragmentation shows Mauritius as far more split than all the other small African island states, and remarkably similar to Trinidad and Tobago, and Fiji.[35] As we saw in the preceding section, ethnic riots accompanied the run-up to independence.

- Population density. The island has one of the higher ratios of population to land area in the world. Unemployment was high in the 1960s, resulting in outmigration. The apparent overpopulation, together with ethnic and political conflict, were major reasons for the pessimism of Meade and Naipaul.
- Volatile monocrop. The economy of 1968 was considered highly dependent on a single crop, sugar, that suffers from high volatility. Today, even more than then, we are aware of the natural resource curse. It is discussed in the next subsection.
- Regression to the mean. The growth literature suggests that, although there is no tendency for countries' income levels to converge unconditionally, there is a significant tendency for gradual conditional convergence. That is, if various factors such as geographical suitability for trade suggest an income level above where a country is at the beginning of a sample period, on average its income can be expected to move slowly in the direction of that long-run equilibrium. But Mauritius in the 1960s had an income level above the Africa average, and perhaps above what would be predicted from its geography. What had been a favorable location a century earlier—a deep-water port well placed for stopping off on the shipping route to India—had become unfavorable when the Suez Canal opened in 1869. Looking forward from the 1960s, one might have predicted downward convergence.
- Last on the list of poor initial conditions at the time of independence

34. Easterly and Levine (1997). One hypothesis is that the relationship is U-shaped, that a very high degree of fragmentation can also be fine for growth (twenty small groups, none of which dominate), and that it is the middle degree that is dangerous (Collier et al. 2007, 393–95; Bates and Yackolev 2002; Collier 2000). They give Botswana as their example of an ethnically homogeneous country and Tanzania as an example at the other extreme. Carroll and Carroll (1997, 465) consider Botswana to be ethnically divided because, even though 80 percent of the population is Tswana, they come from eight Tswana tribes; perhaps, then, the distinction between very high and very low ethnic fragmentation is a subtle matter of definition. (This paper was brought to my attention by Prime Minister Navin Ramgoolam.)

35. The remarkable part is that all three tropical islands, though located in three different oceans, got their ethnic diversity in essentially the same way: Indians were brought to work the sugar fields. Trinidad and Tobago subsequently enjoyed oil wealth, but suffered the natural resource curses of rent-seeking behavior and Dutch disease cycles in a way that Mauritius has been able to avoid by using rents from trade privileges effectively (Auty 2009b, 2–3). Trinidad and Tobago fits right on the international natural resource curse line: 1970–2008 growth was a little substandard in a way that can be statistically associated with the high share of oil in its exports (Frankel 2012, figure 1). Fiji is discussed toward the end of this chapter.

were distortionary trade barriers. It is not that the first government was especially antimarket in philosophy, but import substitution was the fashion of the day. Today it is more widely believed that trade is good for economic performance, less because classical and modern trade theory say so, perhaps, than because of the demonstration of trade-led growth in East Asia and elsewhere.

All in all, one must agree with Meade (1961b) that the initial conditions were not auspicious.

8.2.2   Sugar Wealth

The second possible explanation for the success of Mauritius is the sugar plantations, but natural resources often have undesirable effects.[36] For every Botswana, a diamond-rich and successful state, there is at least one Congo, a mineral-rich and failed state. Indeed, as already noted, dependence on a volatile monocrop economy is on the list of poor initial conditions facing Mauritius at the time of independence. There are many versions of the natural resource curse. Perhaps a majority focus on mineral commodities as the culprit, or more specifically oil; some of these explicitly exclude agricultural products.[37]

But there is a version of the natural resource curse, designed by Engerman and Sokoloff (1997, 2000, 2002) to think about the Americas (Brazil versus the United States), that explicitly includes sugar. The idea is that lands endowed with point-source extractive industries (oil and mining) and plantation crops (sugar and cotton) developed institutions of slavery, inequality, dictatorship, and state control, whereas those climates suited to fishing and small farms (fruits and vegetables, grain and livestock) developed institutions based on individualism, democracy, egalitarianism, and capitalism. When the industrial revolution came along, the latter areas were well suited to make the most of it. Those that had specialized in extractive industries were not, because society had come to depend on class structure and authoritarianism rather than on individual incentive and decentralized decision making.

Several other versions of the natural resource curse apply to agriculture products in general as much as to minerals: external returns to manufacturing, the Dutch disease, and commodity volatility.

Outside of classical economics, diversification out of primary commodities into manufacturing in most circles is considered self-evidently desirable.

---

36. Frankel (2012) offers a survey of the natural resource curse.

37. Sala-i-Martin and Subramanian (2003), Bulte, Damania, and Deacon (2005), and Mehlum, Moene, and Torvik (2006). The latter use the phrase "lootable" resources. Isham et al. (2005) explicitly include coffee and cocoa as plantation crops that are damaging to institutional development, alongside oil and other point-source minerals, rather than as small-scale farm products. (But in Africa cocoa and coffee should perhaps count as small-scale farming.)

Several dubious arguments have been made for it. One is the "structuralist" or Prebisch-Singer hypothesis of secularly declining commodity prices, which is not generally borne out by the long-term data. Another is the mistaken "cargo cult" inference—based on the observation that advanced countries have heavy industries like steel mills—that these visible monuments are necessarily the route to economic development. But one should not dismiss more valid considerations, just because less valid arguments for diversification into manufacturing are sometimes made.

Is industrialization the sine qua non of economic development? Is encouragement of manufacturing necessary to achieve high income? Classical economic theory says "no": countries are best off producing whatever is their comparative advantage, whether that is natural resources or manufacturing. In this nineteenth century view, attempts by Brazil to industrialize were as foolish as it would have been for Great Britain to try to grow coffee and oranges in hothouses. But the structuralists were never alone in their feeling that countries only get sustainably rich if they industrialize. Nor were they ever alone in feeling that industrialization in turn requires an extra push from the government (at least for latecomers), often known as industrial policy.

Matsuyama (1992) provided an influential model formalizing this intuition: the manufacturing sector is assumed to be characterized by learning by doing, while the agricultural sector is not. The implication is that deliberate policy-induced diversification out of primary products into manufacturing is justified, and that a permanent commodity boom that crowds out manufacturing can indeed be harmful.

On the other side, it must be pointed out that there is no reason why learning by doing should be the exclusive preserve of manufacturing tradables. Nontradables can enjoy learning by doing.[38] Mineral and agricultural sectors can as well. Some countries have experienced tremendous productivity growth in the primary sector. American productivity gains have been aided by public investment since the late nineteenth century.[39] Attempts by governments in developing countries to force linkages between the primary sector and processing industries, however, have been less successful.[40]

Some have suggested that the high volatility that afflicts most commodities is the source of the natural resource curse.[41] Highly variable prices on

38. Torvik (2001).

39. In such knowledge are infrastructure institutions such as the US Geological Survey, the Agricultural Extension program, and land-grant colleges (Wright and Czelusta 2006).

40. Hausmann, Klinger, and Lawrence (2008) warn of the pitfalls of assuming that South Africa, for example, can move from diamond mining to diamond cutting. They are not opposed to industrial policy, but rather believe that linkages are more likely where factor intensities and technological requirements are similar across sectors, rather than to upstream or downstream industries.

41. Blattman, Hwang, and Williamson (2007), Hausmann and Rigobon (2003), and Poelhekke and van der Ploeg (2007).

world markets, usually attributable to low short-run elasticities, are the most obvious sort of volatility experienced by agricultural and mineral products. But there are other sorts as well, both on the demand side and the supply side. On the demand side, large swings in the trade policies of the major markets for Mauritian sugar have been a bigger source of volatility during its history than the variance in a world price of sugar. On the supply side, cyclones have caused great damage to the crop, particularly several that hit in the 1960s.

Over the 150 years during which Mauritius was overwhelmingly a sugar economy, it suffered from periodic Dutch disease cycles due to big changes in European barriers/preferences toward its crop. Three booms related to the granting of preferences occurred in the 1830s, 1919–1920, and 1973–1974. Ancharaz (2004, 5) sees in these Mauritian booms the familiar Dutch disease pattern of a rise in public spending "of dubious economic value," budget deficits, inflation (especially in the price of land), and real appreciation of the currency.

Even leaving aside undesirable macroeconomic effects of commodity booms, cyclical shifts of resources (labor, capital, and land) back and forth across sectors may incur needless costs. Frictional unemployment of labor, incomplete utilization of the capital stock, and incomplete occupancy of housing are true deadweight costs, even if they are temporary. A diversified country is indeed probably better off than one specialized in oil or a few other commodities, other things equal.

8.2.3   Openness

Subramanian (2009) attributes to Jeff Sachs[42] the view that an open trade policy contributed to Mauritian success, and then rejects it:

> Mauritius was one of the countries that Sachs and Warner classified as being open or following liberal trade policies. But this categorization of Mauritius as an open economy was misleading, even incorrect. In Sub-ramanian and Roy (2003, tables 4 and 5), we provide estimates of the restrictiveness of Mauritius' trade policy regime. During the 1970s and 1980s, Mauritius remained a highly protected economy: the average rate of protection was high and dispersed. In 1980, the average effective protection exceeded 100 percent, and although this diminished by the end of the 1980s, it was still very high (65 percent). Moreover until the 1980s, there were also extensive quantitative restrictions in the form of import licensing, covering nearly 60 percent of imports.

That Mauritius did not follow free trade policies, at least until relatively recently, does not mean that trade was not a critical part of the story. It seems difficult to escape the conclusion that it was. Exports and imports are each about two-thirds of GDP. But Subramanian and Roy (2003) and Subrama-

---

42. Sachs and Warner (1997).

nian (2001, 2009) discuss two other particular trade-related hypotheses, to which we now turn.

8.2.4 Export Processing Zone and Heterodox Trade Strategy

"Free trade" is normally taken to mean laissez faire, the absence of trade distorting policies, whether antiimport (tariff or nontariff barriers against imports) or proexport (export subsidies and other export-promoting policies, including privileged access to imported inputs).[43] But Rodrik (1998) has suggested that Mauritius' success was the result of a "heterodox" trade policy reminiscent of the East Asian tigers, a strategy that created high returns to the export sector, while preventing resources from being diverted into the protected import-competing sector. The specific institutional mechanism was the export processing zone (EPZ), which was established in 1970.

It accomplished the successful promotion of exports by (a) giving EPZ firms tax advantages, (b) eliminating tariffs on the imported inputs used by manufacturers, and (c) setting laxer labor standards for EPZ workers and a lower minimum wage. Initially the differential between sugar workers and EPZ workers was almost 50 percent. That the EPZ factory workers were mostly women made discriminatory labor laws politically possible.

Although there is a strong a priori case that the development of a manufacturing sector inside the EPZ was an important component of Mauritian success, there are two counterarguments to Rodrik and his heterodox trade policy. First, many countries, including a number in Africa, have established export processing zones without similarly successful results.[44] Second, Subramanian and Roy (2003, 19) compute that the various effective EPZ subsidies in Mauritius (encouraging resources to move into trade) were substantially smaller than subsidies to import-competing sectors (discouraging resources from moving into trade):

> [E]ffective protection for the import-competing sector averaged about 125 percent in the 1980s and about 65 percent in the 1990s. . . . Even allowing for favourable tax breaks, it seems that heterodox opening and intervention (in the form of subsidies in the export sector) did not offset completely the anti-export bias of the restrictive import regime.

8.2.5 Ideas and FDI

Paul Romer (1990, 1993) contributed an approach to growth theory based on ideas (innovations in either products or production methods) as the key

---

43. To the mercantilist minded, import tariffs and export subsidies seem similarly designed: to increase the trade balance. To a trade theorist, the trade balance is determined in other ways in general equilibrium (national saving and investment) and in the very long run is zero; as a result, import tariffs lead to a lower level of overall trade (exports as well as imports) and export subsidies to a higher level (again, on both sides of the trade balance).

44. Subramanian (2009, 15): "Apart from Mauritius, EPZ facilities and the attendant incentives were provided by a host of other African countries such as Zimbabwe, Senegal, Madagascar and Cameroon. . . . The EPZ experiment failed in almost all these countries."

ingredient for development, rather than capital, labor, or other factors of production. Romer (1992) argues that importing ideas from abroad through inward foreign direct investment (FDI) is an effective alternative to growing them at home. Specifically in the case of Mauritius, Chinese businessmen brought the idea of textile and apparel manufacturing to the EPZ, jump-starting the country's industrialization.[45]

Subramanian and Roy (2003) and Subramanian (2001; 2009, 14) argue against Romer's explanation for Mauritian success on the grounds that the share of foreign companies in the EPZ was not all that large: "For example, in 1984, only 12 percent of the total employment in the EPZ was accounted for by wholly foreign-owned operations compared with 72, 42, and 64 percent, respectively, in Korea, the Philippines and Malaysia. It is estimated that about 50 percent of the total equity of firms in the EPZ was owned by Mauritian nationals." This criticism seems a trifle unfair. The idea of "ideas" is that they can be emulated, when observed at close hand. So, it is perfectly plausible that local firms caught on quickly after the Chinese-owned apparel factories were successful. Hausmann and Rodrik (2003) would call it the social benefits of self-discovery.

A more serious objection is that the idea of producing clothing is rather obvious—it is famously the first rung on the ladder of industrialization (though, in fairness, this might not have been so obvious in 1970)—and that something else beyond FDI and the EPZ is needed to explain why it worked in Mauritius and not in other African countries. For Subramanian (2009) a key ingredient is preferential treatment for Mauritian exports in the markets of Europe and the United States. I agree that this was a sine qua non. Under the Multi-Fiber Agreement (MFA) exports of textile and apparel were limited by quotas, but Mauritius benefited from relatively lenient treatment.[46] That Hong Kong had quickly used up its export quotas, and had proceeded to fill the quotas in other Asian countries, explains why its businessmen were willing to start apparel factories in such a far-off country as Mauritius, which had not been using its quota.

Three more ingredients were useful. A key one was a competitively valued exchange rate,[47] which helped offset the antitrade bias of the import tariffs. Another was ethnic links between the Chinese and Chinese-Mauritians, whose ancestors had immigrated long before.[48] Chinese-Mauritians had been instrumental in persuading the government to set up the EPZ in the

45. Also Nath and Madhoo (2008) and Ancharaz (2009).

46. It could be argued that the United States also gave favorable treatment to the exports of Korea and Taiwan during the Cold War.

47. Imam and Manoiu (2008).

48. Global econometrics with the gravity model show that bilateral trade links are significantly stronger when two countries share some population that speaks the same language (perhaps especially so if the language is Chinese). Frankel (1997, 74–75, 104).

first place.[49] Another ingredient was the capital of the Franco-Mauritians, some of whom set up factories in parallel with the Chinese.[50]

8.2.6   Good Institutions

After poking holes in all the other hypotheses—initial conditions, open trade policies, a heterodox trade policy built around the Export Processing Zone, and the importation of manufacturing ideas via foreign direct investment—Subramanian (2009) declares himself for institutions as the explanation. It was good institutions that allowed Mauritius to develop the EPZ effectively, where others might have gotten mired down in corruption. He points out that Mauritius ranks high in the standard measures of the quality of institutions: political participation, rule of law, and control of corruption. As many have noted, Mauritius and Botswana, two star performers, are also the only two African countries to have been democratic continuously since independence.[51]

A prominent trend in thinking regarding economic development is that the quality of institutions, especially property rights and the rule of law, is the fundamental factor that determines which countries experience good performance and which do not,[52] and that it is futile to recommend good macroeconomic or microeconomic policies if the institutional structure is not there to support them.[53] Acemoglu, Johnson, and Robinson (2001) famously use settler mortality rates as an instrumental variable for institutions. Nath and Madhoo (2008) suggest that the settler story applies literally to Mauritius: success is attributed to good institutions, which is attributed to European settlement, and in turn to suitable climate.

8.3   Digging Deeper

8.3.1   Deeper Determinants

Perhaps the most interesting part of the debate on growth over the past decade has been: What are the deeper determinants? Yes, policies regarding taxes, government spending, and tariffs help determine investment,

49. Subramanian (2001). Particularly one E. Lim Fat (Brautigam 1999, 148). The government sent a team to Hong Kong and Taiwan to investigate the export success of these newborn tigers, and the EPZ Act of 1970 was the result of its recommendations.

50. Brautigam (1999, 149) reports that from the beginning, half of the EPZ investment came from the locals.

51. For example, Carroll and Carroll (1997). Radelet (2010) argues that progress toward democracy has contributed importantly to economic progress among a number of African countries.

52. North (1994). Four of the most important empirical contributions are Barro (1991), Hall and Jones (1999), Acemoglu, Johnson, and Robinson (2001), and Rodrik, Subramanian, and Trebbi (2004).

53. Acemoglu et al. (2003).

education, and trade, which in turn are good for growth. But what are the deeper determinants of those policies? Rodrik, Subramanian, and Trebbi (2004) pose the question well. In their view, there are three emerging theories: (a) openness; (b) geography, which I prefer to interpret more narrowly as tropical disease; and (c) institutions. Each theory can be captured by some standard measures, such as trade volume, malaria incidence, and rule of law, respectively. Each has serious endogeneity problems that must be addressed: when countries grow richer they lower tariffs, drain swamps, and adopt accounting standards. The endogeneity of trade has been largely addressed by geographic determinants, such as access to coastline. It ought to be possible to address malaria by purely topographic and climatologic determinants.

That leaves institutions. The settler mortality variable of Acemoglu, Johnson, and Robinson, (2001) is probably the best we have econometrically, but it is just a start on the problem. The very aspects that make it exogenous—colonial history and geographic susceptibility to disease—also raise the question of whether the sort of institutions at stake are so predetermined as to make postindependence mortals powerless to shape them so as to benefit their countries.[54] Fatalist determinism cannot be the answer. Good institutions have been chosen by mortal people in living memory, in countries as diverse as Germany, Singapore, Hong Kong, Chile, Botswana . . . and Mauritius.

8.3.2   Measuring Institutions

We will use measures of institutions in the econometric analysis in the next section, but some are vulnerable to subjectivity. Where they come from surveys (for example, Transparency International's widely cited results on corruption), there is the danger of a "halo effect." Survey respondents "know" that Switzerland is a more successful country than Colombia, and so they tend to give higher ratings to institutions in one place than the other, even when it might not be based on specific familiarity with the facts. Rotberg and Gisselquist (2009) have, since 2007, compiled the Index of African Governance, which attempts to be less subjective than survey-based measures from Transparency International or the Worldwide Governance Indicators (WGI). The cost of eliminating subjectivity is increased reliance on measures that could be regarded as endogenous outcomes, instead of the more

---

54. One might argue that the same is true of trade, as have Rodriguez and Rodrik (2001) in critiquing Frankel and Romer (1999). They ask how we can be sure that the beneficial effects of trade that result from trade policy decisions are similar to the beneficial effects of trade that are observed to result from sea access and other geographic variables. The answer is that, although, as always with instrumental variables, we cannot be sure the effects are the same, (a) those antiglobalizers who question the benefits of trade liberalization generally feel the same when it is technological progress in transport and communications that shrinks the world, and (b) it is possible to measure trade unambiguously. The concept of "better or worse institutions" lacks the unambiguous unidirectionality of "more or less trade."

exogenous institutions that most of us mean by the word "governance." The Index of African Governance data are good for the ranking game, but perhaps more worrisome as the independent variable in a regression. The solution is to drop the three categories of "outcome" components (economic opportunity, safety/security, and health/human development), and focus solely on the two "input" sets of components (rule of law and participation/human rights). The correlation between the rule of law measures in the WGI and in African Governance is .91.

Mauritius ranks first by participation and human rights. It ranks third in rule of law, after Cape Verde and Botswana. Amazingly, the Heritage Foundation in 2011 ranked the island country's economic freedom, not just as first in Africa, but as number eight in the world. Transparency International and the Internet Center for Corruption Research place Mauritius second only to Botswana in freedom from corruption within the region.[55]

It can be hard to square such rankings with common reports from citizens of government corruption that recurrently goes unpunished.[56] Perhaps it is best to conclude that the basic comparison to most other African countries is valid, but Mauritius still does not belong with the Nordic countries. For perspective, when Transparency International gives Mauritius a ranking of number forty-six in its Corruptions Perspectives index for 2011, that is midway between New Zealand's number one and Liberia, Trinidad, or Zambia, which are tied for number ninety-one. Its raw score (5.1) is midway between the United States (7.1) and the three-way tie of Albania, India, and Swaziland (3.1, ranked number 95).

Very few available indicators of the quality of institutions seem able to escape both the Scylla of subjectivity in judgments and the Charybdis of judging by outcomes. To measure fundamental institutional quality, two of the best candidates from the Index of African Governance are the reported number of days to settle a contract dispute and the number of pretrial detainees. Mauritius does not rank as highly if judged by these two statistics as by the other indicators. Does the island paradise thus benefit from a discriminatory halo effect when its institutions are rated? National prison authorities themselves are the sources for the raw detainee data; perhaps the researchers are not able to enforce across countries adequate honesty in self-reporting. We are left short of unambiguous indications of high-quality institutions.

The unusual arrangement whereby the British Privy Council serves as the Supreme Court of Mauritius sounds like a textbook case of a well-designed institution: It can be expected to deliver answers that will be respected by

---

55. Rotberg and Gisselquist (2009).

56. Dukhira (2002, 279–82) and Selvon (2005, 492–94). Crime is another area where local residents (Dukhira 2002, 271–76; Selvon 2005) paint a less idyllic picture than the rankings, which give Mauritius the best possible rating on violent crime (homicides) (Rotberg and Gisselquist 2009, 57, 90).

competing groups who would not necessarily trust home-grown mechanisms. Another observation encourages the notion that Mauritius does actually have effective institutions: A sophisticated cyclone warning system successfully gives warning of coming cyclones on a scale of four alerts, allowing the people to move to higher ground. The system requires both government competence and public cooperation. A new tsunami warning center has also been described as state of the art. These are perhaps clean examples of specific good institutions.

8.3.3   Democracy

As noted, Mauritius and Botswana are the two African countries that have been continuously democratic from birth.

The statistical evidence across countries is at best mixed as to whether democracy per se is good for economic performance. Barro (1996) finds that it is the rule of law, free markets, education, and low government consumption that are good for growth, not democracy per se. Tavares and Wacziarg (2001) find that it is education, not democracy per se. Alesina et al. (1996) find that it is political stability, not democracy per se, that is good for growth.[57] Some even find that, after controlling for important factors such as the rule of law and political stability, democracy has, if anything, a weak negative effect on growth.[58]

One can claim good evidence for the reverse causation, that economic growth leads to democracy, often assisted by the creation of a middle class.[59] Examples include Korea and Taiwan. Of course, democracy is normally regarded as an end in itself, aside from whether it promotes economic growth. Even here, one must note that the benefits of the formalities of elections can be overemphasized. For one thing, elections can be a sham. Such leaders as Robert Mugabe, Hamid Karzai, and George W. Bush have each claimed to have been elected without having, in fact, earned more votes than their opponents. Western style or one-man, one-vote elections should perhaps receive less priority in developing countries than the fundamental principles of rule of law, human rights, freedom of expression, economic freedom, minority rights, and some form of popular representation.[60]

---

57. It is worth noting, however, that many autocracies fail to deliver political stability that survives the term or life of a particular autocrat (leaving aside whether they deliver economic benefits for the people). China is the exception; also Singapore, if it is not counted as a democracy.

58. Collier and Hoeffler (2009) find that when developing countries have democracies, as opposed to advanced-country democracies, they tend to feature weak checks and balances. As a result, when developing countries also have high natural resource rents, the result is on average bad for economic growth.

59. Helliwell (1994), Huber, Rueschemeyer, and Stephens (1993), Lipset (1994), and Minier (1998).

60. Zakaria (1997, 2004).

8.4   The Econometrics

Econometric studies of economic performance worldwide often show a negative dummy variable for Africa. We begin with some econometrics that includes other parts of the world, so as to see to what extent Africa's problems stem from variables such as tropical location. But rather than repeating the sort of 150-country data sets that are so familiar from other papers, we look at a cross section consisting of island countries around the world. There are at least two reasons why this is of interest. First, islands are a test case that can isolate certain factors.[61] For example, national borders are not likely to be endogenous. Second, as noted, not just Mauritius, but three out of the top four performers in Africa are islands, an intriguing fact that invites investigation.

8.4.1   Performance across Island Countries

Table 8.3 reports results of a pure cross section of island countries. Our dependent variable is per capita income in 2006 (PPP basis). The results show a highly significant negative effect for a dummy variable that registers a country's location in the tropics. Since the variables are in log form, a coefficient of −1.8 means that nontropical countries have a sixfold advantage relative to tropical countries, other things equal.[62] The Africa dummy is negative, but not statistically significant when included along with the tropic dummy. The Worldwide Governance Indicators rule of law variable has a highly significant positive effect.[63] Its presence takes two-thirds off of the tropic dummy, confirming the view that tropical lands tend to develop less satisfactory institutions.[64] Surprisingly, the coefficient on size (population) is negative. Normally size is a positive factor for income, presumably due to internal economies of scale and diversity of factor endowments. One conceivable explanation is that all islands are so geographically well-disposed to trade because they, by definition, have good access to the sea that they are able to use trade to make up for the disadvantages of small size.

Within the island data set the trade/GDP ratio has a highly significant positive effect. Remoteness has the expected negative sign, but it is not significant when it has to compete with trade, the main channel through which it is thought to work. When, however, trade is excluded and we also condition on the WGI measure of rule of law, remoteness is indeed signifi-

61. Feyrer and Sacerdote (2009) study a sample of islands as a natural experiment. (Their finding is that the length of the colonial period is an important determinant of income today.)
62. exp(−1.8) = .16.
63. When we tried other measures of institutions from Freedom House, they did not do as well, at least not when they had to compete with the WGI measure.
64. For example, Hall and Jones (1999) and Easterly and Levine (2002). The Acemoglu, Johnson, and Robinson (2001) story about settler mortality is one way this could happen.

Table 8.3   **Islands cross section**

	Log of 2006 GDP per capita, PPP					
Tropicdummy	-1.811***	-1.725***	-0.605*	-1.800***	-1.961***	-0.342
	(0.328)	(0.330)	(0.351)	(0.405)	(0.364)	0.400
L_pop	-0.0870*	-0.0914*	-0.0123	-0.0860	-0.121*	0.032
	(0.0497)	(0.0495)	(0.0441)	(0.0551)	(0.0692)	0.053
Tradey	0.00569***	0.00552***	0.00313**	0.00578***	0.00534***	
	(0.00131)	(0.00129)	(0.00125)	(0.00193)	(0.00126)	
Remoteness	-0.234	-0.140	-0.338	-0.251	-0.601	-0.773**
	(0.463)	(0.477)	(0.346)	(0.439)	(0.568)	0.344
Africa		-0.537				
		(0.457)				
WGI			0.731***			0.826***
			(0.155)			0.183
L_pden				-0.00833		
				(0.124)		
Fragment					4.189	
					(2.905)	
Fragment^2					-3.177	
					(5.902)	
Constant	13.02***	12.31***	11.91***	13.17***	15.79***	15.018***
	(3.789)	(3.819)	(2.796)	(3.488)	(5.076)	2.766
R^2	0.570	0.594	0.694	0.570	0.625	0.6246
Root MSE	0.839	0.830	0.730	0.855	0.836	.77857
Obs.	33	33	32	33	31	37

Note: Robust standard errors are reported below the coefficients in parentheses.
***Significant at the 1 percent level.
**Significant at the 5 percent level.
*Significant at the 10 percent level.

cant, while the effect of the tropic dummy is greatly reduced. Density, too, has the expected negative sign but is not statistically significant. Finally, we tried fragmentation and fragmentation squared to test the hypothesis of a U-shaped relationship between ethnic/linguistic/religious homogeneity and economic success. They are not yet significant. By limiting the data set to islands, we have reduced the sample size to thirty-one, which inevitably raises standard errors, and may possibly explain the statistical insignificance of many of these variables (remoteness, density, fragmentation).

Tables 8.4A, 8.4B, and 8.4C allow for conditional convergence in the islands data set by including initial income as a regressor. The base case has only initial income and size. In table 8.4A the initial year is 1968, the year of Mauritian independence. The coefficient on income is very close to 1, so that we can think of the results as pertaining to average growth rates over the period. That the coefficient is so close to 1 may also indicate that we have not done a good job finding other determinants of equilibrium income. (When the initial year is 1968 and we have only fifteen island observations, nothing

Table 8.4A   **Islands from 1968**

Log of 2006 GDP per capita in constant year 2000 dollars

L_Ypc2k1968	1.003***	1.004***	0.956***	0.967***
	(0.108)	(0.138)	(0.103)	(0.107)
L_Pop1968	−0.017	0.168	−0.004	0.008
	(0.047)	(0.270)	(0.048)	(0.041)
Tradey6872		0.011		
		(0.016)		
L_Pden1968		0.010		
		(0.125)		
Remoteness		−0.731	−0.690**	
		(0.445)	(0.321)	
Fragment				−9.065**
				(3.224)
Fragment^2				11.535**
				(5.115)
Cons	1.138	3.715	7.171**	2.551**
	(0.985)	(5.966)	(2.873)	(0.859)
R^2	0.8325	0.9103	0.8511	0.8793
Root MSE	.66361	.6263	.64503	.59983
Obs.	20	15	20	20

***Significant at the 1 percent level.
**Significant at the 5 percent level.
*Significant at the 10 percent level.

Table 8.4B   **Islands from 1976**

Log of 2006 GDP per capita in constant year 2000 dollars

L_Ypc2k1976	1.035***	1.083***	1.033***	0.977***	1.026***
	(0.096)	(0.082)	(0.089)	(0.089)	(0.113)
L_Pop1976	0.034	0.218**	0.190*	0.038	0.040
	(0.053)	(0.078)	(0.092)	(0.050)	(0.052)
Tradey7680		0.012***	0.010*		
		(0.004)	(0.005)		
L_Pden1976			−0.020		
			(0.086)		
Remoteness			−0.522	−0.802**	
			(0.344)	(0.284)	
Fragment					−6.060*
					(2.990)
Fragment^2					8.412*
					(4.787)
Cons	−0.175	−4.298**	1.215	7.055*	0.727
	(1.194)	(1.641)	(3.930)	(2.456)	(1.300)
R^2	0.8649	0.9215	0.9302	0.8906	0.8800
Root MSE	.57133	.46467	.46616	.52690	.56627
Obs.	24	21	21	24	24

***Significant at the 1 percent level.
**Significant at the 5 percent level.
*Significant at the 10 percent level.

Table 8.4C   **Islands from 1996**

Log of 2006 GDP per capita in constant year 2000 dollars

L_Ypc2k1996	1.037***	1.017***	1.024***	0.918***	0.894***	0.945***
	(0.022)	(0.024)	(0.022)	(0.049)	(0.043)	(0.049)
L_Pop1996	0.000	0.000	0.012	–0.020	–0.017	–0.002
	(0.011)	(0.010)	(0.013)	(0.021)	(0.020)	(0.015)
Tradey9600			0.002**	0.000	0.000	0.001*
			(0.001)	(0.001)	(0.001)	(0.001)
L_Pden1996				0.050	0.040	
				(0.031)	(0.030)	
WGI1996				0.216**	0.233**	0.157*
				(0.097)	(0.089	(0.085)
Remoteness		–0.237**			–0.207*	
		(0.110)			(0.104)	
Cons	–0.106	2.089**	–0.355	0.838	2.797**	0.489
	(0.246)	(1.026)	(0.274)	(0.525)	(0.988)	(0.476)
R^2	0.9793	0.9812	0.9818	0.9896	0.9908	0.9878
Root MSE	.20375	.19711	.19942	.18747	.18214	.19736
Obs.	40	40	36	22	22	22

***Significant at the 1 percent level.
**Significant at the 5 percent level.
*Significant at the 10 percent level.

else is significant. These results are in appendix table 4a.[65] If we drop the trade and density variables then we can expand the sample size to twenty.)

A limited specification estimated on twenty countries is enough to generate some significant results—at least when considering the nonbase variables one by one. Remoteness is significant, with the hypothesized negative effect. Significant coefficients on fragmentation (negative) and fragmentation squared (positive) support the U-shaped hypothesis: The suggestion is that either complete homogeneity or high fragmentation can be good for growth, but that a modest number of large ethnic/linguistic groups is bad for growth.

When the initial year is 1976, we have twenty-one to twenty-four observations, as shown in table 8.4B. Now both trade and size show significant positive effects. (Density is of the hypothesized sign but insignificant.) The negative effect of remoteness is now statistically significant, except when it has to compete with the trade variable. (The explanation could be either multicollinearity or a difference in sample size.) The U-shaped fragmentation relationship is again significant.

When we start the data in 1996, as shown in table 8.4C, we are able to expand the sample size further and also to use the Worldwide Governance

65. The appendix is available in the NBER Working Paper version of this chapter (no. 16569, December 2010).

Indicator Rule of Law index. The WGI is statistically significant, but trade loses much of its significant positive effect. Remoteness becomes a significantly negative influence even when it has to compete with the trade variable. Fragmentation loses statistical significance.

8.4.2   Performance across African Countries

Next we switch to a data set consisting of African countries (table 8.5A). Here we can use the Index of African Governance, which attempts to avoid some of the subjectivity of the other measures of institutional quality. We add a dummy variable for the island countries. We also add a variable defined as the ratio of coastline to land area. This variable will be zero for a landlocked country, small for the Congo, larger for coastal countries, and larger still for small islands. The purpose is to test if access to the sea is the key variable or if something else special about small islands emerges.

We see in table 8.5B that the coastal variable is positive and significant, but only when trade openness is not there to compete with it. A dummy variable for being landlocked is negative as expected, and significant, but again only when it does not have to compete with trade. (A country with at least a little sea access has an advantage of more than 50 percent over one that is landlocked.) It seems clear that the coastal and landlocked variables have their effects via trade. The reader who is concerned about the endogeneity

Table 8.5A   Africa cross section

	Log of 2006 GDP per capita, PPP			
Tradey	0.0108***	0.00968***	0.0111***	0.0100***
	(0.00294)	(0.00311)	(0.00292)	(0.00308)
L_pop	−0.337**	−0.285*	−0.141	−0.0703
	(0.155)	(0.152)	(0.106)	(0.102)
L_area	0.196**	0.214**		
	(0.0873)	(0.0940)		
L_pden			−0.190**	−0.209**
			(0.0872)	(0.0936)
FHdemyrs	0.0257*	−0.00879	0.0257*	−0.00881
	(0.0130)	(0.0166)	(0.0130)	(0.0166)
Rule		0.0347**		0.0347**
		(0.0131)		(0.0131)
Constant	9.172***	6.713***	9.120***	6.658***
	(1.966)	(2.111)	(1.959)	(2.106)
R^2	0.438	0.541	0.435	0.538
Root MSE	0.858	0.785	0.860	0.787
Obs.	43	43	43	43

***Significant at the 1 percent level.
***Significant at the 5 percent level.
*Significant at the 1 percent level.

Table 8.5B   **Africa cross section with coastal variable**

	Log of 2006 GDP per capita, PPP					
Coast_Area	0.00595	0.690**	−0.0363	0.727**	0.0658	0.683**
	(0.528)	(0.341)	(0.539)	(0.346)	(0.514)	(0.330)
Rule	0.0314***	0.0339***	0.0289***	0.0304***	0.0300***	0.0297***
	(0.0105)	(0.00969)	(0.0106)	(0.00979)	(0.0102)	(0.0100)
Tradey	0.00908**		0.0101**		0.00964**	
	(0.00433)		(0.00434)		(0.00424)	
L_pop	−0.293*	−0.402**	−0.293*	−0.415**	−0.294*	−0.416**
	(0.154)	(0.150)	(0.156)	(0.158)	(0.154)	(0.158)
L_area	0.221**	0.225**	0.234**	0.237**	0.218**	0.250**
	(0.0985)	(0.0922)	(0.0990)	(0.0944)	(0.0981)	(0.0972)
Landl	−0.354	−0.519**				
	(0.228)	(0.233)				
Island	0.0286	−0.395	0.237	−0.154		
	(0.516)	(0.446)	(0.511)	(0.436)		
Cons	7.005***	9.327***	6.772***	9.385***	6.966***	9.283***
	(2.212)	(2.183)	(2.256)	(2.290)	(2.136)	(2.178)
R^2	0.560	0.501	0.540	0.454	0.538	0.453
Root MSE	0.790	0.806	0.797	0.832	0.788	0.822
Obs.	43	46	43	46	43	46

***Significant at the 1 percent level.
**Significant at the 5 percent level.
*Significant at the 10 percent level.

of trade will prefer the versions that show coastline and landlockedness in place of trade, as they are much more exogenous. Across the specifications, the coefficient on the island dummy hovers around zero.

Remoteness is never statistically significant (and is omitted from the results reported here). One should not be too surprised that the remoteness variable does not work in the African context, even though it works well in the rest of the world. It uses straight line distances. Thus Tombuctou appears closer to Europe, and less remote, than does Accra, and Kisangani appears less remote than Maseru. These are not the right answers in a meaningful sense.

We add to the Africa regressions the measure of the rule of law from the Index of African Governance. It has a highly significant positive effect on income. The Freedom House measures of democracy do not do as well, though number of years under democracy (since independence) has a significant positive effect when it does not have to compete with rule of law. Population density has a significant negative effect. Size has no significant effect.

Tables 8.6A, 8.6B, 8.6C, and 8.6D allow for conditional convergence in the Africa data set by including initial income per capita as a regressor. The coefficient on initial income is very high, indeed insignificantly less than one. Even if one takes the point estimate at face value (.8 in the sample that starts in 1968, the year of Mauritian independence), it says that income converges

Table 8.6A Africa from 1960

	Log of 2006 GDP per capita in constant year 2000 dollars			
l_ypc2k1960	0.809***	0.743**	0.726***	0.770***
	(0.217)	(0.319)	(0.238)	(0.184)
Tradey6064	−0.002	−0.002	−0.008	−0.014
	(0.008)	(0.008)	(0.010)	(0.009)
L_pop1960	−0.239	−0.203	−0.199	−0.196
	(0.216)	(0.198)	(0.206)	(0.213)
L_pden1960[a]		−0.099	−0.160	−0.212
		(0.223)	(0.209)	(0.204)
Remoteness			2.612	3.933**
			(1.817)	(1.576)
Island				−1.747***
				(0.525)
Cons	4.966	5.064	−16.770	−27.851**
	(3.851)	(4.100)	(14.682)	(12.670)
R^2	0.4065	0.4165	0.5072	0.5940
Root MSE	.86818	.88318	.83387	.77887
Obs.	24	24	24	24

[a] No data for land area in 1960, so density is 1960 population/area in 1961.
***Significant at the 1 percent level.
**Significant at the 5 percent level.
*Significant at the 10 percent level.

Table 8.6B Africa from 1968

	Log of 2006 GDP per capita in constant year 2000 dollars							
l_ypc2k1968	0.851***	0.890***	0.825***	0.780***	0.811	0.902***	0.795***	0.851***
	(0.141)	(0.192)	(0.243)	(0.199)	(0.171)	(0.147)	(0.136)	(0.147)
L_pop1968	−0.176	−0.205	−0.173	−0.213	−0.242	−0.097	−0.172	−0.176
	(0.126)	(0.199)	(0.188)	(0.214)	(0.222)	(0.144)	(0.115)	(0.138)
Tradey6872		−0.006	−0.005	−0.009	−0.013			
		(0.011)	(0.011)	(0.011)	(0.010)			
l_pden1968			−0.098	−0.148	−0.178			
			(0.149)	(0.151)	(0.150)			
Remoteness				1.976	2.834*		1.492	
				(1.498)	(1.422)		(1.150)	
Island					−1.415***			−0.001
					(0.455)			(0.509)
Fragment						−1.170		
						(5.626)		
Fragment²						0.185		
						(4.976)		
Cons	3.661	4.175	4.315	−11.331	−18.038*	2.854	−8.774	3.662
	(2.404)	(3.146)	(3.350)	(10.904)	(10.425)	(2.269)	(8.962)	(2.508)
R^2	0.5719	0.4589	0.4726	0.5351	0.5950	0.5878	0.6019	0.5719
Root MSE	.73975	.7515	.75715	.72619	.69304	.75436	.72696	.75384
Obs.	30	29	29	29	29	30	30	30

***Significant at the 1 percent level.
**Significant at the 5 percent level.
*Significant at the 10 percent level.

Table 8.6C Africa from 1976

	Log of 2006 GDP per capita in constant year 2000 dollars							
L_ypc2k1976	0.940***	0.913***	0.924***	0.881***	0.860***	1.013***	0.880***	0.910***
	(0.117)	(0.133)	(0.124)	(0.113)	(0.121)	(0.124)	(0.107)	(0.120)
L_pop1976	−0.124*	−0.086	−0.082	−0.104	−0.085	−0.002	−0.110	−0.104
	(0.073)	(0.110)	(0.107)	(0.120)	(0.128)	(0.082)	(0.070)	(0.084)
Tradey7680		0.002	0.002	0.000	0.001			
		(0.006)	(0.006)	(0.006)	(0.006)			
L_pden1976			0.053	0.013	0.000			
			(0.090)	(0.102)	(0.105)			
Remoteness				1.263	1.135		1.326*	
				(1.128)	(1.167)		(0.757)	
Island					0.217			0.385
					(0.510)			(0.463)
Fragment						0.474		
						(3.781)		
Fragment²						−1.746		
						(3.427)		
Cons	2.256	1.703	1.421	−8.517	−7.612	0.444	−8.893	2.102
	(1.365)	(1.773)	(1.819)	(8.207)	(8.468)	(1.533)	(6.310)	(1.424)
R^2	0.7309	0.7327	0.7367	0.7530	0.7548	0.7715	0.7527	0.7387
Root MSE	.6172	.62558	.63188	.62329	0.6982	.58863	.60171	.61851
Obs.	33	33	33	33	33	33	33	33

***Significant at the 1 percent level.
**Significant at the 5 percent level.
*Significant at the 10 percent level.

only 20 percent of the way to its long-run equilibrium over the span of thirty-eight years. Most of the other variables are not significant, probably because of the small sample size. When the data sample starts in 1996, we raise the sample size to forty-one. Now size has the expected positive sign, and at moderate significance levels. The other coefficients are of the expected signs, but of low significance. Tables 8.7A, 8.7B, 8.7C, and 8.7D repeat conditional convergence across African countries, but with landlocked dummy now added back in.

8.4.3   Findings from the Econometrics

What have we learned from the regressions, across African countries or across island countries? There is some confirmation, in the island results, that small size is a disadvantage but that trade can help make up for it (less so within Africa). Access to the sea is important. Landlocked African countries are at a disadvantage, as is well known.[66] But beyond sea access, there does not seem to be anything special about islands per se. And straight-line

---

66. Everything else equal, of course. Landlockedness has not stopped Botswana, nor has a long coastline mattered enough to save Somalia.

Table 8.6D   **Africa from 1996**

	Log of 2006 GDP per capita in constant year 2000 dollars					
l_ypc2k1996	1.009***	1.052***	1.050***	1.017***	1.017***	1.009***
	(0.051)	(0.049)	(0.050)	(0.054)	(0.056)	(0.057)
L_pop1996	−0.032	0.042	0.040	0.062*	0.062*	0.068*
	(0.055)	(0.028)	(0.028)	(0.035)	(0.036)	(0.035)
Tradey9600		0.000	0.000	0.000	0.000	0.001
		(0.001)	(0.001)	(0.002)	(0.002)	(0.002)
l_pden1996			−0.007	−0.020	−0.020	−0.029
			(0.023)	(0.026)	(0.026)	(0.030)
Wgi1996				0.101	0.101	0.096
				(0.063)	(0.067)	(0.067)
Remoteness					−0.002	−0.034
					(0.304)	(0.315)
Island						0.145
						(0.162)
Fragment						
Fragment^2						
Cons	0.647	−0.838	−0.784	−0.811	−0.797	−0.571
	(1.075)	(0.587)	(0.617)	(0.682)	(2.506)	(2.544)
R^2	0.8966	0.9636	0.9637	0.9601	0.9601	0.9612
Root MSE	.37575	.21367	.21625	.21651	.21967	.21992
Obs.	45	43	43	41	41	41
l_ypc2k1996	1.045***	1.011***	1.015***	1.015***		
	(0.077)	(0.058)	(0.052)	(0.056)		
L_pop1996	−0.059	−0.032	−0.041	0.003		
	(0.078)	(0.055)	(0.068)	(0.056)		
Tradey9600						
l_pden1996						
Wgi1996	−0.101					
	(0.141)					
Remoteness		−0.025				
		(0.303)				
Island			−0.119			
			(0.205)			
Fragment				−0.151		
				(1.147)		
Fragment^2				−0.215		
				(0.973)		
Cons	0.782	0.849	0.764	0.247		
	(1.096)	(2.873)	(1.231)	(1.171)		
R^2	0.8865	0.8966	0.8974	.38037		
Root MSE	.38052	.38029	.37874	0.8991		
Obs.	43	45	45	45		

***Significant at the 1 percent level.
**Significant at the 5 percent level.
*Significant at the 10 percent level.

Table 8.7A **Africa from 1960 with landlocked dummy**

	Log of 2006 GDP per capita in constant year 2000 dollars			
L_ypc2k1960	0.844***	0.760*	0.615*	0.472
	(0.261)	(0.385)	(0.334)	(0.303)
L_pop1960	−0.220	−0.197	−0.237	−0.303
	(0.213)	(0.209)	(0.211)	(0.205)
Landl	0.110	0.0445	−0.283	−0.809
	(0.390)	(0.386)	(0.508)	(0.517)
Tradey6064	−0.00130	−0.00181	−0.00892	−0.0200**
	(0.00784)	(0.00823)	(0.0112)	(0.00926)
L_pden1960[a]		−0.0948	−0.194	−0.330
		(0.227)	(0.240)	(0.237)
Remoteness			2.924	5.354**
			(2.334)	(2.057)
Island				−2.448**
				(0.870)
Cons	4.422	4.840	−17.95	−35.66**
	(3.897)	(4.666)	(17.40)	(15.52)
R^2	0.408	0.417	0.516	0.655
Root MSE	0.889	0.907	0.850	0.740
Obs.	24	24	24	24

[a]No data for land area in 1960, so density is 1960 population/area in 1961.
***Significant at the 1 percent level.
**Significant at the 5 percent level.
*Significant at the 10 percent level.

Table 8.7B **Africa from 1968 with landlocked dummy**

	Log of 2006 GDP per capita in constant year 2000 dollars							
L_ypc2k1968	0.937***	0.955***	0.884***	0.722**	0.605**	0.977***	0.836***	0.934***
	(0.149)	(0.205)	(0.251)	(0.276)	(0.282)	(0.187)	(0.151)	(0.157)
L_pop1968	−0.154	−0.169	−0.153	−0.236	−0.341	−0.0815	−0.163	−0.151
	(0.114)	(0.185)	(0.184)	(0.223)	(0.209)	(0.137)	(0.109)	(0.124)
Landl	0.249	0.237	0.173	−0.153	−0.579	0.226	0.107	0.253
	(0.342)	(0.340)	(0.310)	(0.462)	(0.534)	(0.343)	(0.318)	(0.345)
Tradey6872		−0.00477	−0.00480	−0.00976	−0.0178			
		(0.0116)	(0.0116)	(0.0120)	(0.0106)			
L_pden1968			−0.0808	−0.170	−0.270			
			(0.141)	(0.185)	(0.201)			
Remoteness				2.211	4.050*		1.377	
				(2.039)	(2.156)		(1.144)	
Island					−1.956**			0.0558
					(0.864)			(0.490)
Fragment						−1.108		
						(5.790)		
Fragment^2						0.171		
						(5.123)		
Cons	2.740	3.107	3.510	−12.48	−24.95	2.057	−8.218	2.704
	(2.024)	(2.680)	(3.090)	(13.85)	(14.95)	(2.548)	(8.973)	(2.125)
R^2	0.581	0.469	0.478	0.538	0.629	0.595	0.603	0.581
Root MSE	0.746	0.760	0.770	0.740	0.679	0.763	0.740	0.761
Obs.	30	29	29	29	29	30	30	30

***Significant at the 1 percent level.
**Significant at the 5 percent level.
*Significant at the 10 percent level.

Table 8.7C   **Africa from 1976 with landlocked dummy**

	Log of 2006 GDP per capita in constant year 2000 dollars							
L_ypc2k1976	1.024***	1.005***	1.038***	0.984***	0.966***	1.069***	0.950***	0.998***
	(0.134)	(0.169)	(0.150)	(0.146)	(0.147)	(0.148)	(0.135)	(0.129)
L_pop1976	−0.0962	−0.0746	−0.0658	−0.0836	−0.0487	0.00373	−0.0939	−0.0651
	(0.0641)	(0.104)	(0.0950)	(0.108)	(0.109)	(0.0803)	(0.0656)	(0.0713)
Landl	0.344	0.334	0.395	0.299	0.349	0.245	0.240	0.401
	(0.237)	(0.255)	(0.250)	(0.233)	(0.234)	(0.227)	(0.245)	(0.244)
Tradey7680		0.00130	0.00107	0.000195	0.00117			
		(0.00601)	(0.00595)	(0.00624)	(0.00624)			
L_pden1976			0.0810	0.0493	0.0335			
			(0.0844)	(0.101)	(0.104)			
Remoteness				0.797	0.513		1.054	
				(1.055)	(1.127)		(0.760)	
Island					0.353			0.507
					(0.425)			(0.444)
Fragment						0.867		
						(3.958)		
Fragment²						−1.953		
						(3.516)		
Cons	1.207	0.904	0.325	−5.682	−3.744	−0.242	−7.340	0.831
	(1.260)	(1.504)	(1.332)	(7.776)	(8.361)	(1.744)	(6.231)	(1.228)
R^2	0.748	0.748	0.757	0.763	0.767	0.780	0.760	0.761
Root MSE	0.608	0.618	0.618	0.623	0.629	0.589	0.603	0.602
Obs.	33	33	33	33	33	33	33	33

***Significant at the 1 percent level.
**Significant at the 5 percent level.
*Significant at the 10 percent level.

distances are not very relevant in Africa, given that most trade has to go to a coastal port first.

Institutional measures make a big difference. Democratic institutions per se are not as important as rule of law. But institutions immediately bring up the question of endogeneity, as does trade. If trade and rule of law lead to good economics in Africa as elsewhere, but remoteness, tropics, and fragmentation can't explain variation in trade, rule of law, and incomes within Africa, what can explain relative performance within Africa? How did a small, remote, ethnically divided country like Mauritius achieve success?

8.5 So What is the Answer?

Mauritian success really divides into two distinct accomplishments The first big accomplishment is that manufacturing took root after independence in 1968. The second is that the country was able to adjust relatively well to subsequent shocks, such as the oil price increases of the 1970s and further trade shocks in later decades, particularly the loss of sugar and textile preferences.

Table 8.7D   **Africa from 1996 with landlocked dummy**

	Log of 2006 GDP per capita in constant year 2000 dollars					
L_ypc2k1996	1.010***	1.070***	1.069***	1.038***	1.045***	1.045***
	(0.0578)	(0.0489)	(0.0499)	(0.0601)	(0.0707)	(0.0723)
L_pop1996	−0.0319	0.0462	0.0458	0.0626*	0.0658*	0.0762**
	(0.0562)	(0.0279)	(0.0282)	(0.0355)	(0.0353)	(0.0333)
Landl	0.00997	0.118*	0.118*	0.0836	0.0923	0.123
	(0.0966)	(0.0666)	(0.0672)	(0.0767)	(0.0897)	(0.0999)
Tradey9600		0.000542	0.000539	0.000561	0.000672	0.000940
		(0.00137)	(0.00138)	(0.00162)	(0.00167)	(0.00165)
L_pden1996			−0.00210	−0.0145	−0.0124	−0.0228
			(0.0216)	(0.0246)	(0.0265)	(0.0285)
Wgi1996				0.0747	0.0753	0.0595
				(0.0688)	(0.0702)	(0.0696)
Remoteness					−0.102	−0.181
					(0.358)	(0.396)
Island						0.201
						(0.154)
Fragment						
Fragment²						
Cons	0.635	−1.066*	−1.049*	−1.027	−0.264	0.229
	(1.165)	(0.595)	(0.617)	(0.719)	(2.780)	(2.957)
R^2	0.897	0.966	0.966	0.961	0.961	0.963
Root MSE	0.380	0.209	0.212	0.216	0.219	0.217
Obs.	45	43	43	41	41	41
L_ypc2k1996	1.061***	1.013***	1.015***	1.014***		
	(0.0904)	(0.0684)	(0.0573)	(0.0619)		
L_pop1996	−0.0593	−0.0316	−0.0412	0.00360		
	(0.0793)	(0.0565)	(0.0715)	(0.0554)		
Landl	0.0664	0.0121	−0.00331	−0.0125		
	(0.0879)	(0.102)	(0.115)	(0.107)		
Tradey9600						
L_pden1996						
Wgi1996	−0.122					
	(0.150)					
Remoteness		−0.0353				
		(0.323)				
Island			−0.120			
			(0.231)			
Fragment				−0.141		
				(1.158)		
Fragment²				−0.229		
				(0.986)		
Cons	0.661	0.917	0.769	0.253		
	(1.146)	(2.864)	(1.372)	(1.211)		
R^2	0.887	0.897	0.897	0.899		
Root MSE	0.384	0.385	0.383	0.385		
Obs.	43	45	45	45		

***Significant at the 1 percent level.
**Significant at the 5 percent level.
*Significant at the 10 percent level.

8.5.1   Policies

One can list many of the specific policies that led to these two achievements:

- **Education.** Mauritius has long invested heavily in quality schooling. Sir Ramgoolam boldly granted free education to all citizens. As a result, the country has achieved a high rate of literacy: 87 percent in 2007. Scholarships promote study abroad. Successful recycling of export rents contributed to the fiscal position that made all this investment in human capital possible.
- **The Export Processing Zone.** We have already noted the importance attributed to the decision to segment manufacturing exports from the rest of the economy by means of favorable tax policy and labor policy, and to encourage foreign direct investment by Chinese businessmen to start the textile and apparel industry.[67]
- **Favorable Trade Preferences from Britain, Europe, and the United States.** We have seen that the discrimination in favor of Mauritian exports in its major markets was more than enough to overcome what, at least at the beginning, was an antitrade bias to national policy. Obviously these preferences were not policies set directly by Mauritians. Good luck must be given its due. This includes the good luck to have had multiple powerful patrons in the world, whether on geopolitical or sentimental grounds, going back to the time when the island was the strategic cross-roads of the East India trade. But Mauritian leaders were not merely passive beneficiaries in winning these trade preferences, their diplomats worked actively to negotiate them.
- **International Diplomacy.** When the United Kingdom joined the Common Market, the Commonwealth sugar preferences were replaced by the 1975 Sugar Protocol of the Lomé Convention. It happened that African, Caribbean and Pacific (ACP) sugar producers were negotiating terms for the access of their product at a time (1974) when world prices were very high. Most chose the option of relatively small European Economic Community (EEC) quotas, seduced by transitorily high world prices. But Mauritius negotiated a large quota at the domestic EEC price. Even though the EEC price was well below the world price then, during most of the time since it has been far above, due to the political power of European farmers domestically. Thus the decision by Mauritius to place priority on quantity turns out to have been a brilliant strategy. Sugar exports to Europe produced large rents for many years thereafter.[68] The government was able to capture part of these rents and

---

67. Brautigam (1997, 1999), Romer (1992), Subramanian (2001, 2009).
68. Sugar rents were 5.4 percent of GDP on average, and in some years much higher Subramanian (2001).

use the revenue for social spending; another part of the rents went to investment.[69] From the beginning Mauritian leaders took diplomatic steps to maintain good relationships with many countries, for example, recognizing a single China very early.

- **A Competitive Exchange Rate.** The IMF-recommended devaluations restored competitiveness in the early 1980s and put exports back on a vigorous footing. But Mauritius had a competitively valued currency during most of its history, compared with many African and Latin American countries.[70] This, like the trade preferences, helped promote trade.

8.5.2   Political Institutions

The question that previous authors have understandably had a harder time answering is why Mauritius made these sound policy choices when so many other countries did not. To be sure, if we were to say that the country was lucky enough to have good leaders who made good decisions, that would not be an altogether discouraging moral. Such a conclusion might help to let modern policymakers realize that they have free will at times when they feel they are completely constrained by history and politics. But some other authors have tried to go further to explain institutional choices, and so should we.

Is it just luck that good decisions were made around the time of independence? If so, what accounts for the second half of Mauritian success, the ability to continue making relatively good decisions to adjust to the various shocks that came along in the 1970s and early in the twenty-first century?

Leadership

An answer to the second question is that many of the good decisions that were made around the time of independence involved the setting up of institutions—or the adoption of practices that soon turned into institutions—and that these subsequently served the country well.[71] The institutions were put in place primarily by a combination of the decolonizers and the first prime minister, Ramgoolam.

Brautigam (1999, 144):

> Indeed, Mauritius was fortunate to have leaders who agreed to conduct their political competition within the boundaries of democratic rules and who saw early on that labor-intensive manufacturing for export could provide the employment required by the rapidly growing population. However once the "defining moment" of independence had passed, the rules

69. Brautigam (1999), Subramanian (2009).
70. Imam and Manoiu (2008); African Economic Outlook (2008, 431).
71. Acemoglu, Johnson, and Robinson (2002) tell an analogous story for Botswana, attributing good policies to good institutions and then in turn tracing back the origins of the good institutions.

of democracy and the other institutions established in that time created the constraints . . . for political action.

Or Brautigam (1999, 158):

> Although the institutions put in place at the time of independence were established to solve the immediate problem of economic and political instability in an ethnically diverse land, they also created a set of norms, procedures, and constraints that continued to shape political and economic strategies and behavior in the post-independence decades.

The Parliamentary System

The rules and institutions that Brautigam has in mind concern first and foremost the Mauritian parliamentary system. During the preparations for independence, elites from different ethnic groups deadlocked over whether delegates should be elected by proportional representation. The British proposed pure proportional representation, but the Labour Party rejected it on grounds that it would fragment the political process too much. They wanted instead single-member districts, which they would dominate. Other ethnic groups, naturally, wanted arrangements that would ensure them more representation. The British brought in the three-member Banwell Commission to work out a solution with the various parties in 1967. The system that resulted features twenty districts with three members each (and two additional from the small island of Rodriguez). The three candidates in each district to get the most votes are elected. But the electoral commission can seat an additional eight of the unsuccessful candidates with the highest number of votes as "best losers," which works to ensure representation by all minority groups.[72] Furthermore, the boundaries of the districts were constructed to give bias to rural constituencies, which counteracts what Bates (1981) sees as a bias to urban constituencies in much of mainland Africa.

The need to form coalitions requires consensus building, encourages inclusion (so that nobody seeks routes outside the system), and produces moderation in policy making. Positions in the government have been shared out. Cabinet posts have been allocated to achieve ethnic balance.[73] Various minorities have also been represented at other levels of public management.[74]

---

72. Bowman (1991, 33–42), Brautigam (1999, 146), Selvon (2005, 436), and Subramanian (2009, fn 17). Some object to the best-loser system because it perpetuates communalism. Ali Mansoor points out that the nation building might have been even more successful if the "best loser" way of assuring minority representation had been supplemented by a provision for seating in parliament some top vote-getters who represented no ethnic group or geographic district, but instead the country as a whole.

73. Auty (2009a).

74. The share of Muslims and Chinese in the Senior Public Service rose in the first three decades after independence. The share of Hindus had been a bit higher than in the general population ever since independence, but had not risen as of 1995. The Chinese had 10 percent

No Army

Another institutional choice made at the beginning was to forego a standing army. As with Costa Rica, its neighbors (such as the Comoros) chose differently; and as with Costa Rica, the "pacifist" route has paid off subsequently. Military spending in Mauritius in 1992 was only $6 per capita, equal to 0.45 percent of GDP or 4 percent of spending on education and health. These statistics for other sub-Saharan countries are far higher, averaging $20 per capita, 2.8 percent of GDP, and 43 percent of education and health spending.[75] Brautigam points out the dual benefit to Mauritius: on the one hand, financial savings, and on the other hand freedom from the military coups that have plagued so many other African countries. One could argue that an island country has less need of an army than a mainland country;[76] but Cape Verde, the Seychelles, and the Comoros all spend substantially higher percentages of GDP on defense.

Institutions Chosen around the Time of Independence

To summarize what we mean by institutions:

- No expropriation or taxing away of the Franco-Mauritians' sugar plantations, which both allowed them to give up political power and established the importance of property rights;
- a politically, economically, and socially stable environment, with rule of law, respect for property rights, and so forth;
- no single elite group was in a position to dominate the others;
- vigorous political opposition and media;
- parliamentary structure: coalition governments and comprehensive participation (representation for rural districts and ethnic minorities, best loser system, power sharing in cabinet); and
- no army.

8.5.3   The Deepest Determinants and Lessons

If good policies were not attributable solely to accidents of personalities or history, but also to good institutions that were put in place at independence, this just pushes the question back another step. When those institutions were put in place, was it attributable solely to accidents of personali-

---

(vs. 2 percent of the population), the Creoles had 13 percent (vs. 28 percent of the population), English/French have been reduced to zero, non-Muslim Indians steady at 68 percent (vs. 52 percent of the population), and Muslims 9 percent (vs. 17 percent of the population) (Carroll and Carroll 1997, 476).

75. Brautigam (1999, 153). Her source is the *Human Development Report 1995* from UNDP.

76. Mauritius has in fact suffered the loss of territory to external military force. The United States and United Kingdom took the Chagos Islands in order to build the base of Diego Garcia, without the permission of either the islanders or Mauritius. Of course Mauritius has hardly been in a position to resist, with or without an army, but small size has not stopped other countries from futile military endeavors.

ties or history? If we dig deeper can we still find some more fundamental determinants as to why here and not somewhere else?

Colonialists

In many ways the British administrators in the end served the future nation well. It is relevant that very few British settlers arrived in the nineteenth century to displace the Franco-Mauriciens, who remained in place as the land-owning elite. Thus when independence came, the British did not have to protect the European settlers to the same extent as in Kenya or other countries. At the time of independence, they helped broker the power-sharing structure, in which the Franco-Mauriciens kept their sugar plantations, while surrendering political power.

It was also useful that the British took their time to prepare the colony for independence in a way that was not true of most African countries. That the process was drawn out to 1968 is to some extent attributable to the lack of enthusiasm for independence on the part of almost half the population.

Cosmopolitanism

Even though Mauritius ceased to be the crossroads of the Indian Ocean when the Suez Canal opened, it retained its cosmopolitan character and mind-set. This is another respect in which it resembles the entrepôt city-states, not just Singapore, but also Hong Kong and Dubai. This cosmopolitanism came in handy in the process of economic development. Ethnic links to China and India led directly to the rise of the textile and apparel sector and the financial center, respectively.

Lessons for Others

There are at least three possible lessons that can be applied to the rest of Africa. First, trade is the key to growth, especially for a small country. Geographic impediments to trade can be counteracted in other ways, including a competitive exchange rate and regional free trade areas. Second, a well-designed electoral system can accommodate ethnic diversity—even harness it for good. Although oppressive rule by a single group is not conducive to development, the opposite extreme of ethnically blind democracy is not necessarily feasible in all countries. Deliberate steps to assure representation of each ethnic group might be necessary. Third, democracies can achieve economic reform, and perhaps in a more sustainable way than autocracies.

The Puzzle

All this has been noted by other authors, but some ingredient seems to be missing. Something having to do with the intriguing puzzle noted at the beginning of the chapter, that four of the most successful countries in Africa are islands. Some superior cultural values of the Indians? No. For one thing, while Mauritius was industrializing, India itself was stagnating with a miserable "Hindu rate of growth." Meanwhile, countries like Cape Verde have done well, with no Indians.[77]

Immigrant Isles

What do Mauritius, Seychelles, and Cape Verde have in common? Each was uninhabited three centuries ago.[78] Everyone who is there came from somewhere else, in modern times. The same is true of famously successful Singapore versus, for example, benighted Sri Lanka.

Why does it help if everyone is an immigrant? Two possible theories. One theory is that migrants self-select for vigor and initiative, and they pass these traits down to their descendants. Another theory is that most countries have nativist factions, children of the soil, who resent newcomers regardless of their merit or perhaps because of their merit. If everyone came from somewhere else, nobody can claim special privileges.

Consider a less successful small country that can serve as a comparator with Mauritius because they have some important things in common: Fiji. The tropical island economy has long been based on sugar, with indentured Indian workers brought to work the fields, and was supplemented more recently by tourism. Ethnic Indians became a majority of the Fijian population in the 1940s.[79] But the first time an ethnic Indian was elected prime minister in 1999 (even though from a party that included many native Fijians), he was soon overthrown in a coup. The climate has been sufficiently bad for the Indians since then, so that a high percentage of them have emigrated. As a result of the political instability and the loss of the Indians, the economy has done poorly. What was the key difference between Mauritius and Fiji? I believe it is that the native Fijians always resented the newcomers, whereas there were no native Mauritians (except the unfortunate dodo bird).

A combination of the two theories, immigrant initiative and absence of nativist resentment, would emphasize the benefits when everyone feels they have a common stake in building a new nation together.

Having said that, Mauritius illustrates that the ideal of an identity-blind meritocracy, however desirable, is not essential. The important thing is for everyone to feel included. Some degree of power sharing along ethnic lines in some circumstances might help achieve this goal rather than hurt it. Another lesson for countries in Africa and elsewhere? History cannot be rewound. But any country can adopt policies that are inclusive to all its ethnic groups

---

77. Macedo and Pereira (2009) conclude that a combination of globalization and governance helps explain the success of Cape Verde, where emigrants' remittances are a major source of income.

78. If we go back to 1493, then we can add São Tomé and Príncipe to the list.

79. Leuprecht (2011) makes much of the fact that, because the Indian migration occurred later in Fiji than in Mauritius, the population was younger and faster growing around the time of independence.

rather than exclusive and that are more welcoming to immigrants, past and future. This is perhaps the fourth of the lessons.

8.5.4 Summary

While tropicalness, remoteness, small size, and landlockedness go a long way to explaining why Africa overall has done less well than some other regions economically, these variables do not help much to explain relative success within Africa (with the exception that access to the sea makes a difference). Tropicalness does not show up because almost all sub-Saharan countries share it. (The exceptions are South Africa, Lesotho, and Swaziland.) Remoteness does not show up, if measured by straight-line distances, because the problem of getting from the interior to the nearest seaport matters more in Africa than in most parts of the world. It is less clear why small African countries do not seem on average to suffer much the usual disadvantage relative to larger countries with economies of scale; it may reflect the success of several small countries, especially the three top-performing island countries—Mauritius, Seychelles, and Cape Verde—itself a puzzle considered by this chapter.

Mauritius has made some policy decisions that have promoted strong economic performance, including the establishment of the EPZ, diplomacy regarding trade preferences, spending on education, avoiding currency overvaluation, facilitation of business, and so on. These policies can be attributed both to successful deliberate choices of individuals and to successful political institutions, particularly a parliamentary system that builds consensus by representing all groups. The successful political institutions, in turn, were the outcome both of decisions made at the time of independence, by the first prime minister together with the outgoing colonial rulers, and of some still deeper underlying causes. Any country can in principle adopt good institutions and good policies at any time. But in the case of Mauritius, the deep underlying origins include a cosmopolitan population with an unusual combination of ethnicities: Franco-Mauritians and Creoles who were willing at the time of independence to trade off their past domination of political power for guarantees under the new system, Indians who were willing to take the other side of the bargain, and Chinese who had links to their country of origin. And, as with the Seychelles, Cape Verde, and São Tomé and Principe, everyone in Mauritius came from somewhere else.

References

Acemoglu, Daron, Simon Johnson, and James Robinson. 2001. "Colonial Origins of Comparative Development: An Empirical Investigation." *American Economic Review* 91:1369–401.

————. 2002. "An African Success Story: Botswana." CEPR Discussion Paper no. 3219, Centre for Economic Policy Research, February.

Acemoglu, Daron, Simon Johnson, James Robinson, and Yunyong Thaicharoen. 2003. "Institutional Causes, Macroeconomic Symptoms: Volatility, Crises and Growth." *Journal of Monetary Economics* 50 (1): 49–123.

African Economic Outlook. 2008. "Mauritius." African Development Bank and Organisation for Economic Co-operation and Development. Washington, DC: Brookings Institution Press.

Alesina, Alberto, Sule Özler, Nouriel Roubini, and Phillip Swagel. 1996. "Political Instability and Economic Growth." *Journal of Economic Growth* 1 (2): 189–211.

Ancharaz, Vinaye dey. 2004. "The Effect of Trade Liberalization on Export-Oriented Output and FDI: A Case Study of the Mauritian EPZ, 1971–1998." *University of Mauritius Research Journal* 5:1–30.

————. 2009. "David v. Goliath: Mauritius Facing up to China." *European Journal of Development Research* 21 (4): 622–43.

Auty, Richard. 2009. "The Political Economy of Hydrocarbon Revenue Cycling in Trinidad and Tobago." Paper prepared for workshop on Myths and Realities of Commodity Dependence: Policy Challenges and Opportunities for Latin America and the Caribbean, World Bank, September 17–18.

————. 2010. "Elites, Rent Cycling, and Development: Adjustment to Land Scarcity in Mauritius, Kenya and Cote d'Ivoire." *Development Policy Review* 28 (4): 411–33.

Barro, Robert. 1991. "Economic Growth in a Cross Section of Countries." *Quarterly Journal of Economics* 106:407–44.

————. 1996. "Democracy and Growth." *Journal of Economic Growth* 1 (1): 1–27.

Bates, Robert. 1981. *Markets and States in Tropical Africa*. Berkeley, CA: University of California Press.

Bates, Robert, and Irene Yackolev. 2002. "Ethnicity in Africa." In *The Role of Social Capital in Development*, edited by C. Grootaert and T. Van Bastelaer. New York: Cambridge University Press.

Blattman, Christopher, Jason Hwang, and Jeffrey Williamson. 2007. "Winners and Losers in the Commodity Lottery: The Impact of Terms of Trade Growth and Volatility in the Periphery 1870–1939." *Journal of Development Economics* 82 (1): 156–79.

Bowman, Larry W. 1991. *Mauritius: Democracy and Development in the Indian Ocean*. Boulder, CO: Westview Press.

Brautigam, Deborah. 1997. "Institutions, Economic Reform, and Democratic Consolidation in Mauritius." *Comparative Politics* 30 (1): 45–62.

————. 1999. "The 'Mauritius Miracle': Democracy, Institutions and Economic Policy." In *State, Conflict, and Democracy in Africa*, edited by Richard Joseph, 137–62. Boulder, CO: Lynee Riener.

Bulte, Erwin, Richard Damania, and Robert Deacon. 2005. "Resource Intensity, Institutions and Development." *World Development* 33 (7): 1029–44.

Bunwaree, Sheila, and Roukaya Kadenally. 2006. "Mauritius, Country Report Based on Research and Dialogue with Political Parties." Stockholm: International Institute for Democracy and Electoral Assistance.

Carroll, Barbara Wake, and Terrance Carroll. 1997. "State and Ethnicity in Botswana and Mauritius: A Democratic Route to Development?" *Journal of Development Studies* 33 (4): 464–86.

Collier, Paul. 2000. "Ethnicity, Politics and Economic Performance." *Economics and Politics* 12:225–45.

Collier, Paul, Robert Bates, Anke Hoeffler, and Stephen O'Connell. 2007. "Endogenizing Syndromes." In *The Political Economy of Economic Growth in Africa:*

1960–2000, (vol. 1), edited by Benno J. Ndulu, Stephen A. O'Connell, Robert H. Bates, Paul Collier, and Chukwuma C. Soludo, 392–418. Cambridge: Cambridge University Press.

Collier, Paul, and Anke Hoeffler. 2009. "Testing the Neo-Con Agenda: Democracy in Resource-Rich Societies." *European Economic Review* 53:293–308.

Dukhira, Chit. 2002. *History of Mauritius: Experiments in Democracy*. New Delhi: Brijbasi Art Press.

Durbarry, Ramesh. 2004. "Tourism and Economic Growth: The Case of Mauritius." *Tourism Economics* 10 (4): 389–401.

Easterly, William, and Ross Levine. 1997. "Africa's Growth Tragedy: Politics and Ethnic Divisions." *Quarterly Journal of Economics* 112 (4): 1203–50.

———. 2002. "Tropics, Germs, and Endowments." NBER Working Paper no. 9106, Cambridge, MA.

Engerman, Stanley, and Kenneth Sokoloff. 1997. "Factor Endowments, Institutions, and Differential Paths of Growth among New World Economies: A View from Economic Historians of the United States." In *How Latin America Fell Behind*, edited by Stephen Haber, 260–304. Redwood City, CA: Stanford University Press.

———. 2000. "Institutions, Factor Endowments, and Paths of Development in the New World." *Journal of Economic Perspectives* 14:217–32.

———. 2002. "Factor Endowments, Inequality, and Paths of Development among New World Economies." NBER Working Paper no. 9259, October, Cambridge, MA.

Feyrer, James, and Bruce Sacerdote. 2009. "Colonialism and Modern Income: Islands as Natural Experiments." *Review of Economics and Statistics* 91 (2): 245–62.

Frankel, Jeffrey. 1974. "Cocoa in Ghana: The Cocoa Farmers, Cocoa Marketing Board, and Elasticity of Supply." MIT. http://www.hks.harvard.edu/fs/jfrankel/cocoa_in_ghana.pdf.

———. 1997. *Regional Trading Blocs*. Washington, DC: Institute for International Economics.

———. 2012. "The Natural Resource Curse: A Survey." In *Beyond the Resource Curse*, edited by Brenda Shaffer and Taleh Ziyadov. Philadelphia: University of Pennsylvania Press.

Frankel, Jeffrey, and David Romer. 1999. "Does Trade Cause Growth?" *American Economic Review* 89 (3): 379–99.

Frazer, Garth, and Johannes Van Biesebroeck. 2010. "Trade and Growth under the African Growth and Opportunity Act." *Review of Economics and Statistics* 92 (1): 128–44.

Gulhati, Ravi, and Raj Nallari. 1990. "Successful Stabilization and Recovery in Mauritius." EDI Development Policy Case Series, analytical Case Studies, no. 5, Washington, DC, World Bank. http://www.worldcat.org/title/successful-stabilization-and-recovery-in-mauritius/oclc/21975239.

Hall, Robert E., and Charles I. Jones. 1999. "Why Do Some Countries Produce So Much More Output Per Worker Than Others?" *Quarterly Journal of Economics* 114 (1): 83–116.

Hausmann, Ricardo, Baily Klinger, and Robert Lawrence. 2008. "Examining Benefication." Policy Brief, Center for International Development, Harvard University, May. http://www.treasury.gov.za/publications/other/growth/01-Overall%20Summary%20and%20Final%20Recommendations/07-Beneficiation_Policy_Brief.pdf.

Hausmann, Ricardo, and Roberto Rigobon. 2003. "An Alternative Interpretation of the 'Resource Curse': Theory and Policy Implications." In *Fiscal Policy Formula-*

tion and Implementation in Oil-Producing Countries, edited by Jeffrey Davis, 12–44. Washington, DC: International Monetary Fund.

Hausmann, Ricardo, and Dani Rodrik. 2003. "Economic Development as Self-Discovery." *Journal of Development Economics* 72 (2): 603–33.

Hawkins, Tony. 2008. "Economy: A Lesson in Reinvention." *Financial Times*, March 11.

Helliwell, John. 1994. "Empirical Linkages between Democracy and Economic Growth." *British Journal of Political Science* 24:225–48.

Huber, Evelyne, Dietrich Rueschemeyer, and John Stephens. 1993. "The Impact of Economic Development on Democracy." *Journal of Economic Perspectives* 7:71–85.

Imam, Patrick, and Camelia Manoiu. 2008. "Mauritius: A Competitiveness Assessment." IMF Working Paper no. 08/212, September, International Monetary Fund.

Isham, Jonathan, Michael Woolcock, Lant Pritchett, and Gwen Busby. 2005. "The Varieties of Resource Experience: Natural Resource Export Structures and the Political Economy of Economic Growth." *World Bank Economic Review* 19 (2): 141–74.

Lange, Matthew. 2009. "Mauritius: Direct Rule and Development." In *Lineages of Despotism and Development: British Colonialism and State Power*. Chicago: University of Chicago Press.

Leuprecht, Christian. 2011. "Migration as the Demographic Wild Card in Civil Conflict: Mauritius and Fiji." *New Directions in Demographic Security, Environmental Change and Security Program Report* 13:34–9. https://www.wilsoncenter.org/publication/new-directions-demographic-security.

Lipset, Seymour Martin. 1994. "The Social Requisites of Democracy Revisited." *American Sociological Review* 59:1–22.

Lutz, Wolfgang, and Anne B. Wils. 1990. "The Demographic Discontinuities of Mauritius." In *Population, Economy and Environment in Mauritius*, edited by Wolfgang Lutz and F. L. Toth, 39–66. Laxenburg, Austria: International Institute for Applied Systems Analysis.

Macedo, Jorge Braga de, and Luís Brites Pereira. 2009. "Cape Verde and Mozambique as Development Successes in Sub-Saharan Africa." NBER Conference on African Successes, Cambridge, MA, December 11–12.

Matsuyama, Kiminori. 1992. "Agricultural Productivity, Comparative Advantage, and Economic Growth." *Journal of Economic Theory* 58:317–34.

Meade, James. 1961a. *The Economics and Social Structure of Mauritius—Report to Government of Mauritius*. London: Methuen.

———. 1961b. "Mauritius: A Case Study in Malthusian Economics." *Economic Journal* 71 (283): 521–34.

Mehlum, Halvor, Karl Moene, and Ragnar Torvik. 2006. "Institutions and the Resource Curse." *Economic Journal* 116 (508): 1–20.

Minier, Jenny A. 1998. "Democracy and Growth: Alternative Approaches." *Journal of Economic Growth* 3:241–66.

Ministry of Finance. 2008. "Additional Stimulus Package: Shoring up Economic Performance." Mauritius.

Naipaul, V. S. 1972. *The Overcrowded Barracoon*. New York: Random House.

Nath, Shyam, and Yeti Madhoo. 2008. "A Shared Growth Story of Economic Success: The Case of Mauritius." In *The Political Economy of Economic Growth in Africa, 1960–2000*, vol. 2, edited by B. J. Ndulu, Stephen A. O'Connell, and Jean-Paul Azam. Cambridge: Cambridge University Press.

North, Douglass. 1994. "Economic Performance through Time." *American Economic Review* 84 (3): 359–68.

Poelhekke, Steven, and Frederick van der Ploeg. 2007. "Volatility, Financial Development and the Natural Resource Curse." CEPR Discussion Paper no. 6513, October, Centre for Economic Policy Research.

Radelet, Steven. 2010. *Emerging Africa: How 17 Countries are Leading the Way.* Washington, DC: Center for Global Development.

Rodriguez, Francisco, and Dani Rodrik. 2001. "Trade Policy and Economic Growth: A Skeptic's Guide to the Cross-National Evidence." In *NBER Macroeconomics Annual 2000*, vol. 15, edited by Ben S. Bernanke and Kenneth Rogoff, 261–338. Cambridge, MA: MIT Press.

Rodrik, Dani. 1998. "Trade Policy and Economic Performance in Sub-Saharan Africa." NBER Working Paper no. 6562, Cambridge, MA.

Rodrik, Dani, Arvind Subramanian, and Francesco Trebbi. 2004. "Institutions Rule: The Primacy of Institutions over Geography and Integration in Economic Development." *Journal of Economic Growth* 9 (2): 131–65.

Romer, Paul. 1990. "Endogenous Technological Change." *Journal of Political Economy* 98 (5): S71–S102.

———. 1992. "Two Strategies for Economic Development: Using Ideas and Producing Ideas." *World Bank Economic Review* 6 (S1): 63–91.

———. 1993. "Idea Gaps and Object Gaps in Economic Development." *Journal of Monetary Economics* 32 (3): 543–73.

Rotberg, Robert, and Rachel Gisselquist. 2009. *Strengthening African Governance: Index of African Governance Results and Rankings.* Kennedy School of Government, Harvard University and World Peace Foundation.

Russell, Alec. 2008. "An Island Bridging Africa and Asia." *Financial Times*, March 11.

Sachs, Jeffrey. 2003. "Institutions Don't Rule: Direct Effects of Geography on Per Capita Income." NBER Working Paper no. 9490, Cambridge, MA.

Sachs, Jeffrey, and Andrew Warner. 1997. "Sources of Slow Growth in African Economies." *Journal of African Economies* 6 (3): 335–76.

Sala-i-Martin, Xavier X. 1997. "I Just Ran Two Million Regressions." *American Economic Review* 87 (2): 178–83.

Sala-i-Martin, Xavier, and Arvind Subramanian. 2003. "Addressing the Natural Resource Curse: An Illustration from Nigeria." IMF Working Paper no. WP/03/139, International Monetary Fund.

Selvon, Sydney. 2005. *A Comprehensive History of Mauritius*, 2nd ed. Mauritius: MDS Editions.

Simmons, Adele. 1982. *Modern Mauritius: The Politics of Decolonization.* Bloomington: Indiana University Press.

Subramanian, Arvind. 2001. "Mauritius: A Case Study." *Finance and Development* 38 (4). http://www.imf.org/external/pubs/ft/fandd/2001/12/subraman.htm.

———. 2009. "The Mauritian Success Story and Its Lessons." UN/WIDER Research Paper no. 36/2009, University Nations University-WIDER. https://www.wider.unu.edu/publication/mauritian-success-story-and-its-lessons-0.

Subramanian, Arvind, and Devesh Roy. 2003. "Who Can Explain the Mauritian Miracle: Meade, Romer, Sachs, or Rodrik?" In *In Search of Prosperity: Analytic Narratives on Economic Growth*, edited by Dani Rodrik. Princeton, NJ: Princeton University Press.

Tavares, José, and Romain Wacziarg. 2001. "How Democracy Affects Growth." *European Economic Review* 45 (8): 1341–78.

Torvik, Ragnar. 2001. "Learning by Doing and the Dutch Disease." *European Economic Review* 45:285–306.

———. 2006. "Resource-Based Growth Past and Present." In *Neither Curse nor Destiny: Natural Resources and Development*, edited by Daniel Lederman and

William Maloney. Redwood City, CA: Stanford University Press and World Bank Publication.

Zakaria, Fareed. 1997. "The Rise of Illiberal Democracy." *Foreign Affairs* November/December. https://www.foreignaffairs.com/articles/1997-11-01/rise-illiberal -democracy.

———. 2004. *The Future of Freedom: Illiberal Democracy at Home and Abroad.* New York: Norton.

Indirect Rule and State Weakness in Africa
Sierra Leone in Comparative Perspective

Daron Acemoglu, Isaías N. Chaves,
Philip Osafo-Kwaako, and James A. Robinson

9.1   Introduction

It is now widely recognized that the "weakness" or lack of "capacity" of states in poor countries is a fundamental barrier to their development prospects. Most poor countries have states that are incapable of or unwilling to provide basic public goods such as the enforcement of law, order, education, and infrastructure. Different scholars use different terminology for this. Acemoglu and Robinson (2012), following the work of political anthropologists such as Evans-Pritchard and Fortes (1940), refer to the lack of "political centralization," indicating that centralized states do not exist and that political power is wielded by other entities.[1] Others, like Migdal (1988), use the word "weak" to refer to states that lack capacity. Mann (1986, 1993) instead broke down the concept into two dimensions, distinguishing between *infrastructural power*, which is "institutional capacity of a central state to penetrate its territories and logistically implement decisions," and *despotic power*, which refers to "the distributive power of state elites over civil society. It derives from the range of actions that state elites can undertake without routine negotiation with civil society" (1986, 59). O'Donnell (1993) and Acemoglu, García-Jimeno, and Robinson (2015) conceptualize state weakness in

Daron Acemoglu is the Elizabeth and James Killian Professor of Economics at the Massachusetts Institute of Technology and a research associate of the National Bureau of Economic Research. Isaías N. Chaves is a PhD student in economics at Stanford University. Philip Osafo-Kwaako is a visiting research associate at the Brookings Institution. James A. Robinson is a university professor at the Harris School of Public Policy at the University of Chicago and a research associate of the National Bureau of Economic Research.

For acknowledgments, sources of research support, and disclosure of the authors' material financial relationships, if any, please see http://www.nber.org/chapters/c13443.ack.

1. This partially follows the classification scheme suggested by anthropologists distinguishing between band, tribe, chiefdom, and state (e.g., Service 1962).

a related way as the physical absence of state institutions and functionaries. Others use terminology that is based more closely on particular practices, which characterize different types of states. For example, Bratton and van de Walle (1997) and Herbst (2000), following Weber's (1978) classification of different types of authority, call weak states in Africa neopatrimonial, which stresses their patrimonial or clientelistic organization that precludes the provision of public goods. Evans (1995) argues that strong states exhibit the property of "embedded autonomy," having bureaucracies that are both embedded in society and understanding its needs, but also autonomous from it and therefore beyond capture. More recent analytical work by Acemoglu (2005) and Besley and Persson (2011) focuses on the idea that a weak state is one that cannot raise taxes. Finally, Acemoglu, Robinson, and Santos (2013), once again building on Weber, emphasize the issue that a weak state lacks the monopoly of violence.

There is as yet little agreement in this literature as to why poor countries do not make their states stronger when there appears to be such obvious benefits from doing so. Nevertheless, several lines of work emphasize certain benefits to those currently holding political power from the continued weakness of the state. The research on neopatrimonialism, for example, sees this as a result of a political strategy used to buy support and control power, and this strategy naturally becomes a fundamental impediment to making the state stronger. For instance, appointments in the bureaucracy are made on the basis of political criteria, as rewards for support, rather than on the grounds of competence for the job.[2] This makes for a weak state, but it is politically attractive. Making the state stronger entails a change in the nature of politics, and Acemoglu and Robinson (2012) argue that this creates the "fear of losing political power," which impedes the creation of a stronger state.

What could explain variation in the intensity of the "fear of losing political power"? Herbst (2000) emphasizes the role of Africa's geography and ecology, which led to very low population densities and discouraged state building.[3] From this perspective, the benefits of state building in Africa are intrinsically low. For Evans (1995), the differential incidence of embedded autonomy is related to idiosyncratic historical processes (such as Confucian bureaucratic legacy in East Asia). Acemoglu, Robinson, and Santos (2013) develop a different argument and suggest that in situations where national elections are important for the allocation of political power, state elites may not wish to establish a monopoly of violence of the state and make it stronger in peripheral areas because this may reduce the support they receive from local elites controlling society and politics. Acemoglu, Ticchi, and Vindigni

2. Robinson and Verdier (2013) provide a theory of why such patronage would take the form of employment.

3. Though Osafo-Kwaako and Robinson (2013) point out that precolonial political centralization and population density in Africa are in fact uncorrelated in the Standard Cross-Cultural Sample.

(2010), relatedly, suggest that national elites may refrain from establishing the monopoly of violence in certain parts of the national territory because this would empower the military or other armed branches of the government as potential rivals to them.

One of the most important ideas about the origins of modern weak states in Africa is that rather than reflecting some deep fundamental difference between Africa and the rest of the world, they are a path-dependent outcome of the nature of colonial governance.[4] There are many different versions of this argument. Young (1994) argued that the authoritarianism of the colonial states set role models and political practices, which transferred themselves to postcolonial politicians. Cooper (2002) proposed that the typical colonial state was a "gate-keeper state," which sat on the coast and was only interested in ruling and extracting natural resources, not building the institutions required to develop the colony. Such states persisted after independence when they were taken over by Africans.

Perhaps the most prominent version of a path-dependent thesis in the context of African politics is that modern state weakness is a legacy of the type of "indirect rule" particularly practiced in English colonies. Indirect rule was a system where colonial powers used traditional rulers ("chiefs") as the local level of government, empowering them to tax, dispense law, and maintain order. Chiefs often maintained police forces and prisons, and were in charge of providing public goods like roads and garnering the resources and manpower necessary to build them. Even during the colonial period there was unease about the impact this system was having on African society. Mamdani's (1966) important work built on this earlier literature (for example, the essays in Crowder and Ikime, eds. [1970]) to emphasize that indirect rule had serious negative effects on the nature of political institutions in Africa. Mamdani's argument was that indirect rule, by making chiefs accountable to the colonial power rather than local people, made them much more despotic. This despotism persisted after independence, influencing both local and national governance. It also played a significant role in the collapse of democracy in postcolonial Africa. There is a mounting body of empirical evidence that indeed suggests that the persistence of indirect rule institutions does have adverse effects on contemporary African development (e.g., Goldstein and Udry 2008; Acemoglu, Reed, and Robinson 2014).

Nevertheless, Mamdani's argument leaves open a great many issues. For one, it does not make precise the mechanisms via which indirect rule persisted and why postindependence African leaders continued to rely on it in some places but not in others. In Guinea, for example, the first government of Sékou Touré completely abolished traditional rulers and traditional mechanisms of social control (McGovern 2013). Similar moves against

4. See Acemoglu and Robinson (2010) present a general path-dependent explanation of African institutions.

previous indirect rulers took place against Mossi chiefs in Burkina Faso, the Buganda chiefs in Uganda, and the Asante chiefs in Ghana (Rathbone 2000a, 2000b). Yet, in Sierra Leone, something quite different happened. Chiefs were not abolished and their powers not attacked. Rather, the powers they had acquired during the colonial period were further institutionalized (e.g., as recently as 2009, the passing of a national Chieftaincy Act froze the institution in the form it had existed at the end of the colonial period). Mamdani's thesis does recognize this variation, positing a distinction between radical reactions such as in Uganda, and conservative ones such as Sierra Leone, but he also argues that this was relatively inconsequential for the main dependent variables of interest, particularly the extent to postcolonial democracy. Just as important, he does not advance an explanation for the variation between radical and conservative reactions. Mamdani's book also does not make precise in what sense a state governed indirectly is weak or lacks capacity. Indeed, in more recent work, Mamdani (2012) denies that indirect rule created weak states because it so powerfully shaped identities.

In this chapter we use a detailed study of the Sierra Leonean case to examine the specific mechanisms via which indirect rule persisted in Sierra Leone and the sense in which it created or contributed to the weakness of the postcolonial state. We also propose a new explanation for the variation in the extent to which the institution of indirect rule persisted in postcolonial Africa.

We argue that indirect rule persisted in Sierra Leone because the postcolonial state was the "bottom up" creation of the traditional rulers who ran the indirect rule system. They formed the first political party and dominated late colonial and postcolonial politics. Thus, in Sierra Leone, the institutions of indirect rule created a political movement that captured the central state at independence in 1961. The system persisted, however, because even when the central state was captured by new movements after 1967, indirect rule mutated into a generalized form of incumbency bias.

The state that indirect rule created was weak in several well-defined ways. First, indirect rule by traditional (and gerontocratic) rulers has made it difficult for the state to establish a monopoly of violence both because it had created an underclass of "lumpen youths" alienated from the society and because it mitigated against the construction of a national identity so that politics stayed local and parochial. Second, as emphasized by Mamdani (1996), traditional rulers were relatively unaccountable and thus able to extract rents and underprovide public goods. This feature was not compensated for by other types of accountability, for example, via a representative national parliament, in large part because of the role chiefs played in managing these higher-level elections. Third, the fact that the local state was based on lineages and ruling families made it an intrinsically patrimonial and non-bureaucratized structure—a defining property of weakness. These factors interacted with others to create huge negative economic consequences from state weakness. For example, the nature of the traditional instruments of control, such as the role of chiefs as "custodians of the land," led to large economic distortions. Finally, though this is harder to measure, logically the model of indirect rule implies that externalities across local areas in the construction of the state or the provision of services will not be properly internalized (Acemoglu, García-Jimeno, and Robinson 2015).

But this did not happen everywhere in Africa. A key difference between a colony like Sierra Leone and one like Uganda was that in the latter there were several large, indeed one dominant, precolonial state—Buganda. This meant that the distribution of power within the system of indirect rule was very different than in Sierra Leone. As Reid (2002) shows, British colonialism in Uganda even allowed the kingdom of Buganda to expand, and British forces helped it defeat its long-term rival, Bunyoro, and annex land from that and other kingdoms. At independence the King of Buganda, the Kabaka, became the president of Uganda, a country named by the British after the precolonial state. Yet the drive toward independence was typically not led by such traditional elites, but rather by more educated, urban, and professional groups. In Uganda the first prime minister, Milton Obote, was not a Ganda (from Buganda), but a Langi from the north of the country. Ruling indirectly via the Buganda chiefs was infeasible or unattractive for him because the Kabaka was too powerful. So when he had the opportunity, he forced the Kabaka into exile in 1966 and changed the constitution to strip him of his powers. It was only in 1986 that a new Kabaka was allowed to return from exile and was much less powerful thereafter. Thus the greater power of traditional elites in Uganda, perhaps at first paradoxically, led to their sidelining and to the weakening of the vestiges of indirect rule after independence. The situation was similar in Ghana.

This contrasts with postindependence dynamics in Sierra Leone. There were no large powerful precolonial states, and though some of the chieftaincies that the British created were directly linked to precolonial polities (such as Banta, Kpa-Mende, or Tikonko), unlike Buganda these got smaller rather than larger and there was little continuity in their political institutions (see Abraham [2003] for Mendeland, or Wylie [1977] for Temneland). This enabled postindependence leaders, even those like Siaka Stevens who had no connection to traditional rulers, to control the traditional rulers.

This theory can help explain the findings of Gennaioli and Rainer (2007) and Michalopoulos and Papaioannou (2013). In their work, the extent of precolonial centralization is positively correlated with current development outcomes today, such as light intensity at night and various measures of public good provision. Phillips (2011) and Bandyopadhyay and Green (2016) find similar things using different data within Nigeria and Uganda. However, it is not clear why precolonial centralization leads to greater state capacity today. Our argument suggests one potential mechanism: where there were important precolonial centralized states, indirect rule tended to be overthrown after independence and its negative legacies ameliorated, making it less likely that the modern state would be dysfunctionally weak, and there would be endemic underprovision of public goods. Our argument can also explain the within-country variation, since it is likely that postindependence states would have intervened and administered more intensely in precisely those parts of the country where the precolonial states were located.[5]

Though Ghana, Uganda, and several other African countries abandoned indirect rule, this does not imply they became development miracles or in fact developed strong effective states. In both countries the abandonment of indirect rule set off other dynamics with other adverse effects. In both cases, in the absence of traditional authority, the state had to rely more on the military, and in both countries the military then overthrew the civilian governments, leading to cycles of violence, predatory rule, and economic decline under Ignatius Kutu Acheampong in Ghana and Idi Amin in Uganda. In Sierra Leone, the persistence of the institutions of indirect rule had different implications for postwar political dynamics and ones that turned out to be perhaps even more violent. For instance, as Richards (1996) argues, the civil war in Sierra Leone can be interpreted as a reaction by alienated youth against the institutions of indirect rule, while neither Ghana nor Uganda have experienced this type of conflict.

The chapter proceeds as follows: In the next section we place the institution of indirect rule within the broader literature on state formation and the forces that make states weak or strong. We discuss what the literature says about the types of incentives and forces that make indirect rule persist and the mechanisms that lead it to be the basis of a weak and ineffective state. In section 9.3 we describe the history of indirect rule in Sierra Leone, and how it persisted after independence in 1961 and the reasons why it has lasted until today, despite many challenges. The latter part of the section examines in more detail the sense in which the postindependence state in Sierra Leone is weak. Section 9.4 examines the two contrasting cases of Uganda and Ghana, arguing that the very different dynamics they experienced at independence was due to the fact that both countries were potentially dominated by a very large precolonial polity. Section 9.5 concludes.

9.2 Weak and Strong States

Though analysis of the importance of the state in providing public goods might be traced back to Hobbes, the most important root of its modern academic study is Weber. A state is obviously made up of many institutions

---

5. There could also be elements of selection here in the sense that, if one considers both Uganda and Ghana, it is clear that the states formed in the ecologically more attractive parts of the country and may have intrinsically higher agricultural productivity today.

and practices. Weber pointed to several key dimensions of states that he thought were critical. His most basic definition of a state emphasized the monopoly of violence:

> A state is a human community that (successfully) claims the monopoly of the legitimate use of physical force within a given territory. (1946, 78)

Weber also pointed to the emergence of rational bureaucracy as another defining process in state formation, noting that:

> In the pure type of traditional rule, the following features of a bureau-cratic administrative staff are absent: (a) a clearly defined sphere of competence subject to impersonal rules, (b) a rationally established hierarchy, (c) a regular system of appointment on the basis of free contract, and orderly promotion, (d) technical training as a regular requirement, (e) (frequently) fixed salaries, in the typical case paid in money. (1978, 229)

Of these two key features of the state, Weber's emphasis on bureaucratization has received the most attention by scholars, particularly in Africa. Many scholars see what Weber described as the transition from a state based on patrimonial lines to a "rational-legal" one to be the defining moment in state formation (e.g., Silberman 1993). Evans's (1995) work is squarely in this tradition, and the empirical work of Evans and Rauch (1999, 2000) suggests that states with "Weberian" characteristics, for example a nonpatrimonial organization, have better public policies and higher rates of economic growth. Africa has yet to undergo this transition.

The issue of the monopoly of violence, or perhaps more generally territorial control, has also been studied in this context. Implicitly, much of the literature on civil war is concerned with this topic. Fearon and Laitin (2003), for example, interpret their finding that income per capita is the dominant determinant of civil war incidence in terms of state capacity (though they do not measure this directly). A more recent literature in political science has considered what it calls "subnational authoritarianism," meaning the presence of regions that the central state does not rule and are instead controlled by local power holders (see Gibson [2005] for examples from Argentina and Mexico).

Other elements of the state that have received recent attention, especially from economists, include the development of a fiscal system, for example, in Acemoglu (2005) and Besley and Persson (2011).

Bearing in mind these different dimensions, we could say that a weak state is one that does not possess a monopoly of violence, does not have a modern bureaucracy, and is unable to raise taxes, particularly direct taxes. In principle, states may be strong in some dimensions and weak in others. However, in reality these three things do seem to covary quite positively, suggesting that the type of forces that keep a state weak make it weak in all three dimensions. For example, if a state lacks a monopoly of violence, it seems likely that it will have a hard time collecting taxes, at least from areas it does not control. Further, we would expect a patrimonial bureaucracy to be very bad at collecting taxes or providing public goods.

There is much less consensus, however, about why all states do not become rational-legal, particularly when there appears to be such large advantages to becoming so. Weber saw the development of such states in Western Europe as deeply bound up with and coevolving with the processes of capitalist modernization driven by, among other things, the Protestant reformation. To the extent that other parts of the world did not undergo similar processes, one would not expect such states to emerge. More recent research has stressed a plethora of mechanisms that may prevent the development of Weberian rational-legal states. They have also stressed other senses in which a state may be weak. The most dominant idea, due originally to Hintze (1975) and developed more fully by Tilly (1975), is that strong states emerge as a consequence of interstate warfare. In other parts of the world, where there has been less interstate warfare, such as Africa (Herbst 2000), rational-legal states have not emerged. Tilly's idea is widely accepted in social science, and even in the recent work by economists on this topic (Besley and Persson 2011; Gennaioli and Voth 2015).

Other scholars have suggested very different mechanisms. Migdal (1988) and Scott (2009), for example, develop the idea that the state may be weak because society is highly organized and refuses to concede authority to a state. This could be for various reasons. For instance, Lebanon does not have an income tax because it is divided into powerfully organized communities, the Sunnis, Shias, Maronites, Druze, and Orthodox, and all are worried that any state might be controlled by another of the groups, and such things as tax policy used against their interests. Similarly, Lebanon has not had a census since 1932. Collecting data on its population might be regarded as a basic function of the state, but in Lebanon each community fears that changes in the relative population shares will destabilize the equilibrium between them (for example, through the intricate electoral system). Hence, nobody dares to collect such information. In Scott's view, the mechanism is that people simply do not want to subject themselves to the coercion of the state and the reduction in autonomy involved with having a strong state, but it might also be local elites vigorously resisting the authority of the central state to protect their own privileges.

The work on patrimonialism and why it does not transition to a rational-legal state focuses on the idea that patrimonialism is, at root, a method of organizing power and exercising control over society. In any society, some rule and some are ruled, but the practice and methods of rule can take many forms, as can the extent of autonomy of the rulers and the extent to which the ruled can participate in decision making. These forms have huge consequences for economic development. If society is organized in a patrimonial way, then the rulers become patrons and the ruled become the clients of the patrons. Patrons typically control scarce resources that they allocate at their discretion to clients in exchange for services, and particularly, loyalty and support. If a client gets access to resources, such as a job, a school place for their children, or essential medical treatment, this does not happen on the basis of some well-defined criteria. Rather, it comes because one's patron has access to the resources. It comes as a reward for loyalty.

As an example of why states become organized in a patrimonial way, consider the political problem facing Joseph Mobutu when he took over the Congolese state in 1965. His first objective was to consolidate his power. He was confronted by a factious "nation" with powerful independence movements bubbling in Katanga and Kasai. The Simba Revolt had already taken over the Kivus and most of the eastern half of the country in 1964–1965. The state was not only short on legitimacy, it was woefully short of human capital and experience. The top echelon of the civil service had been staffed by Belgians who left in 1960, and the first Congolese university graduate arrived only four years before that in 1956.

In 1965 Mobutu, therefore, faced a difficult political problem: how to control the society he had taken over and how to organize political institutions to ensure this. He had a bureaucracy and army of sorts, but he could not rely on anybody's loyalty and he was short of resources. Most of the vast mineral wealth of the country was still controlled by foreigners. Mobutu saw the key to establishing his control as creating a vast web of informal patron-client relationships by dispensing resources and favors to people who in turn dispensed them to others below them, creating a vast pyramid of favors and obligations ultimately flowing from his office and covering the entire state. Such a strategy for consolidating power would work only up to the point where clients could not coordinate on a new patron, so Mobutu also brilliantly sidelined any such candidates. Ministers and political elites were "shuffled" from one position to another, thrown into prison, rehabilitated, and cast into exile, only to be rehabilitated again. Particularly distinctive about the organization of the Mobutu state was, as he himself put it:

> In a word, everything is for sale, anything can be bought in our country. And in this flow, he who holds the slightest cover of public authority uses it illegally to acquire money, goods, prestige, or to avoid obligations. The right to be recognized by a public servant, to have one's children enrolled in school, to obtain medical care, etc. . . . are all subject to this tax which, though invisible, is known and expected by all. (Gould 1980, 485)

Not only was corruption acceptable, within limits, so was preying on society. This apparently perverse organization of the state was actually a brilliant way of allowing Mobutu to extend his vast patronage machine to incorporate far more people than his public finances would otherwise have permitted. A key tool of patronage was employment in the government. People could be hired by the state without payment because just working for the state came with the "option value" of being able to predate on the rest of society. So what looked like—and was of course—corruption was the usual way the politics of the state operated. Naturally, this organization of the state came at huge costs in terms of social welfare and economic development.

The more analytical work in this area also proposes various mechanisms that can account for why weak states persist. For example, in Besley and Persson's (2011) canonical model, it is more attractive to build state strength in the fiscal and legal spheres when the incumbent does not fear losing power (as this makes it less likely that state capacity can be used against itself in the future); when society is more cohesive, so that losing power is not so bad; and when the value of public goods is high (perhaps because of external warfare). In Acemoglu, Ticchi, and Vindigni (2011), an initial political elite facing the threat of democratization creates a weak patrimonial state where bureaucrats extract rents to create a coalition against redistribution, which would entail state reform and a reduction of rents for bureaucrats. Here a weak state is specifically a method of controlling political power and forging a particular coalition. In Acemoglu, Robinson, and Santos (2013), the central state decides not to create a monopoly of violence because warlords provide votes at a lower price than political elites would otherwise have to pay. In Acemoglu, Ticchi, and Vindigni (2010), a state without the monopoly of violence and endemic civil wars persists because the elite controlling the central state are afraid of strengthening the military that can compete against them in the future.

None of the analytical work on state weakness has focused on the idea that indirect rule creates weak states, though both Lange (2004, 2009) and Iyer (2010) present empirical evidence of the impact of indirect rule.

9.3 The Creation, Persistence, and Consequences of Indirect Rule in Sierra Leone

9.3.1 History of the Institution

The Sierra Leonean state is built around the system of indirect rule created by the British in 1896, which is based on a symbiotic relationship between national politicians and local "traditional" (though the tradition is to a large extent invented—see Hobsbawm and Ranger, eds. [1983]) rulers. This system has lasted 118 years, though with some notable adaptations after independence in 1961. It may even have in some sense become stronger after the civil war ended in 2002, when real political competition emerged for the first time since the 1960s. The longevity of the system and the way it was recreated after the civil war suggests that it has quite robust features—even if it leads to a severe underprovision of public goods.

To understand the nature of the current state in Sierra Leone and why it is weak, it is critical to understand the history of how the state was created during the colonial period and what kind of institutional architecture was imposed at the time. In 1896, when the British established a protectorate over what would be the modern territory of Sierra Leone, they set up a canonical version of indirect rule. Local government was to be delegated to the paramount chiefs (PCs) who collected poll taxes and administered justice. The PCs are elected for life, and to be a candidate one must come from a ruling family or ruling house. Chieftaincies, of which there are currently 149, have anywhere between one ruling house (around 10 percent) to a maximum of twelve. The ruling houses are roughly the elites that were recognized by the British in the nineteenth century, possibly descendents of those who signed treaties with the British. In practice, establishing today that a particular family is a ruling house is done by showing that an ancestor of the house was allowed by the British to contest to be PC during the colonial period. There is no formal or written list of ruling houses—the set of acceptable lineages is entirely "local knowledge," and this aspect of the system has never really been institutionalized (Acemoglu, Reed, and Robinson [2014] constructed the list of ruling families by administering a national survey). The PCs are elected from eligible candidates by a secret ballot, where the electorate are the members of the chieftaincy council (formally, the tribal authority). Today there is one member of this council for every twenty taxpayers in the chieftaincy, but the members are selected—not chosen by the taxpayers, let alone ordinary citizens—and are essentially composed of local elites. Underneath the PC is a whole structure of subordinate chiefs, village chiefs, and section chiefs, all of which are automatically members of the council, along with a member of parliament who comes from the chieftaincy and other elites.

This system evolved during the colonial period (Abraham [1978] is the best treatment of the system in action prior to independence). It is in operation today and is still the main way that the national government in Freetown governs the countryside. There are several reasons for this longevity. First, PCs were given disproportionate influence in early representative institutions during the late colonial period. In 1924 the British decided to allow African representation on the legislative council. The protectorate could elect three representatives on a franchise restricted to wealthy adult males (consisting of around 5 percent of adult males; Kilson [1966], 125), which ended in the election of three paramount chiefs. In 1951 the British promulgated a new constitution, which opened up the legislative council further. In consequence the first national political party, the Sierra Leone People's Party (SLPP), formed around Dr. Milton Margai, the protectorate's first doctor and longstanding adviser to the paramount chiefs. Of the fourteen elected representatives, eight were themselves paramount chiefs, the other six included Milton Margai, his brother Albert, and Siaka Stevens, who later formed the opposition All People's Congress party (APC). Margai was a scion of a "ruling family" that had controlled the paramount chieftaincy of Lower Banta since the creation of indirect rule in 1896, and his brother George was the PC of this chiefdom in the 1950s. Apart from Stevens, all of the nonparamount chiefs came from ruling families. As Cartwright (1970, 56) puts it:

> Dr. Margai's wide range of acquaintances enabled him to go to leading men in most towns of the Protectorate and enlist them as the local leaders of the SLPP. But beyond enlisting a few "big men" in each locality . . . the SLPP undertook little political activity.

They controlled elections and got themselves elected to the legislative council and formed the SLPP, which elected the first prime minister at independence, Milton Margai, whose power base rested almost entirely on the paramount chieftaincy. Legislative electoral districts, for example, coincided almost precisely with chieftaincy boundaries. One chief, one member of parliament (Cartwright 1970, 141).

The SLPP then entered into a symbiotic relationship with the chiefs in rather the same way as the British colonial state had done. Cartwright (1970, 88) explains thus:

> While the SLPP leaders negotiated with the British new constitutional arrangements which protected the interests of the chiefs as a class, but at the same time retained for themselves the ability to impose sanctions on any individual chief, the chiefs ensured that their people supported the SLPP.

The local control of PCs over land, the justice system, and forced labor was used to deliver votes in elections. The ability of PCs to use selective punishments and rewards at the local level and their control over resources gave huge political leverage to the SLPP, who had no interest in constructing a national state that might have interfered with this political resource. For the 1957 elections, the last before independence in 1961, there were further changes in the legislative assembly with a broadened franchise. Of the fifty elected members (seven others were nominated by the governor), twelve seats were guaranteed to PCs (one per district) and of the remaining MPs, six were the sons of PCs and of the other thirty-two members, and 64 percent were from ruling houses. Forty-four out of fifty supported the SLPP, including all of the PCs.

Therefore, at independence the SLPP created a political strategy deeply rooted in the colonial institutions. Though the national state constructed by the British was a bureaucratic one, it was primarily staffed by Krios, the Creole people of Freetown who lost out politically as the majority of the electorate was in the interior (see Clapham [1976] on the failed attempt by Krio elites to maintain their power). After independence, the Krios were replaced by supporters of the SLPP from the interior and the national state was "patrimonialized."

It was a liability for the SLPP, however, that all its elites such as the Margais hailed from the south of the country. The APC, formed by Siaka Stevens of Limba ethnicity, from the north of the country to contest the 1962 election, took advantage of this liability. Once in power Stevens reconstructed and operated the same model (Reno [1995] is the best study of the Stevens regime). The APC won the 1967 general election, largely because the SLPP split over whether or not to form a one-party state. Stevens then took over the institutions of indirect rule and continued to use them in the same way, including using the PCs as a way of governing the countryside and mobilizing political support. Stevens even strengthened their powers by abolishing in 1972 the district councils that the British had set up in 1945. At the same time, he aggressively intervened to remove chiefs he did not like (recall the Cartwright quote above on how the SLPP worked), and molded them to be an electoral arm for the APC. With Stevens, and ever since, it is customary for the paramount chiefs to declare loyalty to the government in power and that government expects the PCs to deliver electoral support.

This strategy is still in use today.[6] Chiefs also still appear to be heavily involved in politics. Wyrod (2008, 79) notes that in the 2007 elections, when the SLPP was once again the incumbent, "paramount chiefs tried to deliver votes for the SLPP."[7]

The resilience of indirect rule in Sierra Leone has had both "top-down" and "bottom-up" roots. If at the national level a political equilibrium emerged where the central state had no incentive to invest in making itself stronger (since this might have jeopardized the incumbency advantage delivered by chiefs), the equilibrium also featured local support for the institution. The issue of local attitudes toward chiefs is a complex one because there is a long history of resentment over abuses by chiefs. In 1955–1956 there were extensive riots across the country, fueled by complaints about extortionate taxation and the arbitrary use of powers by paramount chiefs and local authorities. More recently, grievances against the chiefs have been seen by some as crucial to both the start of the civil war and the popularity of the Revolutionary United Front (RUF) with youth (Richards 1996; Mokuwa et al. 2011). Barrows (1976) and Tangri (1976), however, have shown that the rural riots in the mid-1950s were not, in large part, popular

6. Though there is controversy today about the extent to which PCs can control elections, everyone claims they have a major impact. One PC in Kono district, when asked by us whether he was able to influence the way people voted replied, "if I say left they go left, if I say right they go right." A senior member of the SLPP party told us that PCs could control between 20–30 percent of the votes in an election. In our fieldwork we found all rural people willing to talk about how the PCs attempt to sway voting and elections.

7. See Baldwin 2013, one of the very few real studies of the electoral impact of African chiefs. Barrows (1976) is a valuable study that covers some of this ground for Kenema district.

revolts against the institution of paramount chieftaincy itself, but were rather mobilizations by elite opponents against incumbent chiefs. Tangri, for instance, writes that:

> Ruling house competition, amalgamation differences, ethnic antagonisms, personal enmities, and other conflicting interests, all involving men of influence, constituted the underlying causes of the various chiefdom riots of 1955–56. And these divisions among "big men" were expressed within the context of a popular malaise arising from the corrupt, extortionist, and authoritarian behaviour of [incumbent] chiefdom rulers. A symbiotic relationship emerged between opponents of the local establishment, who wanted to further their own interests, and discontented "youngmen," who demanded an end to the abuse of power by the ruling elite. For the "youngmen" [violence] was a means of ending misrule by a particular "ruling" family, while for the elders it was an instrument for unseating and replacing opponents in order to obtain a more equitable share of chiefdom offices and resources between personal rivals, different areas, and various ethnic groups. (Tangri 1976, 318)

As for the arguments about acute current resentment against paramount chiefs, there is the overwhelming finding from recent surveys that chiefs retain legitimacy at the local level. Fanthorpe (2004, 6–7) sums up a large amount of research he conducted for the Department for International Development (DFID) after the end of the civil war on the topic by arguing that:

> Long experience of state corruption has left many Sierra Leoneans extremely distrustful of bureaucracy. . . . In an environment where ruthless pursuit of self-interest among the comparative wealthy and well educated is perceived to be the norm, chiefs continue to be seen as a lesser evil: there is at least some chance that rulers with the appropriate hereditary credentials can be prevailed upon to protect the hereditary rights of the rural populace.

Indeed, while certain reforms of the chieftaincy have had some degree of popular support (for example, the introduction of universal suffrage in elections for PC), other reforms, such as getting rid of the ruling houses, have not. Rural people in Sierra Leone have tended to be suspicious of reforms that might lead to "natives" losing control of the chieftaincy and local institutions.[8] Acemoglu, Reed, and Robinson (2014) argue that this also likely reflects the specific investments that local people make in the patronage networks, which have the paramount chief at the apex. It may also be the case that there are local institutions, such as secret societies like the Poro, that act as constraints on PCs (see Little 1965, 1966); moreover, rural Sierra

---

8. In field work in Kenema, we were forcefully told that it could never be allowed for a stranger to become PC because then strangers could get control over the land—the PC being traditionally the "custodian of the land."

Leoneans see themselves as having far more influence over these local institutions than they do over the central state.

This perspective shows us something interesting about the demand side for state building in Sierra Leone. It is not just that national elites not consider it to be in their best interest to construct a more effective and stronger central state, but also that rural dwellers feel threatened by the central state. This is reminiscent of Scott's (2009) thesis that state formation is a fundamentally coercive process, which is strongly resisted. Such arguments resonate with a wide swath of the literature in African studies (see McIntosh 1999), even if in some cases the resistance comes not from the regular rural dwellers, but the local elites.

9.3.2 Indirect Rule and State Weakness

Does this system of governance necessarily make the state in Sierra Leone weak, and if so in what ways? For the British, indirect rule was a low-cost method for pacifying the periphery of Sierra Leone. The colonial state had little interest in providing public goods or developing the country (particularly after the Hut Tax rebellion, when initial ideas about British settlement were abandoned; see Lange [2009]). However, it did need a way of guaranteeing order and stability and of collecting enough taxes for the state to be self-financing (recall, for example, Cooper's [2002] "gatekeeper state"). The institution of the PC achieved this without entailing any investment in the construction of a national state.

We have already emphasized several ways that a state could be weak: it could lack a monopoly of violence, a modern bureaucracy, and a modern fiscal system. Sierra Leone is weak in all these senses today. The most obvious evidence that it lacks a monopoly of violence is the civil war, initiated by the RUF, that ravaged the country between 1991 and 2002 and that the national army was incapable of fighting. Keen (2005, 34) reproduces a quote from Abu Turay, capturing the extent to which central authority had collapsed in the early 1990s:

> by the end of Momoh's rule he had stopped paying civil servants, teachers and even Paramount Chiefs. Central government had collapsed, and then of course we had border incursions, "rebels" and all the automatic weapons pouring over the border from Liberia. The NPRC, the "rebels" and the "sobels" [soldiers-turned rebels] all amount to the chaos one expects when government disappears. None of them are the causes of our problems, but they are symptoms.

The outbreak of the civil war was the outcome of a long process. Stevens, not trusting the national army that had initially stopped him becoming prime minister in 1967 by mounting a coup to keep the SLPP in power, privatized violence. He created a private security force initially named the Internal Security Unit (the [ISU], which was apparently referred to by his long-suffering people as "I Shoot U") and afterward the Special Security Division ([SSD], or "Siaka Stevens' Dogs"; see Jackson [2004, 63] and Keen [2005, 17] on these acronyms). The APC also recruited marginalized (mostly urban) youth as professional thugs. Kandeh (1998), for instance, has noted how political elites before the war had taken advantage (and fostered the growth) of a class of urban "lumpen youth" as a cheap source of coercive power:

> APC violence and thuggery relied almost exclusively on the recruitment of urban thugs and rural drifters. As Ismail Rashid (1997) points out, most of the thugs recruited by APC patrons in the 1960s and 70s came from peri-urban enclaves like Sawpit, Magazine and Kannikay—all in Freetown. (359)

These lumpen youth were "specialists in political violence"—readily called upon by patrons to intimidate (or eliminate) opponents, raze uncooperative villages, and cow voters during elections (Kandeh 1998, 359–62).[9]

This lack of the monopoly of violence is indirectly linked to the nature of indirect rule in two ways. The PCs had the responsibility for local order and maintaining police, and yet the way that they achieved this and the nature of traditional institutions played an important part in marginalizing youths. As argued in Fanthorpe (2001, 385), this system—whereby rural dwellers depend on a highly exclusionary set of traditional institutions if they want to access property and gain political rights—has historically created a large class of people (mostly young, low-status men) who are practically obligated to become rural drifters or join marginalized populations in the cities. That is, they cannot access political rights by appealing to the modern state, for it is nearly nonexistent in rural areas. But for all intents and purposes, they also cannot do so by appealing to traditional authorities if they lack patronage by those higher up in the chiefdom hierarchy. For example, in many chiefdoms, only those who can validly claim native status are allowed to plant long-term crops. Fanthorpe cites research on a chiefdom in a diamond-mining area, where

> Farmland was allocated according to age and pedigree, forcing newcomers to make farms at a considerable distance from the main settlement. Young people who lacked patronage often faced the prospect of a lifetime's hard labour on a relative's behalf. Yet independent initiatives in wealth-creating among women and low-status men elicited strong disapproval, and were sometimes ruthlessly suppressed. (384)

Moreover, Fanthorpe notes:

9. These lumpen youth formed the bulk of RUF recruits after the initial phase of the war, and specialists believe that the bloody, highly predatory Armed Forces Revolutionary Council regime (an RUF-lower army ranks alliance) was essentially the result of these professional, lower-class thugs becoming independent from their elite patrons. See Kandeh (1998, 361–362) and Abdullah (1998).

In recent times the population obliged to attach itself to a rural settlement in order to obtain a tax receipt, a vote, and other privileges of citizenship has often far exceeded that which is actually resident, and economically supportable, at any given time. The young and those of low inherited status inevitably find themselves in attenuating orders of precedence in access to these privileges. Sierra Leone may therefore represent a case in which alarming numbers of people have become neither "citizen" nor "subject." (385)

For this population of young men, being recruited as the brawn behind a political entrepreneur has offered a much easier, readily accessible route to patronage.

The other obvious implication of this system is that it made it very difficult for a national identity to emerge. As Fanthorpe (2005, 4) puts it:

even today, the vast majority of rural Sierra Leoneans obtain primary rights of residence, land use, and political/legal representation as "natives" of chiefdoms rather than as citizens of the state. It is the prerogative of the chief to recognize and guarantee "native" status. While "native" identities are rooted in history, they have been reshaped by regimes of colonial governance, notably the registration of villages for annual poll tax. In practice "native" status is a privilege conferred by membership of land and title holding groups and attached to villages in which chiefs reside.

Being a native of a chieftaincy, as opposed to a nonnative, referred to as a "stranger" by the locals, confers many benefits. As we noted, typically only natives can grow permanent crops such as cocoa, palm, or coffee. Acemoglu, Reed, and Robinson (2014) show that strangers have weaker property rights than natives. This institution has clearly influenced the extent to which a national identity can emerge and can help explain why voting patterns in elections are still rooted in region and ethnicity and why soldiers in the army identify with their region or ethnicity, not with Sierra Leone. The only option to really establish civilian control over the military is to keep it weak and risk giving up on the monopoly of violence.

Indirect rule does seem to have made the state weak in other well-defined ways as well, which we mentioned in the introduction. As emphasized by Mamdani (1996), traditional rulers were and still are relatively unaccountable. They are able to extract rents and underprovide public goods. Acemoglu, Reed, and Robinson (2014) argue that PCs in Sierra Leone are more powerful in situations where they face less competition and this occurs when there are fewer ruling families. They show, for example, that in chieftaincies with fewer ruling families the paramount chieftaincy is indeed concentrated in fewer families. Using this idea, they then show that in places with fewer ruling families and more powerful paramount chiefs, a whole series of development outcomes are significantly lower. This includes all levels of educational attainment, the proportion of people working outside agriculture, child health, and different measures of asset ownership. The likely mechanism is indeed that more powerful chiefs can extract more rents to the detriment of public-good provision. Acemoglu, Reed, and Robinson (2014) present evidence that a potential channel is through the extra ability of powerful chiefs to control people's access to land. This feature was not compensated for by other types of accountability, for example via members of the national parliament, because of the role chiefs played in managing these higher-level elections.

Moreover, the fact that the local state is based on lineages and ruling families made it intrinsically patrimonial and nonbureaucratized. This patrimonial nature filtered up to the national state after independence and is evident in many dimensions. For example, when the APC returned to power in December 2007, they systematically removed from the civil service over 200 people from the south and east (Africa Confidential 2009, 5). Some of these people were certainly closely connected with the outgoing SLPP government, but others were just competent and dedicated Mende who had to make way for northerners. They were often replaced by people who were not competent, but to whom political favors were owed. For example, an Anti-Corruption Commission was formed in 2000 with a great deal of donor support and pressure and the postwar SLPP government launched its anticorruption strategy in February 2005. However, when the head of the commission, Val Collier, attempted to do his job too vigorously, he was replaced by Henry Joko-Smart, the brother-in-law of the then-president Ahmad Tejan Kabbah. The International Crisis Group (2007, 9) notes:

> While Collier brought charges against ministers, an Appeals court judge and several senior civil servants, Joko-Smart has focused almost exclusively on junior and mid-level officials.

Many appointments in the bureaucracy appear to have been made on the basis of dispensing patronage and they often feature the relatives of powerful people. The new Human Resources Management Office found in 2007 that there were no records for 60 percent of civil servants (9,300 of 16,000) and that there was a huge problem of ghost workers. For example, salaries were paid to 236 people of the senior civil service list but only 125 were found to actually be at their posts (International Crisis Group 2008). The patrimonial nature of the state extends to the military. Evidence for this surfaced in the anonymous "Dream Team" letter to President Koroma on January 1, 2009.[10] The Dream Team is the "Detective Reconnaissance Emergency Action Mission Team . . . is a network of over 850 officers and men in all bases of the Sierra Leone Armed Forces cutting across tribal and political party lines." This report made a series of claims about inappropriate political interventions in the military. For example, it starts by

---

10. Available at http://www.sierraherald.com/dream-team-letter.htm.

demanding that "the decision to handpick [some named] cadet officers . . . to go to Uganda for training be reversed with immediate effect. Eighty percent of these officers are from the Limba ethnic group, the ethnic group of the Minister of Defence." It next demands that the "Government reverses the commissioning of the following [named] officers. . . . Again majority of these officers are Limbas, the Minister of Defence's and the President's tribesmen, many of whom could not read or write. Commissioning these officers flouted all requirements and acceptable procedures of the RSLAF. Their commissioning was done because they were trained in alongside the Minister of Defence in 1977." The report contains a very worrying threat "As these injustices persist and our DREAM Team grows in numbers day by day this pregnant moment in Sierra Leone's history might lead to a tragic birth of something else." Just as in the past, the loyalty of the army could not be assured and the current strategy of the regime is a patrimonial one of filling it with people from the ethnicity of President Ernest Koroma.

9.4   The Diverging Paths of Ghana and Uganda

The particular path of persistence and institutionalization of indirect rule in Sierra Leone has not been the norm, even in British Africa. Sierra Leone firmly deviated from other British colonies, most notably from the Gold Coast (Ghana) and Uganda. In both cases, attempts by the British to set up legislative councils, which were dominated by traditional elites, had to be withdrawn because of strong opposition from urban and middle class groups.[11] In Uganda, however, the Buganda monarchy was so powerful that they were able to have a large initial impact on postindependence political institutions. However, in both Ghana and Uganda, this made postindependence leaders even more unwilling to rule via traditional chiefs or work with traditional elites, ultimately leading to the sidelining of the traditional elites. We now provide a brief account of these political paths.

9.4.1   Ghana

In Ghana, as the British colonial office began moving the country toward independence,[12] the opposition to chiefs and indirect rule was led by Kwame Nkrumah's Convention People's Party (CPP). Rathbone (2000a, 2000b; see also Crook 1986) documents in great detail how the precolonial governments led by Nkrumah between 1951 and 1966 attempted "to break, co-opt and coerce chieftaincy" (2000b, ix).

The CPP, founded in June 1949, was formed of people lacking membership in ruling families, so-called "verandah boys." In this they were quite like

11. Austin (1964, 49–152) discusses this process in the Gold Coast, and Coleman (1958, 271–318) on Nigeria.

12. See Crook (1986) for different views of the British with respect to the chieftaincy in late colonial Ghana.

large segments of Siaka Stevens's APC in Sierra Leone. Stevens was mayor of Freetown in the 1960s when he was building his political machine and a trade unionist, not a traditional elite. But in Ghana, the power of Asante Chiefs and particularly of the king of Asante, the Asantehene, created a context very different from the one that Stevens faced. These chiefs had very powerful bases of support in the Asante country and were much less dependent on the central state than the chiefs of Sierra Leone. As Dunn and Robertson (1973, 93) put it:

> [chieftaincy] neither behaved as an instrument in the hands . . . of the colonial rulers nor . . . drew its political power solely from its capacity to elicit the support of the colonial regime.

Krono Edusei, Nkrumah's lieutenant in the Asante region, had led the Ashanti Youth Association in vehement opposition to the traditional authorities, and he had been fined and imprisoned many times by chiefly courts. Rathbone (2000b, 7) notes "the CPP's struggle against chieftaincy in southern Ghana was, by its own reckoning, at least as important as its dramatic, much better known and ultimately much more successful combat with the British."

By January 1950 Nkrumah himself was on the offensive, writing that "Chiefs in league with imperialists who obstruct our path . . . will one day run away and leave their stools" (Rathbone 2000b, 23) (a stool being the symbol of royal office in Asante). The newspaper of the party, the *Accra Evening News*, began to adopt a Marxist language to talk about the chiefs, referring to their "oppression of the masses" and their "collaboration with the imperialists" (Rathbone 2000b, 22). In particular, and very interesting for the comparison with Sierra Leone, the CPP focused on the mobilization of "youths" or "youngmen." These words are translations of the Twi words "nkwankwaa" and "mmerante," which also have the connotation of a commoner, someone outside the traditional royal lineages.

These were not just idle words. Rathbone (2000a, 54) argues that:

> There is little doubt that the CPP's Central Committee had every intention to scrap chieftaincy as soon as possible. Several prominent members of the Party were widely reported as having made just that commitment before the first general election of 1951.

Rathbone documents how the CPP intervened to take judicial powers away from chiefs (56):

> The substitution of dependable party [in place of] discarded court panel members who were demonstrably royal or clients of chiefs is consistent throughout this long trail of evidence.

Rather than solidifying the judicial powers of chiefs, as happened in Sierra Leone, in Ghana they were stripped away.

Though the CPP dominated the first elections to the legislative council in 1951, its opponents coalesced around a new political party, the National Liberation Movement (NLM), formed in central Asante. Rathbone (2000a, 58) argues:

the NLM was, at heart, an Asante party. It made a patriotic case and underlined it by making common cause with the beleaguered Asante chiefs.

The response by the CPP was to aggressively go after the chiefs and create all sorts of pretexts for removing ones who did not cooperate from office. Rathbone writes of this:

The lists of "destooled" and then de-recognised chiefs, and government-preferred and thus recognised substitutes for the latter part of 1957 and 1958, quite literally involve hundreds of people. (2000a, 62)

Compared with this, the few instances when Stevens's parachuted illegitimate chiefs into power was of marginal importance.[13] Brempong (2006, 30) sums the situation up by noting that:

The Nkrumah government . . . minimized the political and judicial roles of traditional rulers, broke their financial backbone and made them passive appendages to the central government.

After Nkrumah was thrown from power by the military in 1966, there was some change in this. Nevertheless, chiefs have never regained the roles or powers that they had in the colonial period. For example, Rathbone (2000a, 62–63) concludes that:

After its fall in 1966, the military government dismissed all of those chiefs installed or promoted by the CPP . . . and it re-installed the deposed. But it and its successor governments were never to return to chiefs the access to resources which had allowed them to exercise such authority in the later colonial period.

Chiefs did gradually regain more status in the 1969, 1979, and 1992 constitutions, but even this was hedged around with restrictions. For instance, the 1992 Constitution (276.1) bans chiefs from taking part in "active" party politics and stipulates that those who wish to do so should abdicate. There are both regional and national houses of chiefs, but their mandate is restricted to overseeing elections for chiefs and making sure they follow the correct traditional procedures. The 1992 Constitution did allow for the representation of chiefs on local government bodies, but only with limited powers. Brempong (2006, 35) sums it up as:

13. Interestingly, as Reed and Robinson (2012) document, in no case was Stevens able to actually create a legitimate new ruling family using this tactic. Since 2002, the legacies of this period have been completely eradicated.

In effect, the clause meant no consultations with the chiefs or at most only with respect to chiefs supposed to be favorable to the party in power.

A long cry from the situation in Sierra Leone.

9.4.2   Uganda

In the British protectorate of Uganda, the role of the Buganda state was even more institutionalized than the Asante state was in Ghana (see Fallers 1964). Not only was the protectorate named after the state, but the state had expanded with British help to annex surrounding territories, particularly the so-called "lost counties" of Bunyoro, and during the protectorate Ganda governors were appointed by the British in some of the contiguous, previously stateless, societies, for example, Tesoland.

After World War II, Britain began to move its African colonies toward independence (see Mutibwa [1992] and Mwakikagile [2012] for overviews of the relevant history). The new governor of Uganda, Andrew Cohen (appointed in 1952), had the job of opening up the legislative council to elections for Africans. This prospect was seen by the Kabaka of Buganda, Frederick Walugembe Mutesa II, as seriously diluting the power of Buganda, since its population was in a minority in the entire protectorate. In response, he demanded that Buganda be separated from the protectorate. Cohen exiled the Kabaka to London, but his rising popularity in Uganda led to his reinstatement, and in exchange for agreeing not to oppose the creation of a unified Uganda as a state, he was to become the president at independence. The 1950s saw the emergence of a string of new political parties, the most significant being Milton Obote's Uganda People's Congress (UPC). As the 1961 legislative elections approached, the Kabaka became more discontented from the institutional arrangements that the British were proposing for an independent Uganda. He then instructed his people to boycott the election. This strategy not only failed to delegitimize the election, but had the perverse result of allowing the Democratic Party (DP), which had formed in the 1950s to oppose Buganda dominance, to dominate the Buganda homeland on the basis of non-Ganda votes. In response the Kabaka helped to found a new party, the Kabaka Yekka ("king only") party, which went into a coalition with Obote's UPC party at independence. The deal they made included autonomy for Buganda, the right of the Kabaka to nominate the members of the national assembly from Buganda, and assured his position as head of state of Uganda.

However, Obote had no intention of allowing the Kabaka to be either the head of state or to maintain the autonomy of Buganda. He immediately started to strengthen the army and undermine the coalition, which culminated in the 1962 referendum on returning the lost countries to Bunyoro, using it as a way to induce Bunyoro members of the DP to join the UPC. In response the Kabaka tried to create disunity within the UPC, promoting Obote's rivals who, on February 4, 1966, passed a "no confidence" vote against Obote's leadership. Obote's response was to turn to Idi Amin, the young military commander he had been promoting, who helped him to mount a coup d'état and suspend the constitution. The Kabaka ordered that the government quit Buganda territory, but instead Obote ordered Amin to attack the Kabaka's palace on Mengo Hill, forcing him into exile. The new constitution that Obote then introduced in 1967 abolished the autonomy enjoyed by Buganda and the Kabaka's position as head of state.

As in the case of Ghana, the considerable power wielded by the king of a large precolonial state made the continuation of institutions of indirect rule infeasible after independence. Just as it was not possible for Nkrumah to make the Asantehene and other powerful Asante chiefs instruments of his rule, it was not feasible for Obote to govern Uganda in the way the British had done via the king and chiefs of Buganda and the other precolonial states. They had to be abolished.

9.5 Conclusions

In this chapter we have attempted three tasks. We have tried to explain the mechanisms that led the colonial state based on indirect rule to persist to the present day in Sierra Leone. We have also studied the sense in which indirect rule creates state weakness in Sierra Leone. Finally, we provided a hypothesis that has the potential to explain the differential persistence of indirect rule in Africa.

We argued that the persistence of indirect rule after the independence of Sierra Leone was initially caused by the fact that those empowered by indirect rule were able to capture and indeed to structure the postcolonial state. Yet the system persisted after these initial elites lost power because Siaka Stevens, prime minister and then president between 1967 and 1985, was able to exploit the huge advantage that a sitting president had in the system and turn it into a tool of incumbency bias.

Yet indirect rule did make the state weak in at least three clear senses. First, it made it difficult to establish a monopoly of violence because traditional rule created a class of alienated youth who could be easily recruited by politicians or armed groups. This monopoly was further impeded by the fact that the system made it difficult for a national identity to emerge, which made the issue of civilian control over the military harder. The only solution was to keep the military weak, further jeopardizing the monopoly of violence. Second, as developed by Mamdani (1996), traditional rulers were relatively unaccountable and thus able to extract rents and underprovide public goods. This feature was not compensated for by other types of accountability, for example via a representative national parliament, in large part because of the role chiefs played in managing these higher-level elections. Third, the fact that the local state was based on lineages and ruling families recognized by the British made it an intrinsically patrimonial and nonbureaucratized structure—a defining property of weakness.

We then showed that indirect rule, though it was practiced in all British colonies, persisted very differently across different colonies. Indeed, in both Ghana and Uganda, the political elites who captured the state after independence overthrew the institutional structure of indirect rule rather than reinforcing or reshaping it. We argued that the main reason for this was that these countries had large, powerful, centralized precolonial states, Asante and Buganda, which had chiefs that were too powerful to be controlled by postindependence elites. This made indirect rule infeasible for postcolonial political elites.

In explaining the variation in the persistence of indirect rule we are not claiming that this led Ghana and Uganda to move onto radically better development paths. In both cases the civilian governments, which had abolished indirect rule, were overthrown by the army that they had strengthened as part of their state-building projects. Moreover, in most cases they substituted the patrimonialism of the traditional institutions with the patrimonialism of the political parties, as our discussion of the Ghanaian case illustrated. Nevertheless, we also argued that the persistence of indirect rule in Sierra Leone has had significant consequences, in particular generating a pathologically weak state and paving the way to a deadly civil war unseen in either Ghana or Uganda.

References

Abdullah, Ibrahim. 1998. "Bush Path to Destruction: The Origin and Character of the Revolutionary United Front/Sierra Leone." *Journal of Modern African Studies* 36 (2): 203–35.

Abraham, Arthur. 1978. *Mende Government and Politics under Colonial Rule.* Freetown: Sierra Leone University Press.

———. 2003. *An Introduction to Pre-Colonial History of the Mende of Sierra Leone.* Lewiston, NY: Edwin Mellen Press.

Acemoglu, Daron. 2005. "Politics and Economics in Weak and Strong States." *Journal of Monetary Economics* 52:1199–226.

Acemoglu, Daron, Camilo García-Jimeno, and James A. Robinson. 2015. "State Capacity and Economic Development: A Network Approach." *American Economic Review* 105 (8): 2364–2409.

Acemoglu, Daron, Tristan Reed, and James A. Robinson. 2014. "Chiefs: Elite Control of Civil Society and Economic Development in Sierra Leone." *Journal of Political Economy* 122 (2): 319–68.

Acemoglu, Daron, and James A. Robinson. 2010. "Why is Africa Poor?" *Economic History of Developing Regions* 25:21–50.

———. 2012. *Why Nations Fail.* New York: Crown.

Acemoglu, Daron, James A. Robinson, and Rafael Santos. 2013. "The Monopoly of

Violence: Evidence from Colombia." *Journal of the European Economic Association* 11 (S1): 5–44.

Acemoglu, Daron, Davide Ticchi, and Andrea Vindigni. 2010. "Persistence of Civil Wars." *Journal of the European Economic Association* 8 (2–3): 664–77.

Acemoglu, Daron, Davide Ticchi, and Andrea Vindigni. 2011. "Emergence and Persistence of Inefficient States." *Journal of the European Economic Association* 9 (2): 177–208.

Africa Confidential. 2009. "A Family Business." October 8. http://www.africa -confidential.com/article-preview/id/3273/A_family_business.

Austin, Dennis. 1964. *Politics in Ghana, 1946–1960*. London: Oxford University Press.

Baldwin, Kate. 2013. "Why Vote with the Chief? Political Connections and Public Goods Provision in Zambia." *American Journal of Political Science* 57 (4): 794–809.

Bandyopadhyay, Sanghamitra, and Elliott D. Green. 2016. "Pre-Colonial Political Centralization and Contemporary Development in Uganda." *Economic Development and Cultural Change* 64 (3): 471–508.

Barrows, Walter L. 1976. *Grassroots Politics in an African State: Integration and Development in Sierra Leone*. New York: Holmes and Meier.

Besley, Timothy, and Torsten Persson. 2011. *Pillars of Prosperity*. Princeton, NJ: Princeton University Press.

Bratton, Michael, and Nicolas van de Walle. 1997. *Democratic Experiments in Africa: Regime Transitions in Comparative Perspective*. New York: Cambridge University Press.

Brempong, Nana Arhin. 2006. "Chieftaincy, an Overview." In *Chieftaincy in Ghana: Culture, Governance and Development*, edited by Irene K. Odotei and Albert K. Awedoba. Accra, Ghana: Sub-Saharan Publishers.

Cartwright, John R. 1970. *Politics in Sierra Leone, 1947–1967*. Toronto: University of Toronto Press.

Clapham, Christopher. 1976. *Liberia and Sierra Leone: An Essay in Comparative Politics*. New York: Cambridge University Press.

Coleman, James. 1958. *Nigeria: Background to Nationalism*. Berkeley: University of California Press.

Cooper, Frederick. 2002. *Africa since 1940: The Past of the Present*. New York: Cambridge University Press.

Crook, Richard. 1986. "Decolonization, the Colonial State and in Chieftaincy in Ghana." *African Affairs* 85 (338): 75–107.

Crowder, Michael, and Obaro Ikime, eds. 1970. *West African Chiefs: Their Changing Status under Colonial Rule and Independence*. New York: Africana Publishing Corporation.

Dunn, John, and A. E. Robertson. 1973. *Dependence and Opportunity: Political Change in Ahafo*. New York: Cambridge University Press.

Evans, Peter B. 1995. *Embedded Autonomy*. Princeton, NJ: Princeton University Press.

Evans, Peter B., and James Rauch. 1999. "Bureaucracy and Growth: A Cross-National Analysis of the Effects of 'Weberian' State Structures on Economic Growth." *American Sociological Review* 64 (5): 748–65.

———. 2000. "Bureaucratic Structure and Bureaucratic Performance in Less Developed Countries." *Journal of Public Economics* 75:49–62.

Evans-Pricthard, E. E., and Meyer Fortes, eds. 1940. *African Political Systems*. Oxford: Oxford University Press.

Fallers, Lloyd, ed. 1964. *The King's Men*. London: Oxford University Press.

Fanthorpe, Richard. 2001. "Neither Citizen Nor Subject? 'Lumpen' Agency and the Legacy of Native Administration in Sierra Leone." *African Affairs* 100:363–86.

———. 2004. "Chieftaincy and the Politics of Post-War Reconstruction in Sierra Leone." Unpublished Manuscript, Department for International Development.

———. 2005. "On the Limits of the Liberal Peace: Chiefs and Democratic Decentralization in Post-War Sierra Leone." *African Affairs* 105:1–23.

Fearon, James, and David D. Laitin. 2003. "Ethnicity, Insurgency, and Civil War." *American Political Science Review* 97 (1): 75–90.

Gennaioli, Nicola, and Ilya Rainer. 2007. "The Modern Impact of Pre-Colonial Centralization in Africa." *Journal of Economic Growth* 12 (3): 185–234.

Gennaioli, Nicola, and Hans-Joachim Voth. 2015. "State Capacity and Military Conflict." *Review of Economic Studies* 82 (4): 1409–48.

Gibson, Edward L. 2005. "Boundary Control: Subnational Authoritarianism in Democratic Countries." *World Politics* 58 (1): 101–32.

Goldstein, Markus, and Christopher Udry. 2008. "The Profits of Power: Land Rights and Agricultural Investment in Ghana." *Journal of Political Economy* 116:981–1022.

Gould, David J. 1980. "Patrons and Clients: The Role of the Military in Zaire Politics." In *The Performance of Soldiers as Governors*, edited by Isaac Mowoe. Lanham, MD: University Press of America.

Herbst, Jeffrey I. 2000. *States and Power in Africa*. Princeton, NJ: Princeton University Press.

Hintze, Otto. 1975. *The Historical Essays of Otto Hintze*. New York: Oxford University Press.

Hobsbawm, Eric, and Terence Ranger, eds. 1983. *The Invention of Tradition*. New York: Cambridge University Press.

International Crisis Group. 2007. "Sierra Leone: The Election Opportunity." Africa Report No. 129, July 12. http://www.crisisgroup.org/~/media/Files/africa/west-africa/sierra-leone/Sierra%20Leone%20The%20Election%20Opportunity.pdf.

———. 2008. "Sierra Leone: A New Era of Reform?" Africa Report No. 143, July 12. http://www.crisisgroup.org/en/regions/africa/west-africa/sierra-leone/143-sierra-leone-a-new-era-of-reform.aspx.

Iyer, Lakshmi. 2010. "Direct versus Indirect Colonial Rule in India: Long-Term Consequences." *Review of Economics and Statistics* 92 (4): 693–713.

Jackson, Michael. 2004. *In Sierra Leone*. Durham: Duke University Press.

Kandeh, Jimmy. 1998. "Transition without Rupture: Sierra Leone's Transfer Election of 1996." *African Studies Review* 41 (2): 91–111.

Keen, David. 2005. *Conflict & Collusion in Sierra Leone*. New York: Palgrave.

Kilson, Martin. 1966. *Political Change in a West African State: A Study of the Modernization Process in Sierra Leone*. Cambridge, MA: Harvard University Press.

Lange, Matthew. 2004. "British Colonial Legacy and Political Development." *World Development* 32 (6): 905–22.

———. 2009. *Lineages of Despotism and Development: British Colonialism and State Power*. Chicago: University of Chicago Press.

Little, Kenneth. 1965. "The Political Function of the Poro, Part 1." *Africa* 35 (4): 349–65.

———. 1966. "The Political Function of the Poro, Part 2." *Africa* 36 (1): 62–72.

Mamdani, Mahmood. 1996. *Citizen and Subject: Contemporary Africa and the Legacy of Late Colonialism*. Princeton, NJ: Princeton University Press.

———. 2012. *Define and Rule: Native as Political Identity*. Cambridge, MA: Harvard University Press.

Mann, Michael. 1986. *The Sources of Social Power, vol. I.* New York: Cambridge University Press.

———. 1993. *The Sources of Social Power, vol. II.* New York: Cambridge University Press.

McGovern, Michael. 2013. *Unmasking the State: Making Guinea Modern.* Chicago: University of Chicago Press.

McIntosh, Susan K. 1999. "Pathways to Complexity: An African Perspective." In *Beyond Chiefdoms: Pathways to Complexity in Africa,* edited by Susan K. McIntosh, 1–30. New York: Cambridge University Press.

Michalopoulos, Stelios, and Elias Papaioannou. 2013. "Pre-Colonial Ethnic Institutions and Contemporary African Development." *Econometrica* 81 (1): 113–52.

Migdal, Joel S. 1988. *Strong Societies and Weak States.* New York: Cambridge University Press.

Mokuwa, Esther, Maarten Voors, Erwin Bulte, and Paul Richards. 2011. "Peasant Grievance and Insurgency in Sierra Leone: Judicial Serfdom as a Driver of Conflict." *African Affairs* 110 (440): 339–66.

Mutibwa, Phares. 1992. *Uganda Since Independence: A Story of Unfulfilled Hopes.* London: C. Hurst & Co.

Mwakikagile, Godfrey. 2012. *Uganda: A Nation in Transition.* Dar es Salaam, Tanzania: New Africa Press.

O'Donnell, Guillermo A. 1993. "On the State, Democratization and some Conceptual Problems." *World Development* 21 (8): 1355–69.

Osafo-Kwaako, Philip, and James A. Robinson. 2013. "Political Centralization in Pre-Colonial Africa." *Journal of Comparative Economics* 41 (1): 6–21.

Phillips, Jonathan. 2011. "From Caliphate to the Clinic: Traditional Groups and the Provision of Public Goods in Nigeria." Working Paper, Harvard University. http://scholar.harvard.edu/files/jphillips/files/from_caliphate_to_the_clinic_080112.pdf

Rathbone, Richard. 2000a. "Kwame Nkrumah and the Chiefs: The Fate of 'Natural Rulers' under Nationalist Governments." *Transactions of the Royal Historical Society,* Sixth Series 10:45–63.

———. 2000b. *Nkrumah and the Chiefs: The Politics of Chieftaincy in Ghana, 1951–1960.* Suffolk, UK: James Currey.

Reed, Tristan, and James Robinson. 2012. "The Chiefdoms of Sierra Leone." Unpublished Manuscript, Department of Economics and Department of Government, Harvard University. http://scholar.harris.uchicago.edu/sites/default/files/jamesrobinson/files/history.pdf.

Reid, Richard J. 2002. *Political Power Pre-Colonial Buganda: Economy Society and Warfare.* Suffolk, UK: James Currey.

Reno, William. 1995. *Corruption and State Politics in Sierra Leone.* New York: Cambridge University Press.

Richards, Paul. 1996. *Fighting for the Rainforest: War, Youth and Resources in Sierra Leone.* Suffolk, UK: James Currey.

Robinson, James A., and Thierry Verdier. 2013. "The Political Economy of Clientelism." *Scandinavian Journal of Economics* 115 (2): 260–91.

Scott, James C. 2009. *The Art of Not Being Governed.* New Haven, CT: Yale University Press.

Service, Elman R. 1962. *Primitive Social Organization.* New York: Random House.

Silberman, Bernard S. 1993. *Cages of Reason: The Rise of the Rational State in France, Japan, the United States, and Great Britain.* Chicago: University of Chicago Press.

Tangri, Roger. 1976. "Conflict and Violence in Contemporary Sierra Leone Chiefdoms." *Journal of Modern African Studies* 14 (2): 311–21.

Tilly, Charles. 1975. "Reflections on the History of European State Making." In *The Formation of National States in Western Europe*, edited by Charles Tilly. Princeton, NJ: Princeton University Press.

Weber, Max. 1946. "Politics as a Vocation." In *From Max Weber: Essays in Sociology*, edited by H. H. Gerth and C. Wright Mills. New York: Oxford University Press.

———. 1978. *Economy and Society*. Berkeley: University of California Press.

Wylie, Kenneth. 1977. *Political Kingdoms of the Temne*. London: Holmes & Meier Publishers.

Wyrod, Christopher. 2008. "Sierra Leone: A Vote for Better Governance." *Journal of Democracy* 19:70–83.

Young, Crawford. 1994. *The African Colonial State in Comparative Perspective*. New Haven, CT: Yale University Press.

Contributors

Daron Acemoglu
Department of Economics, E18–269D
MIT
77 Massachusetts Avenue
Cambridge, MA 02139

Jenny C. Aker
The Fletcher School
Tufts University
160 Packard Avenue
Medford, MA 02155

Ursula Aldana
Institute of Peruvian Studies
Horacio Urteaga 694, Jesús María
Lima, Perú

Steven Block
The Fletcher School
Tufts University
160 Packard Avenue
Medford, MA 02155

Lorenzo Casaburi
SIEPR, Stanford University
John A. and Cynthia Fry Gunn
    Building
366 Galvez Street Room 228
Stanford, CA 94305–6015

Isaías N. Chaves
Stanford University
Department of Economics
579 Serra Mall
Stanford, CA 94305

Sebastian Edwards
UCLA Anderson Graduate School
    of Business
110 Westwood Plaza, Suite C508
Box 951481
Los Angeles, CA 90095–1481

Jeremy Foltz
Department of Agricultural and
    Applied Economics
University of Wisconsin, Madison
427 Lorch Street
Madison, WI 53706

Jeffrey Frankel
Harvard Kennedy School
79 JFK Street
Cambridge, MA 02138

Douglas Gollin
University of Oxford
Department of International
    Development
Queen Elizabeth House
3 Mansfield Road
Oxford OX1 3TB United Kingdom

Simon Johnson
MIT Sloan School of Management
100 Main Street, E52–562
Cambridge, MA 02142

Michael W. Klein
The Fletcher School
Tufts University
160 Packard Avenue
Medford, MA 02155

Michael Kremer
Department of Economics
Littauer Center M20
Harvard University
Cambridge, MA 02138

Paul Laris
Department of Geography
California State University
1250 Bellflower Blvd.
Long Beach, CA 90840

Jorge Braga de Macedo
Center for Globalization &
    Governance (CG&G)
Nova School of Business and
    Economics
Faculdade de Economia—Campus de
    Campolide
1099–032 Lisbon, Portugal

Sendhil Mullainathan
Department of Economics
Littauer M-18
Harvard University
Cambridge, MA 02138

Nathan Nunn
Department of Economics
Harvard University
1805 Cambridge Street
Cambridge, MA 02138

Stephen A. O'Connell
Department of Economics
Swarthmore College
Swarthmore, PA 19081

Philip Osafo-Kwaako
Economic Research and Policy
    Department
Federal Ministry of Finance
Ahmadu Bello Way
Abuja, Nigeria

Luís Brites Pereira
Center for Globalization &
    Governance (CG&G)
Nova School of Business and
    Economics
Faculdade de Economia—Campus de
    Campolide
1099–032 Lisbon, Portugal

Nancy Qian
Department of Economics
Yale University
27 Hillhouse Avenue
New Haven, CT 06520–8269

James A. Robinson
Harris School of Public Policy
University of Chicago
1155 East 60th Street
Chicago, IL 60637

Richard Rogerson
Woodrow Wilson School of Public and
    International Affairs
323 Bendheim Hall
Princeton University
Princeton, NJ 08544

David N. Weil
Department of Economics
Box B
Brown University
Providence, RI 02912

Author Index

Subject Index